KnifeBible

History & Modern Knowledge

A. J. Cardenal, MSc ICT, MSc GIS
Geographic Information Scientist

with **Sharon Steel,** *as* **Culinary Contributor**

Content Disclaimer:

This book was written with the intent to educate readers on knives and some of their uses. This book covers different types of knives, knife brands, and knife steels. The book or its authors do not encourage readers to purchase such items if the particular jurisdiction where they reside does not grant them the permission to legally purchase and own such items. This book also covers knife exercises, knife maintenance, bushcraft, knife fighting, culinary arts, and knife history. The book or its authors do not encourage readers to engage in activities that can be harmful or hazardous to themselves or others. We also to not encourage readers to engage in illegal activities with any form of item considered a lethal weapon, such as a knife. Before engaging in activities that involve a knife, consult with a local attorney to make sure laws are not broken. In addition, working or training with knives can be physically and mentally demanding, therefore consult with a physician before engaging in such activity. The book or its authors are not responsible for any activity performed by its readers, under any circumstance.

Warning: *Reader discretion is advised. Some of the content in this book is not suited for minors/children under the age of 18. Some of the content might be upsetting in nature and can trigger a negative, unwanted response in certain readers, such as trauma survivors, individuals with common phobias and readers with visual sensitivities. This book contains violent content, which may be too intense for some readers. The content in this book is intended for an older audience.*

For information address Knife Bible, LLC,

P.O. Box 1358, Leesburg, VA 20177

https://www.knifebible.com

FIRST EDITION

Designed by A. J. Cardenal

ISBN 978-0-578-82945-6 (hardcover)

This book is dedicated to our two boys.

"Because we do…. what we do."

About the Author

A. J. Cardenal, MSc. ICT, MSc. GIS

A. J. is a Geographic Information Scientist, with close to 20 years of experience in his field. He holds a Master of Science in Geographic Information Systems from Johns Hopkins University and a Master of Science in Information & Communication Technology, with a Graduate Certificate in Advance Studies of Geographic Information Sciences from University of Denver. In addition, A. J. has a Bachelor of Arts in Geography from Florida International University. He obtained several GEOINT Professional Certifications from the National Geospatial-Intelligence Agency, such as, GEOINT Fundamentals Level I, Cartography Level II and Geospatial Database Management Level II.

A. J. served in the United States Army for 8 years, as a Senior Geospatial Engineer Sergeant. He deployed to Afghanistan with 4th Stryker Brigade, 2nd Infantry Division in Fall 2012 and returned at the end of Spring 2013. While in Afghanistan he served as the Team Lead for the Geospatial Engineer Team, supporting the International Security Assistance Force (ISAF), during Operation Enduring Freedom. His unwavering commitment to the mission earned him an Army Commendation Medal. Upon his return he attended Special Forces Assessment & Selection (SFAS) and Psychological Operations (PSYOPS) Assessment & Selection. His unit recognized the hard work and dedication he gave during the courses and awarded him another Army Commendation Medal. Although A. J. made great strides in his pursuit to become an elite soldier while on Active Duty, he decided to not reenlist due to personal reasons. He then moved onto the United States Army Reserves, where he served in the 478th Civil Affairs Battalion in Miami, FL. While he served in Civil Affairs as a Senior Geospatial Engineer Sergeant, he decided to volunteer for an Active-Duty Tour, where he joined Special Operations, under United States Army South, Civil Military Operations, in Fort Sam Houston, Texas. There, he served as the Civil Information Manager and Senior Geospatial Engineer Sergeant. When his time in service ended, he accepted a job opportunity in Arlington, Virginia at the Pentagon.

A.J. felt he could apply his expertise in other places, not just Department of Defense, and moved on to work in the Intelligence Community for several years, as a Geographic Information Scientist. He worked as a federal contractor at agencies such as the Central Intelligence Agency (CIA) and National Geospatial-Intelligence Agency (NGA).

A. J. now spends his time enjoying the great outdoors and dedicates his weekends to teaching his kids about bushcraft/woodcraft and wilderness survival. He also designs knives for people upon request.

Knife: */nahyf/.* mankind's oldest multi-purpose tool, typically made of a flattened piece of hand forged or machined cut, heat-treated steel that has a sharpened edge, flat cheeks, with some form of handle; used for cutting, chopping, slicing, slashing, or stabbing.

"A knife is a human's original sidearm and true survival companion. A well-made knife paired with strong knife skills can almost guarantee survival for anyone traversing through the unforgiving wilderness of Mother Nature."

—A. J. Cardenal

Author's Notes

You will find a wealth of knowledge embedded in this text, related to what a knife is and why it is humanity's most important tool. It is important to understand what the definition of a knife is before you start reading this book. A knife is mankind's oldest multi-purpose tool, typically made of a flattened piece of hand forged or machined cut, heat-treated steel that has a sharpened edge, flat cheeks, with some form of handle; used for cutting, chopping, slicing, slashing, or stabbing. There are several objects that can be referred to as a form of knife, such as a dagger, sword, machete, parang, golok, kukri, karambit, even a spear. Their dimensions and uses are what set them apart, which is why they were given different names to help distinguish them.

This is not the "holy grail" of knife books, as it covers only topics I personally feel knife owners should know. I will try to cover as much knife knowledge as possible, however, I ask that you do not hold it against me if I miss a few things. I encourage readers to seek additional knowledge related to knives elsewhere to help obtain a different perspective. While a portion of this book is opinion based, it also includes historical facts about knives and how they have evolved over time. This book is intended for a wide range of people, from the knife novice to the knife maker, from the culinary expert to the avid outdoorsman. The book covers a great deal of knife knowledge but does have its limitations. The book covers all the necessary topics related to knives, such as history, culinary arts, bushcraft, knife fighting, knife steels, knife grinds, knife types, knife maintenance, among others. This book is one volume of many that will be released and is designed to serve as more of a general knowledge knife book. The other volumes that follow will be focused on specific types of knives, such as kitchen knives, survival knives, tactical knives, bushcraft knives, carving knives, utility knives, swords, spears, axes, etc. Knife Bible, History & Modern Knowledge is merely the beginning... the first volume of many, that will dive deep into the journey of the knife throughout human existence. What I do promise, is a jaunt that will enlighten some... maybe even fill a void for others.

I am pleased to have written this book and hope readers truly embrace the significance of knives in our lives.

Beware... if you do not already own a knife, this book might encourage you to buy one. Sometimes all you need is a little optimism, a sharp eye, and a knife to give you the confidence to survive in the woods. Safe travels my friend...

Preface

Forged from fire, fury, and passion, hot steel is hammered to its creator's liking, then sharpened into what will be a tool, once wielded for battle and unhinged wilderness survival. The knife… a multi-purpose tool that brings confidence (a sense of security for some), but misery to others. A "well-made" knife is humanity's most important tool—it has served a purpose in our livelihood since the beginning of our existence and will continue to stand true and faithful by our side.

Around the age of six, I was gifted a classic red Swiss Army pocketknife by my older brother. I was thrilled, yet feverishly nervous. Like most new things that require skill and physical contact, the learning stages can sometimes be a little painful. I managed to cut myself when the knife slipped while cutting a piece of wood and the blade closed on my middle finger. The scar is a unique reminder that exploring new things can be a painful, though necessary, endeavor to grow mentally and spiritually as a human being.

Later in my life, carelessness would rise once again, due to confidence taking over, which momentarily effaced my self-awareness. I was twelve years old at the time and trying to open a box that contained a *Super-Soaker*. I used a fixed-blade knife to cut the zip ties that held the water gun in the box. The dull knife slipped from my hands and slashed my right knee near the Lateral Collateral Ligament (LCL), which connects the lower part of the femur bone to the upper part of the fibula bone. I was extremely lucky that it was a straight-cut and did not slice deep enough to injure any major parts of the ligament. That incident was yet another simple reminder that proper training includes maintenance. Part of the maintenance process that we must learn when owning a knife are sharpening skills, because a dull knife is more dangerous than a sharp one. This painful experience, coupled with fourteen stitches, taught me that lesson.

Funny enough, I still feel that my training days never come to an end. At the age of thirty-six, I acquired another "battle" scar while fidgeting with one of my pocketknives. I was being clumsy, and mistakenly closed the blade on the distal interphalangeal joint of my right index finger. This required a lengthy heeling period, but it taught me to always be incredibly careful when handling knives. Even the most skilled knife handlers can get hurt, if not careful. Knives are not meant to be played with—they are tools that serve a greater purpose. When using knives for onerous tasks, wearing proper protection is important. Wear gloves that are made with kevlar or are thick enough to provide adequate cut protection. It is also important to keep your body parts away from the direction you are cutting, to avoid slicing, slashing, or stabbing yourself. Learn proper knife handling skills so that you can prevent unwanted injury.

Pass down knowledge to loved ones, as you would a cherished object that you would like your family to carry forever. Sharing knowledge is a beautiful act of generosity that is of great value. As a father of two amazing boys, it is my duty to pass down my knowledge to my kids. I have learned over the years that knife handling requires a lot of patience and technique. Never rush through tasks with a knife because you are more prone to inflict an injury on yourself or someone else. A well-made knife, along with proper knife skills, can bring years of pleasure, enjoyment, and personal fulfillment.

A knife has no substitute; it is a unique multi-purpose tool. It can be used to make fire by striking a flint stone or scraping a ferrocerium rod with the knife's 90-degree spine. The sparks generated from this process can ignite a flame if there is tinder sitting in the way of the flying sparks and the ground. By performing techniques known as chopping and batoning, a knife can also process the wood that can be used to sustain the fire, skills that will be covered in the "Bushcraft" section in this book.

A knife can also be used for hunting and cleaning wild game, as well as prepping food for cooking. Knives have been used for centuries for hunting and skinning game. A knife can be used for gutting and field cleaning duties. Knives are a primary tool used for slicing, chopping, mincing, or deboning in the kitchen and must always be sharp to avoid injury. When I was in my mid-twenties, I hunted my first wild boar with an ESEE 6 Survival Knife. I stabbed the boar through the ribs, penetrating the lungs, killing it instantly. The boar was then skinned, processed, cooked, and eaten.

Knives are important to me, because they have been a part of my life for an exceptionally long time, and I understand their usefulness. When I deployed to Afghanistan in Fall 2012 with the United States Army, 4th Stryker Brigade, 2nd Infantry Division, part of my everyday carry was an ESEE 3 Survival Knife. My primary weapon was an army-issued Colt AR-15, but maintaining a good, fixed blade knife by my side proved to be useful in the field. I used my ESEE 3 for multiple tasks, such as cutting paracord and opening boxes and MREs, in addition to hammering nails with the pommel. I also pried open a few containers/crates and luckily never broke the tip.

I currently use my knives for camping, bushcraft/woodcraft, hunting, and wilderness survival training. My collection currently stands at over three hundred knives, in addition to nine machetes, five *Gransfors Bruk* hatchets, five *Gransfors Bruk* axes, and two *Karesuando* hatchets. Some would consider me a knife enthusiast. In my opinion—and it is just an opinion—knives carry more value than a firearm. Many may think I am foolish for suggesting that, but it is not the monetary value I am referring to, instead, a wilderness survival value. Even though it is ideal to legally carry a firearm for self-defense, when the ammunition runs out, we are left with a firearm that is as good as a paper weight. A knife can outlive a firearm's usefulness in certain situations

Knives are multi-purpose tools. A knife can be used to build a shelter, process food, and make fire—things that cannot be done with a firearm. A knife will always be the ultimate survival tool, and paired with a good quality axe, a survivalist can make a campsite habitable for long-term use. Given its immense importance, a knife should always be considered a person's primary tool. It is also important to note that people should never buy inferior quality knives. It is important to go the extra mile and purchase high quality knives because your life depends on it. Never try to cut corners or be cheap when it comes to your tools. A well-made, high-quality tool means there less probability of it malfunctioning or simply breaking on you, potentially causing an injury to you or someone else. Knives are not all built the same; therefore, use your knife for what it was intended to be used for. Owning a high-quality tool also means it can be handed down to loved ones and remain in your family for a long time.

On several occasions, I have travelled to unsafe locations as a soldier, contractor, and civilian, carrying only a small foldable pocketknife. I have found that it is important to adapt to one's surroundings, blending well into what certain situations may dictate and avoid uncomfortable scenarios. There were occasions when I worked for the Intelligence Community, where any type of object that could be used as a weapon was strictly prohibited. If a person can legally carry a knife, whether a foldable pocketknife or fixed blade, then I highly recommend it. It is essential to always abide by the laws set in place by the town, city, state, and country in which you live, as they pertain to knives. Not every location is the same, therefore the laws can vary. Adapt your lifestyle accordingly. If you will spend time in the great outdoors camping, hunting, fishing, or doing survival training, then absolutely take a knife with you, but check your local and state laws to make sure what you will be carrying is legal. If permitted (depending on where I am going), my everyday carry is either an ESEE—Izula, TOPS MSK 2.5, LionSTEEL M1, Benchmade—Mini Bugout, Giant Mouse—Biblio, Clyde, GMF1-F, or Swiss Army—Walker. When not in a work facility or location where they are prohibited, my everyday carry blades are all below the 3-inch blade length legal limit for the state of Virginia.

At home, I use my knives heavily to process wood for my firepit and fireplace, in addition to practicing bushcraft/woodcraft in the backyard with my kids. While enjoying the great outdoors, performing survival training, bushcraft or camping chores, I usually rotate between the following knives: ESEE 3, ESEE 6, Bark River Kephart, Bark River Bravo, Bark River Aurora, Bark River Gunny, KA-BAR Kephart, KA-BAR Becker BK2, KA-BAR Becker Bk9, TOPS Fieldcraft B.O.B, TOPS Tanimboca Puukko, Condor Bushlore, L. T. Wright Bushcrafter, L.T. Wright Genesis, L.T. Wright Bushbaby, LionSTEEL M4, LionSTEEL M1, Fallkniven F1, or Helle Algonquin. The knife steels that I use are typically 1075, 1095, CPM 3V, AEB-L, A2, M390, Cru Wear, or Triple Laminated. As far as the grinds go, I enjoy using Convex, Full Flat, Saber, or Scandi. Sometimes the grinds do have a secondary convex micro-bevel to help with cutting edge strength and edge retention. If I plan to go on a fishing trip, then there is only one knife that fits the environment best, and that is my Spyderco—Pacific Salt in H1 steel, due its anticorrosion properties and amazing toughness. When processing wood for fire, I carry my trustworthy Gransfors Bruk Axe or hatchet. I interchange gear all the time, depending on how I am feeling or the task I want to achieve. If I do not want to take my axe, I will sometimes use a saw. I enjoy using a Silky saw or Bahco. On the occasions when I prepare food for cooking, either in the kitchen or on the barbeque, using the right knife is important. Not all knives are created equal, and each serve different purposes, which will be covered throughout this book. Before getting into the different purposes of knives, steel types, grinds, etc., I will cover their historical significance and evolution over time.

It is with much pleasure that I present to you *Knife Bible*.

Photograph taken by A.J.

Acknowledgements

Sharon Steel, your contributions helped immensely and helped take this book to another level. A big heartfelt thank you for giving this book a huge creative twist.

Holly Caldwell, PhD, this was a challenging project, and we could not be happier with all your contributions. You went above and beyond, and we are touched and grateful. Thank you for all you have done.

L.T. Wright, thank you for the unwavering support, kindness, and contributions. God bless you now and always.

Shane Adams, from ESEE Knives, was our point of contact and huge supporter of this project. We owe you a huge level of gratitude for everything you contributed to this book.

Victorinox was kind enough to contribute not only to the modern knives section but also the wood carving section. Special thanks to world-renowned Bushcraft and Victorinox Pocketknife Instructor Felix Immler. We owe a high level of gratitude to Leah Pepper, Alexa Quinn, and Nina Poosikian for being amazingly helpful and a splendid point of contact throughout this entire process.

Gransfors Bruk, the world's best axe maker, contributed quite heavily to the axe section, to include images and commentary. Emelie Torstensson and Ida Lindström were absolutely amazing. They provided unconditional support and provided wonderful contributions to the book. We are extremely grateful. We owe a special thank you to Emelie for taking such amazing pictures and sharing them with us for the book. We also want to thank Samuel Uneus for providing exceptional photography.

Craig Powell is not only the General Manager for TOPS Knives, but also a great knife designer. We owe tremendous gratitude to Craig for all the support throughout our journey to get the book published.

We owe a special thank you to Gianni Pauletta, Owner & CEO of LionSTEEL, for contributing a wealth of information about LionSTEEL, and also want to thank Andrea Mazzoli for providing fantastic images for the book.

Peter Hjortberger, renowned Swedish knifemaker and Fallkniven's Founder, provided amazing insight about Fallkniven. We are incredibly grateful for all your contributions and generosity.

A special thank you to Jessica Leitch, US Marketing Manager for Opinel and Alex Delecroix, Director of US Sales and Operations for Opinel. Jessica and Alex worked really hard in providing us with exceptional content for the book. We are truly appreciative for everything you did.

Dan Wowak from Coalcracker Bushcraft was kind enough to contribute a few images where he is performing bushcraft techniques using a knife. We appreciate your help greatly.

Work Sharp contributed a great deal of content, which was displayed in the knife sharpening section. We are grateful for all your support, kindness, and generosity. Josh Warren, we appreciate everything you did for us, and for providing excellent images for the book.

STAY SHARP, STAY TUNED...

A.J.

Acknowledgements

When I first sat down to write, I had a hard time finding "the voice" I wanted to share. It was the excitement and curiosity shared by friends and family, the enlightening conversations with the wonderful makers, and the all-present, unintimidated encouragement from my partner that made me realize, my voice was the only one needed to be shared. Thank you, reader, for taking the time to wander through our book. Thank you for hearing our voice.

From the very beginning Kikuichi has been a wonderful partner. Harry you were pleasantly welcoming, and a wonderful help. Your words set the tone for what was "expected." Ikuyo, your story is one that I am honored to continue to share. Your leadership is guided with your heart and conscience, both evident in the company's values and evolution. I look forward to seeing your influence grow! Duomo Arigatou!

Andrea, grazie mille per tutti quello che hai fatto per questo libro. Veramente e stato un piacre conoscere la tua storia. Grazie per aver creduto in noi e per averci dato l'opportunita di condividere Coltelleire Berti con il mondo. Ci avete accolto a casa vostra e per questo siete tutti benvenuti nella nostra.

Messermeister, you were a class-act! Marc, it was a pleasure to speak with you and I hope to share further conversations in the future. Kirsten and Chelcea, it is safe to say that the company is in wonderful hands. It is an inspiration to see what two women have been able to do for such a renowned knife company. You have done your father, Bern, and your mother, Debra, proud. I am excited to see what is next for the company and am honored that you were glad to be represented in our book.

Chelsea Miller. Girl, what can I say…? I loved your knives instantly but, honestly, I love the person you are, even more. Your multifaceted life is reflected in the personality of your knives, but it is your heart that drives their design. I am so glad that we had the chance to speak and work together. I can only hope that a delightful friendship arises from this experience. Thank you for your honesty and time.

To the phenomenal Pirolo's, Michael & Jacqueline, thank you for indulging my dream of working with you. The problem is that this was way too quick, and now I will have to search for another way to team up soon. You are both wonderful individuals who harmoniously produce experiences meant to become cemented recollections of memorable evenings. Always excited to see what the future holds for you. Always applauding you. Bravo!

A special thanks to the entire team at The Whole Ox. Amanda and Derek, you guys have something truly special going on, both in and out of the shop. We honestly appreciated your patience and flexibility to make this happen. Family is without a doubt a huge factor in your daily lives, as was shown when you welcomed our youngest during the interview and photography sessions. The Whole Ox has an amazing future with you behind it!

Cristina, eres un brava y ha sido un honor tenerte parte de este libro. Gracias por darme la oportunidad de representarte y gracias por todo lo que has hecho por tantos en la sociedad. Es necesario compartir tu historia, porque es importante inspirar nuestras comunidades hacia el "mejor camino." Esto es solo un ejemplo de la magia de la cocina. Cristina, Ben, y a todos de la familia South Philly Barbacoa, ¡sigan haciendo un trabajo fenomenal!

Finally, Opinel, you guys are truly a wonderful team. From the very beginning you were excited to participate and were just great to work with. The quality in your service is reflective in your product, no doubt. Your knives are truly significant in our family. Merci Opinel!

AJ, there are not enough words… ever. Thank you for believing in me… for believing in us... for believing in this.

B and N, this is for you.   - *S.*

TABLE OF CONTENTS

Introduction

Knives cannot be strictly categorized as lethal weapons, built with a sole purpose to take a life. In reality, they are tools… multipurpose tools, created to make certain tasks easier to accomplish. They are the very objects that gave humans an advantage over other living species, to be able to defend themselves, but also sustain a formidable diet that made us who we are today. Knives gave us the ability to hunt, cultivate, build, bond, defend, forage, and sustain life on this wild planet. These sharp tools enabled us to break free from our caves and navigate through treacherous environments that seemed nearly impossible. Its these tools that helped us gain a higher level of consciousness, by allowing us to use our imagination in ways that were unattainable. These multipurpose tools functioned in such a way, that we were able to create clothing and shelter from animal hide to keep us warm in the winter, as we traversed through unimaginable places throughout our planet. We were able to introduce new foods to our diet, we also modified these tools so that we could cultivate the land, build fortified settlements, defend ourselves from threats, and bond with other humans to build stronger communities. To place a knife in the same category as a firearm is absolutely ignorant and demonstrates a real lack of education. A knife is without a doubt the most useful tool humankind has ever created, so much so, that even today… millions of years later, the general design remains nearly unchanged. Knives are NOT a symbol of violence; they are symbol of hope and strength.

Humans are vulnerable creatures by nature. A willingness to survive, to fight, not flee… is what drove us to create the knife. Knives gave us the ability to become warriors, to conquer fear, and establish ourselves as the dominant species on this planet. It became our responsibility to provide a safe haven for those we love, to protect and sustain what we have worked so hard to build. It is this tool, that gave us the motivation we have, because it gave us the undeniable advantage, the opportunity to dream. This was the first tool humanity mastered. We learned the capability of the knife as we migrated into other realms of human consciousness and cemented our existence on earth. We are all survivalists at heart, and it is the knife that will continue to push humanity to unprecedented heights.

There is no better way to explain the abovementioned text, than to take a deeper look at our past. Without further ado, lets transport back in time, to the beginning of humanity and cover how the knife has been the most significant object for humankind since the stone age.

The History of the Knife

(a glimpse)

Imagine your life today, without the use of a knife. Keep in mind that a knife can take many forms, such as a kitchen knife, multi-tool/pocketknife, hunting knife, survival knife, combat knife, bushcraft knife, carving knife, foraging knife, throwing knife, dagger, sword, spear, arrow, axe, saw, chisel, machete, shovel, scalpel, razor, even scissors. The list goes on… Remember the definition of what a knife is, "one of mankind's oldest multi-purpose tools, typically made of a flattened piece of hand forged or machined cut, heat-treated steel that has a sharpened edge, flat cheeks, with some form of a handle, used for cutting, chopping, slicing, slashing, or stabbing." All the items mentioned fit the definition of what a knife truly is; we just assume that some of them are not knives. The truth is, they are just different forms of knives, each given a specific name and designed for a specific purpose. We are surrounded by different forms of knives and they are as useful today as they were thousands of years ago. What has changed over time is the material, the shape, and the use of the knife. We are attached to the knife forever. It allowed humans to not only coexist but thrive as a civilization.

Educate yourself on knife handling and then wield it like a master of the craft, as a magician of sorts, because this mystical dance can only be performed by those dedicated to the art. Respect the power of the blade and use it as if it is an extension of your body. When you hold a knife, remind yourself, that you are holding the very object that enabled us to break free from our ancient raw caves and evolve into an intelligent species . . . capable of conquering foreign lands in treacherous environments and building cities and empires.

Fig. 2.
Object: Nine Bifaces
Date: 700,000–200,000 B.C.
Culture: Acheulean
Medium: Flint, quartzite
Classification: Tools
Credit Line: Purchase, Arthur Ochs Sulzberger and Friends of Arms and Armor Gifts, Arthur Ochs Sulzberger Bequest, and funds from various donors, 2018
Accession Number: 2018.51.1–.9
Met Museum

STONE AGE

Archaeological discoveries suggest cutting tools were used by early civilizations dating back millions of years ago. In the early Stone Age, stones were flint knapped into cutting tools and used primarily for hunting, skinning game, preparing food, shaping wood, and self-defense. Early flint knapping styles were known as "direct percussion," where stone was struck with hard rocks, or hard wood, to break small pieces off and cautiously bring it to a desired shape. It could very easily be that during this process, the stone/flint was hit with enough force with a particular rock to create a spark. This discovery of the spark could have easily led to the discovery of fire. It is not entirely known when fire was first used by humans, but there is some evidence to suggest *Homo erectus* was using fire about 400,000 years ago.

Most of the discoveries during this period were likely accidental. Methods related to using cutting tools for cooking and eating may have evolved soon after the discovery of fire. Cutting tools existed before our race, *Homo sapiens*, came into existence. Archaeological fossil discoveries found in Africa dictate *Homo sapiens* came into existence over 300,000 years ago. Also known as humans, *Homo sapiens* were nomadic and travelled long distances in search for food. They would migrate according to shifts in climate, as did the herds and flocks of animals they were hunting. *Homo sapiens*, though, were not responsible for the development of the first stone tools, rather, *Homo habilis/Australopithecus habilis* deserve that credit. *Homo habilis* was one the earliest representatives of the human genus and inhabited areas of sub-Saharan Africa roughly between 2.4 million to 1.5 million years ago. The earliest forms of flint knapped stones had blunt edges and were not particularly useful for stabbing or slashing. Cutting tools were used more for digging, scraping, carving, light hammering, and chopping. With the emergence of *Homo sapiens*, stone tools became more refined. Hand axes were also used quite heavily during the Stone Age, making its first appearance about 1.6 million years ago. The hand axe could possibly be the longest-used tool in human history. It was made of a large stone and flint knapped into a teardrop shape with a primitive point, such hand axes were used up until 35,000 BC. The stones typically used during this period for flint knapping were flint, quartzite, or obsidian. There is no doubt that tools helped humans evolve into an intelligent species, competent enough to achieve higher consciousness, required for cultural growth.

Roughly 60,000 years ago, planet Earth was right in the middle of an Ice Age. This extreme shift in climate was harsh and prevented humans from traveling too far north. Some areas of the southern hemisphere, like the African continent, suffered horrible droughts. This Ice Age nearly wiped out all human existence from the planet. But it was also during this time that humans made an astonishing leap forward related to stone tool development and communication. Humans realized that they performed better as a collective, so they began to develop organized social groups. Although these social groups existed several million years ago, they were especially important during this time. Ultimately, humanity needed to form bonds to navigate through the ongoing severe climate change in order to survive.

As humans started refining their tools and experimenting with crops and irrigation, they began to settle in areas for longer periods, eventually creating permanent communities. Flint knapping techniques consequently improved over time. The archaeological discoveries of stones dating back 12,000 BC, demonstrate a more refined flint knapping technique. Around this period, these techniques demonstrate a careful and skillful removal of flint flakes, to produce cutting tools more closely related to a knife, with a sharp blade and a tapered grip. Stone saws made of flint first appeared between 50,000 BC and 11,000 BC. Small tools that resembled a saw, with geometric microliths that were shaped into triangles, were a major development for this period. Archaeological findings show that small, sharp micro blade tools existed within the Magdalenian culture, between 11,000 to 17,000 years ago, from the Upper Paleolithic and Mesolithic period. Located primarily in Western Europe, the Magdalenian culture was named after a rock site that was discovered in the Vezere Valley, located in France's Dordogne department, "La Madeleine." The Magdalenian and their intricate stone tool developments marked the final stage in the stone tool development journey.

Shovels are important to mention because they too are a form of knife. The shovel was an incredibly important multi-purpose tool that was developed around this period, with findings suggesting they were created sometime between the Neolithic and Bronze Age. While no one truly knows exactly when and where shovels were developed, some archaeologists believe they were made from an ox's scapula (shoulder-blade) and modified to be used as an effective digging tool. They served as a multi-purpose tool, used for agricultural purposes or self-defense. As shovels evolved over time, edges and shape were modified, handles and blades were replaced for stronger and more durable material. Stones were also flint knapped into spear heads that were used as hunting tools, which could easily pierce the flesh of animals. Knives were also used for cutting and shaving hair. Prehistoric drawings depict clam shells, shark teeth, obsidian, and even sharpened flint were used as shaving instruments.

In the Neolithic period (c. 10,000 BC), also known as the New Stone Age, humans began to focus more on settling in more defined areas, versus wandering around nomadically. In this period, stone tools were polished via grinding methods, using polishing stones. Archaeological discoveries in Europe demonstrate that tools such as axes, chisels, and gouges were beautifully polished during this time.

When humans finally came across metal, stones were not entirely ignored. Some archaeological discoveries suggest that stone knives were still being made 2,000 years into the Bronze Age. It was a slow transition that occurred in different places at different times around the world. For example, indigenous cultures throughout the Americas used primarily stone tools up until the fifteenth and sixteenth centuries AD, at the point of European encounter.

Fig. 2. Object: Biface
Date: ca. 400,000–150,000 B.C.
Culture: Acheulean
Medium: Flint
Dimensions: L. 9 3/4 in. (24.8 cm); W. 4 3/4 in. (12.1 cm); D. 1 7/8 in. (4.8 cm); Wt. 2 lb. 12.9 oz. (1271 g)
Classification: Tools
Credit Line: Purchase, Friends of Arms and Armor Gifts, 2019
Accession Number: 2019.422
Met Museum

COPPER AGE

Stone can be a difficult material to work with and can only be fashioned into a limited number of useful shapes. If broken, stone blades cannot be repaired or recycled. These limitations made it easy for early civilizations to adopt a new material—metal. Archaeological discoveries in northern Iraq indicate that around 9,000 BC, copper was already being used in certain areas. As primitive knives evolved and became more polished, had sharper, refined edges, and were made of stronger material, this marked a transition from the Neolithic, Stone Age to the Eneolithic, Copper Age. Smelting copper may have started between 7,000 or 6,000 BC, in "the cradle of civilization," (also known as the Fertile Crescent), located in the Middle East.

Not every culture embraced copper as much as the Egyptian and Middle Eastern societies during the Copper Age. This was probably because not all cultures were as well established as these societies and did not have the same resources to extract copper deposits. There were multiple human migrations that took place during this period, with humans traversing as far north as Europe, until they finally settled. A stable climate made migrating less arduous and dangerous as compared to the early Stone Age which had suffered more shifts. Due to the lack of widespread use of copper during the Chalcolithic Period (Copper Age), it is not considered part of the Three Age System—Stone, Bronze, Iron—that traditionally defines early human development. All things considered, the Copper Age fell within the transitory period between the Stone Age and the Bronze Age. However, some consider this period part of the last stages of the Stone Age which ended between 4,000 and 2,000 BC.

In the Eastern Hemisphere, the Copper Age was confined to certain areas in the Middle East and Egypt, but the use of the material also extended to the Western Hemisphere and influenced cultures in North America. In this region, Indigenous tribes, such as the nomadic peoples who crossed through Beringia (commonly known as the Bering Strait), an icy land bridge that connected Asia with the Americas about 18,000 years ago, were experimenting with copper. Archaeological discoveries in the nineteenth and twentieth centuries of the Lake Superior Basin in North America suggest that Indigenous tribes who dwelled near the Keweenaw Peninsula mined copper using primordial excavation methods. Using makeshift wedges and hammer stones, they would loosen the natural deposits of native copper that was exposed on the surface. Ancient artifacts that have been recovered in the Keweenaw area demonstrate that tools were being made from copper, such as axe heads, small knives, arrow heads, chisels, and needles (awl). These findings date back to the Archaic stage in North America, which took place between 7,000 and 1,000 BC. In sequence of North American pre-Columbian cultural stages, the Archaic stage followed a Lithic stage and was superseded by the Formative stage. Currently, there have been no signs of casting or smelting ever discovered in this area, which means the tools where being fashioned using simply cold hammering methods.

Stone tools were not entirely replaced with copper ones, although the smaller tools were. While copper can be a very resilient metal, it is exceptionally soft. Tools made of copper had limitations, and depending on the dimensions and use, a tool could easily bend, chip, or disintegrate. Shorter tools/weapons performed better when using copper. Daggers were the weapon of choice because of the size and thickness. They were the first metal-edged weapon used for self-defense. Daggers typically had a double-sided medial ridge cast on the blade's spine (center) to provide support and increase strength. By 4,000 BC, medicine was a known science and civilizations during this period were already using small cutting tools/knives to perform surgeries. Obsidian, for example, was being used as surgical blades because it was easier to attain a razor-sharp edge, than with copper, at the time. Egyptian physicians had designated specialties, focusing on specific parts of the body, such dentists, neurosurgeons, ophthalmologists, gastroenterologists, and proctologists.

Knife handles changed over the years as well. In the neolithic era, a knife handle may have started out as a rounded, or blunt, extension from the actual knife blade. This changed over time to bone or thick, stacked layers of animal hide for additional comfort and grip. In 1991, in the Tyrolean Alps along the Italian-Austrian border, a flint dagger found on a Copper Age mummy (which archaeologists named Otzi) changed our understanding of how people during this period used knives. Found in the Tisenjoch pass of the Similaun glacier, Otzi's dagger demonstrates the significance in using knife handles made of wood. Based on this discovery, people living during the Copper Age were forcing sharp flint blades into wooden handles for better grip and comfort. The blades were bound with animal sinew and a string attached to the end of the handle to keep the blade in place. A 12 cm sheath was also found, made from lime tree bast. The blade was resharpened with a *retoucheur*, made from a stripped branch of a lime tree, and carved into pencil shape. This tool was used for precision work, to chip away small fragments of the flint blade to keep it sharp; it was the first of its kind to ever be discovered. Several other tools were discovered on Otzi, such as a quiver made of deer hide, a long bow with arrows, and a copper axe made of 99.7% pure copper.

Linear-Band-Keramik (LBK) Culture (5,700 BC)

The Linear-Band-Keramik (LBK) culture was identified by German archaeologist, Friedrich Klopfleisch, in the nineteenth century. The LBK were also known as the Linear Pottery culture because of their ceramic pottery designs. Radiocarbon dating suggests the LBK originated around 5,700 BC, in the Hungarian plains as well as parts of Austria, southern Bohemia, Moravia, eastern Germany, and the Danube Valley. Their first settlements were discovered in the Rhine Valley, which includes Belgium, the Netherlands, and southern Poland. Around 4,900 BC, their territory spanned as far as Ukraine, Moldavia, northern Romania, and France. They cultivated land, hunted, domesticated animals such as pigs, sheep, goat, and cattle, and supplemented their diet with whatever they could gather from the wilderness. Their tools were typically made of flint knapped stone, from which they would carefully knap the stones to the shape of their liking. Archaeological discoveries, at some of the earlier settlement sites, show how skillful they were at flint knapping, developing axe heads, narrow blades, end scrapers, sickle blades, and armatures. Some of their later settlements, such as the ones in western Europe, reveal how their flint knapping techniques evolved over time with the production of flint tools with more triangular points. They were an extremely self-sufficient culture that thrived over most of Europe during the Copper Age (Chalcolithic period) into the early Bronze Age. Though it was once believed that their territorial expansion was peaceful, new evidence drawn from several of their early and late-stage sites has shown that they were, in fact, rooted in a violent past. Warfare was present during this time and human remains show death by trauma. It can be assumed, in some instances, that there must have been conflict between nomadic hunter-gatherers and the incoming settlers. Massacre sites, which have been unearthed specifically in the Rhine Valley, show skull head injuries, potentially caused by heavy blows with self-defense weapons of the time. Over time, the LBK culture evolved, merging with other cultures, and later giving rise to the Funnel-beaker culture, which will be covered in detail in the Bronze Age.

BRONZE AGE

As early civilizations began processing more metal, this led to the discovery of bronze around 3500 BC. This period marked the transition from the Stone Age to the beginning of the Bronze Age. Many technological advances occurred during the Bronze Age, such as the creation of the first writing instruments and the invention of the wheel. When bronze was used for knives, people realized they stumbled onto a much stronger and durable metal that retained an edge for a longer period of time.

The discovery of bronze gave civilizations that used it an advantage over those that did not. Civilizations in the Middle East started combining tin and copper alloys to produce bronze and people began smelting and casting metal ores to create several objects made from bronze, such as spears, daggers, swords, and axes. Knives used for self-defense and hunting were not the only items produced during this period. Tools for cultivation and agriculture were also developed, such as the bronze plow/plough.

The Bronze Age lasted from 3300 to about 1200 BC throughout the Middle East and some parts of Asia and gave rise to the ancient Mesopotamian civilization of Sumer around the fourth millennium BC. As prolific farmers, Sumerians grew a plethora of grains, which enabled them to comfortably form larger settlements. They established approximately a dozen city-states spread throughout Mesopotamia, a land they called "Kiengir," known today as Iraq.

Cucuteni-Trypillia Culture (5000–2800 BC)

When looking back at the Bronze Age, the first civilizations that often come to mind are the Sumerians or the Egyptians. However, several groups, clans, tribes, and cultures were developing at the same time all over the world. A perfect example is the Cucuteni-Trypillia culture, which flourished in eastern Europe between 5000–2800 BC. They were a society of farmers who cultivated the land with early forms of agricultural tools, such as the plow/plough made of copper or bronze. Over time, the Cucuteni-Trypillia developed advanced irrigation systems which eventually supported their well-established settlements and communities. Their territory spanned to what is known today as Romania, Ukraine, and Moldova, and extended northeast from the Danube River Basin, near the Iron Gates (Carpathian Mountains), to the Black Sea and Dnipro River, just above Kyiv. Archaeologists have uncovered more than 3,000 sites, ranging from small, rudimentary settlements to large, sophisticated settlements.

The Cucuteni-Trypillia culture was not a sudden development, but rather, a population transfer or human migration that took place over time. Several tribes and clans from various areas across central and southern Europe migrated to the Steppe region and eventually banded together to form the Cucuteni-Trypillia culture. In the Neolithic period, there were several thriving cultures throughout Europe already laying the foundations for more advanced civilizations to emerge. They fished, domesticated animals, cultivated the land, and worked with clay to make pottery, statues, and amulets. Most of these settlements were located near rivers. Copper used was extracted from riverbeds and mined from Ukraine. As discovered on archeological sites, in the early stages of their culture they worked with copper to create jewelry and small ornate items. Over time they developed better hunting techniques and used tools such as axes and plows/ploughs forged out of copper or stone.

This culture acquired a great deal of copper tools via trading with neighboring cultures. Towards the end of the Cucuteni-Trypillia culture, the use of clay began to taper off as more items were made of copper, a result of their metallurgical methods improving over time. Eventually, bronze made its appearance around 3000 BC, leading to greater use of bronze made tools. The Cucuteni-Trypillia culture made great strides with their use of cutting tools, cultivation methods, and animal domestication. Even though they were primarily an egalitarian society, there was some form of social stratification. The Cucuteni-Trypillia were a peaceful society, therefore making it easy for aggressive cultures to overtake them. Warfare and raiding were common among tribal agriculturalists in the Steppe region during this period and were the major factors for bringing an end to the Cucuteni-Trypillia culture.

Funnel-Beaker Culture (4300–2600 BC)

The Funnel-Beaker culture emerged from the Linear-Band-Keramik (LBK)/Linear Pottery Culture and the Mesolithic hunter-gatherers of southern Scandinavia, the Netherlands, Northern Germany, and Poland. They flourished between 4200–2650 BC, meaning they began establishing themselves nearly 1000 years before the Bronze Age. Therefore, they are considered more of a Bronze Age culture as opposed to a Stone Age culture. The Funnel-Beaker farmed, domesticated animals such as pigs, sheep, and cattle, and supplemented their diet by hunting wild game and fishing. They mined flintstone and used advanced flint knapping techniques to create axe heads and other small items. They also imported copper daggers and axes from Central Europe. Archeological findings from burial sites show unique ceramic vessels, jewelry, and flint axes belonging to this society.

The Funnel-Beaker culture gave rise to the Corded Ware culture, which settled around most of northern and western Europe, between 2900 and 2350 BC. The Corded Ware culture will be covered later in this section.

Maykop Culture (3700–2900 BC)

The Maykop was a Bronze Age culture that thrived between 3500 to 3000 BC in the northern and western Caucasus region, from the Taman Peninsula in the north to the Kura River in the south. Their territory fell within modern-day southwestern Russia and some parts of northern Georgia. To the south they bordered the Kura-Araxes culture (an early trans-Caucasian culture), and to the north they bordered the Yamnaya culture. Their ethnic identity is unknown but is believed to be Indo-European in origin. The Maykop had extensive contact with early civilizations of the Mesopotamia region during the Uruk/Protoliterate period (c. 4000–3100 BC). This contact with neighboring societies helped them evolve to a highly sophisticated culture. They participated in regional trade, cultivated the land, and domesticated animals such as pigs, cattle, sheep, goats, and horses. The Maykop were also one of the first societies to make practical use of the horse for transportation, an advancement which supported trading capabilities. Some researchers have also credited them with potentially being the first to use the wheel, as archaeologists believe the Maykop developed the first versions of the chariot.

The mountains of the Steppe region were abundant in rich deposits of precious metals and stones, aiding the Maykop culture to acquire a great deal of wealth. During this time, metal production in the Middle East, Asia, and Eastern Europe consisted of arsenic, copper, tin, iron, gold, silver, lead, arsenic bronze, and tin bronze. Groups in these regions often traded valuable commodities and the Maykop knew they held large deposits of these precious metals within their territory, which also assisted them in amassing their vast material wealth. Archaeological findings of Maykop tombs show that this culture had developed an array of bronze tools and weapons, such as axes, broad blades, daggers, spear heads, awls, and chisels. Discovered in the tombs of their elite leaders were vast amounts of jewelry made from gold, silver, and semi-precious stones. Their clay pottery served a multitude of purposes, such as storing water and grains. Archaeological discoveries have revealed that they quite possibly obtained valuable commodities through trade and exchange with southern regions, such as Mesopotamia, as they possessed jewelry made from precious metals, namely gold, as well as weapons made of bronze.

They produced their own bronze tools locally, such as plows/ploughs and axe heads. As molds used to cast the metal material into the shape of these tools were discovered, their metallurgical methods improved over time, leading to an explosion of growth for the Maykop, as more effective tools equated to more efficient production. Recent findings by archaeologist A. Rezepkin demonstrate that the Maykop were also developing swords dating as far back at the second-third of the 4th millennium BC. His discovery of the most ancient bronze sword was found in a Maykop tomb near Novosvobodnaya. The sword has a total length of 24.8 inches and a hilt length of 4.5 inches and can be seen on display at the Hermitage in St. Petersburg, Russia.

Supply of new material and valuables began to dwindle in Mesopotamia due to climate change, creating conflict across the southern regions. This ultimately led to essential shortages for the Maykop culture. Their ancient burial traditions were one of the many reasons why the culture eventually crumbled. Unlike other cultures, Maykop elite leaders hoarded riches and were buried with them, rather than handing them down. Mesopotamia held the greatest influence in the region, therefore, when their internal conflicts inadvertently led to war, the region was completely destabilized. The inevitable collapse of Mesopotamia led to the end of adjacent cultures around the same time. The power of the Maykop chiefs depended on material circulating from the south and when that vanished, it negatively impacted their influence and power. The collapse of trade routes around 3,100 BC, coupled with the potential of damaging foreign interference, may have brought the Maykop culture to its demise. These foreign interferences may have manifested themselves as severe climate change, internal conflicts, economic collapse, or foreign invasion. Although the disappearance of the Maykop culture is still somewhat of a mystery today, what *is* certain is that when they vanished, the Yamnaya culture spread into the former Maykop territory. It is because of the Yamnaya culture that the influence of the Maykop culture remained present in the region, even after their demise, as a result of the Yamnaya embracing various cultural aspects of the Maykop. Note that it is estimated that around 3100 BC, while the Maykop began to be phased out, other regions began to flourish around the same time, such as the Egyptians.

Yamnaya Culture (3300–2600 BC)

Around 5,000 years ago, nomadic herdsman arrived in Europe. These people, known as the Yamnaya, originated in the Eurasian Steppe region (modern-day Ukraine and Russia), just north of the Black Sea. During this time, Indo-European languages began to take shape as a result of the Yamnaya people, which later evolved to the European dialects we know today, including English. DNA studies show links between the Corded Ware and Yamnaya cultures, in which the former are unquestionably descendants of the latter, who migrated to northern Europe via mass migration.

The Yamnaya were undoubtedly an advanced culture, with several influential inventions, such as the creation of the wheel and the use of horses as a means of transportation. Although these were previously regarded as Maykop breakthroughs, it is difficult to determine which of the two cultures were truly the first to introduce these inventions so it remains a topic of debate amongst researchers and archaeologists. The Yamnaya had a healthy relationship with the Maykop which led to a great deal of trade between the two groups. As a result, it is possible to assume that during their exchanges, one may have shown the other what could have been the first rendition of the wheel. Likewise, the same may be implied regarding the use of horse for transport. That said, the Yamnaya did, in fact, invent axled wagons which eventually led to their arrival in Europe. They were able to carry enough goods to travel long distances without having the need to set up campsites for long periods of time.

Mass migration was easier due to the invention of the wagon, as opposed to traveling on foot and simply carrying whatever was possible by hand or on your back. Horseback riding and the use of the wagon gave the Yamnaya an opportunity to explore the world in a way that had never been possible before. The use of horses as a means of transportation changed the course of history and was an important factor in the rise of civilizations. In Yamnaya settlements, archaeologists discovered that their diet consisted of mostly meat from cattle, horse, sheep, pig, and antelope, as well as whatever they could forage from their natural surroundings. Some Yamnaya did farm crops, like millet and amaranth, but cultivating and harvesting was uncommon practice.

The Yamnaya also had warlike tendencies and possibly raided the settlements of other early European groups. Early European settlers where docile by nature and did not really have the weaponry or infrastructure to fend off a hostile Yamnaya takeover. Europe's early settlers had sporadic settlements which consisted of mostly small to medium-sized tribes during this period, from 3000 BC to 2700 BC. The Yamnaya are sometimes referred to as warrior horseman, and if accurate, early settlers stood little chance against them. Although it is still unclear if they conquered everything in their path, early European settlers were eventually replaced by the Yamnaya.

Burial mounds, also known as *kurgans*, demonstrate that the Yamnaya people used copper or bronze daggers and small flint tools. The Ural Mountains provided the main source for copper and stone during this period. Archaeologists found a *kurgan* at the Kutuluk grave site located near the Russian city of Samara which contained a 25-inch, 1.11-pound copper clublike weapon with flared pommel. The blade is diamond-shaped in cross-section with semi-sharp edges and a flattened end, versus the traditional pointed end. This weapon would have been used for self-defense, to bash enemies during conflict. The Yamnaya people carried war clubs made of copper or bronze, in addition to spears with bronze or copper spearheads. Archaeologists are evermore convinced that the Yamnaya culture was indeed, extremely warlike, and ruthlessly massacred enemy societies in Europe. Most of modern-day Europe is descendant of the Yamnaya culture, which in some parts, transitions to the Corded Ware culture.

Corded Ware Culture (2900–2350 BC)

The Corded Ware culture is derived from a merger, or amalgamation, of the Yamnaya and the Funnel-Beaker cultures. The term "Corded Ware culture" was coined by German archaeologist Friedrich Klopfleisch in 1883. The name symbolizes the cord ornamentation on the surface of pottery, discovered in archaeological sites throughout extensive areas of Central and Eastern Europe. These items have been discovered over a vast amount of territory, which implies that the people who created these earthenware artifacts are historically significant. In the early twentieth century, artifacts pertaining to the Corded Ware culture were collected and preserved, such as stone axes, beakers, arrowheads, amphorae, and flint flakes. As more discoveries were made, some researchers concluded that the Corded Ware did have warriorlike roles, implying that the hunter-fighter held the highest prestige in their communities. Key findings of hunting or self-defense tools such as battle-axes, bow & arrows, and knives provide evidence that further support the notion that they embraced warriorlike tendencies.

The territory that the Corded Ware occupied is still somewhat debated. Based on the location of the archaeological sites studied, the Corded Ware spanned most of Northern Europe, from the Rhine River in the west to Volga River in the east. Today, their territory would include modern-day Germany, the Netherlands, Denmark, Poland, Lithuania, Latvia, Estonia, Belarus, the Czech Republic, Austria, Hungary, Slovakia, Switzerland, parts of Romania, northern Ukraine, as well as some parts of Russia. Evidence of the Corded Ware people has also been discovered in parts of Southern Norway, Southern Sweden, and Finland.

The period of their disappearance is still contested among researchers. Most have concluded, though, that it may have taken place roughly between 2300 BC and 2400 BC. It is not that the Corded Ware people simply vanished. On the contrary, their amalgamation with other emerging cultures ultimately led to the "disappearance" of their culture and way of life. Their settlements began to disappear between 2300–2440 BC, with the last sites located in Russia, disappearing approximately around 2000 BC.

Battle Axe Culture (2800–2300 BC)

The Battle Axe culture was an offshoot of the Corded Ware culture, which eventually replaced the Funnel-Beaker Culture in southern Scandinavia. The Battle Axe culture coexisted with the Pitted Ware culture, another native Scandinavian people who settled in the area long before the Battle Axe. After about three centuries of cohabitation, the Pitted Ware were eventually absorbed by the Battle Axe. What made the Battle Axe so unique, was the shape of the axe heads they used. The distinctive design was unique to this culture, as the axe heads looked like a small sea vessel, leading some researchers to refer to these people as the Boat Axe culture. Archaeologists have discovered in their burial sites over 3,000 precision-worked axe heads made of polished flint stone with an interesting, curved shape. They served a dual purpose, with one end sharpened like a traditional axe and the other end similar to a rounded hammer used for smashing objects. Some of these axe heads were used for ceremonial purposes, demonstrating social status within the culture, but it is unquestionable that these tools were also used in warfare, as several unearthed burial sites reveal skulls with crushing head wounds. These findings led Swedish writer, Herman Lindqvist, to name this period (2800–2300 BC) the "Age of Crushed Skulls." The merger between the Battle Axe and Pitted Ware cultures led to the Nordic Bronze Age. Eventually the axe heads used by the Battle Axe transitioned from flint to bronze but for the most part maintained the same shape.

The Koryos (2200–1300 BC)

A feared warrior tribe that raided settlements along the Steppe region with intent to conquer and loot, the Koryos was made up of mostly young males, presumably between seventeen and twenty years old. Indoctrination to the Koryos consisted of a series of tests, including a yearlong journey with other candidates, where they "roughed it out" in the wild with only their weapons. The point of these trials was to help the candidates develop strong character, confidence, and survival skills. Upon return from their wilderness experience, these young men were initiated into the Koryos and could now engage in activities of pillaging settlements, military duties, and conquering foreign territory. They behaved incredibly beastly, animal-like, and even dressed themselves in animal skins to embody the nature of wolves or feral dogs. The purpose of immersing themselves in wolf-like behavior was to eliminate human taboos and live outside of human cultural norms. One could assume that the folklore surrounding the legend of the "werewolf" or "man-wolf" derived from this beast-like behavior embodied by these early warrior tribes or clans. Typically armed with axes made of either stone, copper, or bronze, the Koryos also kept clubs and spears in their arsenal. Axe heads were hafted to a wooden handle by wedging method. Birch-tar, rawhide lashings, or other cordage was used to reinforce the head onto the wooden handle—similar in shape to what we see in modern day, a cast, solid bar, with slightly convex cheeks and a cutting edge. Copper and bronze axe heads were cast into the desired shape, then refined using other methods, such as hammering and polishing. The Koryos were formed from alliances between warrior tribes and were the foundation of what would later become known as the Gallic tribes.

Note: Archaelogists David Anthony and, his wife, Dorcas Brown, along with their excavations and findings in Krasnosamarskoe, (located in the Russian steppes), helped legitimize the existence of the Koryos.

Egyptian Empire (3150 BC–671 BC)

To cover the formation of the Egyptian Empire we need to travel back in time, to around 3100 BC, when the empire was conceived with the unification of Upper and Lower Egypt. This endeavor was led by Egypt's first pharaoh, Narmer, also known as King Menes. King Menes of Upper Egypt sent an army down the Nile River and defeated the king of Lower Egypt, unifying Egypt. After relocating to Lower Egypt and establishing his new capital in the city of Memphis, King Menes declared himself pharaoh of Egypt and established the First Dynasty. Egypt developed a strong central bureaucracy, engaged in widespread commerce, and developed a strong military. The empire expanded its territory by conquering neighboring regions. When they conquered the Kingdom of Kush, Egypt amassed copious amounts of gold. As a result, Egyptians fashioned jewelry, personal adornments, and ritual tools out of the precious metal.

During the Bronze Age, though, copper was not entirely forgotten. Copper was mined in the Sinai Peninsula, located between Egypt and Western Asia. In the southwestern portions of the peninsula, two sites seem to be the most important, Magharah and Serabit el-Khadim, where primarily copper ore and turquoise were found. Copper razors have been discovered in Egyptian tombs as old as the 4th millennium BC. Regardless of wealth or social status, Egyptian men and women were known to shave their entire bodies from head to toe, as shaving was a form of ritual cleansing as much as it was a sanitary endeavor. The act of shaving assisted in acclimating to the extreme heat and to prevent a lice breakout. Egyptians wore wigs to hide their bald heads and protect themselves from the sun. Nobles also customarily wore artificial beards as a sign of divinity. Shaving was not a habit, nor customary, amongst the earliest human civilizations until about the fifth century AD. Today, we now know the Romans to be the first to have adopted the act of shaving as a societal standard and fashion statement.

In addition to razors, Egyptians used copper saws during this period. Documentation of archaeological findings state that unframed saws have been found in tombs, such as tomb No. 3471 in Saqqara, dating back to the reign of Djer, between 3,100 BC and 2,686 BC. This tomb was near the Pyramid of Teti and part of the First Dynasty Necropolis tombs. Copper saws were not the only items found in some of the tombs. Items such as needles, scissors, pincers, axes, razors, arrow tips, and knives have also been discovered.

Although a portion of Egyptian weapons were still made of copper, they would eventually shift to bronze as the primary metal for weaponry. Knives were shaped to a more dagger-like form and swords looked simply like long daggers. Egyptian weaponry went through a major transformation between the Middle Kingdom of Egypt and the New Kingdom of Egypt around 1700 to 1500 BC. The Hyksos, a people with whom Egyptians traded goods often, played a major role in Egypt's transition of weapons to more sophisticated ones. The Hyksos were from western Asia and were exposed to different cultures. They introduced to the Egyptians the sickle-shaped sword, known as the *khopesh*, as well as full-tang daggers made of bronze. The *khopesh* sword was cast completely of bronze with handles wrapped in animal hide for comfort. They also shared the technology of improvised bows made from wood reinforced with animal horn and introduced the horse and the horse-drawn war chariot. The New Kingdom Army of Egypt was now heavily equipped, thanks to the Hyksos.

As the Egyptian Empire grew, it began rubbing borders with the Hittite Empire, located in present-day Turkey. Conflict soon arose between the Egyptians and the Hittites, who were led by King Muwatalli II, over the city of Kadesh. With over 50,000 troops taking part, the Battle of Kadesh (1274 BC) was the largest fought during this period. It was during this battle that the Egyptians were introduced to iron. The Hittites were large producers of iron and known to be excellent metallurgists. Most of their weapons were made of iron. During the battle, Ramesses II of Egypt realized that he was at a disadvantage because iron is a stronger metal and its properties outweighed those of bronze. In 1258 BC, a peace treaty between Ramesses II (Ramesses the Great) and Hattusili III, successor to Muwatalli II, enabled a new relationship to take place, which led to a sharing of knowledge. Egypt began manufacturing weapons made of iron. At first, the empire produced low quantities of weapons because iron required charcoal from burnt lumber as part of the strengthening process. Egypt's geographic location was at a disadvantage because there were few trees that could be used to produce charcoal. Egypt eventually entered its Iron Age between 1000 and 900 BC.

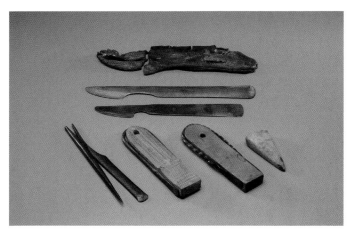

Fig. 3. (left)
Object: Cosmetic Instruments.
Period: New Kingdom.
Dynasty: Dynasty 18. Date: ca. 1550–1295 B.C. Geography: From Egypt, Upper Egypt, Thebes.
Medium: Bronze or copper alloy.
Credit Line: Rogers Fund, 1912.
Accession Number: 12.182.7d
Met Museum

Fig 4. (right), Object: Razor and mirror, Period: New Kingdom Dynasty: Dynasty 18, early, Reign: reign of Thutmose II–Early Joint reign, Date: ca. 1492–1473 B.C., Geography: From Egypt, Upper Egypt, Thebes, Sheikh Abd el-Qurna, Tomb of Hatnefer and Ramose (below TT 71), inside Basket "L", MMA excavations, 1935–36, Medium: Bronze or copper alloy, boxwood; copper alloy, Dimensions: Razor: Handle: L. 11.8 cm (4 5/8 in.); Diam. 1.5 cm (9/16 in.); Blade: L. 9.3 cm (3 11/16 in.) Mirror: Overall: h. 16.8 cm (6 5/8 in.); W. 8.5 cm (3 3/8 in.); Th. 2 cm (13/16 in.), Credit Line: Rogers Fund, 1936, Accession Number: 36.3.69,.13-related, Met Museum

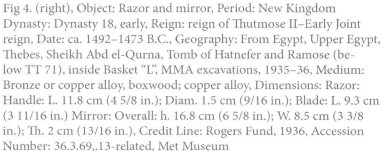

Fig 5. (above), Object: Dagger, Period: Middle Kingdom–Early New Kingdom, Dynasty: Dynasty 12–18, Date: ca. 1981–1550 B.C., Geography: From Egypt, Medium: Bronze or copper alloy, ivory, Dimensions: L. 21.7 cm (8 9/16 in, Credit Line: Rogers Fund, 1912, Accession Number: 12.182.18, Met Museum.

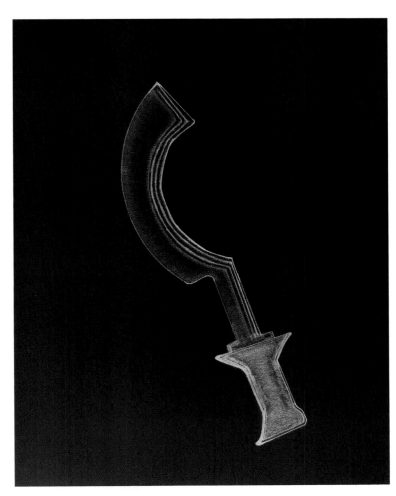

Fig. 6. (left), Drawing made by A.J., depicting a Khopesh on display at Liberty Biblical Museum, in Lynchburg, VA. The item is ca. 1500 BC, late Bronze Age, with a total length of 23 inches, and a blade length of 18 inches.

Fig. 7. (above), Object: Arrow or Javelin Point of Neferkhawet, Period: New Kingdom,Dynasty: Dynasty 18, early, Reign: reign of Thutmose I–early sole Thutmose III, Date: ca. 1504–1447 B.C., Geography: From Egypt, Upper Egypt, Thebes, Asasif, Tomb of Neferkhawet (MMA 729), west chamber A, Burial of Neferkhawt (I), MMA excavations, 1934–35, Medium: Bronze or copper alloy, Dimensions: L. 11.6 cm (4 9/16in); W. 1.6 cm (5/8 in); greatest thickness 0.5 cm (3/16 in.), Credit Line: Rogers Fund, 1935, Accession Number: 35.3.88, Met Museum.

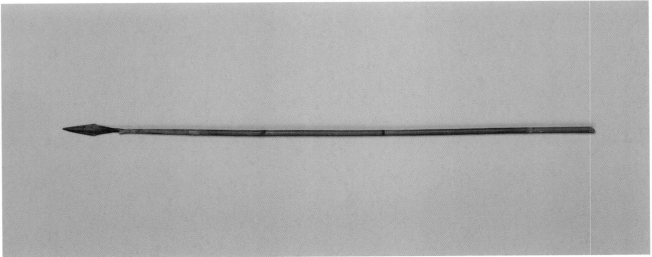

Fig. 8. (above), Object: Javelin shaft (see 36.3.207a), Period: New Kingdom, Dynasty: Dynasty 18, Reign: Joint reign of Hatshepsut and Thutmose III, Date: ca. 1479–1458 B.C., Geography: From Egypt, UpperEgypt, Thebes, Sheikh Abd el-Qurna, Tomb of Senenmut (TT 71), below, deposit of hunting weapons, MMA excavations, 1935–36, Medium: Reed, Dimensions: L. 74 cm (29 1/8 in), Credit Line: Rogers Fund, 1936, Accession Number: 36.3.206c, Met Museum.

IRON AGE

It is difficult to determine precisely when the Iron Age began because regions entered this stage of technological advancement at different periods. The Iron Age is the last epoch of the three eras of early human development. It is also the most important, because iron is the strongest of the three metals (copper, bronze, and iron). The Iron Age did not begin to influence northern Europe until about 500 BC, and the Germanic Iron Age of Scandinavia did not end until about 800 AD, when the Viking Age began. During this period, knives were highly improved because smiths realized, maybe accidently, that by adding carbon/charcoal to iron strengthens its properties and transforms it to what we know today as alloy steel. The development of steel also led to the creation of more brutally lethal weaponry and stronger body armor. Over time, different methods were explored around the world for ways to harden steel to make it tougher and more durable. Carbon steel is ideal for knives because it is strong, durable, and easy to sharpen. The only problem with carbon steel is that due to low chromium content, it corrodes easily if left unattended.

Although the Iron Age ended around 330 BC, there were major advancements during this period, such as superior weaponry, tools, utensils, armor, structures, etc. Although it is difficult to pinpoint when particular ages began and ended because their introductions were different for everyone there is a consensus that, for most of the world, the Iron Age ended around 330 BC.

Zhou Dynasty (1029–258 BC)

The Zhou Dynasty was among the most culturally important and longest lasting in China. While it is commonly split into two periods, the Western Zhou (1029–771 BC) and Eastern Zhou (771–258 BC) these dates are still being revised due to new archaeological discoveries. The Zhou Dynasty established a feudal system, which divided areas into semi-independently governed states that took orders from the king. During the period known as the Hundred Schools of Thought, great intellectuals and philosophers like Confucius, Mencius, Mo Ti, Lao-Tzu, and Sun-Tzu contributed to developments in philosophy, military organization, and literature. The Zhou Dynasty maintained power for over 800 years during which time it made important cultural enhancements in agriculture, education, music as well as the arts and metallurgy.

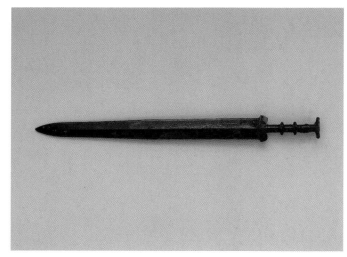

Fig. 9.
Object: Sword
Period: Zhou dynasty (1046–256 B.C.)
Culture: China
Medium: Bronze with lacquer-like patina
Dimensions: L. 18 in. (45.7 cm)
Classification: Metalwork
Credit Line: Fletcher Fund, 1924
Accession Number: 24.172.2

Met Musuem

Bronze chopsticks were among the new inventions introduced during the Zhou Dynasty and became one of the primary utensils used to consume food. China was the first country to use chopsticks, called "*zhu*" during ancient times, and has used eating utensils for over 5,000 years. The Zhou Dynasty was not the first to use chopsticks, though, as it is recorded in the *Liji*, the *Book of Rites*, that chopsticks were already being used during the Shang Dynasty (1600–1100 BC). As a matter of fact, the *Shiji*, the *Chinese Book of History*, notes that the last king of the Shang Dynasty used ivory chopsticks.

Given its superior characteristics, iron tools slowly replaced bronze ones. However, the transition from bronze to iron did not fully unfold until the sixth century BC, when iron became widespread and an important factor in everyday life. Examples of weapons used during this period included the dagger-axe (resembling a reaphook or sickle), spear, halberd (fusion of the spear and dagger-axe, reaching a length of 3 meters), bow, and sword.

Eventually the feudal system established by the Zhou Dynasty collapsed in 258 BC, giving rise to the Qin Dynasty. It was not until the Han Dynasty (206 BC–220 AD) that China truly transitioned from a Bronze Age to an Iron Age. Iron technology, as we now know, brought a new generation of weaponry because it was far cheaper and easier to produce tools. Weapons such as the spear, pike, battle axe, and dagger could now be made readily accessible to even the common infantry man.

The Sword of Goujian

The Sword of Goujian was discovered in 1965 inside an ancient tomb in Hubei, China. The sword is believed to have been created between 771 BC and 403 BC. What makes this sword so astonishing is its unique razor sharpness and resistance to tarnish, despite having been buried for over 2,000 years in a damp environment. The sword displays incredible craftsmanship, well advanced for the period. It is a double-edged, straight sword made of bronze, weighing about 2 lbs., with a length of 22 inches. The blade is about 1.8 inches wide at the base. The scabbard was also intact with a nearly airtight fit around the blade. The sword features beautiful markings engraved on one side in a script known as bird-worm seal script. Six of the eight characters have been deciphered and read, "*King of Yue*" and "*Made for Personal Use.*" Archaeologists and Chinese linguists agree that the sword most likely belonged to Goujian, ruler of the Kingdom of Yue from 496 BC to 465 BC. Jian swords are the earliest form of swords in China and are greatly respected due to their mythological ties. Chinese folklore describes these knives as "The Gentleman of Weapons."

Emperor Goujian ruled during a very tumultuous time in the Zhou Dynasty known as the Spring and Autumn period which lasted from 771 BC–476 BC. A series of military quests took place during this period, which led to more refined weaponry with greater strength and durability. Bladesmiths in the Yue region in South China reached incredibly high levels of skill in metallurgy, to the point that they were already incorporating rust-proof alloys into their knives.

The Scythians (900–200 BC)

The Scythians were a male-dominated society of nomadic warrior horsemen, who originated in what is now southern Siberia. This ancient warrior tribe dominated the Pontic-Caspian Steppe around the seventh century BC until third century BC. The Scythians were one of the greatest cultures of the barbarian world. They flourished in the area east of the Altai Mountains, a mountain range in Central and East Asia where Russia, China, Mongolia, and Kazakhstan intersect. As the climate warmed up quite significantly in the region, it enabled the Scythians to move more freely. They performed reconnaissance of sorts, where they gathered information on neighboring settlers, which eventually led to raiding those settlements. Overtime, they developed predatory tendencies and engaged in massive pillaging of the simple pastoral people who lived in the steppe region. They carried bow & arrows, short swords (akinakes), and battle axes (sagris) with razor-sharp edges and hammer ends on the opposite side. They also carried lances, maces, war picks, shields, and armor for protection. They were expert horseback archers, which gave them a clear advantage over foot soldiers. They implemented a combination of techniques in battle, from guerilla warfare to scorched earth tactics. The Scythians amassed a great deal of wealth from their raids. Around the sixth century BC, the Scythians had established themselves on the west of the steppe. They had driven the Cimmerians out of the south Russian steppe and eventually, established themselves as the ruling culture of the Pontiac Steppe. The Saka and Massagetae, (to whom the Scythians considered brethren), formed a realm of cultural domination that extended over vast regions across Eastern Europe to the borders of China. South of the Scythian territory was the Persian Empire, which also grew rapidly during this time.

Contrary to popular belief, the Scythians actually dressed quite well. Their garments were beautifully stitched, decoratively dyed, and embroidered with ornate patterns which, at times, included generous amounts of gold thread. Some men dressed in well-made sheepskin coats, insulated with wool, and fashioned decorative belts with gold and bronze fastenings. The Scythians were very spiritual people who believed in deities and in the afterlife. Similar to the Egyptians, they were buried with works of art, weapons and armor, parts of wagons, carpets and textiles, household items, and food and wine sealed in claylike jars.

The Scythians were essentially the first Central Asian nomadic empire. The ancient Greek writer and geographer Herodotus wrote in the fourth century BC that the Scythians were an "invincible force." As fearsome warriors they upheld this reputation by defeating the Assyrian Empire at the Battle of Nineveh in 612 BC. They formed an alliance with the Babylonians, Persians, Medes, and Chaldeans, with the intention of together defeating and driving out the Assyrian Empire from Iran. It was an assault that lasted months, and when they finally arrived at the palace of Nineveh, they set it on fire.

There was a period when the Scythians remained quite dormant and did not engage in a great deal of warfare, even though the Persians continued to grow under the rule of Cyrus the Great. As the Persians managed to conquer the Medes and Babylonians around mid-500 BC, their territory grew rapidly, extending as far east as the Indus River and as far west as Asia Minor. Cyrus the Great established the largest empire the world had ever seen. The Persian Empire, also known as the Achaemenid Empire, wanted to stretch their reach to the north and so they went to battle against the Scythians. The Persian Empire was defeated numerous times by the Scythians, most notably, in a battle in which they were brutally massacred by a Scythian tribe known as the Massagetae, which was under the fearless leadership of Tomyris, Queen of the Massagetae. The Persians and Scythians had a love-hate relationship for centuries.

The Scythians began to underestimate their opponents and found themselves losing a confrontation with the Macedonians. They lost a battle against Phillip II of Macedon in 339 BC, which led to the conquest of Thrace in 340 BC. The Scythians and Persians, then under the Rule of Darius III (r. 336–329 BC), united to fight against a common enemy, Alexander the Great of Macedonia. In 331 BC, the Persians fought against Alexander the Great at the Battle of Gaugamela and lost. This battle was the final nail in the coffin for the Persians, as it marked Alexander the Great's glorified conquest of the Persian Empire. At the Battle of Jaxartes in 329 BC, Alexander defeated the Scythians and marked the end of an era for the nomadic warriors of the steppe. Their reputation as fearsome warriors declined, and they simply assimilated to overwhelming changes emerging in the political landscape around them. The defeat against the Macedonians was one event from which they would never fully recover. In the early Middle Ages, the Scythians and Sarmatians were assimilated and absorbed by the early Slavs.

Fig.10.
Object: Short Sword (Duan Jian)
Date: ca. 4th–1st century B.C.
Geography: Xinjiang
Culture: Eastern Central Asia
Medium: Steel, bronze, gold
Dimensions: L. 26 3/8 in. (67 cm); W. 2 in. (5.1 cm); Wt. 1 lb. 6.5 oz. (637.9 g)
Classification: Sword
Credit: Purchase, Bashford Dean Memorial Collection, Funds from various donors, by exchange, 1998
Accession Number: 1998.418
Met Museum

The Persian Empire (550–330 BC)

Around 550 BC, an ancient Iranian empire emerged known as the Persian Empire. Founded by Cyrus the Great, it became one of the largest empires in history. Cyrus the Great began his conquest of nearby kingdoms, merging them under one government to include the Media, Lydia, and Babylon. The Persian Empire, often referred to as the Achaemenid Empire, managed to amalgamate three principal sites of early human civilization under their rule: Mesopotamia, Egypt, and the Indus Valley. What they accomplished was no easy task and required a great deal of tactic and maneuverability. Climate played a significant role in how their army behaved and what they wore. In order to adapt to the hot climate of the Middle East, their armor was lightweight and they tried to keep close combat at a minimum. The stance on combat was to be swift and eliminate as many enemies as possible by employing expert archery and high-speed advance. The Persian army did have quite a collection of weaponry at their disposal, which included spears, recurved bows, arrows, daggers, and swords. Their preferred combat weapon was the bow and arrow. In battle, the Persian archers would fire massive barrages of arrows toward their opponents. They were also equipped with light javelins/ spears, known as *palta*. The spears were about four feet in length and had an iron spear head. The Persians knew how effective the Scythians were with their *akinakes* (short swords) so they developed a version of their own. The blade was double-edged, made of iron, and typically used for cutting or stabbing. Based on Greek artwork and archaeological findings, it is believed the Persians also used a Scythian-style battle axe, known as the *sagris*. They also employed horse-soldiers, or mounted warriors, due to the fact that two of their greatest foes fought with horse-soldiers—the Scythians and the Medes.

When the Persian army conquered the Medes, they adopted their horseback warfare tactics. The Persians eventually mastered horseback warfare, and it became a primary method of fighting taught even to their nobles. Juvenile males, between five and twelve years of age, were taught three key things: to ride a horse, draw a bow, and speak the truth. Even though the bulk of the Persian army mastered the rapid approach and combat at a distance, they did have an immensely powerful infantry. Elite soldiers known as "The Immortals," comprised of 10,000 soldiers, were fearsome warriors who enhanced their infantry to levels unseen before. The Immortals created the illusion of immortality, because the instant one elite soldier fell, there was another to immediately replace the fallen. The intent was to always maintain 10,000 elite soldiers, ready, willing, and able to fight. The Immortals were those who were trained to use the *akinakes* and the ones who used it the most in battle. The common soldier carried a spear, recurved bow, and arrows. The Immortals were also employed by Darius I (r. 522–486 BC) when he unsuccessfully attempted to invade Greece at the Battle of Marathon in 490 BC.

Ten years later, the Persian army would attempt to strike the Greeks again under Xerxes I (r. 486–465 BC), but this time they would be confronted by the Spartans at the Battle of Thermopylae. Led by General Leonidas I (c. 490–480 BBC), only 300 Spartans along with 6,000–7,000 soldiers from neighboring Greek city-states, managed to defeat a Persian army that far outnumbered them. The Spartans would hold this position of strength until they were betrayed by a Greek citizen by the name of Ephialtes, who had a strong desire to acquire wealth and popularity among the Persians. Ephialtes informed the Persian army of a path that went around Thermopylae Pass where they could surround the Greek soldiers and attack from behind. Much of the Greek force retreated and this horrible turn of events inevitably led to the massacre of Leonidas and his army of 300 Spartans, as well as the Thespians and Thebans who had remained behind to fight the enemy. If it were not for the betrayal of Ephialtes, the Greek army would have continued chipping away at the Persian army until there was nothing left. The Persians continued their pursuit to expand and conquer foreign lands.

The Persians engaged in many conflicts with the Scythians, suffering great losses, and sneaking few wins here and there. It was not until the Persians and their elite Immortals fought against the Macedonians at the Battle of Gaugamela (331 BC), where they were obliterated. Alexander the Great of Macedonia led his troops into battle and employed his skillful military tactics, coupled with his superior weaponry, to conquer the Persian Empire. After his death in 323 BC, the Persians fell under the rule of Seleucus I Nicator, one of Alexander's generals. He became the founder of the Seleucid Empire (312–363 BC), which succeeded the Persian Empire. It was eventually conquered by the Parthians, who emerged from the steppe region as a Scythian tribe, known as Parni.

Fig. 11.
Object: Arrowhead
Date: 4th–3rd century B.C.
Geography: Iran, Pasargadae
Culture: Achaemenid or Seleucid
Medium: Bronze
Dimensions: 1.18 in. (3 cm)
Credit: Purchase, H. Dunscombe Colt Gift, 1978
Accession Number: 1978.93.16

Met Museum

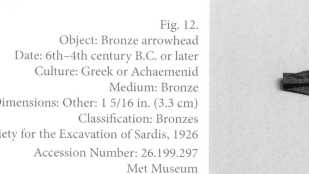

Fig. 12.
Object: Bronze arrowhead
Date: 6th–4th century B.C. or later
Culture: Greek or Achaemenid
Medium: Bronze
Dimensions: Other: 1 5/16 in. (3.3 cm)
Classification: Bronzes
Credit: Gift of The American Society for the Excavation of Sardis, 1926
Accession Number: 26.199.297
Met Museum

Sparta (also known as Lacedaemon 430–371 BC)

The ancient warriors of southern Greece, known as the Spartans, were an extremely powerful people who dominated the area from 434–404 BC. At a young age, Spartan boys began their intense military training, known as the *Agoge*. The *Agoge* was a system focused on duty, discipline, and endurance. Unlike most of Greece, where learning was centered on arts and philosophy, the Spartans were a warrior culture. Typically, these well-trained, elite soldiers would carry a large bronze helmet, a breastplate, ankle guards, a shield made of bronze, a long spear (*dory*), and a short sword (*xiphos*). Some Spartan soldiers elected to carry an alternative to the *xiphos*, and instead preferred the larger, thicker, and more curved-like iron sword, known as the *kopis*. Their shields were used to bash their opponents in battle, knock them down, or create distance so they may strike with another weapon. They wore red cloaks and had long hair, with some displaying beards. Much of their battle gear was family heirlooms, handed down from father to son, and displacing battle gear was viewed as a disgrace. Spartans were later defeated in 371 BC, by Thebes at the Battle of Leuctra. As a result, a long period of decline followed shortly thereafter.

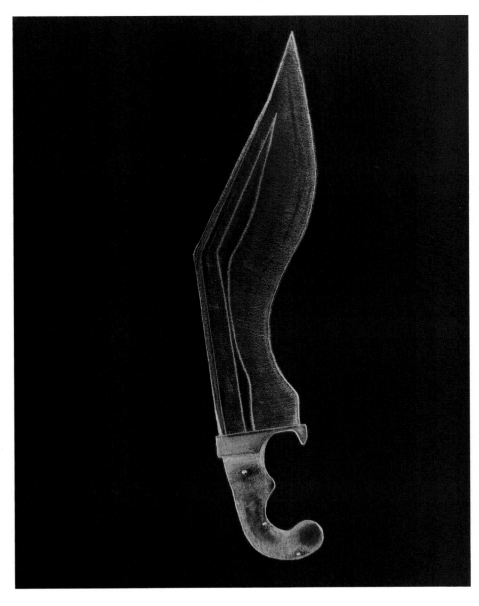

Fig. 13. Drawing made by AJ Cardenal, resembles a Greek Kopis, on display at the Met Museum. Object dates between 5th and 4th millenia century B.C., made of iron.

The Kopis at the Met Museum has the following details:
Dimensions: 22 1/4 in., 1.5 lb. (56.5 cm, 0.7 kg)
Credit: Rogers Fund, 2001.
Accession Number: 2001.346

Macedonia – Alexander the Great (r. 336–323 BC)

Macedonia was a small kingdom located in the north of the Greek peninsula. This area was dominated by great city-states, such as Athens, Sparta, and Thebes. Alexander III was born in 356 BC to King Philip II and Queen Olympias. Alexander learned a great deal from his teacher, the philosopher Aristotle, and became highly interested in science, medicine, philosophy, but most importantly, military. At the age of twenty, Alexander became king following his father's assassination in 336 BC. The young man understood the consequences of being king and had his rivals killed before they could contest his sovereignty. He then continued his father's quest in expanding Macedonia's dominance. One of history's magnificent military minds, Alexander ultimately earned the title of "Alexander the Great." His army carried a small double-edged sword (*xiphos*) for close combat, 18-foot spears (*sarissa*), and strong shields made of bronze called *aspis*, which could be shoulder carried if travelling long distances.

During his time as ruler, Alexander the Great encouraged his soldiers to shave, so that during close combat the enemy could not grab them by their beards. His recommendation made shaving fashionable, which later led to more innovation and techniques introduced to the act of shaving. This decision to motivate his soldiers to shave their beards occurred in 331 BC, just before the violent showdown with the Persians. The act of shaving may have been performed using either their daggers, or small razor-like devices.

Alexander the Great was accompanied by several medical professionals during his expeditions. There were times when they were short on medical instruments and resorted to using their swords to perform surgical operations on the wounded. Some tasks performed by physicians during battle included amputations, pus drainage, sterilization, and healing fractures. Alexander's physicians carried medical instruments such as tweezers, scalpels, and even extractors for arrowheads. None of these instruments would exist without the evolution of the knife.

Alexander led his army through many brutal battles and victories. In 326 BC, he expanded Macedonia's territory as far east as India and the Indus River. Within ten years, he managed to overthrow the Persian Empire, reach the mouth of India, and expand his dominion farther than any had ever seen in the ancient world, spanning over 3,000 miles. Indeed, Alexander the Great had the most powerful army of his time, but he would not maintain that for long. In 323 BC, he became mysteriously ill and died at the age of thirty-two in Babylon. After Alexander's passing, the empire was divided among four of his generals, including Seleucus I, who ruled central Asia and Mesopotamia, which later became the Seleucid Empire (312–63 BC).

Fig. 14.
Object: Plate 4: Alexander Battling the Persians, from The Deeds of Alexander the Great
Artist: Antonio Tempesta (Italian, Florence 1555–1630 Rome)
Publisher: Johannes Baptista Vrints (Netherlandish, active Antwerp, ca. 1575—1610)
Date: 1608
Medium: Etching, first state of two (Bartsch)
Dimensions: Sheet: 8 11/16 × 11 1/8 in. (22 × 28.3 cm)
Classification: Prints
Credit Line: The Elisha Whittelsey Collection, The Elisha Whittelsey Fund, 1951
Accession Number: 51.501.4087

Met Museum

The Parthians (247 BC–224 AD)

A Scythian tribe with a unique fighting style emerged from the steppe region and managed to conquer the Seleucid Empire. This tribe, formerly known as the Parni, became a powerful empire known as the Parthians. They favored a feudal and decentralized system but did take advantage of the social structure built by the Seleucids, which condoned the creation of vassal kingdoms. They employed melee style fighting in the field, approaching their enemies from all directions, wreaking havoc, and dismembering their opponents with their powerful spears. With this method, they managed to conquer territories as far west as the Mediterranean to as far east as India and China.

The Parthians were so effective at their military tactics that they even fended off the Roman Empire on several occasions. Their military was a well-oiled machine, with their cavalry as the piston force propelling them forward, shattering everything in their path. Their cavalry's maneuverability was simply unmatched at the time. Their elite cavalry were the cataphracts (mounted warriors), which carried a lance (*Kontos* – typically 4 meters in length), sword, and bow & arrows. The spear was mighty and had the ability to pierce through two men at once. They were equipped with armor and helmets. Their horses also wore a blanket of chain-linked scales, made or bronze and steel, for protection. The light cavalry units mostly carried bow & arrows, with a dagger-like short sword. The cataphracts used their spears and swords to finish picking off clusters of fighters throughout the battlefield. According to Greek philosopher and historian Plutarch, their arrowheads were made of horn or bone and contained barbed tips. The arrows were fired with such strength and velocity that they would easily fracture armor and pierce though all sorts of protective covering, entering the flesh of their enemies. Based on Plutarch's description of the barbed tips, it could easily be assumed that the Parthian army was using metal arrowheads. The sword used by their archers measured about 3 feet (1 meter) in length, was double-edged, and made of iron. Meanwhile, the cataphracts, aside from their spear and bow, also carried a long sword.

The Parthians employed psychological warfare, applying deceptive tactics to trick their enemies into thinking the layout of their troops was simply only the portions seen by the human eye, while there were thousands more hiding. The intent was to call upon the soldiers who were hiding at precise moments so they could strike when the enemy was most vulnerable. The Parthians defeated quite a few Roman Emperors—one after another. The most notable was the defeat of Crassus and Mark Anthony. The Roman Empire was persistent, and managed to weaken the Parthians overtime, but never truly conquered them. In 224 AD, the weakened Parthians were finally brought down by the arrival of the Sasanian Empire (also known as empire of the Iranians). The Sasanian Empire was the last Neo-Persian Empire to dominate the area before the arrival of the Muslim conquest (633–651 AD), led by the Rashidun Caliphate.

Fig. 15.
Object: Arrowhead
Period: Parthian
Date: ca. 1st century B.C.–1st century A.D.
Geography: Iran, Shahr-i Qumis (ancient Hecatompylos)
Culture: Parthian
Medium: Bronze
Dimensions: 0.33 x 1.34 in. (0.84 x 3.4 cm)
Credit Line: Purchase, H. Dunscombe Colt Gift, 1978
Accession Number: 1978.93.59

Met Museum

Han Dynasty (206 BC–220 AD)

The Han Dynasty was the second great imperial dynasty of China, from 206 BC to 220 AD. It succeeded the Zhou Dynasty and became the longest ruling dynasty, with over 400 years of rule. The Han Empire embraced a Confucian ideology that camouflaged the authoritarian policies of the establishment. Improvements in iron casting enabled the production of stronger, double-edged swords, known as *jian* and later single-edged knives known as *dao* (highly favored during the Ming Dynasty). The *dao* had round grips and ring-shaped pommels, with an average length of 33 inches. The most commonly used sword during this period, the *jian* was slender, had a double edge, and measured about 32 inches in length, with a hilt that measured close to 7 inches. Typically, this sword could be maneuvered with one or two hands. This sword did a particularly great job at severing body parts and cleaving skulls in the battlefield. As tactics and equipment evolved, the *jian* was eventually replaced with the *dao*. Their famous long-range crossbows outranged any weapon possessed by their adversaries. Enhancements to their crossbow made it more accurate and lethal.

The Han Dynasty studied the teachings of Sun-Tzu and applied his principles in military operations. All men from the ages of twenty-three to fifty-six had to serve in the army for at least two years. The Han military was immensely powerful and rid China of nearly all its enemies. A stronger military also meant they had the means to expand their kingdom throughout other areas of Asia. The army had a well-organized chain of command and intricate troop formations. The best fighters were grouped into elite teams within the units. Even the most perfect systems inevitably develop minor weaknesses over time which leads to failure, so every year, the Han army went through general inspection where they corrected any flaws. The Han Empire was constantly at war with potential invaders, such as the Kazakhs, the Mongols, the Jurchens, and the Xiongnu. The Sino-Xiongnu Wars lasted from 133 BC to 89 AD and may have been the weakening point for the Han Dynasty in China; as the empire struggled to keep their well-oiled machine functioning properly. Internal corruption and rebellion caused the empire to fall and opened a gap in technological evolution, leaving the country in great disarray for several centuries. China experienced a huge setback with the fall of the Han Dynasty.

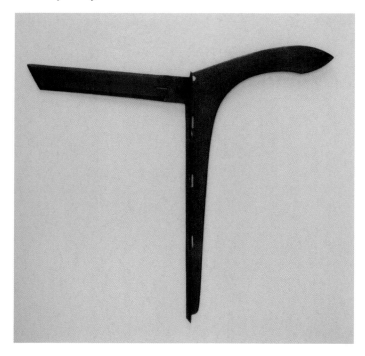

Fig 16.
Object: Pair of Dagger-Axes (Ge)
Date: 4th–3rd century B.C.
Culture: Chinese
Medium: Bronze, lacquer
Dimensions: Dagger-ax (a); H. 15 3/16 in. (38.6 cm); W. 16 3/8 in. (41.6 cm); Wt. 1 lb. 7.4 oz. (663.4 g); Dagger-ax (b); H. 15 1/4 in. (38.7 cm); W. 16 1/4 in. (41.3 cm); Wt. 1 lb. 8.3 oz. (688.9 g)
Classification: Shafted Weapons
Credit Line: Purchase, Henry Keasby Trust, and Kenneth and Vivian Lam Gift, 2000
Accession Number: 2000.262a, b
Met Museum

*Note: These style of knives were more prevalent during the end of the Western Han Dynasty

Celts of Britain (750 BC–43 AD)

The Celts of Britain were the mightiest people in Central and Northern Europe. Comprised of a conglomerate of tribes; the three major groups were the Gauls, the Britons, and the Gaels. The Celts dominated large parts of Europe, spanning modern-day Austria, Switzerland, France, Spain, Belgium, and Britain, before the Romans conquered them and drove them out in 43 AD. During this period, they were simply known as Britons, not Celts (which means "barbarian" in Greek), a term that was adopted in the eighteenth century. The Celts were known to be excellent warriors, who covered themselves in blue paint to inspire fear as they fought in battle. A Celtic belief held that the root of spiritual power resided in the head, therefore by lopping off the heads of their enemies they believed they were absorbing their spiritual power. They would then display the heads as war trophies. Naturally, this was not a justification for hacking off the heads of enemies and retaining them for keepsake, but rather, part of their ritualistic beliefs. In the period before the Iron Age, people in Britain used bronze, an alloy of copper and tin, to make tools. Celtic warriors, however, rode on horses, carried oval shaped shields, daggers, spears, and long slashing swords made of iron. The Celts were also known for bringing war chariots into battle, as described by the Romans. The Celtic tribes, though, lacked a unified front. They were at constant conflict with one another over status and power. This lack of unity was the major reason they were ultimately conquered by the Romans in 43 AD.

Fig. 17.
Title: Sword and Scabbard
Date: ca. 60 B.C.
Culture: Celtic
Medium: Iron blade, copper alloy hilt and scabbard
Dimensions: Overall: 19 5/8 x 2 5/8 x 7/8 in. (49.8 x 6.7 x 2.2 cm)
Classification: Metalwork-Bronze
Credit Line: Rogers Fund, 1999
Accession Number: 1999.94a-d
Met Museum

Germanic People (750 BC–526 AD)

The Germanic tribes occupied Northern Europe, east of the Rhine and north of the upper and middle Danube Rivers. Known as Germania, the territory spanned modern-day Germany, Poland, the Czech Republic, Slovakia, Hungary, and Austria. Germanic tribes were descendants of Indo-Europeans that migrated north into Europe from the steppe region, known as the Yamnaya. The Yamnaya merged with early European settlers known as the Funnel-Beaker. This amalgamation produced both the Corded Ware and the Battle Axe Cultures (an offshoot of the Corded Ware). Much of contemporary Western and Northern Europe has ancestral background rooted in Germanic tribes, such as the Dutch, Swiss, Austrians, Flemish, Swedes, Norwegians, Danes, and Germans. All these countries are, in some form, modern speakers of Germanic dialects, which evolved from Indo-European languages.

Germanic tribes lived off the land, performing small-scale cultivation and harvesting of crops, although they preferred hunting as their primary source of food. They also domesticated animals, such as cattle, goats, pigs, sheep, and at a later period, horses. The plough was the most popular tool out of their agricultural equipment. They grew mostly grains, like barley and wheat, and also participated in foraging, gathering what they could from the forest. Their diet consisted of mostly meat, cheese, and milk. Drinking was very common in social gatherings among the Germanics and they were known for brewing beer and preparing mead.

Germanic people were made up of several independent tribes, which allied and fought common enemies as needed. They even engaged in warfare amongst each other to gain control of territories and resources. They were fearless fighters who fought ferociously and defeated their enemies at all costs. They typically carried a small knife, with a blade about 2.7 to 4.8 inches in length. A machete-like sax/seax, roughly 18 inches in length, was also fairly common, and mainly used for chopping and slashing. It was also common for some Germanic people to carry a double-edge sword, similar to Celtic sword, which measured about 24 to 30 inches in length. Their weapons for the most part were made of iron mixed with low amounts of carbon. The low level of carbon was not immensely helpful at adding much strength, because the higher the carbon content, the harder the blade. However, the blade will become brittle as a result of the high carbon content. Because Germanics added small amounts of carbon, their weapon steel remained ductile. Therefore, to compensate for this disadvantage, they made their blades with thicker spines.

Axes were quite popular, though more common within those who knew how to wield them, well. People who were not as experienced with an axe typically had a battle-club. The battle axes (Dane axe) they used were strong enough to break through bone and enemy shields, but also small enough to be thrown with great precision. The axe heads were made of iron and were razor-sharp. Referred to as *frameae*, lances were also used in battle as much as they were used for hunting, as they had barbed points made of iron. Germanic tribes carried an *angon*, a type of javelin, with a barbed head and long narrow shank made of iron, mounted on a wooden shaft. Spears, known as *atgeir*, would puncture enemy body armor/chainmail once Germanics began using it in later decades.

Over the decades, these tribes merged and formed kingdoms, with six major Germanic tribes rising to prominence over the years: Visigoths (Western Goths), Ostrogoths (Eastern Goths), Vandals, Burgundians, Langobards, and Franks. The Romans referred to the Germanic people as "barbarians" due to the way they behaved on the battlefield, these tribes eventually became the Roman Empire's greatest enemy. While the name could have also been given as a result of the Romans' utter disdain for the Germanics, they did praise their intensity in battle and mastery in wielding the sword. The Germanics' victory over the Roman Empire will be covered later in the Iron Age section, under the Roman Empire.

Punic Wars (264–146 BC)

The Punic Wars were fought between Rome and Carthage. They were both great superpowers of their time, with strong armies seeking to expand their territories. Carthage was situated on the coastal region of northern Africa and Rome was situated just north of Carthage, across the Mediterranean Sea. The Punic Wars were fought in three episodes between 264 BC and 146 BC. The First Punic War (264–241 BC) lasted over twenty years with battles fought over the island of Sicily and the surrounding sea.

During this period, Roman knives had transitioned to large daggers, used as a sidearm, with the sword being the primary weapon in battle for some. Armies also depended on spears, bow and arrows, battle axes, and shields. There were also highly effective, larger weapons of destruction such as the catapult and battering rams, which were used as siege weapons. Carthaginians used a sickle-shaped style knife derived from the Iron Age. The *falcata* was a popular single-edged sword during this period. *Falcata* blades were made from three layers of forged steel that had been put through an aging process to reduce weakness, then reheated in the furnace and tested to meet the quality control set by the Carthaginian bladesmiths, making Carthaginian *falcata* blades superior to the swords used by the Romans.

The Second Punic War (218–201 BC) also lasted nearly twenty years, with Carthage led by Hannibal. Heavily armed with weapons, Hannibal led his armies through the Alps to fight the Romans in northern Italy. He also used elephants in battle to crush the Romans. Carthaginians used the *falcata* to slash, stab, and give devasting overhand blows to their enemies. The fighting in the north went on for roughly sixteen years, until Hannibal decided to retreat because the Romans began assaulting Carthage. The last battle of the Second Punic War was known as the Battle of Zama, where the Roman General Scipio Africanus finally defeated Hannibal.

The Third Punic War (149–146 BC) was led by Rome attacking the city of Carthage with such force, they destroyed the walls and lit the city on fire, burning it to the ground until it was reduced to ashes. Rome had shown deep bravado, making sure everyone in the region understood who was the dominant superpower.

Fig. 18.
Object: Sword (Falcata)
Date: 5th–1st century B.C.
Culture: Iberian
Medium: Iron alloy
Dimensions: H. 20 15/16 in. (53.2 cm); H. of blade 17 in. (43.2 cm); W. 2 5/8 in. (6.7 cm); D. 13/16 in. (2.1 cm); Wt. 1 lb. 0.7 oz. (473.4 g)
Classification: Swords
Credit Line: The Collection of Giovanni P. Morosini, presented by his daughter Giulia, 1932
Accession Number: 32.75.260
Met Museum

*Note: This sword has a modified modern handle, not the original one. This falcata closely resembles the Greek swords used by the Spartans and the Macedonians. It also shares similarities in design to a kukri.

Roman Empire (31 BC–476 AD)

Rome went through major changes in territorial growth and leadership over the next hundred years following the Punic Wars, which included the rise of Julius Caesar.

The First Triumvirate was formed between Julius Caesar, Crassus, and Pompey, around 59 BC, as Caesar became senior Roman consul, with the help of Crassus and Pompey. Marcus Licinius Crassus was the wealthiest man in Rome at the time. Gnaeus Pompeius Magnus (a.k.a. Pompey), was married to Caesar's daughter, Julia, and also held tremendous political power and influence over Rome.

Gallic Wars—(58–50 BC)

Julius Caesar successfully led major war campaigns against the Gauls from 58–50 BC. The Britons, however, would not succumb easily and employed guerilla war tactics against the Romans. Due to the sheer size of the Roman army, a traditional standoff was unacceptable, which pushed Britons to use other alternatives to fight back. The Gauls had a uniquely informal way of fighting in battle. Their fighting style was barbaric, yet highly effective, hacking away at their opponents with their large heavy swords. They also mastered shorter weapons, leaving little space between them and their enemies on the battlefield. When the Gauls faced the Romans, they were outnumbered and stood against a well-formed opponent, known for using organized war tactics. The Romans were more disciplined and crushed the Gauls using tight troop formations and spears. Roman spears were long and provided enough distance to keep the Gauls from using their short weapons against them.

Fig. 19.
Object: Scene from the Gallic Wars: The Gaul Littavicus, Betraying the Roman Cause, Flees to Gergovie to Support Vercingétorix
Artist: Théodore Chassériau (French, Le Limon, Saint-Domingue, West Indies 1819–1856 Paris)
Date: ca. 1838–40
Medium: Oil on canvas
Dimensions: 13 1/2 x 17 3/4 in. (34.3 x 45.1 cm)
Classification: Paintings
Credit Line: Gift of Lisa and William O'Reilly, 2001
Accession Number: 2001.720

Met Museum

The Gauls understood that fighting in a more conventional way was unproductive. Cassivellaunus and his tribe, the Catuvellauni, were the most successful at guerrilla warfare against the Romans. Inevitably, the Catuvellauni lost, and the remaining tribe moved further north, establishing a capital in proximity of St. Albans. Their most famous battle was fought in 52 BC against Vercingetorix, leader of the Gallic army. The Battle of Alesia was the fight that finally broke the Celtic people and their dominance of the region (modern-day France, Belgium, Switzerland, and northern Italy). Ultimately, Julius Caesar gained a great deal of respect and honor by winning the Gallic Wars and successfully expanding Roman territory. Rumors spread amongst the Roman people, in particular the Roman Senate, that Caesar wanted to declare himself king of Rome. Gaius Cassius Longines and Marcus Junius Brutus led an uprising against Julius Caesar, resulting in his assassination, in which he was stabbed to death by members of the Roman Senate in 44 BC.

Following the assassination of Julius Caesar, the Second Triumvirate was formed in 43 BC between Octavian Caesar (great-nephew to Julius Caesar), Mark Antony, and Marcus Aemilius Lepidus. Roman territories were divided among them, establishing a sharing of power. Mark Antony was given the western territory. In 41 BC, Mark Antony was in Tarsus (modern-day Turkey), when he sent a convoy to Egypt to ask for Cleopatra to meet him. Mark Anthony first met Cleopatra in Rome several years earlier when she was a mistress to Julius Caesar. This moment marks the beginning of their affair, which raised eyebrows and "poisoned the air" within the Second Triumvirate. In 37 BC, Octavian had Mark Antony ousted and considered him a traitor to Rome. Five years later, Octavian declared war against Cleopatra and by association, Mark Antony, resulting in a loss against Octavian. It is rumored that they escaped the battle during the final hours and fled to Egypt, where they later committed suicide.

The Roman Empire was formed in 31 BC, when Octavian Caesar, successor to Julius Caesar, declared himself the first emperor of Rome. During this time, he had his name changed to Augustus and managed to double the size of the Roman Empire. He secured tight alliances and amassed riches from all over Europe and parts of Africa. In 14 AD, Augustus passed away and his adopted son Tiberius became his successor. The rule of Tiberius marks the beginning of the Pax Romana (literally "Roman peace"), a period of unprecedented economic growth and stability in the empire that lasted nearly 200 years. At the turn of the century, a man with divine abilities and relentless drive to make the world a better place, was gaining an incredible amount of attention. This man was Jesus (Yeshua) of Nazareth, also known as Jesus Christ.

Fig. 20.
Object: Plate 3: Emperor Tiberius on Horseback, from 'The First Twelve Roman Caesars', after Tempesta
Series/Portfolio: The First Twelve Roman Caesars
Artist: Matthäus Merian the Elder (Swiss, Basel 1593–1650 Schwalbach)
Artist: After Antonio Tempesta (Italian, Florence 1555–1630 Rome)
Date: 1610–50
Medium: Etching
Dimensions: Sheet: 11 11/16 × 9 1/16 in. (29.7 × 23 cm)
Classification: Prints
Credit Line: The Elisha Whittelsey Collection, The Elisha Whittelsey Fund, 1951
Accession Number: 51.501.3488
Met Museum

As the empire was enjoying its period of peace, Jesus was viewed as a political threat to their newly formed stability, as he not only refused to conform to the required pagan worship, but was also converting people to a new message of faith—which would become Christianity. In 33 AD, he traveled to Jerusalem for Passover. While visiting the temple, Jesus grew angry upon seeing the traders and moneylenders engaging in business in the holy site, so he turned over their tables and wrecked their stalls. His outburst upset religious leaders and he was arrested on the count of treason. Emperor Tiberius was present at Jesus's trial and gave the final authorization to crucify him on account of Pontius Pilot's order. To the Romans, Jesus was considered a common criminal and his punishment was to be brutally beaten, publicly humiliated, and fatally crucified. To Christians, his suffering and crucifixion symbolized the ultimate sacrifice, was a demonstration of his love for humankind, and marked the beginning of a new religion—Christianity. Today we know that Christ's beliefs spread throughout the world, converting billions of people to Christianity, through a path of righteousness.

The Holy Lance

The Holy Lance, also known as *the Spear of Destiny* or Lance of Longinus, was the spear that was used by a Roman soldier (centurion, specifically), to pierce the side of Jesus Christ as he hung on the cross. Some consider the centurion's act one of mercy, while others deem it an act of ruthlessness. The bottom line is that the spear represented the final thrust which condemned Jesus to his death. In the King James version of the Bible, John 19:34 states, "But one of the soldiers with a spear pierced his side, and forthwith came there out blood and water." The whereabouts of this spear is unknown; however, several countries have claimed to have it in their possession. The truth as to which country may have the actual spear, though, is still uncertain. France, Italy, Armenia, and Austria all claim to have the spear. Solely based on design, style, and analysis, the one in Vienna, Austria appears to be the most authentic. Whether it is the genuine Holy Lance, however, is still open to interpretation. There was a time in our history when, because of their symbolic value and power of influence over populations, the fabrication of holy relics became widespread practice. Over the centuries, people have fought and died for relics and continue to do so today.

Fig. 21.
Object: Jésus en Croix (Jesus on the Cross)
Artist: Jacques Callot (French, Nancy 1592–1635 Nancy)
Publisher: Israël Henriet (French, Nancy ca. 1590–1661 Paris)
Date: 1621–35
Medium: Etching; second sate of two (Lieure)
Dimensions: Sheet: 3 9/16 x 2 13/16 in. (9.1 x 7.2 cm)
Plate: 3 3/8 x 2 5/8 in. (8.6 x 6.7 cm)
Classification: Prints
Credit Line: Th Elisha Whittelsey Collection, The Elisha Whittelsey Fund, 1967
Accession Number: 67.764.1

Met Museum

The Batavian Revolt—(69–70 AD)

Batavians were a people who lived in the Netherlands between two rivers, the Waal and Rhine. This area was poor and unexploitable by the Romans. The two major contributions Batavians could offer to the Roman Empire were manpower and weapons. The exact root of the Batavian revolt is unclear, but what is certain is that it was led by Julius Civilis. In addition to his innate hatred for the Roman Empire, he wanted revenge for the slaying of his brother. There were several wins and losses on both sides, but in the end, the Romans massacred Batavians under the leadership of Roman General Quintus Petillius Cerialis. The Batavian Revolt serves as a point of reference that depicts the degree to which the Roman Empire was beginning to crack and further decline. People were growing tired of the empire and the disagreeable rule over vast territory. Change in leadership in the Roman Empire created inconsistencies in management and created weaknesses under their control.

Fig. 22.
Title: Plate 3: Claudius Civilis Arrested and his Brother Paulus Beheaded, from The War of the Romans Against the Batavians (Romanorvm et Batavorvm societas)
Artist: Antonio Tempesta (Italian, Florence 1555–1630 Rome)
Artist: After Otto van Veen (Netherlandish, Leiden 1556–1629 Brussels)
Date: 1611, Medium: Etching, first state of two, issue 1 (Bartsch), Dimensions: Sheet: 6 1/2 × 8 1/4 in. (16.5 × 21 cm)
Classification: Prints, Credit Line: The Elisha Whittelsey Collection, The Elisha Whittelsey Fund, 1951
Accession Number: 51.501.3439, Met Museum

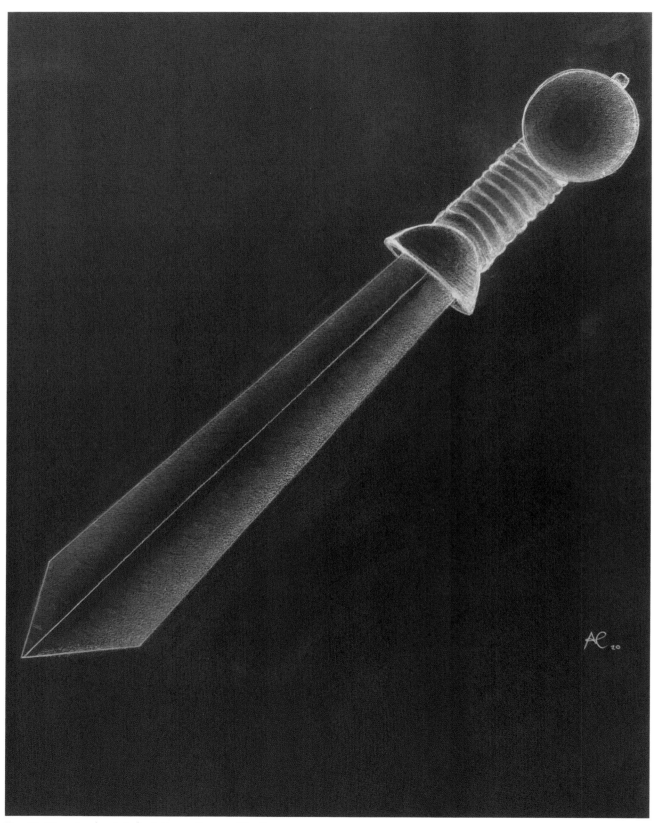

Fig. 23. Drawing by A.J. depicting a Roman Gladius.

Gladiators—(265 BC–5th c. AD)

Gladiators were individuals who fought in arenas throughout Rome around 265 BC, peaking around the first century AD and ending around the fifth century AD. Gladiators were prisoners of war, slaves, criminals, and sometimes volunteers. They had no rights in Roman society, but they did have the opportunity to win back their freedom if they proved themselves victorious in the arena at the decree of the emperor. As a token of victory, they were given a *rudis*, a wooden sword symbolizing their newfound freedom. This sword was named after their newly given title of *Rudarius*, meaning "gladiator who was granted freedom." There were several types of gladiators, though the more popular ones were known as *murmillo, thraex, retiarius, eseedarius, dimachaerius, sagittarius,* and *hoplomachus*. The *murmillo* were armored and carried swords (*gladius*) along with their large shields. The *thraex* wore similar armor to the *murmillo* but carried a smaller square shield and a short, curved sword called a *sica*. The *retiarius* were equipped with a large net and a long trident. The *essedarius* were mounted gladiators who carried either a spear or sword. The *dimachaerius* carried two small daggers, and for the most part, only fought other *dimachaerius*. The *sagittarius* were dressed with a bow, light armor, and rode on horseback. Lastly, the *hoplomachus* carried a throwing spear, a small sword, and a round, concave shield. All gladiators endured vigorous training where misbehavior was not tolerated and anyone who defied the rules could be punished by death. Some additional weapons used in battle were swords (*gladius, spatha, semispatha, sica*), daggers (*pugio*), spears (*hasta, lancea, pilum*), tridents (*fascia*), nets, bows (*arcus*), and boxing gloves (*caestus*).

Construction on the Roman Colosseum began around 72 AD under Emperor Vespasian and was completed around 80 AD under Emperor Titus. The Colosseum saw nearly four centuries of use before it was completely abandoned due to the outlawing of gladiator events. These "games" were outlawed by Constantine I in 325 AD; however, small events still took place from time to time until the mid-fifth century AD.

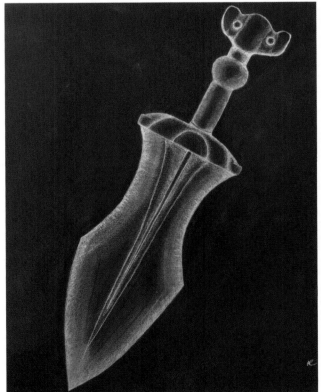

Fig. 24. Drawing by A.J. depicting a Roman Pugio.

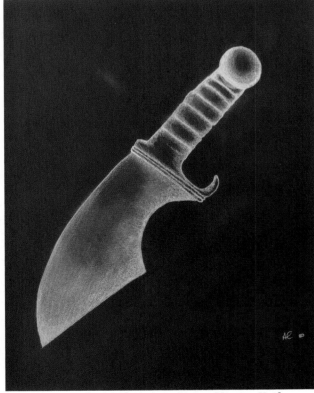

Fig. 25. Drawing by A.J. depicting a Roman Hunting Knife.

Fall of the Roman Empire—(5th century AD)

The Roman Empire was divided into two halves—the Western and the Eastern. As the Eastern Roman Empire grew wealthier, over time, the Western Roman Empire was steadily becoming weaker. The decline of the Western Roman Empire was the landmark event that defined the end of the ancient world and marked the beginning of the Middle Ages in the Western World. Multiple events contributed to its decline, such as major economic woes caused by constant wars, military overspending, and overexpansion. In 285 AD, Emperor Diocletian made the decision to formally divide the empire, an early contributing factor to its inevitable decline. Major government corruption and instability also added to the empire's growing list of troubles. As the Western Empire fought to maintain control it was consumed by civil war, leading several people to assume the throne, only to be assassinated. The emperor's private bodyguards, the *Praetorian*, assassinated at will and instated new sovereigns. At one point, the *Praetorian* even attempted to auction the throne to the highest bidder. Inevitably, the Romans lost interest and trust in their leadership. A weakened state signified vulnerability and opportunity for other tribes and empires to invade. As the rise in Christianity shifted mindsets in the Western Empire and led to an erosion of traditional Roman values, the empire struggled to recruit Romans to join the military. The military was therefore pushed to enlist foreigners, most of whom were Germanic mercenaries. These mercenaries eventually made up most of the soldiers in the legions and began to turn on their emperors. Due to centuries of entanglement and war between the two groups, the Germanic tribes had an endless thirst for Roman blood. After several attempts, the Germanic tribes finally won enough battles to wreak havoc and instability within the Roman Empire. The decline of the Western Roman Empire was due to a combination these various uncontrollable events.

A sign of changing times for the Roman Empire were its significant losses in battle against the Germanic tribes. The series of defeats began with the Battle of the Teutoburg Forest/Kalkriese in the ninth century AD, when Germanic tribes annihilated three Roman legions. This was known as "the battle that stopped Rome," as coined by Peter S. Wells, author of *The Battle That Stopped Rome*. Roman legions were led by Arminius, a former Germanic Prince, from the Cherusci tribe. The twist in the story is that Arminius betrayed the Romans and led them into an ambush, where Germanic tribes annihilated the Romans. This claimed a victory so significant that the Roman Empire had to realign their military operations and assess plans for any future movement into Germania. Rome withdrew all their bases in Germania and decided to consolidate closer to home in order to prevent potential invasion. It took six years for the Roman Empire to gain the courage to return to the place they had been slaughtered, and with good reason. The empire documented the scene as the most horrific they had ever witnessed—delimbed bodies and severed heads were stuck onto trees, marking the ceremonial sites where Germanic tribes had sacrificed Roman soldiers who had been captured alive. In sending a campaign after Arminius, leader of the Cherusci tribe, the empire decided to strike the Germanics once again. The campaign marched into the wilderness and returned defeated, terrified, and nearly lifeless—never to return. Arminius was hailed as the first national hero of Germania.

The Roman Empire's defeat against the Germanic tribes, coupled with their government corruption and economic instability, opened the door to additional barbarian invasions and the eventual collapse of the empire. In 410 AD, invading armies led by Alaric of the Visigoths managed to breach the walls of the Eastern Roman Empire and sack the capital. Rome, which had been looted, pillaged, and burned down, fell under control of the Visigoths. Led by Odoacer, the Western Roman Empire was conquered by the Germanics in 476 AD, marking the year of the Roman Empire's complete defeat and dissolution.

The Gupta Empire of India (320–550 AD)

The Gupta Empire of India was another powerful dynasty, which, like the Roman Empire, ruled during the Iron Age. Founded by Sri Gupta (r. 240–280 AD), the Gupta Empire maintained control of northern India between early third century to late sixth century AD. Some historians say that between 320 to 466 AD marks the "Golden Age" for India, when a significant amount of Hindu culture was created during this period, with contributions in literature, art, architecture, mathematics, medicine (Ayurveda), science, and philosophy. The empire's first ruler was Chandra Gupta I (r. 319–335 AD), whose reign united the Guptas via marriage to Princess Kumaradevi of the Kingdom of Magadha. He assumed the title of *maharajadhiraja*, meaning "King of Kings." Samudra Gupta, son of Chandra Gupta I, expanded their territory by conquering neighboring kingdoms. Although Chandra Gupta I and his son Samudra Gupta were great rulers, it was the rule of Chandra Gupta II that made the greatest impact.

During the rule Chandra Gupta II, son of Samudra, the *navartna* was established. The *navartna* was a group of nine scholars that developed impressive advancements in several academic fields. Their research and literary works established major concepts of medicine (Ayurveda), the first advanced numerical system, the game of chess, and developed a standard work for sexual behavior, known as the *Kama Sutra*. The Gupta Empire was primarily focused on promoting Hinduism, though also supported Buddhist and Jain cultures.

Advancements in chemistry played a major role in the improvements of metallurgy and blade smithing during this period which resulted in the fabrication of stronger swords with better designs. Foot soldiers and nobles of the Gupta Empire typically carried a double-edged straight sword known as the *khanda*. The *khanda* proved remarkably effective on the battlefield and was also used for ceremonial purposes, as it was even featured in religious writings. Its hilt was designed to secure a good grip to prevent slippage and the cutting of one's hands on the blade, and the pommel contained a spike that was used to strike opponents. Soldiers/archers used a bow and arrow made of metal, instead of the typical wood used in earlier periods. Used to eliminate threats while keeping a safe distance, the bow was another popular weapon during the Gupta Dynasty.

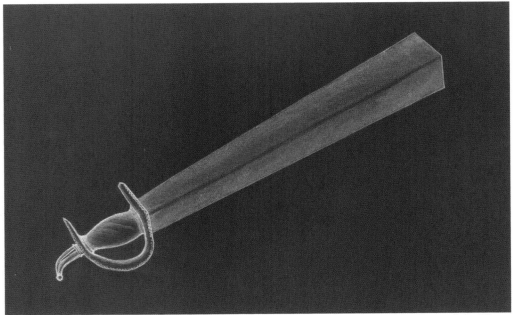

Fig. 26. Drawing by A.J. depicts a Khanda style sword. There were many variations of the Khanda sword, this drawing is just one variation.

MIDDLE AGES

Medieval Period (Middle Ages, or "Dark Ages"), from 5th to 15th century AD, which began after the fall of the Western Roman Empire.

Weakened central governments in need of protection from invaders, raiders, and bandits relied on skilled armed men as their first line of defense. Knights appeared in Europe around the ninth century with the purpose of protecting monarchies, villages, cities, and/or monasteries. The single most important weapon during the Middle Ages was the sword, and for knights, the sword was a chivalric symbol and sign of noble status. The sword's blade of this period typically measured about 3 feet in length and, due to its heavy weight, was held with both hands. Swords could easily sever limbs with a single thrust, producing a psychological distressing effect on the inflicted person. Knights would receive extensive training from about the age of ten until they mastered the difficult skill of effectively wielding a sword. Around the age of twenty-one, if the squire (boy in training) was proficient at using the sword, he could then be knighted by the lord. Swords during this period were double-edged, made of steel, and heat treated over a charcoal fire. Swords weighed several pounds, from the *broadsword* which weighed around 3.5–5 pounds to the *greatsword* which weighed about 6–10 pounds.

This period has rarely been portrayed correctly in movies, where we are shown chivalrous, aristocratic warriors fighting nobly with a sword. The fact is, though, that this period was grisly and cold blooded, where medieval warriors would slaughter their opponents with a combination of murderous tools. Due to cheap production costs, other weapons were also popular during this time, such as the lance. Lances were used to perform horse-mounted attacks, wherein the lance would crushingly penetrate the opponent's body on impact. Therefore, this weapon was rendered single use, as it would shatter upon contact. Spears, axes, and mace were all popular during this time as well. The spear was used as a defensive block to dismount cavalry from their horses and deflect foreseeable danger. Through evidence of shattered skulls or completely dismembered opponents, skeletal remains from this period reveal the dreadful blows from these weapons. In Medieval Europe, knives were multi-purpose tools, used not only for self-protection, hunting, and processing food, but also as eating utensils.

Due to their ability to penetrate vulnerable spots in armor, daggers, also played an important role because despite their small size, they were highly effective in exposing vulnerabilities and killing. The *rondel/roundel* dagger was a medieval weapon associated with knights and denoting status. The purpose of this knife was to bypass armor, via jabbing between vulnerable gaps. Its specialized grip provided more security when handling. The earliest versions of the *rondel* had only one discoidal guard. Later versions had two: one as a finger guard and the other as a pommel. Both discoidal guards were about an inch thick. Discoidal guards provided protection from the blade when stabbing into objects. The *rondel* shape also varied depending on who made it and where it was made. The guard and pommel's discoidal shape were not always round, as some were made octagonal, hexagonal, or even fluted at times. Therefore, location of origination and maker might have influenced the shape/style of the *rondel*.

Fig. 27. Object: Roundel Dagger, Date: 14th century, Culture: possibly British, Medium: Steel, Dimensions: L. 13 in. (33 cm); L. of blade 9 7/16 in. (24 cm); W. 1 3/4 in. (4.4 cm); W. of blade 9/16 in. (1.5 cm); thickness of blade 3/8 in. (1 cm); Wt. 7 oz. (198.4 g), Classification: Daggers, Credit Line: Gift of Jean Jacques Reubell, in memory of his mother, Julia C. Coster, and of his wife, Adeline E. Post, both of New York City, 1926, Accession Number: 26.145.31, Met Museum.

Fig. 28. Object: The Four Horsemen, from The Apocalypse, Artist: Albrecht Dürer (German, Nuremberg 1471–1528 Nuremberg), Date: 1498, Medium: Woodcut, Classification: Prints, Credit Line: Gift of Junius Spencer Morgan, 1919, Accession Number: 19.73.209, Met Museum.

Attila the Hun and The Sword of Mars (434–453 AD)

Attila the Hun was an exceptional warrior whose legendary tales complemented his barbaric lifestyle. He was known as the *"scourge of God,"* because of his crushing raids on the Eastern Roman Empire during the fifth century AD. One of the more popular legends belongs to the sword he carried in battle. Legend has it that the sword was presented to him by a Hunnic sheep herder who dug it up in his farmland while his flock was grazing the field. Attila believed this magical sword was a gift from the gods, specifically Mars, the Roman god of war. He displayed the sword to his troops and claimed it the "Sword of Mars," meant to give him victory during all his battles. He carried the sword until his death in 453 AD. The sword was never recovered and remains fable until the day it is unearthed once again. There are no documented facts regarding this sword—only rumors of its existence and how it was Attila's weapon of choice in battle.

The Vandals (435–534 AD)

Germanic Barbarians, formally known as the Vandals, who may have originated in southern Scandinavia, migrated to Silesia (Southwestern Poland) around 130 BC. Vandal warriors carried swords, spears, lances, pikes, and various throwing weapons, including the battle axe. The Vandals had armor, helmets, and shields for personal protection, but obviously, none compared to what the Roman army held. There were no major distinct changes in weaponry among the Vandals, aside from the usual weapons used during this time. That said, it is important to discuss the Vandals due to their significant impact on history.

The Vandals were a violent tribe, known for their unique relationship with the Roman Empire. Some historians such as Peter the Patrician, referred to them as allies with Rome, while Eutropius expressed the opposite. Historian Cassius Dio found the Vandals to be neither enemies nor friends with Rome. The Vandals simply coexisted with the Roman Empire for a period, but eventually, disputes between both parties inevitably led to war. They managed to set their issues aside for a brief moment during the invasion of the Huns. The Vandals felt betrayed by the Romans after they pulled back and left the Vandals to fend for themselves. As expected, Rome's decision did not bode well for the empire, later resulting in negative consequences.

In roughly 406 AD, the Vandals ripped through Gaul and continued onward to Hispania (Iberian Peninsula), where they eventually settled. While in Hispania, they confiscated the most important Roman ports and built a navy to keep Rome at bay. The Visigoths, who were the predominant people in the region, felt threatened by their arrival. The Visigoths had bigger plans for the time being, and so in 410 AD, they conquered and set ablaze the Eastern Roman Empire. Rome was left in shambles after this invasion, with no strong infrastructure to keep any potential invading armies at bay. In 418 AD, the Visigoths engaged in warfare with the Vandals and the Alans, eventually defeating the Vandals and assuming control of the southcentral portion of the Iberian Peninsula, forcing the Vandals to relocate to another region.

Around 429 AD, King Gaiseric (428–478 BC), emerged as the most prolific king of the Vandals. During this time, he led thousands of troops from the Iberian Peninsula into North Africa with the intent of conquering and establishing a permanent territory. They first took the city of Hippo, moving on to conquer city after city in North Africa, including Carthage (in present-day Tunisia). The Vandals' incredible naval fleet dominated the Mediterranean Sea for many years. As a result, the Romans were furious and tried everything possible to destroy the Vandals but were unsuccessful. During this period, the empire found itself fighting battles on all fronts, with the Huns on one end and the Vandals on the other. Eventually, the Roman Empire fell back and signed a treaty with the Vandals in 442 AD. The treaty was signed between Valentinian III and King Gaiseric. Based on Gaiseric's account, Valentinian III was murdered by Petronius Maximus shortly after, nullifying the treaty.

Gaiseric then gathered a huge army and went off to Rome, where he met with Pope Leo I, who begged Gaiseric to take mercy on them and not set the capital on fire. It is important to recall that the Romans were still attempting to recover from the earlier assault the Visigoths had inflicted upon them. This resulted in an informal sack of Rome as the Vandals were unwillingly let in by the Romans, who, at the time, were suffering a major famine and economic instability. The Romans knew they did not have the ability to confront Gaiseric's army. Gaiseric also realized that it would be pointless to rip apart a city that was already in pieces. The Vandals proceeded to take anything of value and left the city.

In 460 AD, the Romans managed to muster a sizable army and decided to attack the Vandals. Gaiseric was always a proactive person, especially regarding the Romans. He found out the Romans were heading his way and launched a counterattack. His quick response successfully destroyed the Roman fleet, which included every Roman soldier onboard the ships. Rome had no choice but to succumb and renegotiate terms with the Vandals. Gaiseric said they wanted a reinstatement of the 442 AD Treaty and negotiated for the Vandals to have free reign.

In 452 AD, Attila the Hun breached the walls of Rome and was approached by Pope Leo I, who once again, pleaded that the city be left alone. Yet again, Pope Leo I pleas were successful, and Attila the Hun took whatever valuables he could find and left. Rome was completely devastated—slowly dissolving and now judged by history for the legacy they left behind. It had suffered several invasions and would never rise to the "glorified Rome" it once was. In 476 AD, the Western Roman Empire succumbed to another defeat when it was conquered by the Germanics, led by Odoacer. The empire's nexus of power would later emerge in its eastern counterpart, the Byzantine Empire.

When Gaiseric, king of the Vandals, died in 478 AD, so did the accolades bestowed upon him. The Vandals began their descent from a well-built, warlike kingdom, to a subpar ruling system with poor leadership. Founded under Constantine I, the Byzantine Empire (also known as the Eastern Roman Empire), had emerged in 330 AD. Two hundred years later, the Byzantine Empire was rapidly gaining momentum and power. Emperor Justinian I was waiting for the right time to strike back at the Vandals and take back the territory that once belonged to them. Since Justinian knew the Vandals were in a weakened state, he decided to take full advantage of the situation and sent his army to invade and overthrow the Vandals in 533 AD. The Byzantine army was led by Commander Flavius Belisarius, who was also responsible for reconquering most of the Mediterranean territory the Western Roman Empire had lost nearly a century earlier. The following year, the Vandals' leader Gelimer was captured and sent back to Constantinople. Due to the horrific defeat against the Byzantine Empire, the Vandals collapsed and scattered, never to regain their rule over the region.

Byzantine Empire (330 AD–1453 AD)

The location of Byzantium's capital Constantinople was carefully chosen. Named after Emperor Constantine I, this ancient city was located in what is now Istanbul, Turkey, and rested on a triangular peninsula of land that split the Bosporus from the Sea of Marmara. Interestingly, people living in the Eastern Roman Empire adopted many practices from the Hun people, who previously invaded and looted Rome. The Byzantine military implemented a "rapid approach system," where speed and precision, coupled with sheer firepower and accuracy, were the key components when facing adversaries. Byzantine soldiers went through vigorous training to build and enhance their archery skills, combatives, and fast decision-making. Their heavy cavalry carried long lances, short bows, small axes, broadswords, daggers (pugio style), and small shields. The cavalrymen and their horses wore chainmail armor to protect them while on the battlefield. The infantry was organized into regiments, consisting of highly specialized soldiers accompanied by light infantry. At one point, the military recruited heavy infantry mercenaries from the Frankish, and later, the Varangians.

The Byzantine Empire was phenomenally successful and managed to conquer a large amount of territory, which included modern-day Italy, the Balkans, Greece, Asia Minor, Syria, Egypt, North Africa, and southern Spain. As one of the great empires of the medieval world, the Byzantine Empire succeeded in adapting to the changing political and military climate of the time. In the sixth century, the military reinvented itself once again, with the intent to become archer and cavalry centric. Contrary to earlier Roman military tactics, which relied more on foot-soldiers, the newly transformed Byzantine military had mounted troops that carried out a significant amount of the heavy fighting. A great deal of these tactics were learned from the Hunnic military but perfected by the Byzantine army, such as mastering the use of the stirrup which allowed them to maneuver their horses more effectively on the battlefield.

Sophisticated trainings and routine interval refresher trainings enabled these soldiers to build wonderful muscle memory on the battlefield. The Byzantine Empire employed a number of military tactics and military science to defeat their enemies. Together, they perfected their skills as a single unit, and together "danced in the battlefield," annihilating their enemies. The use of siege machines, spies, psychological warfare, and specialized weaponry are just a few examples of their tactics. The Byzantines also mastered the art of axe throwing, dart wielding, spear thrusting, and hand-to-hand combat. They also educated themselves through famous military manuals such as the *Strategikon*, an exemplary handbook that taught soldiers about proper formations (tagma), cavalry tactics, infantry, siege warfare, logistics, proper movement, ambushes, surprise attacks, and coping techniques for the psychological effects of war.

Under Emperor Justinian I, a myriad of warrior-like people sought the opportunity to serve in the Byzantine army, such as the Huns, the Gepids, the Goths, the Heruli, the Slavs, the Bulgars, and the Berbers. These different groups learned from each other in battle, which resulted in new and improved fighting tactics and techniques. The Byzantine military was not partial with regard to who served within its high ranks. On the contrary, they had foreign leaders who rose up to its highest positions, such as the rank of general. Flavius Belisarius was one of Justinian's generals who led the effort to reconquer their territories, which included obliterating the Vandals in the process. There is no doubt that a properly educated army is more effective in the battlefield. Because of this, the Byzantines also focused on intelligence gathering, reconnaissance operations, and careful analysis of their enemy, prior to striking. The Byzantine Empire's clandestine operations were carefully conducted by a chosen few elite, formidable scouts.

Over the years, the Byzantine Empire fought several peoples with intentions of conquering, while also defending, their territory. Since they had a well-established military institution, it was not their military approach that finally brought them to their knees—it was religion. At the turn of the first millennia AD, the empire was split between Greek Orthodox and Roman Catholic beliefs, resulting in the Great Schism, which led to ever-increasing tension between the two denominations. Constant conflicts with Muslims, such as with the Arab and Turkish armies, placed an additional strain on the empire. As history has illustrated, no matter how sophisticated a military is, once internal conflicts occur within the ranks it is only a matter of time before the threads that bind them begin to weaken. Similar to other great empires and cultures, the Byzantine Empire began to slowly show its cracks and weaknesses.

In early 1200 AD, the Crusades were already in full motion and going strong. During this period, the Fourth Crusade was in progress, with the Byzantine Empire in a vulnerable position and Constantinople ripe for the taking. In 1204, crusaders broke through walls and took the city, looting and damaging whatever they could. In 1261 AD, the Byzantine Empire managed to muster some strength under Emperor Michael VIII Palaiologos, liberating the capital city. Constantinople was reconstructed and its citizens felt a short-lived optimism that life might return to its past glory, but they later realized their hopes were false. The damage Constantinople had suffered during the sack of 1204 AD was not simply superficial—it ran deep into the hearts of every man, woman, and child. Everyone tried to save face and embrace these false hopes with the little dignity they had left, but that damage would never properly heal. In 1453 AD, another foe came knocking at their door—the Ottoman Empire. Even though nearly 200 years had passed, the Byzantine Empire was no longer the powerhouse it once was and there was no way to stop the Ottoman Empire from invading. Once again, Constantinople was captured—this time, by Sultan Mehmed II and his incredibly motivated army.

Charlemagne (Charles the Great) and the Sword of Joyeuse (768–814 AD)

A medieval emperor who ruled a large area of Western Europe from 768 to 814 AD, Charlemagne was one of the most influential people of his time. Around 771 AD, he became king of the Franks, a Germanic tribe that lived in what is today Belgium, France, Luxembourg, Netherlands, and western Germany. An expert military planner who spent an extensive amount of time involved in warfare throughout his reign to achieve his intentions, he wanted to unify all Germanic tribes and convert them to Christianity. In 800 AD, Pope Leo III crowned Charlemagne emperor of the Romans; his empire was referred to as the Carolingian Empire. What was fascinating, yet feared, by many, was the legendary sword he carried by his side known as the Sword of Joyeuse. This was the very sword that helped Charlemagne unite Europe, bestowing upon him the title of the "Father of Europe."

The Sword of Joyeuse, or "joyful" in French, was forged by the famous blacksmith Galas. Legend has it that the sword was said to change colors thirty times a day, and that whomsoever wielded it would be impervious to poison. In battle, it would shine with such luminosity that it would blind enemies on the battlefield. The sword measures about 41 inches in total length, with the blade measuring about 33 inches. It is about 1.78 inches wide at the base, with a total weight of 3.6 lbs. It has a laboriously sculpted gold pommel, made of two halves, that bears a resemblance to a bulky, Oakeshott type B. It has a 4-inch-long gold grip, which is ornately decorated with fleurs-de-lis inside a beautifully intricate diamond pattern surrounding the handle. Finally, the Sword of Joyeuse features a gold cross guard in the shape of two winged dragons with lapis lazuli beads for eyes. The sword became such an important part of history that it was used to coronate several French kings, namely, Philip the Bold and Charles X. In Europe, the Sword of Joyeuse gained so much popularity that it was later recognized as "the sword that conquered Europe."

The Viking Age (793–1066 AD)—*During the Middle Ages and Germanic Iron Age*

Vikings are known to be mostly comprised of Scandinavian people. New archaeological findings show that other people, including groups from southern Europe and even Asia, could have joined these Norsemen on their voyages. Vikings were seafaring warriors who left their Scandinavian homes in search of great riches. These fierce Norse sailors arrived on their oak-made ships, adorned with carvings of serpents or ravens, both appearing to come to life at sea. They acquired most of their wealth by raiding coastal settlements throughout Europe, including parts of modern-day Russia and North America. It is well documented that around 1000 AD, Leif Erikson, son of Erik the Red, reached the coastal provinces of modern-day Canada, such as Newfoundland and Labrador. Christopher Columbus was not the first explorer to discover America, and contrary to popular opinion, the Genoese explorer never even made it to what is now United States.

The incident that launched the beginning of the Viking Age was the attack on the Lindisfarne monastery, located off the coast of Northumberland, England, in 793 AD. After this event, European coastal settlements were on edge because they knew that due to their vulnerability, they could at any point become victim to a Viking raid. Around the ninth century AD, Ireland, Scotland, and England became primary targets for Viking raids and settlements. During 1000 AD, the Vikings had spread their reach to Iceland, Greenland, and Newfoundland.

Vikings carried several bone-crushing weapons to overcome their victims and aid in their conquests. These weapons depended on what they could afford financially, but regardless of what they could afford (as far as weaponry), Vikings always carried some form of weapon. The most common weapons were the axe, sword, spear, bow & arrow, and seax. Their battle axe typically had a long handle, which gave them a fighting advantage over their opponents. The cutting edge was anywhere from 4 to 16 inches. Their swords where very heavy, with a cutting edge of about 36 inches. Swords were highly sought after and quite expensive because they were made of iron, and therefore, usually only owned by elite military leaders or wealthy individuals. The *ulfberht* swords were forged from high-carbon steel and were known for their astonishing strength, durability, and razor sharpness. The spear they used ranged in length from 4 to 10 feet and was primarily used for throwing, stabbing, and striking. Some spears were designed for close combat while others were made for throwing. Their bow and arrows were used to inflict pain or death from a distance before they even engaged in close combat. Nearly all Vikings carried some form of a knife. Large in size with a clip point style blade, the seax was the most popular style and was much larger than the typical knife. Discoveries illustrate how Vikings used friction folder knives as well as clasp-style folders that appear to have contained a catch to hold the blade open.

Vikings were associated with the Berserkers, whom historian Tacitus referred to as "fantastic elite warriors among the tribes of the north," in his book *Germania*. Berserkers were also known as "wolfskins," and said to be elite Viking warriors who shared a resemblance to the ancient Koryos, another group that wore *ulfheonar*, or wolf or bear skin as war garments. Described by Vikings as Odin's special warriors, these elite soldiers were invincible, fearless warriors who would violently rip apart their enemies in battle using their spears, swords (Viking/Carolingian–8th c.), and short battle axes. The axes were used aggressively in battle, splitting heads down to the jaw. Berserkers would hurl their battle axes at their opponents with head-splitting force, to inflict the most damage possible. Some suggest that these people were simply a legend, surviving only in the realm of famous Viking sagas, although old scriptures confirm that they did, indeed, exist. Berserkers were known for their engagement during attacks—howling like wild dogs with fearsome expressions and beastly mannerisms. There was no way of taming Berserkers to fight more orderly, which contributed to the downfall of several Nordic leaders.

The Battle of Stiklestad (1030 AD), was the "turn of the tide" for the Vikings, who were known to be the greatest sailors of their time. King Olaf II Haraldsson of Norway (995–1030 AD) was determined to transition Norway out of heathenism and move the country towards Christianity. The "fantastic elite warriors" upon whom the Vikings depended were the same individuals who turned against King Olaf during this battle—an unexpected move which resulted in the death of this Viking king. Some believe that Olaf's decision to place the Berserkers on the front line was the primary reason as to why the war was lost. But actually, this was secondary to the fact that it has been alleged that the Berserkers had been previously "bought out" by Cnut the Great, the leader on the opposite end of the sword in the Battle of Stiklestad. Cnut's bribing of King Olaf's warriors essentially allowed for his takeover of Norway and his proclamation as king. Cnut the Great (995–1035 AD), who is referred to by some as the "most effective king in Anglo-Saxon history," also held great power and influence with the Catholic Church. He was the first to rule over all of England since the fall of the Roman Empire. His victory at the Battle of Stiklestad marked the opportunity for his self-proclamation as king of the "North Sea Empire," which included modern-day England, Denmark, Norway, and parts of Sweden.

This particular moment in Norse history is important as it depicted how the Vikings and their leaders were seeking not only physical riches, but those of the spiritual kind, as well. A year after King Olaf's death, he was granted sainthood at the pontification of Pope Alexander III, where the Roman Catholic Church canonized him Saint Olaf (St. Olave) in 1164. St. Olaf remains ever present in Norway today, as a symbol of Norwegian independence and pride, which is represented in the national coat of arms, depicted as the axe.

The Viking Age came to an end in 1066 AD, after suffering several loses during battle with England, the most famous being the Battle of Stamford Bridge. Coastal cities were more fortified by this point with modified structures to deter Vikings from invading. It was no longer profitable to raid costal settlements, which led to a reduced number of raids, until they finally stopped. The Vikings were never really conquered, they just seemingly stopped raiding. Most had already settled in communities around modern-day Sweden, Finland, Norway, Iceland, and Greenland, where they also gained positions of power and wealth.

Fig. 29.
Object: Viking Sword
Date: 10th century
Culture: European, probably Scandinavia
Medium: Steel, copper, silver, niello
Dimensions: L. 37 3/4 in. (95.9 cm); L. of blade 31 7/8 in. (81 cm); W. 4 5/16 in. (11 cm); Wt. 2 lb. 4 oz. (1021 g)
Classification: Swords
Credit Line: Rogers Fund, 1955
Accession Number: 55.46.1

Met Museum

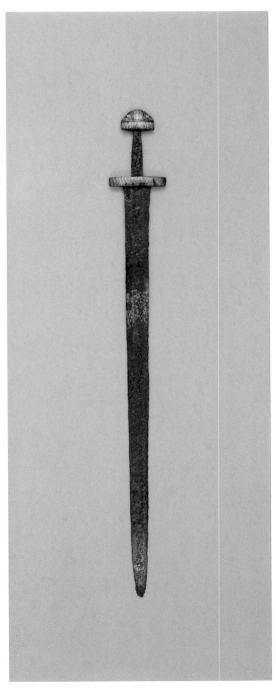

Fig. 30. Drawing by A.J. depicts a 10th-century Viking Seax, resembling the "Seax of Beagnoth," also known as the "Thames Scramasax," currently on display at the British Museum in London.

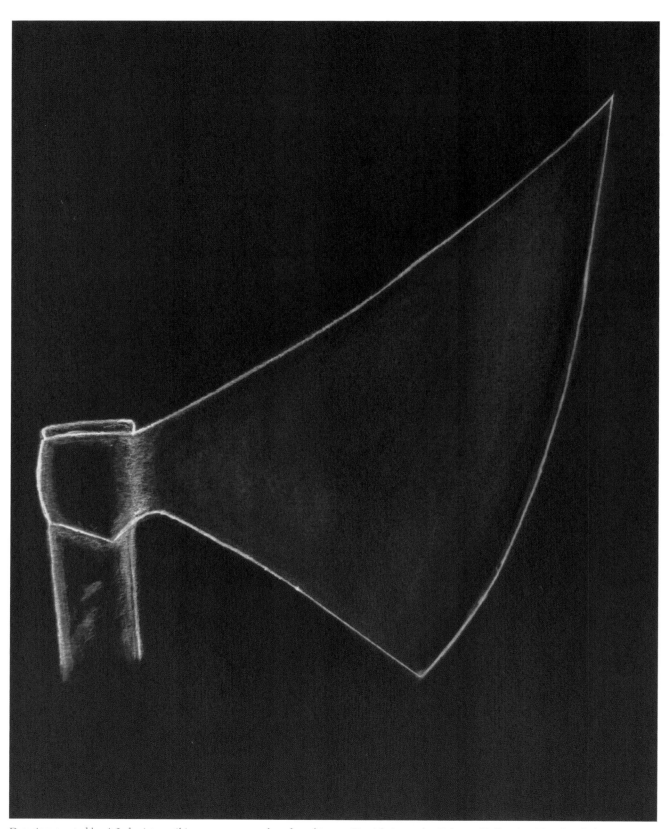

Drawing created by A.J. depicts a viking axe, commonly referred to as a Danish Axe, a.k.a Poleaxe (Pollaxe) or Two-handed Axe.

Photograph taken by A.J. depicts a knife made by Helle from Norway, called Saga Siglar. Its a traditional viking style puukko.

Kievan Rus (882–1240 AD)

In 840 AD, Scandinavian Vikings, known as the Varangians, ruled over the Slavic tribes of Eastern Europe. Over time, the Varangians and the assimilated Slavs would become known as the Kievan Rus and form the first East Slavic state. Initially ruled by Viking King Rurik (830–879 AD), this state was first established in Novgorod. Before his passing, King Rurik personally appointed Oleg of Novgorod as successor since his son Igor was too young to reign. After conquering Kiev in 882 AD, King Oleg declared the city their new capital and the Kievan Rus relocated to a territory located in what is modern-day Belarus, Ukraine, and parts of Russia. The army used weaponry such as axes, bow and arrows, hunting spears (*rogatina*), swords, and maces. There is little evidence that shows any significant blade manufacturing during the early stages of their civilization.

Most of the knives they used were of Viking style, as they were imported from Scandinavia. They originally had a Petersen design, with later variations containing decorated guards. Compared to other people in the region like the Druzhina, the Kievan Rus army was more of a militia, with moderate training and a small armament. As they began to modify and modernize their military, their swords changed as well. They altered cross guards and pommels to suit the needs of horseback soldiers. They also imported sabers with a curved blade design from Central Asia. The Kievan Rus did the best they could to adapt to modern times and their surrounding environment.

After King Oleg's death in 913 AD, he was succeeded by Igor of Kiev, son of his predecessor, King Rurik. Although much of Igor's reign remains a mystery, we know he engaged in a series of successful military campaigns which resulted in the acquisition of vast quantities of material wealth. Igor felt that these gains were not enough, and therefore sought to impose higher tributes from his people. In 945 AD, after a series of financially selfish decisions, King Igor was untimely and gruesomely assassinated by the Drevlian tribe. Like Igor, his son was also too young to assume control of the throne from his father, so Igor's wife, Olga of Kiev, stepped in as intermediate ruler. Her first priority was to seek revenge against those involved in her husband's horrendous assassination.

Without lifting a finger, Olga's vengeful plans began to take form after the Drevlians vaingloriously arrived at her court. These negotiators were sent with the intent to "convince" her to marry their Prince Mal, whom she suspected was behind King Igor's death. Olga artfully agreed to their terms and invited them to return the next day for a "proper welcoming." What the Drevlian negotiators were not expecting was that in accepting this invitation, they would soon be buried alive. Olga had commanded trenches to be dug so that upon the return of these "ambassadors," they would be tricked and carried by her people into their unanticipated graves. Unaware of the fate of the previous messengers, the Drevlians agreed at Olga's request to send another group of "diplomats." Upon their arrival, she invited them to "freshen up" in her bathhouse. Once they entered the building, Olga commanded her soldiers to set the baths ablaze, where they all burned alive. Surprisingly enough, the Drevlians had not discovered that their previous groups had met their demise, and yet again, agreed to a third meeting. This time, a feast was planned at the site of King Igor's death, Iskorosten, so she might pay her final respects. After a night of inebriated indulging, Olga ordered her guards to massacre those who remained. Her vengeful war persisted for another year, until she finally decided to "negotiate" with the Drevlians.

Promising an end to the war, she requested three pigeons and three sparrows in return from each Drevlian household. Ecstatic with her terms, they complied, unaware of her dark intentions. Olga instructed her army to bind bits of cloth wrapped sulfur onto the birds, and upon nightfall, light the material on fire and release the birds to their nests. The entire city caught fire instantly. Olga of Kiev achieved her retribution against everyone involved in her husband's unforeseen death. Though her actions would be considered unorthodox today, ironically, it is said that she was the first ruler of Kiev to adopt Orthodox Christianity.

In 963 AD, Olga abdicated the thrown and passed it to her son, Sviatoslav I. King Sviatoslav was a far more aggressive ruler than his predecessors, Oleg and Igor. He engaged in a series of military campaigns to expand their territory and gain more power over the region. He defeated the Khazaria, the Volga Bulgars, the Alans, and the Danube Bulgars, gaining a full dominion over most of Eastern Europe. Sviatoslav ruled over the largest kingdom in medieval Europe by territory alone.

As the Mongol Empire gained momentum in the thirteenth century, the Kievan Rus were on their radar. In 1237, the Mongols invaded the Kievan Rus, setting ablaze, raping, pillaging, and looting several cities, including Ryazan, Kolomna, Moscow, Vladimir, and Kiev. The invasion lasted several years, ending in 1242. Over 100,000 Mongol soldiers swept through the region, destroying every- thing in sight. They carried spears, daggers, long knives, and at times, single-edged swords, but their greatest attribute was their speed. The Mongols were expert warrior horsemen with astonishing maneuverability on the battlefield. The composite bow was their primary weapon, as it would fire arrows great distances and hit targets with perfect precision. They mastered archery on the move and could fire arrows with high accuracy. The arrowheads were originally made of bone, but later tran- sitioned to metal. Their quivers contained both light and heavy arrows, with around thirty to forty of each variety. The mounted soldier typically carried two to three bows, and in the event that one failed, he could quickly replace it. Aside from their weaponry, they were also expert military plan- ners that employed reconnaissance and military intelligence, to collect as much information on the enemy before an attack. The Kievan Rus stood no chance against this massive war machine, hurtling toward them.

It took over 100 years for Russian territories to recover from the devastation brought on by the Mongols. The Mongols did not want full control over the region, they just demanded stable tributes. Russian territories were eventually divided into principalities, where each committed to paying the Mongol Empire their scheduled tributes. These tributes, or taxes, were collected every month by the *baskaks*, or Mongol taxmen. In 1266, the Tatars of the Mongol Golden Horde separated themselves from the Mongol Empire. All future tributes paid by the Rus people were then redirected to the Golden Horde. Over the years, the princes who ruled each of the Rus principalities began to nego- tiate deals with the Golden Horde, which eventually led to greater power and wealth. As the princi- palities gained strength, the Golden Horde weakened. Eventually the principalities stopped paying tributes to the Golden Horde, resulting in conflicts between the two groups.

The Battle of Kulikovo, which occurred in 1380, was a major turning point for the Rus people be- cause they managed to defeat the Tatars and began to reestablish prominence in the region. During the battle, the Rus principalities were led by Dmitry Ivanovich of Moscow and Vladimir Andreyev- ich the Bold, while the Golden Horde was led by Mamai Muhammad Bolak. The victory did not mean the Mongols were entirely defeated in the region, as more conflicts ensued. Finally, the Musco- vites won their independence, resulting in the establishment of the Russian State.

Samurai (794–1868 AD)

The samurai were elite warriors who were highly trained in sword and bow fighting. They emerged during the Middle Ages, around the tenth century AD in Japan. Initially, they were provincial warriors during the Heian period (794–1185 AD) until the country fell into the hands of a feudal dictatorship known as the shogunate, in the twelfth century. The samurai backed the authority of the shogun and because of their abilities, the shogun gained enough strength to overpower the *mikado* (emperor of Japan). The period of transition began with the success of Minamoto Yoritomo (samurai leader) during the Genpei War (1180–1185 AD). Yoritomo's clan defeated the Taira, which led to the triumphant leader's inevitable control over Japan. As a result, the samurai controlled the Japanese government for a lengthy period, most notably known as the Kamakura Period (1185–1333 AD). What followed this time was great civil unrest, which resulted in a reformation and unification of Japan. This period of unification led to over two centuries of peace in the kingdom. The Meiji Restoration took place in 1868 and led to the abolishment of the feudal system, which, by default, led to the end of the samurai.

Legend has it that the first *tachi*-style sword was created in 700 AD by Amakuni Yasutsuna, a Japanese swordsmith employed by the emperor of Japan. Amakuni noticed his swords kept breaking in battle, so he began to reconsider the overall design in order to create a stronger, more effective sword. For seven days and seven nights, Amakuni pleaded to the Shinto gods for inspiration and guidance, during which time, he found the best sand ore to create *tamagahane*, a type of rare steel made in the Japanese tradition. He worked relentlessly for thirty days, and what materialized was an exceptionally sharp, single-edged sword. Essentially, what Amakuni produced may be considered the first variation of the *tachi*. In addition, the sword had a slight curve for ergonomics and balance. It is important to note that there were some *tachi* variations already being used prior to Amakuni's redesign of the blade. According to the legend, Amakuni is considered the "father of the samurai sword." Today, the *Kogarasu Mara*, a unique samurai sword, which embodies qualities of both the Chinese *jian* and Japanese *tachi*, is on display at the Japanese Museum of the Imperial Collections and is rumored to have been produced by Amakuni.

The most popular Japanese swordsmiths emerged between 900–1450 AD. In the year 900 AD, a smith known as Yasutsuna from the Hoki Province (known today as the western part of the Tottori Prefecture) made a name for himself by forging exceptional samurai swords. They were made of the best iron and sand ore, with an approximate length of roughly 3–4 feet, and little has changed in the style since Yatsusuna's initial creation. Eighty percent of the swords produced were from smith schools in five provinces, known as Bizen, Yamashiro, Yamato, Soshu, and Mino. These became known as the "Five Schools."

The samurai were known to carry various types of swords, with the *katana* being the most famous. First produced around the fifteenth century during a transitional period in Japan, the *katana* became king in the battlefield, dominating opponents by slicing off limbs with great ease. The *katana* functioned like a magical wand in the hands of the samurai and it was said to be an extension of the wielder's soul. A majestic battle dance took place between the samurai and their sword, and those who stood in the way of this dance would suffer the consequences. The graceful dance took on the name of "martial art" and the rest… is history.

In addition to the *katana*, the other edged weapons in the samurai kit were the *wakizashi*, the *tanto*, the *nodachi*, and the *tachi*. The *wakizashi* was about 19 inches in length and usually carried along with a *katana*. When these items were "worn together," they were referred to as *daisho*, which translates to "large and small." The *tanto* was a traditional Japanese dagger, primarily used for stabbing opponents, with either a single or double edge. The *nodachi*, also known as the "great sword," was used by foot soldiers to take down cavalry. Lastly, the *tachi* was a curved sword, which measured about 29.5 inches and was predecessor to the *katana*. The *tachi* was primarily used by horseback warriors, and only as a last resort, to slash their way through the crowds on the battlefield.

During the time in which the samurai controlled the Japanese government, they revived the *bushido,* or "way of the warrior," as their basic code of conduct and honor. Japanese society had to abide by the *bushido* or suffer exclusion. The samurai did not always control the country by means of military force. There was a period when the country suffered through civil instability, known as Sengoku-Jid-ai. Though historians have not agreed on an exact date when this era ended, there are three distinct events which may have led to the end of the Sengoku: the Siege of Odawara Castle (1590), the Battle of Sekigahara (1600), and the Summer of Siege of Osaka Castle (1615). Therefore, it would be safe to presume that by 1615, the Sengoku-Jidai had come to an end. During this era, Japan was on a path towards unification and was at peace for over 200 years. This time was known as the Edo period, when the samurai had become the highest-ranking social caste in Japan. They governed Japan through civic duty and loyalty, prioritizing citizens and government. This age of peace also immersed Japanese society into the Buddhist and Confucian way of life.

Throughout the nineteenth century, Japan was undergoing economic hardship and was influenced by the United States to open its borders to international trade. A treaty was eventually signed between Japan and the United States, which shifted Japanese political views and influenced the signature of several other treaties with Britain, France, and Holland. As a result, support reemerged for a Meiji-style of governance in Japan, which eventually led to the Meiji Restoration. During this time, the feudal system was abolished and the samurai were no longer permitted to carry their swords in public.

Fig. 31. (right), Object: Blade for a Sword (Katana), Swordsmith: Blade inscribed by Masazane (Japanese, Ise, documented 1515–26), Date: dated 1526, Culture: Japanese, Medium: Steel, Dimensions: L. 36 1/8 in. (91.8 cm); L. of blade edge 29 9/16 in. (75.1 cm); D. of curvature 3/32 in. (2.4 cm), Classification: Swords,

Credit Line: Purchase, Arthur Ochs Sulzberger Gift, 2001, Accession Number: 2001.574, Met Museum

Fig. 32. (above), Object: Blades and Mountings for a Pair of Swords (Daishō), Swordsmith: Long sword (katana) blade inscribed by Sukemitsu of Bizen (Japanese, Bizen, Muromachi period, active ca. 1440), Swordsmith: Short sword (wakizashi) blade attributed to Yasumitsu (Japanese, Muromachi period, 15th century), Fittings maker: Set of sword mountings by Iwamoto Konkan (Japanese, Edo period, 1744–1801), Date: sword (katana) blade, dated 1440; short sword (wakizashi) blade, 15th century; mountings, late 18th century, Culture: Japanese, Medium: Steel, wood, lacquer, copper-silver alloy (shibuichi), gold, copper, rays-kin, silk, Dimensions: L. of sword (katana) 34 1/8 in. (86.7 cm); L. of sword (katana) blade 25 1/4 in. (64.1 cm); L. of sword (katana) scabbard 28 1/4 in. (71.8 cm); L. of short sword (wakizashi) 26 in. (66.0 cm); L. of short sword (wakizashi) blade 20 3/4 in. (52.7 cm); L. of short sword (wakizashi) scabbard 19 3/4 in. (50.2 cm); L. of knife (kozuka) for short sword (wakizashi) mounting 8 3/4 in. (22.2 cm), Classification: Swords Credit Line: The Howard Mansfield Collection, Gift of Howard Mansfield, 1936,

Accession Number: 36.120.417a, b, .418a–c, Met Museum.

Fig. 33., Object: Samurai, Yokohama, Artist: Felice Beato (British (born Italy), Venice 1832–1909 Luxor), Date: 1864–65, Medium: Albumen silver print from glass negative, Dimensions: Image: 17.9 x 14.6 cm (7 1/16 x 5 3/4 in.), Classification: Photographs, Credit Line: Gilman Collection, Purchase, Robert Rosenkranz Gift, 2005, Accession Number: 2005.100.566, Met Museum

El Cid and His Mystical Sword Conquer Valencia (11th c. AD)

There is no doubt that knives contain some form of "power," which can be harnessed through proper training. A sword with unknown origins said to pose special properties, feeding onto its wielder great abilities, emerged in the eleventh century. Legend states that the power is bestowed upon whoever holds it. This mystical sword, which bears the name of *Tizona*, or Tizon, was carried by the famous Rodrigo Diaz de Vivar, "El Cid," a masterful field commander who ruled Valencia from 1094 until his death in 1099. The sword has a double-edge blade which measures at a length of 36 inches and weighs about 2.5 lbs. Most importantly, down the greater part of the blade runs a groove containing gold hieroglyphic lettering, which has not yet been deciphered. The *Tizona* was an incredibly special sword and it was said that its very appearance would frighten opponents into surrendering in battle. The *Tizona* was used by "El Cid" to defeat the Moors in Valencia, Spain. In 1099, following his death, Valencia fell to the Moors once again.

Fig. 34.
Title: Plate 11 from the 'Tauromaquia': The Cid campeador spearing another bull
Artist: Goya (Francisco de Goya y Lucientes) (Spanish, Fuendetodos 1746–1828 Bordeaux)
Date: 1816
Medium: Etching, burnished aquatint, burin
Dimensions: Plate: 9 13/16 × 13 3/4 in. (25 × 35 cm)
Sheet: 12 1/16 × 17 5/16 in. (30.7 × 44 cm)
Classification: Prints
Credit Line: Rogers Fund, 1921
Accession Number: 21.19.11
Met Museum

Medieval India & the Mughal Empire (600–1600 AD)

The Medieval era lasted several centuries under various Indigenous rulers, including the Chalukyas, the Pallavas, the Pandayas, the Rashtrakutas, the Muslims, and the Mughal Empire. Around mid-500 AD, following the fall of the Gupta Empire, India was dominated by three rival kingdoms: the Cheras, the Pandayas, and the Cholas. During this period, India developed strong Islamic influences derived from invasions by foreign countries in the fourteenth century AD.

Like many regions during this time, the Indian subcontinent developed formidable knives whose characteristics evolved over time. When Alexander the Great invaded northwest India around the fourth century, local Indian smiths known as *kamis* may have been inspired by the blades used by the Macedonian army. The knife may have evolved due to blending the designs of the *kopis* (Greek sword) and the *machira* (Macedonian cavalry sword).

The most famous was the *kukri*, a recurved, steel blade with a razor-sharp edge, designed to dismember opponents. Although the exact origin of the *kukri* is unknown, some say it originated in northern India, while others claim it originated in Nepal. (As an independent country, Nepal has never been a part of India nor was it ever formally colonized). The *kukri* is recognized as Nepal's national blade, and possibly obtained its origin from the Mallas, who came into power in the thirteenth century AD. The *kukri* was used by the Nepalese *gurkha*, elite soldiers, who were eventually commissioned by several countries throughout the region to assist during moments of external conflict. Every Gurkha soldier carried a *kukri* as their primary weapon.

The *kukri* has several name variations, such as: *kukri, khukuri, kukuri, khukri and kookuri*. Because this legendary knife has rooted origins in both India and Nepal, many folklores have been passed down through the centuries. One superstition behind the *kukri* states that one cannot draw the knife from the sheath and re-sheath it without the sword "tasting blood." It is also said that a man with a *kukri* represents a man with honor, dignity, courage, and loyalty. For many, carrying a *kukri* symbolized the end of their childhood and the beginning of manhood.

During the Chola Dynasty (ca. 9th c. AD), metallurgy involved a casting method, typically using metals such as copper, zinc, tin, gold, and silver. At times, the metals were combined to produce national statues. In addition to casting the statues of Nataraja and Vishnu, the regime also produced tri-metal coinage (silver, copper, and gold) through their fully functioning minting system. The *talwar* (talwaar or tulwar), a scimitar-shaped sword, was also used during this period, and primarily found in South Asia in places such as India, Pakistan, and Bangladesh. Early forms of this sword may have been developed around 1300 AD. It was a single-edged curved blade with a pointed tip. The blade had a unique disc hilt meant to help protect the hand from the blade when performing a draw cut or stabbing. The *talwar* was typically used by soldiers, such as cavalry and/or infantry. Some variations of this sword have a spike on the pommel that could have been used to strike an opponent.

The Mughal Empire was founded in the early sixteenth century AD by Babur, a Chagatai Turkic and descendant from the Turkic conqueror Timur on his father's side, as well as a descendant of Mongol ruler Genghis Khan on his mother's side. The *kukri* style sword was not the only knife used during the medieval period in India. During the Mughal Empire metallurgy bloomed, leading to the development of many unique knives, such as the *talwar* (sword), the *shamsher* (small, curved blade), the *sirohi* (scimitar style blade), and the *gupti* (concealed walking stick). They also used several battle-axes, such as the *zaghnol*, which, due to its pointed head and two cutting edges, was coined a "crow's beak." The *tarangalah* was another battle-axe, which was longer with a crescent-shaped head. The Mughals also used a *tabar zaghnol*, a double bit axe known for its broad cutting edge on one side and pointed edge on the other. The *tahar* was a battle-axe with a broad cutting edge and was triangular in shape.

The Mughal Empire also used spears of various shapes and sizes during this time. The *sang* was made entirely of iron and measured 7 feet, 11 inches in total. The *nezah* was a cavalry lance with a small steel head attached to a long bamboo shaft. They used a *gandasa*, which is type of billhook or pole axe. Daggers were popular during this period, most notably the *katar/katari*, a lightweight knife used for thrusting during close combat. The weapon had an H-shaped horizontal grip, meaning the blade rested above the knuckles. This knife was created in southern India, during the Vijayanagara Empire, around the fourteenth century AD. The Turks, as well as the Persians and Indians, used the *khanjar* a fairly popular dagger with a double curve and a hilt like a sword, which measured about 12 inches in length. The *peshkaj/peshkabz* was a pointed, Persian-style dagger with a thick straight spine, designed to puncture through armor. Bow and arrows were also still used during this period, until pistols and cannons were developed, when powdered weapons became the primary weapons of combat. Lastly, the *gurz* (mace) was also used, which had a head composed of steel blades and a circular steel shaft ending in a sword-hilt. It had a circular pommel that could be used to bash people over the head. The *gurz* measured around 25 inches in total. Maces were used as weapons, but at times could be used as symbols of office.

Abu al-Fath Jalal-al-Din Muhammad Akbar, also known as Akbar the Great, was one of the most powerful emperors of the Mughal Empire from 1556 to 1605 AD. He extended the empire over most of the Indian subcontinent, resulting in a unified kingdom. Through reformation and centralization of his administration and financial system, he was able to gain the loyalty of Indian citizens, to include non-Muslim populations. Akbar the Great encouraged cultural expression through the arts and religion. He never rejected Islam, nor any religion for that matter, and abolished the taxation imposed on non-Muslims in lieu of military service. However, Akbar the Great demonstrated no mercy to those who refused to accept his supremacy.

The Mughal Empire eventually grew large enough for it to encompass almost all South Asia, from Afghanistan to the southern tip of India, and from the Indus River to Burma. Much of the territorial expansion was attributed to their major successes on the battlefield. The Mughal military reached full maturity under his reign. The use of gunpowder during this time grew considerably, which is why the Mughal Empire, much like the Mongol Empire, is known as one of the "gunpowder empires." The empire developed small firearms that were stronger, more accurate, and more efficient than those being produced in Europe at the time. The Mughal Empire began to decline around the eighteenth century when a large portion of its territory fell under the control of the Marathas. The last Mughal emperor was Bahdur Shah II, who reigned from 1837–1857.

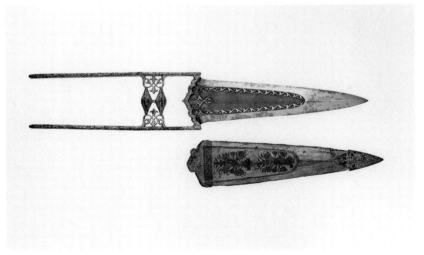

Fig. 35.
Object: Dagger (Katar) and Sheath
Date: 17th century
Culture: Indian, Mughal
Medium: Steel, leather, gold
Dimensions: L. 19 in. (48.26 cm)
Classification: Daggers
Credit Line: Bequest of George C. Stone, 1935
Accession Number: 36.25.973a, b
Met Museum

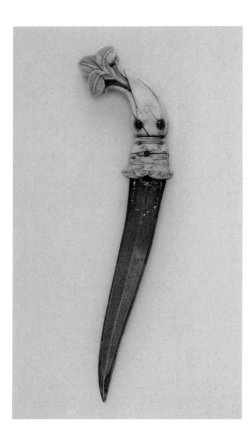

Fig. 36.
Object: Dagger (Khanjar)
Date: mid-17th century
Culture: Indian, Mughal
Medium: Steel, ivory (elephant), gemstone, gold
Dimensions: H. 13 13/16 in. (35.1 cm); H. of blade 8 7/8 in. (22.5 cm);
W. 4 in. (10.2 cm); Wt. 8.5 oz. (241 g)
Classification: Daggers
Credit Line: Bequest of George C. Stone, 1935
Accession Number: 36.25.675

Met Museum

Fig. 37.
Object: Dagger (Jambiya) with Sheath and Carrier
Date: 18th century
Culture: Indian, Mughal
Medium: Steel, silver, jade, leather, wood, lacquer, velvet
Dimensions: Dagger (a); H. with sheath 15 1/4 in. (38.7 cm);
H. without sheath 14 1/2 in. (36.8 cm); H. of blade 10 in. (25.4
cm); W. 3 5/8 in. (9.2 cm); Wt. 14.4 oz. (408.2 g); sheath (b);
Wt. 5.1 oz. (144.6 g); carrier (c); L. 7 1/2 in. (19.1 cm); Wt. 2.6
oz. (73.7 g)
Classification: Daggers
Credit Line: Bequest of George C. Stone, 1935
Accession Number: 36.25.980a–c
Met Museum

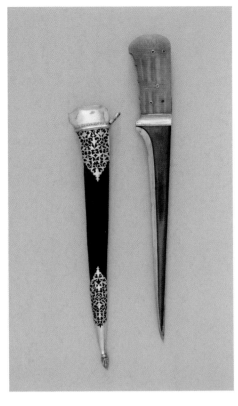

Fig. 38.
Object: Dagger (Pesh-kabz) with Sheath
Date: late 18th–early 19th century
Culture: Indian, Mughal
Medium: Jade, steel, silver, wood, velvet, ruby, gold
Dimensions: L. with sheath 17 13/16 in. (45.2 cm); L. without sheath 15
7/8 in. (40.3 cm); L. of blade 11 1/4 in. (28.6 cm); W. 2 1/8 in. (5.4 cm);
Wt. 1 lb. 2.3 oz. (518.8 g); Wt. of sheath 4.3 oz. (121.9 g)
Classification: Daggers
Credit Line: Bequest of George C. Stone, 1935
Accession Number: 36.25.700a, b

Met Museum

Fig. 39., Title: Hunting Sword (Shamshir Shikargar) with Modern Scabbard, Date: 18th–mid-19th century, Geography: Rajasthan, Culture: Indian, Rajasthan, Medium: Steel, gold, textile (velvet), wood
Dimensions: H. without scabbard 36 1/2 in. (92.7 cm); W. 4 3/4 in. (12.1 cm); Wt. 2 lb. 3.5 oz. (1006.4 g); Wt. of scabbard 3.1 oz. (87.9 g), Classification: Swords, Credit Line: Bequest of George C. Stone, 1935, Accession Number: 36.25.1506a, b, Met Museum.

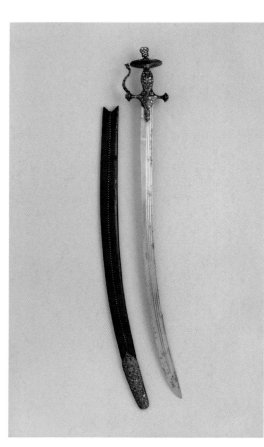

Fig. 40.
Object: Saber (Talwar) with Scabbard
Date: blade, dated A.H. 835/ A.D. 1673; hilt, 19th century
Culture: Indian
Medium: Steel, silver, diamonds enamel, leather
Dimensions: L. 36 5/8 in. (93 cm); L. of blade 31 1/2 in. (80.3 cm);
Wt. 2 lb. 11 oz. (1220 g); Wt. of scabbard 12 oz. (348 g)
Classification: Swords
Credit Line: Bequest of George C. Stone, 1935
Accession Number: 36.25.1591a, b

Met Museum

Fig. 41.
Object: Crutch Dagger (Zafar Takieh, "Cushion of Victory") with
Sheath
Date: 18th–19th century
Culture: Indian, Mughal
Medium: Steel, silver, gold, jade, ruby, turquoise, emerald
Dimensions: L. with sheath 22 5/8 in. (57.5 cm); L. without sheath 18
3/4 in. (47.6 cm); W. 5 1/4 in. (13.3 cm); Wt. 12.3 oz. (348.7 g); Wt. of
sheath 7.1 oz. (201.3 g)
Classification: Daggers
Credit Line: Bequest of George C. Stone, 1935
Accession Number: 36.25.1001a, b

Met Museum

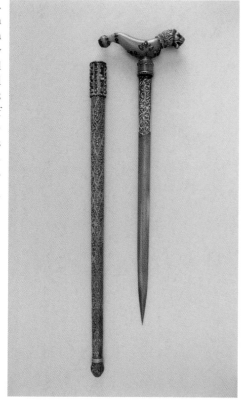

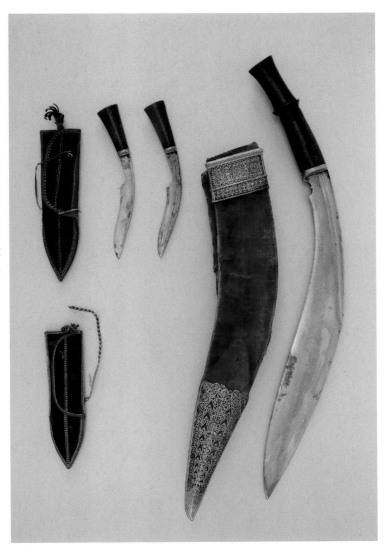

Fig. 42.
Object: Knife (Kukri) with Two Sheaths, Two Small Knives, and Two Sharpening Pouches
Date: 18th–19th century
Culture: Indian or Nepalese, Gurkha
Medium: Steel, horn, gold, leather, velvet
Dimensions: H. with sheath 18 1/2 in. (47 cm); H. without sheath 17 3/8 in. (44.1 cm); W. 1 11/16 in. (4.3 cm); Wt. 14 oz. (396.9 g); Wt. of sheaths 9.1 oz. (258 g); small knife (c); H. 6 1/4 in. (15.9 cm); W. 7/8 in. (2.2 cm); Wt. 1.3 oz (36.9 g); small knife (d); H. 6 1/4 in. (15.9 cm); W. 7/8 in. (2.2 cm); Wt. 1 oz. (28.3 g)
Classification: Daggers
Credit Line: Bequest of George C. Stone, 1935
Accession Number: 36.25.714a–g
Met Museum

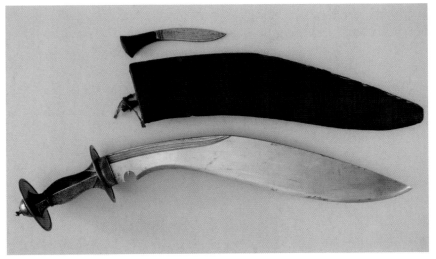

Fig. 43.
Title: Knife (Kukri) with Sheath, Small Knife and Pouch
Date: 19th century
Culture: Indian or Nepalese, Gurkha
Medium: Steel, wood, leather
Dimensions: Knife (a); H. with sheath 17 3/8 in. (44.1 cm); H. without sheath 17 3/8 in. (44.1 cm); W. 3 in. (7.6 cm); Wt. 1 lb. 15.1 oz. (881.7 g); sheath (b); Wt. 4.1 oz. (116.2 g); small knife (c); H. 5 3/16 in. (13.2 cm); W. 1 1/4 in. (3.2 cm); Wt. 1.6 oz. (45.4 g)
Classification: Knives
Credit Line: Bequest of George C. Stone, 1935, Accession Number:36.25.828a–d
Met Museum

Genghis Khan & Mongol Empire (1206–1368 AD)

The Mongol Empire was primarily made up of Mongolians, not to be confused with the Mughal Empire, which was comprised of ethnic Turks. Founded by Genghis Khan in 1206 AD, the Mongols originated in the steppe grassland belt located in Central Asia, which extends about 5,000 miles from Hungary to Manchuria. The empire's territory grew to reach over nine million square miles (23 million square km) of land. It spanned from the Pacific Ocean in the east (China) to the Danube River and the Persian Gulf in the west. To the south, it kissed the borders of India and in the north, touched the forest belt of Siberia. The Mongol Empire was the largest continuous land empire in human history. Genghis Khan was on a mission to rule the world. He believed that a world under his dominion would, by default, be a unified kingdom.

The Mongols excelled at diplomacy, espionage, and terrorism, enabling them to have an advantage over their adversaries in battle. Due to their light, swift cavalry and exceptional bowmen, the battles they fought were already won before there was any form of military confrontation. The Mongol military was constantly evolving, adapting new tactics learned from their enemies. Their soldiers were nicknamed "the devil's horsemen," as they were fearsome warriors who fought valiantly in battle, showing no mercy against their opponents. Military training was a priority and therefore, a way of life. Disobedience was not tolerated. Those who broke the rules would be severely punished by receiving lashings or even death sentences. The Mongols began their training during childhood, by engaging in athletic competitions, hunting, archery, horse racing, and wrestling. By taking part in these contests at a young age, they entered the military with a strong proficiency in bow, spears, battle axes, daggers, long knives, and swords. Unlike traditional military institutions, the Mongol military was unisex, both men and women fought side by side—an application also ahead of its time.

Mongolian warriors used three different styles of arrows, with each serving a different purpose. One type of arrow consisted of an iron head that could travel over 200 yards. Another arrow had a V-shaped tip, used for piercing through the flesh of enemies. The third type of arrow had holes running through it, and when shot, would whistle to alert of its direction. The wood used to make these arrows was either willow, birch, or juniper. The Mongols also had the tendency to smear their arrows with a poison, called *khoron.* It was a plant-based poison derived from the aconite plant, often referred to as "monks-hood." They would also smear their arrows with venom from the steppe viper or adder. The Mongols also favored the composite bow, which had the ability to hit enemy soldiers at twice the distance, compared to the traditional bow.

Two of the most popular blades were the halberd and the Mongol sabre. The halberd was a double-sided blade, mounted on a six-foot pole, and extremely popular amongst those who could afford them. The halberd was generally used on a horse to swing at foot soldiers on the ground. A single swipe could hit several enemy soldiers at once.

The Mongol sabre, also known as the Turco-Mongol sabre, was another popular weapon given to all soldiers in the army. It had a 24 to 30 inch curved, single-edge steel blade. The blade was so powerful that it could puncture through armor and helms. The Mongol sabre was highly effective for foot soldiers, but also used on horseback.

Low-ranking troops typically received spears and lances. The spears served foot soldiers as well as those on horseback. They could be thrown several yards or used to decapitate enemies while riding on horseback. The spears measured several feet and had spear heads made of steel or iron, with "hair-popping sharpness."

In addition to the different types of bows and blades used, the Mongol Empire was also already using gunpowder weapons during this period, which is how they came to be known as the one of the "gunpowder empires." The gunpowder weapons were more for incendiary purposes, rather than explosive. Incendiary weapons were the precursor to the explosive gunpowder weapons we are most familiar with today. It is possible that gunpowder was already being used before this time, however, the Mongol Empire used it to its maximum effect, in every aspect of war.

The Mongol Empire was known for their psychological warfare and art of deception, in which they would lead their opponents to believe something entirely different other than what was actually taking place, was occurring—what we would refer today as gaslighting. Their most popular tactic was to instill terror by massacring their enemies in battle, therefore depressing resistance against them. Unlike the Roman Empire, the Mongols did not maintain garrisons and preferred to annihilate entire areas that seemed troublesome. As a result of these horrific acts, they maintained a fearsome title and a healthy financial system.

Genghis Khan died in 1227 AD, but the empire was far from decline. It was not until 1294, with the death of Kublai, that the empire fragmented. Following a series of weak successions, the Mongol Empire's Yuan Dynasty fell in China around 1368.

Fig. 44.
Drawing by A.J. depicts a Mongolian Cavalry Saber/Sabre, resembling one on display at the Military Museum of Mongolia. The saber at the museum has an iron blade. Date: 13 - 14th century.

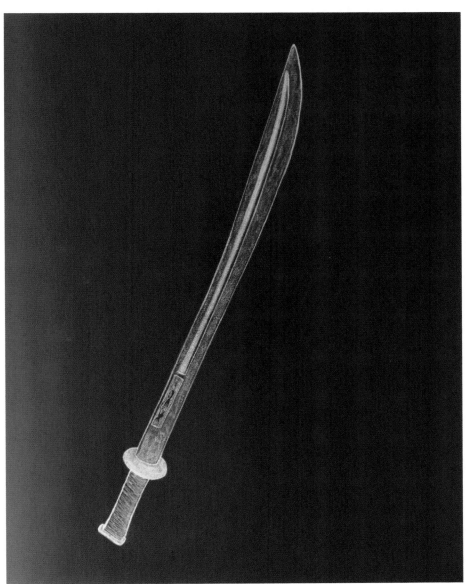

William Wallace—Battle of Stirling Bridge (1297 AD)

William Wallace was—and still is—a perfect example of what it means to fight for freedom, not only to Scotland, but around the world. Wallace engaged enemies that were nearly at the peak of their military capabilities. Britain was shaped by the turbulence between its nations, the agitation between Church and state, and the desire to expand its territory. Centuries of rigidity and quarrel forged the brawn, at the core, in one of the greatest empires the world has ever seen. The British committed atrocities as they sought to conquer Ireland and Scotland—two nations most affected by Britain's attempt at dominance.

William Wallace was said to have fought with a two-handed sword made of carbon steel that measured 5 feet 4 inches in total length and weighed approximately 5.95 lbs. There is a sword said to be his on display at the National Wallace Monument in Stirling, Scotland, though it is debated as to whether the sword on display at the monument actually belonged to Wallace. The fact is, over the years the sword underwent several alterations and repairs and was even stolen a few times. After examining the sword, Dr. David Caldwell states that based solely on design, it does not date as far back as the fourteenth century. Could William Wallace have held a sword similar to the one displayed at the National Wallace Monument? Sure, I believe so, just not one with that particular design. A lot of the characteristics of the sword on display would match up with a fourteenth-century sword, with the exception of the hilt. It is documented that King James IV paid for a new hilt and other fittings. There is a chance that certain parts of the sword, such as the blade, are truly authentic and belong to the original. It is undeniable that the sword is a symbol of freedom, perseverance, and bravery, and it is no wonder why it has been dubbed "The Liberator." The sword on display at the National Wallace Monument is a beautiful historical piece, and if ever in Scotland, well worth taking a moment of time to admire it.

U.S. National Archives: The Heart of Scotland, National Archives Identifier: 169140876, Local Identifier: 30-N-44-2474, Creator(s): Department of Commerce. Bureau of Public Roads. 8/20/1949-4/1/1967 (Most Recent), From: File Unit: Foreign - Scotland, 1896 - 1963, Series: Historical Photograph Files, 1896 - 1963
Record Group 30: Records of the Bureau of Public Roads, 1892 - 1972, Original caption: From "The Call of the Blood" Country Life, Sept. 3, 1927.

The Ottoman Empire (1299–1922)

The unification of Turkish tribes created one of the most powerful empires in history known as the Ottoman Empire. They ruled the Anatolia region and beyond for more than 600 years. The Ottoman Empire followed the footsteps of the Roman and Byzantine Empire by conquering an enormous part of the world. At their peak, they were an unmatched force, with a territory that included modern-day Bulgaria, Egypt, Greece, Hungary, Jordan, Lebanon, Israel, Palestinian territories, Macedonia, Romania, Syria, portions of Arabia, and a substantial part of the North African coast. Their military, like the Byzantine military, was mostly composed of foreign mercenaries. These mercenaries were not obligated to convert to Islam; they just had to heed to their Ottoman military leaders and obey certain rules, which included paying taxes. Though the empire tolerated other religions, its subjects lived under a millet system which categorized them into a communal structure, thus giving them limited power or authority to control their personal affairs.

The Ottoman Empire did an incredible job transitioning their military from Old World weaponry to contemporary firearms. If there is an empire that utterly understood where progress and technology were heading as far as warfare and weaponry, it was them. They transitioned from a Turkish recurve bow, Ottoman mace, and spears to more sophisticated swords, like the *kilij*, the *yatagan*, and even embraced firearms, like the volley gun, the dardanelles gun, and others. The Ottomans rapidly adapted to modern times—and even beyond—by developing and introducing firepower of their own. Though the *kilij* and the *yatagan* were the predominantly used knives, the Ottoman Empire also used a variety of weapons that were introduced by their mercenaries.

The *kilij*, also known as the Ottoman Cavalry Sabre, was a variation of the Turko-Mongol Sabre that appeared around the fifteenth century. With its crescent-shaped steel blade, where the curve is more pronounced at the distal half, this sword has an incredibly unique design. It is very sharp on the entire front, convex cutting edge, and has a sharp opposite edge, down to about 8 inches from the point. The sharpened back edge is known as the *yelman*, which is a signature design specific to the *kilij*. The handle, or hilt, was curved at the end, and fashioned a nice guard with scabbard. Unlike the *yatagan*, the *kilij* changed overtime, specifically in the eighteenth century, where it transitioned to a shorter, stouter blade, with a wider yelman tip.

The *yatagan* was an Ottoman knife that was created somewhere in the mid-sixteenth century, and was used up until the late nineteenth century. These short swords were made in every major city, such as Constantinople, Bursa, and Filibe (Plovdiv). It was a single-edged, slightly curved steel blade, modestly fanning out at the top, then tapering back down at the edge. Think of a *kukri*, but with a much straighter spine. It measures about 32 inches in length, with a bone or ivory hilt, and a flared round pommel. This magnificent *yatagan* was used by the Ottoman army, navy, and most importantly, the Janissaries. The higher in status, the more decorated the *yatagan*, some of which included beautifully ornate designs encrusted with gold on portions of the blade. Most notably was a *yatagan* sword made by jeweler Ahmed Tekel for the Ottoman Sultan Suleyman the Magnificent (1520–1566). Some of the designs for the more affluent, higher-ranking officials were Chinese inspired, specifically the gold-inlaid cloud bands and foliate scrolls on the ivory grips. This sword style was nearly unchanged until the late nineteenth century.

The Ottoman empire hit its pinnacle between 1520 and 1567, under the rule of Suleyman the Magnificent. In the nearly fifty years of Suleyman's rule, the empire rose to its highest status of wealth and power. But shortly after his death, the Ottoman Empire began to decline. In the early 1600s, Europe entered the heart of the Renaissance period, when new innovative technology began emerging, and Europe began amassing hordes of gold and other precious metals via conquest of the New World. Europe was better equipped to handle invaders, with stronger infrastructure and advanced weaponry. In 1683, the Ottoman Empire was defeated at the Battle of Vienna, further adding to their declining status as a global superpower. As time passed, the Ottoman Empire began losing territory due to countries fighting back for their independence, such as Greece in 1830. In 1878, Romania, Serbia, and Bulgaria all were declared independent by the Congress of Berlin.

In 1912, the Ottoman Empire was faced with another hurdle—the Balkan Wars. By the end of the conflict, the empire had lost a significant amount of land in Europe and they were in a position where they thought it would be nearly impossible to recover the lost territory. In 1914, World War I kicked off and the Ottoman Empire decided to join the Central Powers with the intent of potentially winning back some of this lost territory. Most of us know what happened in 1918—the Central Powers got their asses kicked. This was the "last nail in the coffin" for the Ottomans. Shortly after, the Ottoman Empire officially ended its 600-year run in 1922. The following year, Turkey was declared a republic, which was founded by Mustafa Kemal Ataturk (1881–1938), who became the country's first president.

Fig. 45.
Object: Sword (Kilij) with Scabbard
Date: 19th century
Culture: Turkish
Medium: Steel, horn, silver
Dimensions: H. with scabbard 35 1/4 in. (89.5 cm); H. without scabbard 33 in. (83.8 cm); W. 6 in. (15.2 cm); Wt. 1 lb. 6.5 oz. (637.9 g); Wt. of scabbard 1 lb. 4.3 oz. (575.5 g)
Classification: Swords
Credit Line: Bequest of George C. Stone, 1935
Accession Number: 36.25.1342a, b

Met Museum

Fig. 46.
Object: Sword (Kilij) with Scabbard
Date: 19th century
Culture: Turkish
Medium: Steel, horn, silver
Dimensions: H. with scabbard 35 1/4 in. (89.5 cm); H. without scabbard 33 in. (83.8 cm); W. 6 in. (15.2 cm); Wt. 1 lb. 6.5 oz. (637.9 g); Wt. of scabbard 1 lb. 4.3 oz. (575.5 g)
Classification: Swords
Credit Line: Bequest of George C. Stone, 1935
Accession Number: 36.25.1342a, b
Met Museum

Fig. 47.
Object: Sword (Kilij) with Scabbard
Date: 19th century
Culture: Turkish
Medium: Steel, wood, turquoise, coral, emerald, gold
Dimensions: L. 35 1/2 in. (90.2 cm)
Classification: Swords
Credit Line: The Collection of Giovanni P. Morosini, presented by his daughter Giulia, 1932
Accession Number: 32.75.300a, b

Met Museum

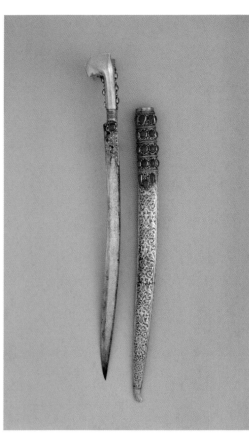

Fig. 48.
Object: Yatagan with Scabbard
Date: dated 1802–3
Culture: Anatolian or Balkan
Medium: Steel, silver, gold, coral
Dimensions: L. with scabbard 31 1/8 in. (79 cm); L. without scabbard 29 in. (73.7 cm); L. of blade 23 1/8 in. (58.7 cm); W. 2 1/4 in. (5.7 cm); Wt. 1 lb. 14 oz. (850 g); Wt. of scabbard 1 lb. 10 oz. (737.1 g)
Classification: Swords
Credit Line: The Collection of Giovanni P. Morosini, presented by his daughter Giulia, 1932
Accession Number: 32.75.261a, b

Met Museum

Fig. 49.
Object: Short Sword (Yatagan) from the Court of Süleyman the Magnificent (reigned 1520–66)
Sword maker: Workshop of Ahmed Tekelü (possibly Iranian, active Istanbul, ca. 1520–30)
Date: ca. 1525–30
Geography: Istanbul
Culture: Turkish, Istanbul
Medium: Steel, gold, ivory (walrus), silver, turquoise, pearls, rubies
Dimensions: L. 23 3/8 in. (59.3 cm); L. of blade 18 3/8 in. (46.7 cm); Wt. 1 lb. 8 oz. (691 g)
Classification: Swords
Credit Line: Purchase, Lila Acheson Wallace Gift, 1993
Accession Number: 1993.14

Met Museum

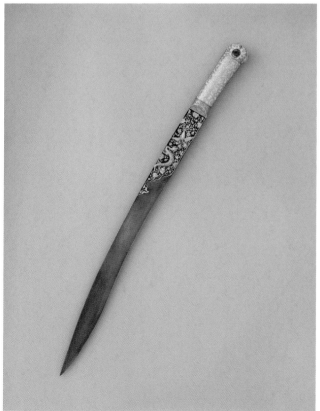

The Aztecs (Mexica) (1300s–1521)

The Aztecs, known as the Mexica in their native language of Nahuatl, were a nomadic tribe that eventually settled in present-day Mexico. They arrived at Mesoamerica in the thirteenth century AD. The Aztecs were a dominant civilization in the region, with a complex society and logistics. They built an impressive capital, known as Tenochtitlán, an island city full of elaborate structures with unique meaning. Warfare was a way of life for the Aztecs, as it was their way to amass a great deal of wealth and strong labor force, and by the fifteenth century, they had assumed nearly full control of the region's city-states. From a young age, Aztec warriors were trained to master weapons such as spears, bows, clubs, and darts. Warriors also held small round shields to help protect them against heavy blows in battle. Their battle weapons had razor sharp blades made of obsidian that were fragile, but if used effectively, could easily rip through an enemy's body. Their spears were short and typically used for stabbing the enemy in close combat.

The Aztecs' cutting tools were not only used for battle and self-defense; they also used small daggers made of obsidian, or flint, which were knapped to razor sharpness and attached to wood (cedarwood) handles for ceremonial purposes. The most notable is the *tecpatl*, a double-edged dagger typically used for human sacrifices. In ceremony, the knife was used to cut open the chests of sacrificial victims and extract the still beating heart. The intent of this ceremony was to feed the gods and please them enough to bring the Aztecs many blessings.

Agricultural tools are what helped the Aztecs flourish in the region. They developed cutting tools/knives used for farming, such as the copper axe and the wooden digging stick, and used knives to shape small wooden branches into fire-making tools. They would create fire through friction techniques, where they would voraciously rub fire kindling sticks together at high speeds, eventually creating enough heat to ignite a flame.

Metallurgy in the Aztec community was mostly used to fashion small personal items or jewelry. They learned metallurgy from by the Tarascans, the second largest state at the time who settled just west of the Aztecs, and were very skilled at making bronze and copper tools. The Aztecs used gold and silver to make ornaments, decorations, plates, and jewelry, and stone chisels to create amazing (accurate) calendars and monumental stone sculptures. They were truly a remarkable civilization until their untimely collapse in 1521 due in large part to the introduction of smallpox and other diseases introduced by the Spanish and the military campaign waged by Spanish conquistador Hernan Cortés.

Fig. 50., Object: Blade, Date: 13th–16th century, Geography: Mexico, Mesoamerica, Culture: Aztec, Medium: Chert, Dimensions: Overall: 3 1/2 x 11 1/4 in. (8.89 x 28.58 cm), Other: 3 1/2 in. (8.89 cm), Classification: Stone-Implements, Credit Line: Museum Purchase, 1900, Accession Number: 00.5.1044, Met Museum.

THE RENAISSANCE PERIOD (14TH–17TH CENTURIES)

There was an emergence of new sword designs during the Renaissance. This time was known to produce remarkably ornate swords, daggers, and pocketknives. The handles of these knives would have been either quite simple or more intricate in design, with the inclusion of exotic materials. This period marked not only new beginnings for Western society but also a shift in cultural expression. Therefore, accessorizing became paramount in the distinction of wealth and status. The dagger, along with ornate cloaks, elaborate jewelry, and other fine weapons, became indispensable in everyday life, thus resulting in what many have coined as "the golden age of the dagger."

Spain was the first country to introduce the rapier style sword in the early 1400s, with Italy, Germany and England adopting it soon after. By the 1600s, the use of the rapier was widespread. Its precursor was the cruciform-hilted sword, often referred to as the longsword, which measured between 27–39 inches in length. The rapier was typically dressed with a curved cross guard and multiple hilt bars to counterbalance the weight of the blades. The sword was thin and used for personal defense or as a civilian dueling weapon. Meaning *espada ropera* in Spanish, or "sword of the robe," as it was designed to be worn with civilian attire, it was a true sign of gentlemanliness. Thus, it was not meant to be used in combat, as its thin blade could easily snap when striking a heavy object. The rapier also had an exceptionally large spherical pommel which, in conjunction with the ornate guard, helped counterbalance the sword. Rapiers were originally manufactured in Toledo and Valencia, Spain. Later, they were also manufactured in Solingen and Passau, Germany, as well as in Milan and Brescia, Italy.

The *cinquedea* was a popular Italian dagger that appeared during the Renaissance. Due to its resemblance to a Venetian dagger which measured five fingers in length, the *cinquedea* became known as the "five fingers" dagger. The actual length of the *cinquedea* was between 10 and 28 inches, and was frequently carried in lieu of a sword or large dagger. A weapon of prestige, it was typically carried by people of status. It featured a double-edged blade with a wedge-like shape that measured about 3.5–4 inches wide at the guard that tapered steeply towards the point. In the 1500s the *cinquedea* was fashioned with more elaborate designs, decorated pommels, exotic handle materials, intricate etchings, and gilded with precious metals.

Hunting has traditionally been a popular pastime amongst those of noble ranks and a desirable activity of the wealthy. It was during this period that the falchion also underwent its own "rebirth." Though previously used in ancient Greece as an infantry weapon, it reemerged as the precursor to the hunting sword. In proper Renaissance fashion, the falchion had beautifully elaborate designs on its guard, handle, and pommel. A saw-back was later added to the sword to ease penetration, cutting, and processing of the kill.

The Renaissance also witnessed an increase in the production of "execution swords." These swords were double-edged, had rounded points, and were of a cruciform-hilted design. The eponymously named executioner swords typically depicted engravings condemning the mischievous and ill-behaved prisoners who nervously awaited their death sentences. These swords were more common in Germany than in other countries of Europe. The blade had to be kept razor-sharp, so that it would sever the head of the prisoner with a single, heavy blow.

5.   HG. fe.   I. de gheyn sculp

Dupla ego pro meritis mereor stipendia; nempe
Insigni reliquis strennuitate prior.

Fig. 51., Object: Soldier, Armed with Broadsword and Shield, from Officers and Soldiers,
Series/Portfolio: Officers and Soldiers, Artist: Jacques de Gheyn II (Netherlandish, Antwerp 1565–1629 The Hague),
Artist: After Hendrick Goltzius (Netherlandish, Mühlbracht 1558–1617 Haarlem), Date: 1587, Medium: Engraving;
first state of two (New Hollstein), Dimensions: sheet: 8 7/16 x 6 1/8 in. (21.5 x 15.5 cm), Classification: Prints, Credit
Line: Bequest of Phyllis Massar, 2011, Accession Number: 2012.136.351, Met Museum

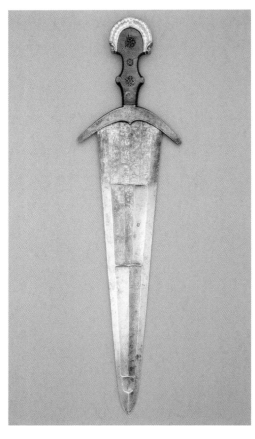

Fig. 52.
Object: Cinquedea
Date: ca. 1500
Geography: possibly Emilia
Culture: Italian, possibly Emilia
Medium: Steel, gold, copper alloy, horn, brass
Dimensions: L. 23 in. (58.42 cm); Wt. 2 lb. (907 g)
Classification: Daggers
Credit Line: Gift of William H. Riggs, 1913
Accession Number: 14.25.1266

Met Museum

Fig. 53.
Object: Dagger
Date: late 15th century
Culture: French
Medium: Steel, bronze, bone
Dimensions: L. 13 9/16 in. (34.5 cm); W. 1 3/4 in. (4.5 cm);
D. 1 1/4 in. (3.2 cm)
Classification: Daggers
Credit Line: Gift of Jean Jacques Reubell, in memory of his
mother, Julia C. Coster, and of his wife, Adeline E. Post,
both of New York City, 1926
Accession Number: 26.145.43
Met Museum

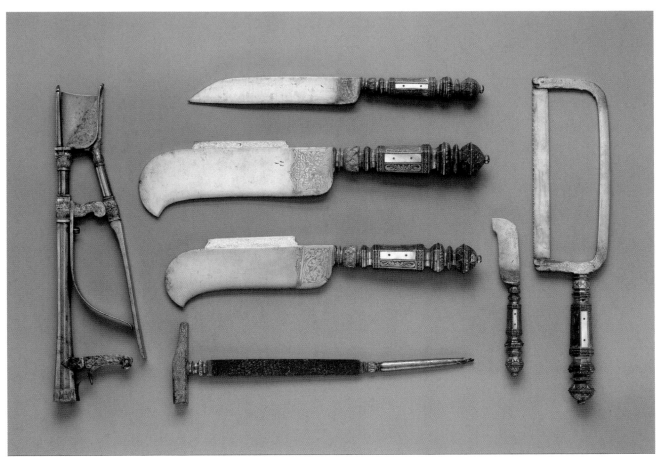

Fig. 54.
Object: Set of seven pruning tools
Date: 1575–1600
Culture: French, Moulins
Medium: Steel, partly gilded; mother-of-pearl
Dimensions: Overall (tool .1470): 3 5/16 × 5/8 × 12 in. (8.4 × 1.6 × 30.5 cm);
Overall (knife .1471): 1 × 6 5/8 × 7 in. (2.5 × 16.8 × 17.8 cm);
Overall (knife .1472): 1 1/4 × 1 × 12 in. (3.2 × 2.5 × 30.5 cm);
Overall (saw .1473): 3 1/8 × 13 3/4 × 1 1/8 in. (7.9 × 34.9 × 2.9 cm);
Overall (clippers .1474): 3 9/16 × 13 1/8 × 1 1/16 in. (9 × 33.3 × 2.7 cm);
Overall (knife .1475): 2 7/8 × 1 3/8 × 12 3/4 in. (7.3 × 3.5 × 32.4 cm);
Overall (knife .1476): 3 1/8 × 1 1/2 × 14 in. (7.9 × 3.8 × 35.6 cm)
Classification: Metalwork-Steel
Credit Line: Gift of Irwin Untermyer, 1964
Accession Number: 64.101.1470–.1476

Met Museum

Fig. 55.
Object: Serving Knife
Date: 15th–16th century
Culture: Austrian
Medium: Steel, brass, wood, bone, mother-of-pearl
Dimensions: Overall: 17 7/16 x 2 11/16 x 5/8 in.
(44.3 x 6.9 x 1.6 cm)
hilt: 4 11/16 x 2 3/16 x 5/8 in. (11.9 x 5.6 x 1.6 cm)
Classification: Metalwork-Steel
Credit Line: Rogers Fund, 1951
Accession Number: 51.118.3
Met Museum

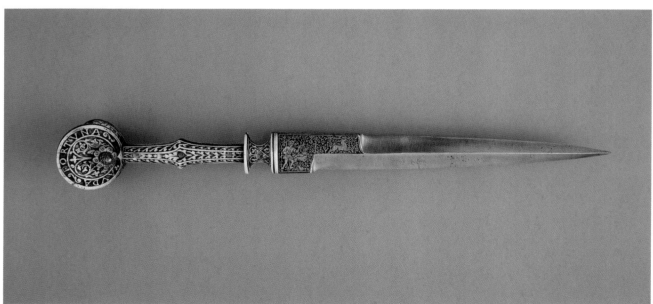

Fig. 56., Object: Eared Dagger, Date: 1540, Culture: Spanish, Medium: Ivory, steel, gold, Dimensions: L. 17 in. (43.2 cm); W. 2 in. (5.1 cm); Wt. 1 lb. 1.4 oz. (493.3 g), Classification: Daggers, Credit Line: The Collection of Giovanni P. Morosini, presented by his daughter Giulia, 1932, Accession Number: 32.75.99, Met Museum.

Fig. 57.
Object: Basket-hilted Sword
Bladesmith: Blade by Johannes Wundes the Younger (Germany, Solingen, active mid-17th century)
Date: blade dated 1662
Culture: hilt, British; blade, German
Medium: Steel, wood, silver
Dimensions: L. 39 7/8 in. (101.3 cm); L. of blade 34 1/4 in. (87 cm); W. 5 in. (12.7 cm); Wt. 2 lb. 6 oz. (1077 g)
Classification: Swords
Credit Line: Rogers Fund, 1909
Accession Number: 09.210.2
Met Museum

Fig. 58.
Object: Basket-hilted Sword
Bladesmith: Blade by Johannes Wundes the Younger
(Germany, Solingen, active mid-17th century)
Date: blade dated 1662
Culture: hilt, British; blade, German
Medium: Steel, wood, silver
Dimensions: L. 39 7/8 in. (101.3 cm); L. of blade 34 1/4
in. (87 cm); W. 5 in. (12.7 cm); Wt. 2 lb. 6 oz. (1077 g)
Classification: Swords
Credit Line: Rogers Fund, 1909
Accession Number: 09.210.2
Met Museum

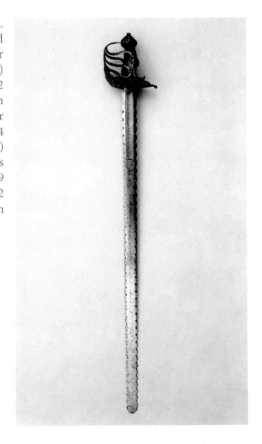

Fig. 59., Object: Rapier, Bladesmith: Andreas Munsten, German, Solingen, active ca. 1600, or Peter Munsten (German, Solingen, mentioned 1591–1627), Date: ca. 1620–30, Geography: Solingen, Culture: hilt, Italian; blade, German, Solingen, Medium: Steel, gold, iron, wood, Dimensions: L. 47 1/8 in. (119.7 cm); L. of blade 40 3/4 in. (103.5 cm); W. 9 1/8 in. (23.2 cm); Wt. 2 lb. 6 oz. (1077 g),Classification: Swords Credit Line: Rogers Fund, 1904, Accession Number: 04.3.7, Met Museum.

Hundred Years' War (1337–1453)

The Hundred Years' War was a bloody conflict that lasted, as the name implies, for 100 years between France and England (1337–1453). The primary reason for the war was that France and England were involved in a dispute over territories, with England looking to expand their holdings and France seeking to liberate the territory held by the English. A series of brutal battles took place between both countries, with France proving victorious in the end. Several notable people fought in these battles, such as Edward the Black Prince, Henry V, and Joan of Arc. The Hundred Years' War also saw the introduction of various new weapons, such as firearms and cannons, with the longbow being the most famous. While it was not a new weapon, it was responsible for causing a great deal of carnage. The longbow gave the English a tactical advantage over the French, who relied more on the crossbow which had greater limitations. Two-handed swords were also used heavily. A common weapon of the Middle Ages, it typically weighed about 5–8 pounds and measured about 5 feet in length. Naturally, the heavier the weapon, the more powerful the blow it could inflict.

In addition to a great side arm, daggers were common in the event that a soldier's sword failed to perform or was dropped during battle. The dagger could easily find its way into small vulnerable spots between a soldier's armor, easily puncturing through flesh. The dagger used throughout the war was known as the ballock dagger (ca. 1300), and acquired its name from the two large lobes at the base of the grip, which carried a similar resemblance to that of the male genitalia. A stiletto-style dagger was also quite popular during this period, known as the *misericorde*. Slender in design, this longer, narrower knife was often used to kill off the fatally wounded, as it was considered a "mercy knife." However, according to popular belief, the name was actually inspired by a knight's cry for mercy after having been overthrown during battle to avoid being slain.

The use of war hammers was also favored among foot soldiers during the Middle Ages. These weapons consisted of a double-sided steel hammer, mounted on a wooden pole, and were dedicated to dismantling and crushing armor. The hammer was also used to knock off knights from their horses by smashing the horse at the knees. Another weapon that was also extensively used during this war was known as the halberd. Known as a spear with an axe head attached to it, the halberd was a longer version of the one-handed battle axe, therefore making it the two-handed "big brother." Because we now know that other weapons already existed during the late Middle Ages, one may assume that they were already being used during the Hundred Years' War. It is speculated that weapons such as the morning star (club with head of spikes) and the flail (ball of spikes attached to a chain and small pole), were mostly deployed in Germany and Central Europe during the late Middle Ages.

In 1453, the French were well underway to victory, having liberated much of the territory held by the English. The English suffered a great defeat at the Battle of Castillon near Libourne on July 17, 1453. This loss was a major turning point, the proverbial final straw, which defined a significant shift in the war. The war ended on October 19, 1453, when Bordeaux finally surrendered by leaving Calais as the final territory of English possession. The French were victorious and gained a great deal of respect for their accomplishments and sacrifices in the region.

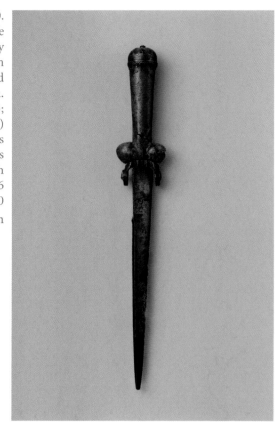

Fig. 60.
Title: Ballock Knife
Date: late 15th century
Culture: possibly French or German
Medium: Steel, wood, lead
Dimensions: L. 14 5/16 in. (36.3 cm); L. of blade 9 5/16 in. (23.7 cm); W. 2 in. (5.1 cm); W. of blade 13/16 in. (2.1 cm); thickness of blade 7/16 in. (1.1 cm); Wt. 8 oz. (226.8 g)
Classification: Daggers
Credit Line: Gift of Jean Jacques Reubell, in memory of his mother, Julia C. Coster, and of his wife, Adeline E. Post, both of New York City, 1926
Accession Number: 26.145.10

Met Museum

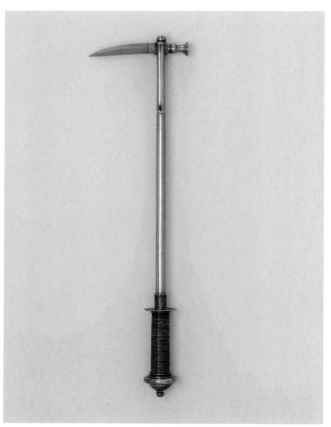

Fig. 61.
Object: War Hammer
Date: mid-16th century
Geography: Saxony
Culture: German, Saxony
Medium: Steel, silver
Dimensions: L. 22 1/2 in. (57.2 cm); L. of head 5 in. (12.7 cm); W. 6 1/8 in. (15.6 cm); Wt. 2 lbs. 8 oz. (1134 g)
Classification: Shafted Weapons
Credit Line: Bashford Dean Memorial Collection, Funds from various donors, 1929
Accession Number: 29.158.674
Met Museum

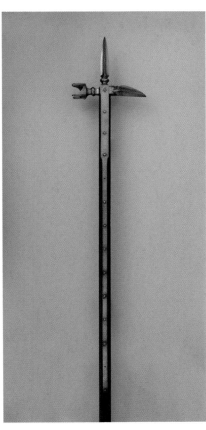

Fig. 62.
Object: War Hammer
Date: 15th century
Culture: Italian
Medium: Steel, wood (oak)
Dimensions: L. 79 7/8 in. (202.9 cm); L. of head 8 1/2 in.
(21.6 cm); W. 9 5/8 in. (24.5 cm); Wt. 7 lbs. 8 oz. (2608.2 g)
Classification: Shafted Weapons
Credit Line: Gift of William H. Riggs, 1913
Accession Number: 14.25.465

Met Museum

Fig. 63.
Object: Pollaxe
Date: ca. 1450
Geography: Burgundy
Culture: French, Burgundy
Medium: Steel, wood (oak)
Dimensions: L. 81 7/8 in. (208 cm); L. of head 12 1/2 in.
(31.8 cm); W. 8 1/4 in. (21 cm); Wt. 5 lbs. 7 oz. (2466.4 g)
Classification: Shafted Weapons
Credit Line: Gift of William H. Riggs, 1913
Accession Number: 14.25.302

Met Museum

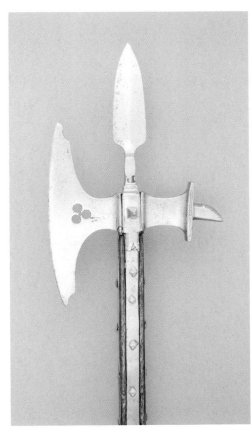

Fig. 64.
Object: Sword
Date: 1500
Culture: Italian
Medium: Steel
Dimensions: L. 31 1/4 in. (79.4 cm); L. of
blade 26 in. (66 cm); W. 4 3/16 in. (10.6
cm); Wt. 1 lb. 14 oz. (850.5 g)
Classification: Swords
Credit Line: Gift of Christian A. Zabrisk-
ie, 1936
Accession Number: 36.149.14
Met Museum

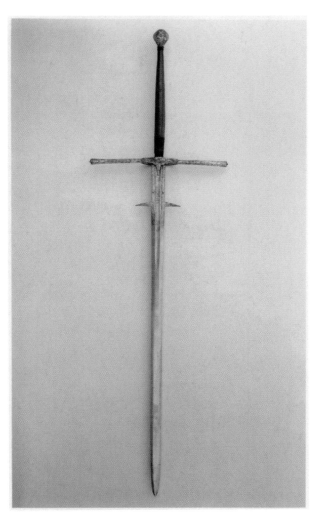

Fig. 65.
Object: Two-Hand Sword
Date: ca. 1570
Geography: Venice
Culture: Italian, Venice
Medium: Steel, gold, wood
Dimensions: L. 63 in. (160 cm); L. of blade 45 1/8 in. (114.6 cm); W. 17 3/4 in. (45.1 cm); Wt. 6 lb. 5 oz. (2863 g)
Classification: Swords
Credit Line: Rogers Fund, 1904
Accession Number: 04.3.290

Met Museum

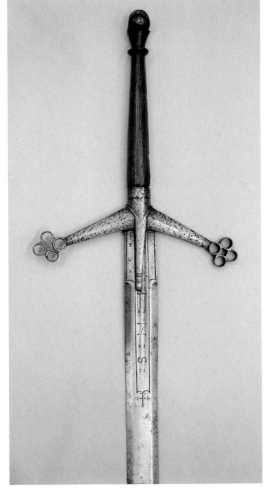

Fig. 66.
Object: Claymore
Date: 16th–17th century
Geography: Solingen
Culture: hilt, Scottish; blade, German, Solingen
Medium: Steel, wood
Dimensions: L. 53 1/2 in. (136 cm); L. of blade 40 3/4 in. (103.5 cm); W. 11 1/4 in. (28.5 cm); Wt. 4 lb. 9 oz. (2068.5 g)
Classification: Swords
Credit Line: Bequest of Alan Rutherfurd Stuyvesant, 1954
Accession Number: 54.46.10

Met Museum

Ming Dynasty (1368–1644)

The Ming Dynasty was founded by Emperor Taizu, a member of the rebel group known as the White Lotus Society. He led the invasion in the city of Nanjing and its success ignited a movement to overthrow the warlords in the region. In 1368, he successfully captured Beijing from the Mongolians and kickstarted the Ming Dynasty. Emperor Taizu was very well respected and those who displayed disrespect towards the dynasty would be beaten nearly to death. He did not trust his own people and therefore converted the palace guard into a "secret service," that would extract betrayers and investigate conspiracies. In 1380, he launched a decade-long campaign which resulted in a massive internal investigation that led to over 30,000 executions. A very paranoid ruler, Taizu's reign led to the executions of an additional 65,000 government officials.

The Ming Dynasty was not solely about betrayal and mischief, it also cemented itself as an influential dynasty that represented a period of restoration and reorganization for China. By allowing foreigners to visit and document their impressions to share with the world, the Ming Dynasty gave the world its first glimpse into Chinese society. Due to an increase in publishing, the country was flooded with literature of all sorts, from novels to reference books. The Ming Dynasty was proud of its accomplishments, such as reaching the highest literacy rate in history and embarking in massive trade negotiations throughout Asia, the Middle East, and Europe. In addition, the Ming Dynasty fortified its country's borders, strengthened its military capabilities, and restored the practices of Confucianism.

Qi Jiguang is recognized as one of the most victorious generals of the Ming Dynasty. He instilled a system of intense regimental training and extreme discipline. Jiguang specified that the cutting edge of a sword must be created by the best steel, free of impurities, with excess metal material filed and smoothed away where the back of the blade evenly unites with the edge. This sword design, which he clearly described, is what we know today as the "convex" grind.

The *dao*, also known as a saber, is a Chinese single-edged, curved sword used in battle. Its design was loosely based on that of the saber-type swords carried by the Central Asian nomadic tribes. The *dao* was a favored close combat weapon among warriors in the Ming Dynasty. Although the *dao* was a favored battle weapon, Chinese nobility still gravitated toward the *jian*— a multipurpose sword used for cutting, thrusting, and literally capable of slicing limbs off opponents in the battlefield. Throughout Chinese history, there have been distinct variations of the *jian* in terms of length, balance, and weight, but it is a straight, double-edged sword, with a typical length of 32 inches and a hilt of nearly 7 inches.

Another variation of the *dao* used by the Ming Dynasty was the *yanmaodao* (goose-quill saber). This variation was a hybrid of a straight and curved sword and had a thicker spine, which gave it greater strength over its forerunners. This hybrid had a unique semi-curve along the last quarter of the cutting edge toward the tip, which provided the swordsman the capability to convey ruinous wounds. The distinctive shape of the sword also provided the ability to perform linear thrusts. The successor of *yanmaodao* sword was the *liu ye dao* (willow-leaf saber), which became the military's favored choice. The *liu ye dao* was a common Chinese sword that was slightly curved along the entire length of the blade, versus the *yanmaodao* which had a small curvature toward the tip of the blade. The sword measured about 36 inches and typically weighed about 3 pounds. The change in balance and shape made it a formidable slasher, as opposed to an accurate thruster, and was therefore popular among cavalry and infantry as a sidearm. The *liu ye dao's* unique dimensions made it an ideal weapon for effectively ripping through clusters of foot-soldiers during battle.

In the early seventeenth century, the Ming Dynasty began to suffer from an economic crisis, in part driven by a lack of silver currency and widespread famine in China. The government did little to aid the suffering of its population, which created discontent among the Chinese populace. As a result, the final emperor of the Ming Dynasty, Emperor Chongzhen (Zhu Youjian), committed suicide in the imperial garden, which led to the simultaneous fall of the Ming Dynasty in 1644 AD and the rise of the Qing Dynasty. The Qing Dynasty was founded by descendants of the Jurchen People, known as the Manchus of Manchuria (in what is now considered northeastern China).

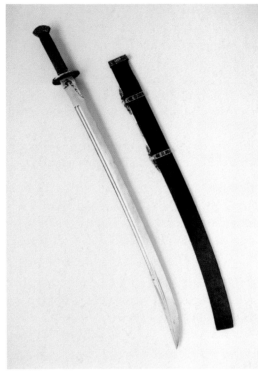

Fig. 67.
Object: Sword with Scabbard
Date: 17th century
Culture: Chinese
Medium: Steel, mother-of-pearl, coral, shark skin, textile, gold, semiprecious stones
Dimensions: H. with scabbard 36 in. (91.4 cm); H. without scabbard 35 1/4 in. (89.5 cm); W. 3 in. (7.6 cm); Wt. 1 lb. 9.7 oz. (728.6 g); Wt. of scabbard 8.1 oz. (229.6 g)
Classification: Swords
Credit Line: Rogers Fund, 1914
Accession Number: 14.48.2a, b
Met Museum

Fig. 68.
Object: Saber with Scabbard and Belt Hook
Date: probably 18th century
Culture: Chinese
Medium: Steel, iron, silk, leather, wood
Dimensions: L. 36 in. (91.4 cm); blade L. 28 1/2 in. (72.4 cm)
Classification: Swords
Credit Line: Bequest of George C. Stone, 1935
Accession Number: 36.25.1477a, b
Met Museum

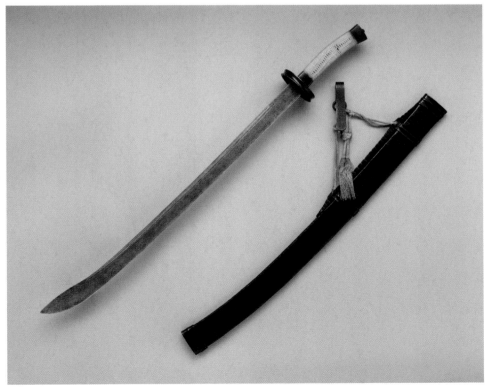

The Landsknechts (15th–16th c.)

Founded by Archduke Maximillian I von Habsburg in 1486, the Landsknechts were highly skilled and sought-after mercenaries, who, during the early sixteenth century, became the most feared soldiers in Europe. Their most favored weapons were halberds (poleaxes), pikes, *katzbalgers* (short swords), and *zweihanders* (two-handed swords). A chronicler of the time wrote, "even the devil refused to let them into hell, because even he, was terrified of them."

Katzbalgers were small arming swords recognized for their unique guard, which formed an almost perfectly circular S-shape. These swords were usually double-edged and tapered from guard to point. The *zweihander* was a two-handed sword, often referred to as a "greatsword," *bidenhander*, or *schlachtschwerter*. The sword measured about 4 feet, 7 inches (1.4 meters) and weighed approximately 5.5 pounds (2.5 kilograms). It was double-edged with a straight blade and made of steel. This sword was created as a result of modern adjustments made to the *langschwert* (longsword) design. Unlike other swords of the late Middle Ages, which were carried in a sheath of sorts, the *zweihander* was carried across the shoulder similar to a halberd. The *zweihander* became the signature weapon of the Landsknechts during the Italian Wars (1494–1559).

The Landsknechts played major roles in several European conflicts, such as the Navarrese War (1512–1524), the Battle of the Spurs (1513), Henry VIII's invasions of France (1513 and 1543), the Battle of Marignano (1515), the Battle of Bicocca (1522), the Battle of Pavia (1525), and the First Revolt of Espada (1526), to name a few.

As Europe experienced a period of inflation and political unrest in the late sixteenth century, the use of hired mercenaries declined significantly. As the prestige of being a European mercenary fell, so did the quality of the service. Eventually, the use of mercenaries was banned altogether in some European countries. By the end of the sixteenth century, many of the mercenary units in Europe simply disintegrated.

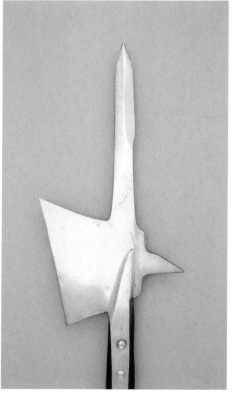

Fig. 69.
Object: Halberd
Date: late 15th century
Culture: German
Medium: Steel, wood (oak)
Dimensions: L. 81 3/8 in. (206.6 cm); L. of head 16 in. (40.6 cm); W. 8 3/4 in. (22.2 cm); Wt. 4 lbs. 12 oz. (2154.6 g)
Classification: Shafted Weapons
Credit Line: Gift of William H. Riggs, 1913
Accession Number: 14.25.51

Met Museum

Polish Winged Hussars (1503–1770)

The Polish Winged Hussars (a.k.a. the angels of death) were cavalry units that originated in Serbia and dominated eastern regions of Europe during the early to mid-1500s. They were mercenaries who fled Serbia after the Ottoman Turks defeated the Serbs in 1389. Their primary weapon was the *kopia*, a lance made of firewood measuring about 15 feet in length that was built to shatter on contact, as seen in jousting competitions. The lance shaft was made of two halves of hollow wood, which were attached at the ends with a double-edged iron spearhead fitted at the top. The spearhead measured from 9 to 12 inches in length. They also used a *koncerz*, a straight-pointed carbon steel sword used for stabbing and thrusting. It resembled a *rapier*, but was a bit rigid and much longer.

The Hussars also used a curved sabre made of carbon steel, known as *szabla*. It had an open hilt with a cross-shaped guard fashioned with quillons, with upper and lower langets. First introduced in the late sixteenth century, the *szabla* was the best sabre-style sword of the period and became a precursor to several other such European swords. They also carried a war hammer known as a *nadziak*, which was a metal horseman's pick. In 1576, King Stephen Báthory of Poland transformed the Hussars into a shock cavalry. Known for their ferocious battlefield tactics, these men rode on special horses that were a cross between Polish and Tartar horses. Not only were they absolutely beautiful beasts, but these horses were also exceptionally fast and held incredible maneuverability on the battlefield. The Hussars wore light steel armor that was tough enough to handle heavy impact while also light enough to not slow them down. They fought and won several battles in Europe, with their most significant being the Battle of Vienna in 1683, when they defeated the Ottoman Turks. The Ottoman Janissaries were no match for these "angels of death." The Hussars ripped the Ottomans apart, and among those who survived narrowly escaped.

In 1702, the Hussars were finally defeated by the Swiss Army at the Battle of Kliszów. The loss to the Swiss Army was a significant blow to Poland, as well as a wake-up call to the Hussars. In the eighteenth century, wars were being fought with advanced weaponry where shock cavalry was simply not enough to win. As firearms improved, even heavily armored horsemen were too exposed and considered a weak point. In the late 1770s, the Polish parliament abolished the Hussars altogether. These once feared legendary warriors simply became a part of historic tales.

Fig. 70.
Object: Polish hussar in profile facing right with wings attached to his back, a circular composition, from 'Figures on Horseback' (Cavaliers nègres, polonais et hongrois)
Series/Portfolio: 'Figures on Horseback' (Cavaliers nègres, polonais et hongrois)
Artist: Stefano della Bella (Italian, Florence 1610–1664 Florence)
Date: ca. 1651
Medium: Etching
Dimensions: Plate: 6 7/8 x 6 15/16 in. (17.5 x 17.6 cm)
Classification: Prints
Credit Line: Bequest of Grace M. Pugh, 1985
Accession Number: 1986.1180.666
Met Museum

Early Settlers of America (1607)

The first British colony was established in Jamestown, Virginia, in 1607. During the time of this first settlement, small amounts of iron ore were found around 1608 and sent back to England for processing. The successes of the Jamestown settlement were impermanent, as the inhabitants of the colony vanished and what actually occurred remains a mystery.

In the 1620s, the Pilgrims arrived at Plymouth, Massachusetts, and established the first permanent settlements in America. The Pilgrims fled Europe due to religious persecution and were seeking a fresh start elsewhere. They would not have been successful, however, if it were not for the help and guidance of local Native American tribes.

The Native Americans were the first to establish settlements in America and no one knew the land better than them. There is no verifiable truth behind the notion that Native Americans were a "savage people." They had a tribal system set in place, with an established means of self-governance. They had intricate settlements, seasonal agricultural and hunting methods, as well as an economic system in place. Native American tribes had a barter system in place with other neighboring tribes. Their way of life cannot be considered simply primordial, as it had much more sophistication and meaning than what many people commonly believe. Inevitably, poor communication and education, along with a sense of fear (to say the least), led to major conflicts between the first European settlers and the Native Americans. The battles that ensued from their disagreements resulted in gruesome mass deaths. The conflicts between Native Americans and colonists include the Powhatan Uprising, King Philip's War, and the Yamasee War, to name a few.

In 1622, colonists created a small structure for smelting ore in the colony at Falling Creek. During the Powhatan Uprising, which claimed the lives of 347 people, the smelting site was torn down. This was the first site of iron smelting in early colonial America. Early settlers often used knives that were shipped from overseas. Long knives and jackknives were used as utility knives to aid in camp chores, clearing vegetation, and self-defense. Axes and saws were also imported during this time and were used for building shelter and homes. It wasn't until the 1650s, when ironworks were established in Massachusetts, that the early colonies began producing their own metal products rather than relying on imported knives.

KNIVES OF THE 1600S

Dining Knife

The seventeenth-century outfit was not complete without a knife as a sidearm. Knives were incredibly personal and never shared, as they were considered an extension of one's body and tailored to the owner's specifications. During this period, the knife was as unique as one's wedding ring. As a result, knives could range from quite plain to rather ornate, with intricate handle designs—in the same manner as one would personalize a wedding band today. Daggers were used as a utensil, to slice and cut practically anything on the plate, ranging from cheese to beef. The carver was the first person known to professionally slice meat dishes. Due to their skillful carving abilities, the carver retained more prestige than the cook.

In the 1630s, French Cardinal Richelieu loathed eating at the dinner table with sharp, double-edged knives because he felt that such blades denoted violence at the dinner table. In Richelieu's view, eating with a pointed knife (i.e., weapon) was an unsettling gesture with "barbaric roots." He convinced King Louis XIV to ban the use of pointed, double-edged knives for the purpose of dining, as eating with rounded tipped knives appeared "less violent." The decree gave rise to the blunt head knife we all know today as "the dining knife." The use of dining knives was popularized throughout Europe, with America being the last place to embrace this utensil at the table. Until forks were introduced to the table in the late Renaissance period, individuals depended on their trustworthy personal knife as the primary utensil at the table. The dining knife inspired the use of the fork, to aid in holding meat or any food needed to be cut, and by the eighteenth century, the use of the fork and knife at the dining table had become standard across most of Europe.

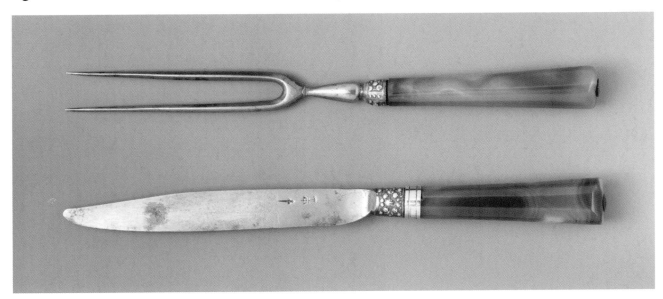

Fig. 72., Object: Table knife and fork, Maker: William Laughton (British, active London, recorded 1676), Date: 17th century, Culture: French, Medium: Steel, silver, blue agate, Dimensions: Length (knife .22): 9 3/8 in. (23.8 cm); Length (fork .23): 9 1/4 in. (23.5 cm), Classification: Metalwork-Steel, Credit Line: Gift of R. Stuyvesant, 1893, Accession Number: 93.13.22, .23, Met Museum.

Early Western European Folding Knives

During the seventeenth century, the French were renowned knife makers, exporting knives throughout the world. They shipped knives to Spain, Italy, and Asia, via the ports of Bordeaux or Nantes. During the Age of Exploration in the early 1600s, French Canadian traders often exchanged French folding knives, known as "clasp knives," with Native Americans. These transactions took place in French-influenced territories extending from northern Canada down to Louisiana. The French pocketknife was one of the first knives imported into North America. Typically, the French pocketknife of this period had a wooden handle, which the blade would fold into. The blade measured between 3 to 4 inches, depending on the manufacturer. The pocketknife was a style of friction folder and used as a multi-purpose tool from skinning game to eating meals. When people were seated during meals, they were expected to pull out their own knife and use it as their cutting utensil.

During this period, people also used a foldable, pistol grip "Gully" knife, typically used for self-defense. This knife had a narrow wooden pistol grip and a 3.5–4-inch carbon steel blade.

Around 1650, the "peasant knife," also known as the "penny knife," became widely distributed around the world, due to its affordability. Sheffield, England, became the primary place of production for this knife, which was extremely popular among farmers. The Opinel company of France still makes knife designs like the penny knife today.

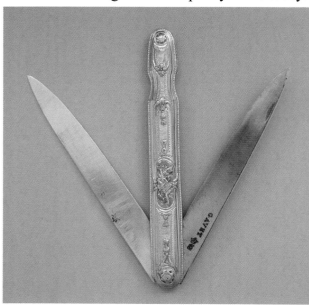

Fig. 73.
Object: Pocket knife
Maker: Probably by Jean Gavet (cutler to the King 1757, master goldsmith 1769, recorded 1781)
Date: 1766–67
Culture: French, Paris
Medium: Gold, steel
Dimensions: Length (closed): 4 1/8 in. (10.5 cm);
Length (open): 7 11/16 in. (19.5 cm)
Classification: Metalwork-Gold and Platinum
Credit Line: Bequest of Catherine D. Wentworth, 1948
Accession Number: 48.187.498

Met Museum

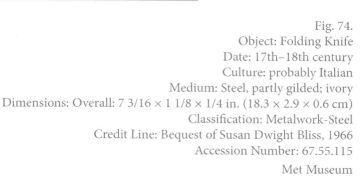

Fig. 74.
Object: Folding Knife
Date: 17th–18th century
Culture: probably Italian
Medium: Steel, partly gilded; ivory
Dimensions: Overall: 7 3/16 × 1 1/8 × 1/4 in. (18.3 × 2.9 × 0.6 cm)
Classification: Metalwork-Steel
Credit Line: Bequest of Susan Dwight Bliss, 1966
Accession Number: 67.55.115

Met Museum

Slipjoint-style Knife

The slipjoint-style knife was first developed in 1660. The "Barlow knife," manufactured by the John Russell Cutlery Company in 1875, is a good adaptation and representation of this style of pocket-knife. These knives were said to be built to outlast their owner, at a price of only a few coins. John Russell Cutlery Company was an American manufacturer of knives, known today as the Russell Harrington Cutlery Company/Dexter-Russell, Inc., located in Massachusetts. Even though the Barlow-style pocketknife was first created in the early 1600s in Sheffield, England, some people refer to the Barlow knife as being "as American as baseball." George Washington carried a Barlow knife throughout his military career and while he served as president of the United States. The Barlow was the knife of American heroes and a symbol that marked the transition from childhood to adulthood. Mark Twain wrote a great deal about the Barlow knife in his great literary accomplishments, such as the *Adventures of Huckleberry Finn* and *Tom Sawyer*.

Different styles of pocketknives later emerged, such as the Canoe, the Trapper, the Congress, the Whittler, the Texas Toothpick, the Copperhead, the Muskrat, the Swayback, and the Lockback. Some of these styles, namely the Lockback, were first introduced around the fifteenth century, while others, such as the Trapper, the Canoe, the Congress, and the Toothpick, emerged in the late eighteenth and early nineteenth centuries.

Fig. 75.
U.S. National Archives
National Archives Identifier: 193874198
Local Identifier: 138052
Creator(s): Department of the Interior. Patent
Office. (1849 - 1925) (Most Recent)
From: Series: Utility Patent Drawings, 1837 -
1911
Record Group 241: Records of the Patent and
Trademark Office, 1836 - 1978
This item was produced or created: 4/22/1873
The creator compiled or maintained the series
between: 1837 - 1911

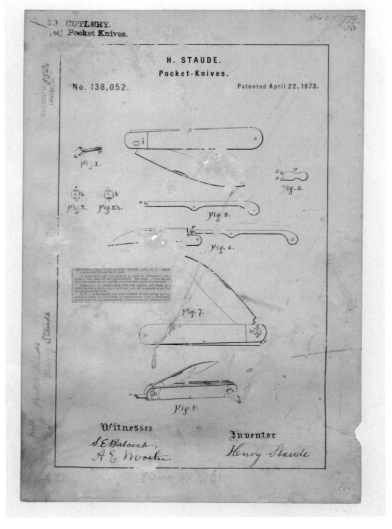

Spanish Navaja

The Spanish navaja was developed in the 1600s as a folding fighting knife in Andalusia, Spain. The Spanish navaja was much larger than the typical folding knife, as blades measured anywhere from 10 to over 16 inches, which easily folded into its ornate handles. The blades were made of carbon steel, consisting of a flat grind and featuring a sharp, curved edge. Locking mechanisms where not part of the initial models, but rather, were introduced in later models.

Inspiration for the development of these knives was due to the restrictions of carrying/wearing swords and other weapons by those outside of the Spanish nobility. The Spanish navaja could easily be concealed and effectively deployed when needed. These knives were used for dueling and vigorous fighting. The navaja-style knife was also considered an heirloom knife, meant to be handed down, along with the proper fighting technique.

Modern ingenuity and the development of a reliable spring steel (i.e., low-alloy manganese, medium or high carbon steel), led to the Spanish navaja adopting a tempered steel and a mounted backspring. The addition of a backspring meant that the knife could finally be used for more tasks. As a result, popularity of the knife rapidly spread throughout Europe, and in particular, France.

Fig. 76., Object: Clasp Knife, Date: 18th century, Culture: Spanish, Medium: Steel, horn, brass, Dimensions: L. 15 in (38.1 cm); W. 2 in. (5.1 cm); Wt. 4.9 oz. (138.9 g), Classification: Knives, Credit Line: Gift of Rutherfurd Stuyvesant, 1891, Accession Number: 91.16.80, Met Museum.

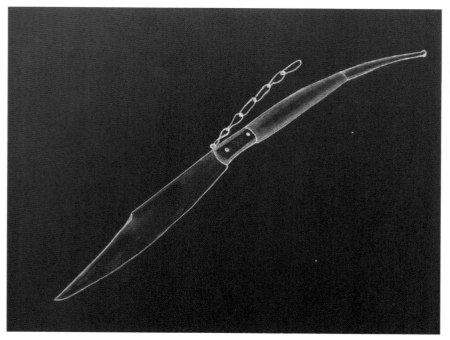

Fig. 77. Drawing by A.J. depicts a Spanish Navaja. The blades on some of these navajas measured anywhere between 10 to 16 inches. They were basically foldable short swords.

The First Steel-Edge Straight Razor

In the 1680s, the first steel-edged straight razors were being produced in Sheffield, England. By the 1690s, the razors were manufactured with beautiful, silver-plated handles, as they began their world-wide distribution. Straight razors became the primary method of shaving. The straight razor (a.k.a. cutthroat razor) of this era did not have a hollow grind, but more of a wedge shape. The blades had no tang, and if they did, it was ridiculously small. The typical handle materials for this period were horn, wood, or bone. The handles were flat, unlike the curved handle scales that were later introduced and still used today. The blade would rest between the handle scales when not in use and was simply unfolded when it was time to shave. The razor was attached to the handle via a pin, or set of pins, made of brass. Designs changed over time to include the addition of the words "warranted" or "cast steel," so as to demonstrate the type of blade material used, a detail introduced in 1740 by Robert Huntsman from Sheffield, England.

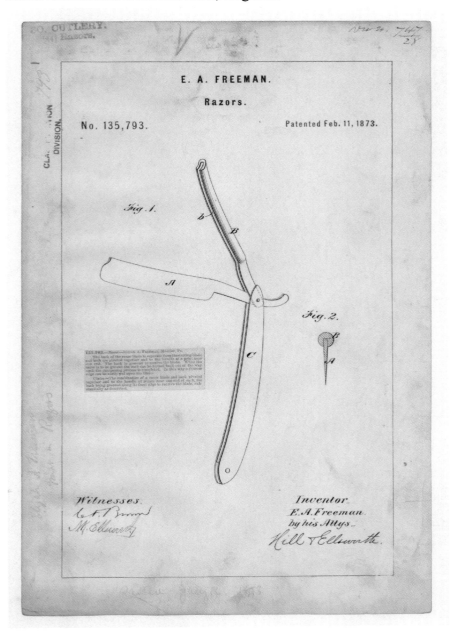

Fig. 78.
U.S. National Archives
National Archives Identifier:
178973583
Local Identifier: 135793
Creator(s): Department of the Interior. Patent Office. (1849 - 1925) (Most Recent)
From: Series: Utility Patent Drawings, 1837 - 1911
Record Group 241: Records of the Patent and Trademark Office, 1836 - 1978

This item was produced or created: 2/11/1873
The creator compiled or maintained the series between:

1837 - 1911

Colonial Ironworks

Around 1680, Lewis Morris established the first successful ironworks in North America—in Tinton Falls, New Jersey. The first three ironworks that were initially built in the 1650s in Massachusetts, Connecticut, and Delaware, failed because they were too costly to maintain due to the high cost of shipping items to Europe. Once shipping costs dropped due to the increased availability of ships, it became possible to export more iron to England. Once there was a growing demand for iron in North America as the colonies were expanding and populations were growing, Maryland and Pennsylvania followed en suite to its New Jersey partner and also built largely successful iron companies later in the 1680s.

Eating Utensils in Colonial America

Although there were local ironworks producing iron products, there was a shortage of forks, which meant early colonists still used pointed knives and spoons as eating utensils. As more products from Europe trickled in by ships, colonists were exposed to the aforementioned round-tip dining knife, which became the new norm and replaced the pointed-tip knife. The only problem, though, was that due to the shortage of forks, colonists had to adjust their table manners and eat with blunt-tip knives sans fork. It was an inconvenient process, as they now had no pointed utensil to pick up the food from their plates. Because of this annoyance, they had to transfer food onto their spoons, which became the primary vehicle to bring food to their mouths. For some colonists, this practice was less than ideal, so they returned to using their pointed knives as an "all-around" eating utensil. This method of eating persisted until forks became more readily available.

Fig 78.2
Title: Fork
Date: 1740–50
Culture: American
Medium: Silver
Dimensions: L. 4 1/4 in. (10.8 cm); 5 dwt. (8.2 g)
Credit Line: Gift of Estate of Mrs. Abraham Lansing, 1929
Accession Number: 29.159.8

Met Museum

THE AGE OF ENLIGHTENMENT (18TH C.)

A movement emerged in Europe known as the Age of Enlightenment, where politics, philosophy, science, arts, and communications were rejuvenated. This movement came as a direct result of the Thirty Years' War, during which time society became weary of long, dragged out wars fought for monarchs and their own personal wealth and power. "Enlightened thinkers" of this period included Sir Thomas Paine, Isaac Newton, John Locke, Thomas Hobbes, Montesquieu, Voltaire, and Jean Jacques Rousseau, to name a few. These renowned individuals, known as *philosophes*, argued that traditional authority deserved an overhaul and cradled the notion that humans could be enhanced through logical transformation. Also known as the "Age of Reason," this period churned out copious amounts of literature, inventions, scientific discoveries, and revolutions. The Enlightenment and its ideals of liberty, equality, fraternity ignited the American and French Revolutions, and pushed forward new concepts of independence. The vision was that to improve one's way of life and pave a revitalized path, one needed to rid themselves of old authorities, therefore alluding to the fact that independence was a direct result of the "enlightened" being. The three main ideas of the Enlightenment were: the use of reason, the scientific method, and progress. This period "cast a light" on man's discovery of the world around him, shedding the previously instilled fear "taught" to him during the medieval period.

Seven Years' War/French and Indian War (1754–1763)

The Seven Years' War was a conflict between Britain and France for global dominance that inevitably pulled other countries into the mix—the Austro-Hungarian Empire, Russia, Sweden, and Saxony allied with France, whereas Prussia and Hanover allied with Britain. Spain remained neutral for most of the war, but eventually signed an agreement stating that it would declare war on Britain should the conflict not end by May 1, 1762. Naturally, the French dragged the war on well beyond the 1762 date, hoping that Spain would fight alongside them.

The Seven Years' War was an interesting moment in history, as it was also a proxy war between the French and the British fought on North American soil in which Native Americans were used as pawns. In North America, a "scalping war" fired up, in which French colonists offered payments to the Natives for British scalps. Native Americans sided with the French, with the intention of pushing British colonies out of North America and forcing them to settle elsewhere. The tables, unsurprisingly, turned as the British began offering bounties for the scalps of Natives. These incidental exchanges gave rise to what people referred to as the "scalping knife." The act of scalping, on both living and dead victims, persisted for 100 years.

Other knives used in the Seven Years' War were: the French officer's sword, the British sergeant's sword, the British bayonet, the French bayonet, and European daggers. The French officer's sword had a high-carbon steel blade that measured about 36 inches in length. Its slim and lightweight blade provided good maneuverability in battle. The British sergeant's sword had more of a claymore (broadsword) design with a highland basket-hilt.

Knives were not the only weapons used during the war, as muskets, carbines, and mortars were used as well. Powdered guns were often inaccurate, as the bullet travelled a limited distance prior to losing velocity and height. Firearms were not ideal weapons, as they opened the potential of having the soldier wounded or killed while reloading. Because armies understood this possibility, bayonets ("plug" type) were fitted directly into the barrel of the musket. This enabled muskets to become effective weapons for close combat, by using the bayonet as a stabbing knife. The "plug" bayonet was an offshoot of the French hunter musket, where a knife was stuck on the end of the barrel, typically used for hunting wild boar. The French realized the effectiveness of this hunting method, and so they began to use it in warfare. The "plug" bayonet was later succeeded by the "socket" bayonet, which simply fit over the muzzle of the barrel versus inside the barrel. The principal reason as to why the latter was more effective was because it allowed the musket to be fired with the bayonet still attached.

When the war raged on beyond Spain's stipulated May 1, 1762 deadline, they entered the war and sided with France. The Spanish attempted to invade Portugal, who were allies of Britain, but failed miserably. In return, the British seized Spanish Cuba, the French Caribbean Islands, and the Philippines. In 1763, French and Spanish ambassadors sought to establish peace with the British, resulting in the signing of the Treaty of Paris. As part of the negotiations, the British acquired vast amounts of territory in North America, including Florida and all French territories east of the Mississippi River.

There are never gains without losses. The British Empire was experiencing financial hardship due to the Seven Years' War, and so decided it would be "wise" to impose higher taxes on the American colonies. Higher taxes, coupled with the intervention of the British to stop colonists from expanding into Native American territories, did not settle well with colonists and inevitably led to rebellion and the Declaration of Independence.

Butterfly Knife, a.k.a. Balisong

Discoveries have shown that in the early 1700s, the French developed the "butterfly knife," also known as the balisong. However, its origin is debated quite heavily in the Philippines, as they claim to be the first to have introduced it. Butterfly knives (balisong) feature two handles that conceal the knife's blade, which, when flipped open, reveal the blade. This knife was typically used for self-defense but is also used as a pocket utility knife.

There are rumors which suggest that the balisong's origins date back to 800 AD, but there are no legitimate supporting facts to such claims. Scholars state the knife originated in the Philippines as a self-defense, utility knife. The French, however, claim that the butterfly-style knife originated within its country's borders around the early 1700s. There is always the possibility that it could have originated in two different places at two different periods of time, but that will just have to be open for debate. This book will discuss both French and Filipino origins.

Fig. 79.
Drawing by A.J. depicts a butterfly knife,
a.k.a balisong.

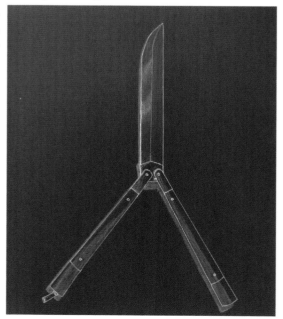

THE INDUSTRIAL REVOLUTION (1760–1840)

The Industrial Revolution marked the beginning of a new era for humanity. Industrialization led to machine mass production of goods, which resulted in the replacement of rigorous handmade work-flows. The meticulous approach that went into producing crafted items was now the job of machines. Iron making, textiles, and various other industries were influenced by many new innovations of the nineteenth century. The Industrial Revolution, which began in Britain, rapidly gained momentum as it was reproduced throughout the world, impacting the traditional lifestyles of all social classes. The infrastructure of countries changed dramatically, as now there were more rapid ways to commute, communicate, and manufacture goods. As the wheels of industrialization spun faster, engines burned greater fuel, thereby releasing more energy into the atmosphere. This period, though necessary for bringing forth the modern age, also marked an important transition where this robust locomotive was steaming toward a new epoch, with little sign of slowing down. Advancements in metallurgy made it possible for the development of stronger, more efficient steels, which could be used in a number of applications, one of which was knives. Stronger knife steels meant that blades would not break as often and could maintain an edge for longer periods of time.

Switchblades

In the mid-eighteenth century, switchblades made their first appearance in Sheffield, England. These knives became popular for their spring-loaded blades, which would "fold out" from the handle with the simple push of a button. Around the late eighteenth century, spring-operated knives were used as folding spike bayonets, also referred to as "pigstickers," on flintlock guns. By the nineteenth century, the design of the knife changed, offering a more pocket-friendly style that gained widespread pop-ularity in Europe. Over time, several variations of the switchblade were created by French, Span-ish, Italian, and American knifemakers, each offering their own unique variations on how the blade would be exposed. These variations were either via pushbutton or lever-lock. With the arrival of the Industrial Revolution, switchblades began to be mass produced and sold at lower costs, therefore making them more readily available. In the early 1900s, George Schrade, Founder of Geo. Schrade Knife Co., dominated the American switchblade market, with his automatic versions of jackknives and pocketknives. When the mid-1900s rolled in, these knives were mass produced by various com-panies worldwide, and advertised as "compact, versatile multi-purpose tools." George Schrade died in 1945, and his sons sold Geo. Schrade Knife Co. in 1956 to the Boker Knife Co. of New Jersey.

When American soldiers returned from Europe after World War II, they brought back the stilet-to-style switchblades to the States. First introduced in Italy in the 1950s, this style of switchblade appeared more threatening, due to its double edge and needle tip design. The simultaneous rise in crime on American streets by people who just so happened to be carrying switchblades, raised eyebrows in communities and did not help to subdue its already threating appearance. News outlets had a field day misrepresenting the stiletto-style switchblade, further pushing a heightened state of fear into the community. By this point, people viewed the knife as a violent, lethal weapon that had no place in our society. In the late 1950s, the switchblade was condemned, and anyone seen with this knife was categorically viewed as a criminal. Negative news portrayal of the knife ultimately gained the attention of the United States Congress, resulting in the banned sale of switchblade knives, which led to the inevitable closure of the Geo. Schrade Knife Co. in 1958. The ban on switchblades not only occurred in the United States though, as countries throughout Europe also prohibited the sale of these knives.

The closure of the Geo. Schrade Knife Co. did not mark end of the company, because earlier in 1946,

Schrade Cutlery Co. (Schrade's second knife company), was purchased by Imperial Knife Associated Companies. Long story short, the modern Schrade company is derived from this predecessor.

Laguiole

In 1829, Laguiole was founded by Pierre-Jean Calmels in Laguiole, France, a commune located in the Aveyron department of southern France. In 1829, Calmels conceived of the very first knives. One was a pocketknife called the *capuchadou*, meant to be used during one's daily tasks from field to table. The other was a variation of the original Spanish navaja. This pocketknife was approximately a quarter of the size and slimmer in design, in comparison to the original. Calmels's "navaja" sometimes featured a corkscrew, which in 1880, was included in the knife's permanent design. This effortless feature linked his Laguiole to the emergence of a "bottled wine society."

Hoe-shaped Razor

In 1847, a man by the name of William Henson invented the hoe-shaped razor, though it did not gain widespread popularity until 1880. In the early twentieth century, King Camp Gillette, a travelling salesman, combined the hoe-shape razor with a double-edge disposable/replaceable razor. The problem at the time was that the razors were not as easy to manufacture. After some thorough research and a partnership with MIT Professor William Nickerson, Gillette figured out a way to stamp out the blades from thin sheets of high carbon steel. Their efforts resulted in the first batch of *Gillette* razors that were released for use by 1903.

Fig. 80.
U.S. National Archives
National Archives Identifier: 7451921
Local Identifier: 775134
Creator(s): Department of the Interior. Patent Office.
(1849 - 1925) (Most Recent)
From: Series: Utility Patent Drawings, 1837 - 1911
Record Group 241: Records of the Patent and Trademark Office, 1836 - 1978

This item was produced or created: 11/15/1904
The creator compiled or maintained the series between: 1837 - 1911

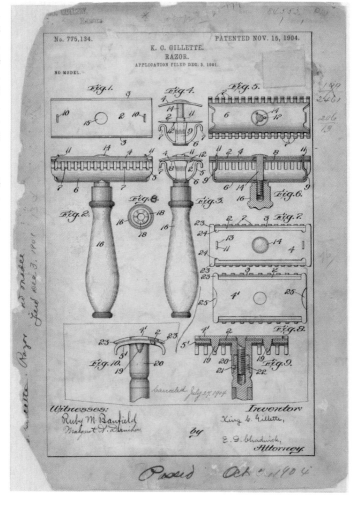

American Revolutionary War and Declaration of Independence (1776)

By this time in history, there were various multi-purpose cutting tools available to people. From small pocketknives to 36-inch swords, knives were everywhere, including everyone's household.

There are moments in time when people come together to fight for a common cause. Due to a series of events that soiled their relationship, American settlers realized that they needed to end their ties with the British Empire. After the Crown spent a significant amount protecting their territory in the American Colonies to win the war against France, they enacted the Stamp Act. The act required American Colonies to pay heavy transaction taxes back to the British Crown, so the empire could recuperate some of the funds lost during the Seven Years' War. American colonists found the act outrageous, as they not only had to purchase goods from the British Empire but also pay taxes on those goods. Long story short, those taxes were never paid. As a result, the British Parliament reinforced its authority by enacting the Townshend Act, which directed British customs commissioners to collect taxes on goods sent to American colonies while simultaneously attempting to eradicate smuggling. Naturally, this was viewed negatively by American colonists and major boycotting followed soon after. One afternoon in March 1770, the situation between Britain and the colonists reached a breaking point, when tensions escalated between a few British troops that occupied the Boston area and 200 colonists. The confrontation between both parties ended tragically as British troops opened fire and killed several colonists in an event known as the Boston Massacre. This incident resulted in even more palpable tension between the colonists and the British Empire.

In an effort to try and ease tensions, the British withdrew their troops from Boston and adjusted the Townshend Act. However, the tax on tea was still in full effect. In 1773, the Tea Act was enacted in support of the British East India Company as a financial aid. This act gave the company the exclusive right to sell tea at unfavorable prices to American merchants. Yet again, eyebrows were raised as colonists contested that they were being told to purchase tea through specific countries—only those that would benefit the British Crown. Essentially, colonists wanted the freedom to purchase from whomever they pleased and opposed the monopoly Britain was creating. A radical group, known as the Sons of Liberty, confronted the British when they jumped onboard British ships in Boston Harbor and destroyed over 90,000 pounds of British tea by throwing it into the water. This event, which took place in December 1773, is now known as the Boston Tea Party.

Naturally, their actions did not settle well with the British Empire and was viewed as another act of defiance. In response to the Boston Tea Party, the British Parliament enacted the Coercive Acts of 1774—or from the standpoint of the colonists, the Intolerable Acts—meaning the Boston Harbor would remain closed until the colonists reimbursed the Crown for the destroyed tea. In addition, Parliament gave full authority to General Thomas Gage to take control of the situation in the colonies. As a result of the Quartering Act, British soldiers were now granted the right to occupy certain houses and buildings in town rather than reside in the countryside. The colonists, thus, had to provide food and hospitality to these soldiers. The Quartering Act was proverbial the straw that broke the camel's back. In 1775, General Gage led British troops from Boston to Lexington to capture colonial leaders, such as Sam Adams and John Hancock. Colonist spies found out about the plan and gave colonists a chance to prepare. Their will to fight for what they believed in demonstrated that, despite the fact that many of those fighting lacked formal military training at first, American colonists would not go down without a fight. In 1776, the British launched an attack on colonial coastal towns, which kickstarted the American Revolutionary War. In the end, America won despite all odds and the Declaration of Independence was signed into effect. As men took to the battlefields, some women disguised themselves as men to fight alongside their male counterparts. Others accompanied their husbands so that they could serve soldiers on the battlefields. Many brave American men and women died in this gruesome war fighting for freedom, with the hope of establishing a path toward a more unified nation… one that stands together.

Knives were highly important during the war because muskets were fairly inaccurate, so soldiers would rely on close combat. There was no set standard as to what type of knife should be carried because most of the men were volunteers that brought their own weapons from home. The most common types of knives used were the bayonet and the rifleman's knife. Carried by the infantrymen of the Continental Army, the bayonet was fixed to the end of the musket and was very important since only about 18 percent of the lead projectiles fired from muskets actually hit their target. The rifleman's knife had a single edged blade made of carbon steel. It was a multipurpose tool and was used not only for hand-to-hand combat, but also for woodcraft, skinning game, and as an eating utensil.

Cutlass swords and sabers were also used during the war. The cutlass sword's blade was either straight or slightly curved, single edged and made of carbon steel. Officers also carried a saber, which was a single edged blade with a slight curve, made of carbon steel. A tomahawk was also quite popular during the Revolutionary War. It was small, hatchet-like, and with a straight shaft. The tomahawk was used as either a throwing weapon or for hand-to-hand combat. The head of the tomahawk was made of carbon steel.

Fig. 81., Object: The Declaration of Independence, July 4, 1776, Artist: Waterman Lilly Ormsby (American, Hampton, Connecticut 1809–1883 Brooklyn, New York), Artist: After John Trumbull (American, Lebanon, Connecticut 1756–1843 New York), Date: 1876, Medium: Engraving, Dimensions: plate: 25 5/8 x 32 1/4 in. (65.1 x 81.9 cm) sheet: 27 1/4 x 36 1/4 in. (69.2 x 92.1 cm), Classification: Prints, Credit Line: Gift of William Loring Andrews, 1888, Accession Number: 88.1.1, Met Museum.

The United States and Territorial Expansion

North America was not entirely uninhabited, as Native Americans had settled in various areas centuries prior. But the newly minted United States was at a point where territorial expansion was necessary for continued development. Several waves of immigrants from all corners of Europe began to flee their homelands to settle in America. Due to the lack of opportunity, rigid governments, and discrimination in their homelands, European immigrants left seeking a better way of life as there was opportunity in America. Many arrived aspiring to acquire fertile land, have a say in government, rise in social status, and have freedom to practice the religion of their choice. Others fled hoping to obtain proper education and maintain steady employment. The difficulty the United States faced during this time was the unfortunate fact that a large percentage of the land was already claimed and occupied by Native Americans.

How to deal with claimed land stood in the way of the much-needed territorial expansion in order to accommodate the ongoing growth. A country's development process is perplexingly intricate as it entails acquiring commodities, such as land, which will have direct social and economic impacts on populations and infrastructure. Land is considered valuable because within that territory there could be valuable natural resources. An abundance of territory also means there is room for towns, cities, and states to flourish, which means there is room for population growth, an opportunity to establish institutions, and the potential for economic growth. A strong economy is needed to support a strong military. As a new and vulnerable nation, the leaders of the United States saw the need to expand the nation's territory in order to grow both economically and develop a strong defense system because there was always fear that the British would break their agreement and attempt to invade. The conflict that the earliest colonists had faced soon surfaced once the new nation became free of the British Crown—Native Americans had already settled in the areas needed by the United States to successfully expand.

The understandable resentment and pushback by Native American tribes, coupled with the settlers' quest to occupy new land, led to additional conflicts over the decades. The narrative of how these disputes were put to an end is controversial, to say the least, and far beyond the scope of this book. Native Americans were looking to defend their land and tribes while newly independent Americans and European settlers viewed the situation from their own vantage points. Yet, not all European settlers acted one way, just as not all Native Americans acted in a particular way. The period of territorial expansion was a harsh time in North American history when drastic decisions resulted in great turmoil and the suffering of countless innocent bystanders. Poor decisions caused these conflicts, which resulted from an incompatible relationship, which, like many conflicts, resulted in only one side as the "victor."

The 1780s were an incredibly challenging time for the thirteen states that made up the United States of America. The Treaty of Paris meant there was peace and a newfound independence for the United States, but that a centralized system of government still needed to be established. There were disputes between the states over ownership of western territories, which eventually led them to voluntarily turn over their territories to the national establishment. Two ordinances prepared the young nation for success: the Land Ordinance of 1785 and the Northwest Ordinance of 1787. These ordinances created territorial government, developed procedures for the addition of new states, divided land into measurable units, and separated land in each township for public utilization. Ordinances paved the way for the United States' territorial expansion.

During this time, the iron industry was a highly developed, well-oiled machine. The United States was mining hundreds of tons (possibly tens of thousands even), of iron ore per year. There were three types of metal being used during this period: cast iron, wrought iron, and steel. Steel was used to produce knife blades, files, saws, springs, and musket ramrods.

While the United States was independent and free, it was shunned by Europe. Trade opportunities were restricted, as only European powers had access to trade rights with other colonies outside of North America. Even though the United States was finding its place in the world, there was still several hurdles to jump. This, however, did not stop frontiersmen from exploring the West.

In the 1790s, Congress passed a tariff legislation to save the iron industry from overseas competition. The legislation had a positive impact on US businesses because it enabled the price of iron to remain high in the domestic market, and by default, allowed local businesses to maintain profitability.

Fig. 81.2
Object: The Rocky Mountains, Lander's Peak
Artist: Albert Bierstadt (American, Solingen 1830–1902 New York)
Date: 1863
Culture: American
Medium: Oil on canvas
Dimensions: 73 1/2 x 120 3/4 in. (186.7 x 306.7 cm)
Credit Line: Rogers Fund, 1907
Accession Number: 07.123
Met Museum

AMERICAN FRONTIER

Between 1790 and 1867, the period of the American frontiersmen was birthed. These formidable, gallant men always carried a knife by their side, so these knives needed to be a reliable companion that performed as intended under extreme conditions. Although pocketknives were popular during this time, frontiersmen typically carried a belt knife or butcher-style knife. The art of self-reliance was at a peak during this period, and the knives a frontiersman carried needed to meet certain standards in terms of capability so that they could be used for many tasks, for example, hunting, fishing, trapping, skinning game, fire making, shelter building and self-defense. Typically, these knives had handles made of wood, bone, or stag, with blade sizes varying in size from 6.5 to 15 inches.

Mountain men immersed themselves into the dense, rigid wilderness with aspirations of expanding what is known today as the United States of America. The first eighty years in American history were brutal and ruthless but gave birth to some of the boldest men in modern history. John Coulter, Meriwether Lewis and William Clark, Davy Crockett, Joel Estes, Christopher "Kit" Carson, and Daniel Boone deserve recognition for paving their way through the mysterious and wild regions of North America.

Just as our ancestors practiced a great deal of bushcraft/woodcraft, people venturing into new territories during this period also relied upon these skills extensively as they began to explore new lands and settle in rural locations. Understanding the surrounding land and how to make the most of its resources was crucial when attempting to traverse great distances across the wilderness. Bushcraft is a significant part of wilderness survival and being a skillful craftsman can increase one's chances of staying alive.

Fig. 82.
Object: The Mountain Ford
Artist: Thomas Cole (American, Lancashire 1801–1848 Catskill, New York)
Date: 1846
Culture: American
Medium: Oil on canvas
Dimensions: 28 1/4 x 40 1/16 in. (71.8 x 101.8 cm)
Credit Line: Bequest of Maria DeWitt Jesup, from the collection of her husband, Morris K. Jesup, 1914
Accession Number: 15.30.63
Met Museum

James Bowie and his Infamous Fighting Knife

James Bowie was taught to use a knife, ride horses, hunt, and trap by his avid outdoorsman father. His father also taught him how to shoot with a pistol and rifle. James did not live the purest of lifestyles and was engaged in what many would consider unethical activities, ranging from very heavy alcohol consumption to involvement in the slave trade. He joined the army later in life, rising to the ranks of colonel. Despite his troubled background, James is recognized as a hero for his patriotism and involvement in the Texas Revolution. He fought and died in the Battle of the Alamo in San Antonio, Texas. That said, James Bowie is a recognizable figure today for his contributions to the knife community.

James was reported to have a terrible temper and feared knife fighting skills. It is said that he carried a custom personal knife that originally belonged to his brother. Some believe it was created by Louisiana blacksmith Jesse Clift, while others claim it was Arkansas blacksmith James Black. Nevertheless, it is said that James Bowie extracted his custom knife from its sheath during a brawl known as the 1827 Sandbar Fight. He managed to slash, stab, and cut through several opponents, leaving them lifeless on the floor. Rumors circulated that he used the knife during several other fights, ripping through his threats "like a hot knife, through butter."

Although questions remain concerning the details due to inconsistencies in the story, James and his personal knife gained popularity and people began to refer to the style and design of the knife as the "Bowie knife." Measuring about 12–18 inches, the Bowie knife had a cross guard to prevent accidental injury of the wielder during a fight and a clip-point-style blade that was about 5–12 inches in length.

James Bowie died in 1836 during the Battle of the Alamo. Since so much of his life was poorly documented, including the legendary tales with his infamous knife, a great deal of debate based on rumors and no legitimate documentation persists. What is certain, though, is that his personal knife was a custom-made fighting knife. The design and style were hard to overlook since it was used in many bloody brawls. Because of James's unique knife fighting skills and success in the brawls, this style of knife was named after him.

Fig. 83.
Drawing by A.J. depicts a bowie knife that resembles the James Bowie knife.

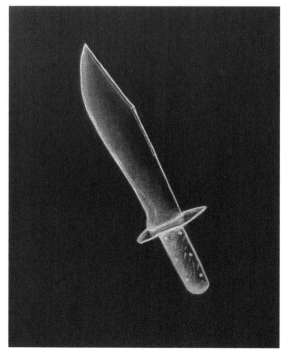

American Civil War (1861–1865)

The United States of America doesn't always stand united. There are quite a few instances in history when Americans were divided, for example, all the issues which led to the American Civil War. It was the bloodiest conflict ever fought on American soil, with over 620,000 soldiers killed and millions of others injured. The war was primarily fought over the issue of slavery, along with the inhumane treatment and economic factors attached to that system. The northern states consisted of mostly urban and suburban communities, with small-scale farming areas. The southern states were the opposite, as their economy relied on mostly large-scale farming; therefore, "dependent" on forced labor. For the most part, those living in the northern states believed slavery was unconstitutional and that the United States needed to rid itself of that system in order to grow as a "free" and prosperous country, where everyone's rights *should* be respected. The election of Abraham Lincoln would cause the southern states to secede from the Union and eventually kickstart the war, under the reorganized Confederate States of America.

Confederate soldiers typically carried large Bowie knives with 14-inch carbon steel blades. The Confederate "D" guard Bowie knife, which was large enough to be considered a short sword, was carried in conjunction with their rifle-musket and/or revolver. Confederate cavalry officers also carried a sabre used for slashing, thrusting, or stabbing in battle, but their main weapon was the rifle-musket and revolver. When the gunpowder ran out, they would pull out their swords or large Bowies and hack at their opponents. Most swords in the years leading up to the war were imported from Europe. Confederate soldiers brought their own edged weapons from home, in addition to using whatever was issued to them.

Union Army soldiers were also issued swords, typically the model 1840 and 1860 cavalry sabers. Union soldiers carried a pocketknife, which featured a take-apart fork, knife, and spoon. They carried bayonets attached to their rifle-musket that they would use in close combat as needed as well as a revolver as a sidearm. The navy would carry a 1860 cutlass-style knife, in addition to having access to harpoons, axes, and grappling hooks.

The war ended on April 9, 1865, when Robert E. Lee surrendered to Ulysses S. Grant at Appomattox Courthouse, Virginia. It took sixteen months after the surrender of Robert E. Lee to formally declare the war was over in August 1866. The reason behind the delay was that Robert E. Lee was just one of many Confederate forces scattered throughout the country, so several back-and-forth struggles between the remaining Confederate forces and the Union Army continued for many months. Eventually, a domino effect took place and each of the Confederate forces surrendered one by one. On April 2, 1866, President Andrew Johnson issued a proclamation, stating that the insurrection had ended in all southern states but one—Texas. That same year, Texas went through internal reconstruction issues but managed to sustain itself with some independence from the United States. Texas did not rejoin the Union until 1870. The rejoining of Texas to the Union was not a smooth process; it took a great deal of communication, cooperation, and finally, acceptance.

Fig. 84.
Title: Light Artillery, Sergeant Major
Artist: Attributed to Oliver H. Willard (American, active 1850s–70s, died 1875)
Date: 1866
Medium: Albumen silver print from glass negative with applied color
Dimensions: Image: 20.3 x 15.2 cm (8 x 6 in.)
Mount: 33.3 x 25.7 cm (13 1/8 x 10 1/8 in.)
Classification: Photographs
Credit Line: Purchase, Saundra B. Lane Gift, in honor of Charles Isaacs, 2010
Accession Number: 2010.36

Met Museum

Fig. 85.
Title: The Battle of Gettysburg, Pa., July 3rd, 1863
Publisher: Currier & Ives (American, active New York, 1857–1907)
Date: 1863
Medium: Hand-colored lithograph with blue tint stone
Dimensions: Image: 15 11/16 x 22 3/8 in. (39.8 x 56.8 cm)
Sheet: 19 13/16 × 25 13/16 in. (50.3 × 65.6 cm)
Classification: Prints
Credit Line: Bequest of Adele S. Colgate, 1962
Accession Number: 63.550.512
Met Museum

Fig. 86.
Object: [President Abraham Lincoln, Major General John A. McClernand (right), and E. J. Allen (Allan Pinkerton, left), Chief of the Secret Service of the United States, at Secret Service Department, Headquarters Army of the Potomac, near Antietam, Maryland]
Artist: Alexander Gardner (American, Glasgow, Scotland 1821–1882 Washington, D.C.)
Person in Photograph: Allan Pinkerton (American (born Scotland), Glasgow 1819–1884 Chicago)
Person in Photograph: Abraham Lincoln (American, Hardin County, Kentucky 1809–1865 Washington, D.C.)
Person in Photograph: John Alexander McClernand (American, Breckinridge County, Kentucky 1812–1900 Springfield, Illinois)
Date: October 3, 1862
Medium: Albumen silver print from glass negative
Dimensions: Image: 20 x 18.5 cm (7 7/8 x 7 5/16 in.)
Mount: 22.8 x 21.3 cm (9 x 8 3/8 in.)
Mount: 34.1 x 27 cm (13 7/16 x 10 5/8 in.)
Classification: Photographs
Credit Line: Gilman Collection, Gift of The Howard Gilman Foundation, 2005
Accession Number: 2005.100.1220
Met Museum

Fig. 87.
Title: The Fall of Richmond, Virginia, on the Night of April 2nd, 1865
Publisher: Currier & Ives (American, active New York, 1857–1907)
Date: 1865
Medium: Hand-colored lithograph
Dimensions: Image: 15 3/4 x 22 1/8 in. (40 x 56.2 cm)
Sheet: 17 15/16 × 24 in. (45.5 × 61 cm)
Classification: Prints
Credit Line: Bequest of Adele S. Colgate, 1962
Accession Number: 63.550.11
Met Museum

A Return to Nature

"The lover of nature is he whose inward and outward senses are still truly adjusted to each other; who has retained the spirit of infancy even into the era of manhood. His intercourse with heaven and earth, becomes part of his daily food. In the presence of nature, a wild delight runs through the man, in spite of real sorrows. Nature says,—he is my creature, and maugre all his impertinent griefs, he shall be glad with me."

—Ralph Waldo Emerson, "Nature"

In the 1880s, George W. Sears, also known as "Nessmuk," played a major role in reigniting the love for bushcraft/woodcraft with the publishing of his book *Woodcraft* in 1884. He was a sportswriter for *Forest and Stream* magazine in the 1880s and a conservationist at heart. Today, people can purchase knives that have a similar style to the ones he used for wilderness survival and bushcraft. Nessmuk spent his time in the Adirondacks, where he found peace in the woods, one of earth's greatest gift to humans. This famous line from his book expresses his true motto for life, "We do not go to the woods to rough it; we go to smooth it—we get it rough enough in town. But let us live the simple, natural life in the woods, and leave all frills behind." (Woodcraft)

Nessmuk believed that America was an overworked nation, where most would age before their prime due to stress. He thought returning to nature was the only way to cure stress and possibly slow the aging process.

He expressed that an outdoorsman should always carry a fixed-blade knife, an axe or hatchet, and a foldable pocketknife, when going into the woods. He later wrote, "A word as to knife, or knives. These are the prime necessity, and should be of the best, both as to shape and temper." (Woodcraft) Nessmuk's writings influenced people like travel writer and librarian Horace Kephart to explore nature, live off the land, and leave one's troubles behind. Best known for the 1906 groundbreaking book, *Camping and Woodcraft*, which became a classic outdoor guide for the wilderness explorer. Today, people can also purchase similar style knives to those used by Nessmuk and Horace Kephart, when they explored the great American wilderness and practiced woodcraft.

Fig. 88.
Object: Camp Fire
Artist: Winslow Homer (American, Boston, Massachusetts 1836–1910 Prouts Neck, Maine)
Date: 1880
Culture: American
Medium: Oil on canvas
Dimensions: 23 3/4 x 38 1/8 in. (60.3 x 96.8 cm)
Credit Line: Gift of Josephine Pomeroy Hendrick, in the name of Henry Keney Pomeroy, 1927
Accession Number: 27.181

Met Museum

THE 1900S

The 20th century was a time that brought with it great changes, not only in the United States of America, to the world. The early 1900s was an era of boisterous activity as far as business expansion goes. This time also brought with it, progressive reform in the United States. During this time the United States launched into a period of peace, prosperity, and progress. Cities flourished, factories had maximum output, small businesses thrived, and incomes jumped to an all-time high.

During the early 1900s stainless steel ('rustless' steel) was invented. Though there were several scientists around the world that made similar discoveries around the same time, it was Harry Brearley who was given the credit. The invention of stainless steel was a major breakthrough that revolutionized most modern industries.

The 20th century was not always full of joy, happiness, and prosperity. Humanity also faced several major confrontations that led to millions of fatalities, fell into a great depression that affected the lives of billions, and overcame a severe pandemic that infected an estimated 500 million people globally.

Fig. 88.2, Object: Waterfront, Artist: Joseph Kaplan (American, 1900–1980), Date: ca. 1940, Medium: Gouache on paper Dimensions: 15 1/8 × 21 in. (38.4 × 53.3 cm), Classification: Drawings, Credit Line: Gift of New York City W. P. A., 1943 Accession Number: 43.47.19

World War I (1914–1919)

In 1914, as darkness fell over humanity, the world was covered in a veil of ash and gun powder. Times were changing and society was yearning for a sign of hope during those relentless times. The assassination of Archduke Franz Ferdinand of Austria-Hungary and his wife, Sophie, by a Bosnian Serb nationalist kicked off what later became known as the Great War in June 1914. Involved in this historic conflict were the countries of Germany, Austria-Hungary, Bulgaria, and the Ottoman Empire—or the Central Powers. They battled against Great Britain, France, Russia, Italy, Romania, Japan, and eventually, the United States—collectively known as the Allied Powers. These nations also used manpower and resources derived from their colonies and territorial holdings, which magnified the scale and impact of the conflict. The war was almost entirely fought on French soil.

"Eyes"

Eerie... this war is just so raw and frightening. I am overtaken by uncontrollable shivering, my body is completely filthy, and over-exhausted. I find myself numb, to the ballistic sounds and the mud caked grounds supporting my worn-out boots. I run through the trenches with my comrades, terrified, yet with the hopes that one day, this deadly confrontation will end. This insatiable desire to finally overpower the enemy and win this battle, sometimes devours me at night. It's cold, wet, the air smells of sulfur oxide, coal, and decaying corpses. Sometimes I wonder how I can keep moving, breathing, knowing I haven't eaten for days. At night, my eyes see red lit skies, and my ears hear young men's cries. In this hell, there are no lullabies to help sooth your pain. My hands smell and taste like metal and gunpowder. No matter how much I try to rub away this nauseating stench, it does not leave. The smell lingers, as if to remind me I may never make it back home. I may never see my wife, nor meet my newborn son. Here, in this dreadful place, there is no sun, because the lingering smoke blocks all light and overall sight. There are days we must conserve our ammunition and others when we overwhelm our opponents through attrition. On the days we conserve our ammunition, we traverse the battle grounds stealthily in the hours before dawn. We sneak up behind the sentries patrolling their perimeter and use our knives to quietly make the silent kill. These trustworthy edged tools we carry are a symbol of hope in moments of despair. Whether I manage to make it back home or not, my mind is already damaged beyond repair. My eyes have seen Satan's Kingdom, they have experienced gruesome scenes, and unholy events. There are times I see myself in the enemy's eyes, as I end their life with a single thrust of my blade. I cover their mouth, shush them as the knife punctures through their flesh, and see my soul in their eyes as their face goes pallid. I still pray every night for forgiveness, even though I could never forgive myself for committing these discordant acts. I don't have the right words to define what War is. I do have faith that my feeble body will push through this ghastly event, and one day I will be home with those I cherish.

—AJ Cardenal

The Great War swallowed everyone and reshaped humanity forever. Countries were experiencing unease and rushed frantically to develop improvised tools and equipment for the brave soldiers who went off to meet the Grim Reaper in blood-tainted, leaden, muddy trenches. At the beginning of the war, the Allied Powers had a large shortage of combat knives. Troops were being issued kitchen and hunting knives. In the minds of the dog-tired troops, "trench knives," were born by divine intervention and gave life to constructive creativity. The invention of the trench knife galvanized troops' spirits, as it was an engineered sign of hope, in a period of gut-wrenching despair. Trench knives pushed these tenacious men to meet their enemy face-to-face and fearlessly fight in close combat. Close combat is the complete embodiment of what survival of the fittest truly represents during battle—when ammunition eventually runs out and all that is left is the trustworthy blade by your side. Trench knives were used for everything from self-defense and food preparation to the mundane camp chores. For easy access, trench knives were kept in a sheath attached to a waist belt or kept in a boot. The muddy trenches were tight spaces to move through, and sometimes the bayonet attached to the end of the rifle was inconvenient, so troops would modify the bayonet to use it as a trench-style knife. They knew what worked, and because they were on the front lines, they understood what had to be done to survive. Modifications to bayonet knives led to what we know today as the Bowie-type fighting knife. Trench knives were the silent weapons that quietly ended lives of many in the dense fog that blanketed the mud-caked trenches during the Great War.

During the war, the French had a massive shortage of combat knives. They lacked large cutleries in the country that could mass produce combat knives, unlike the Germans, who had dozens of internationally recognized cutleries located in Solingen, Germany. As a result, the French government had to rapidly devise a solution, so they decided to purchase civilian knives that were already in circulation and hand them to the troops. French soldiers were given navaja-style folders, modified butcher knives, and utility knives. Hundreds of thousands were issued and put to the test in the battlefield. Most of the modified knives were double-edged, with a steel blade that measured anywhere from 6 to 9 inches.

German knifemakers, typically known for their hunting knives, manufactured higher quality, more durable trench knives, than those produced in France. Some of the mass-produced combat knives in Germany consisted of a 6-inch steel blade with a metal cross guard and wooden handles. Other combat knife models had checkered wooden grips and steel pommels. There was no set standard as far as the design of the trench knife, and so various styles of combat/trench knives were introduced to the battlefield. Every country had multiple combat knife styles produced by multiple cutleries during the war.

The M1918, Mark 1, also known as the "knuckle knife," was an American trench knife used during the war which had a 6.75-inch, double edge blade made of carbon steel. With a handle made of brass coupled with brass knuckles, it was difficult for an enemy to take the knife from its wielder. This knife had better steel than its predecessor, the M1917, and would not break as easily. This knife was used for thrusting and stabbing an opponent.

Seventeen million were reported to have died in battle and over twenty million were wounded. The war ended on November 11, 1918, when Germany formally surrendered. However, the war officially ended on June 28, 1919, with the signing of the Treaty of Versailles.

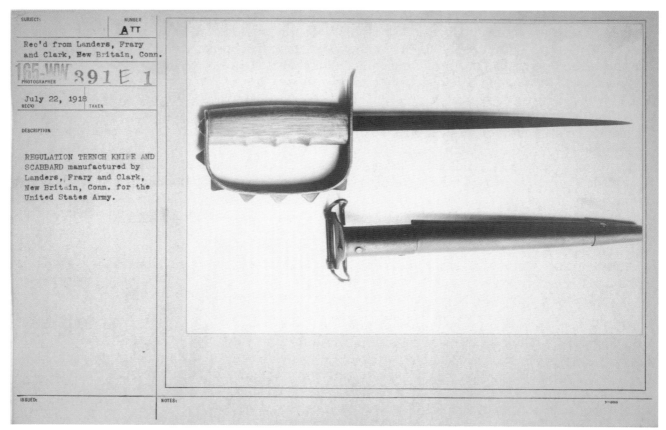

Fig. 90. U.S. National Archives, National Archives Identifier: 45525434, Local Identifier: 165-WW-391E-1, Creator(s): War Department. 1789-9/18/1947 (Most Recent), From: File Unit: Ordnance -, Types - Knives, 1917 - 1918, Series: American Unofficial Collection of World War I Photographs, 1917 - 1918. , Record Group 165: Records of the War Department General and Special Staffs, 1860 - 1952.

The above image is an example of what a WWI trench knife looked like.

Fig. 91. U.S. National Archives National Archives Identifier: 45539480
Local Identifier: 165-WW-463A-51
Creator(s): War Department. 1789-9/18/1947 (Most Recent)
From: File Unit: Propaganda - Motion Pictures, 1917 - 1918
Series: American Unofficial Collection of World War I Photographs, 1917 - 1918
Record Group 165: Records of the War Department General and Special Staffs, 1860 - 1952

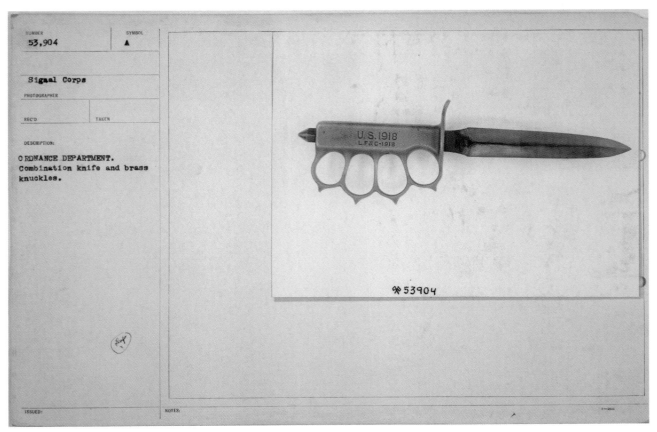

Fig. 92.
U.S. National Archives
National Archives Identifier: 86713012
Local Identifier: 111-SC-53904
Creator(s): Department of Defense. Defense Audiovisual Agency. 6/21/1979-9/30/1985 (Most Recent)
War Department. Army War College. Historical Section. World War I Branch. ca. 1918-ca. 1948 (Predecessor)
Department of Defense. Department of the Army. Office of the Chief Signal Officer. Signal Corps Pictorial Center. (ca. 1953 - 2/1/1956) (Predecessor)
Department of Defense. Department of the Army. Office of the Deputy Chief of Staff for Operations and Plans. Training Directorate. U.S. Army Audiovisual Center. U.S. Army Still Photographic Library. (1978 - 10/1980) (Predecessor)
From: Series: Photographs of American Military Activities, ca. 1918 - ca. 1981
Record Group 111: Records of the Office of the Chief Signal Officer, 1860 - 1985
Level of Description:
Item Type(s) of Archival Materials: Photographs and other Graphic Materials
This item was produced or created: 1919
*Note: Above image depicts the M1918 Trench Knife, used during WWI.

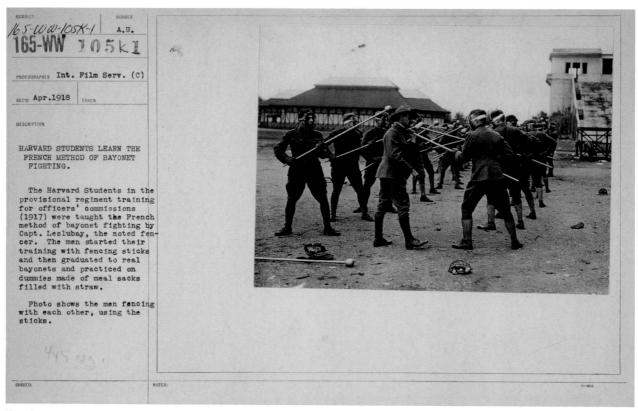

SUBJECT: 165-WW-105K-1 NUMBER: A.U.
165-WW 105K1

PHOTOGRAPHER Int. Film Serv. (C)

REC'D Apr.1918 TAKEN

DESCRIPTION

HARVARD STUDENTS LEARN THE
FRENCH METHOD OF BAYONET
FIGHTING.

The Harvard Students in the
provisional regiment training
for officers' commissions
(1917) were taught the French
method of bayonet fighting by
Capt. Leslubay, the noted fen-
cer. The men started their
training with fencing sticks
and then graduated to real
bayonets and practiced on
dummies made of meal sacks
filled with straw.

Photo shows the men fencing
with each other, using the
sticks.

ISSUED: NOTES:

Fig. 93.
U.S. National Archives
National Archives Identifier: 26426254
Local Identifier: 165-WW-105K-1
Creator(s): War Department. 1789-9/18/1947 (Most Recent)
From: File Unit: Colleges and Universities - Harvard University, 1917 - 1918
Series: American Unofficial Collection of World War I Photographs, 1917 - 1918
Record Group 165: Records of the War Department General and Special Staffs, 1860 - 1952

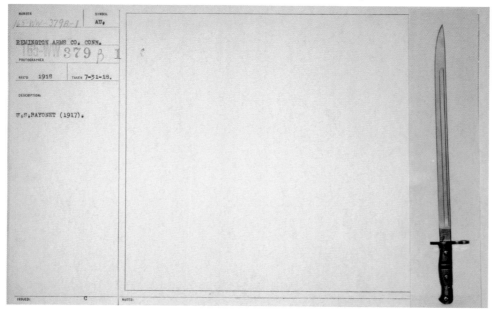

NUMBER: 165-WW-379B-1 SYMBOL: AU.
REMINGTON ARMS CO. CONN.
165-WW 379 B 1
PHOTOGRAPHER

REC'D 1918 TAKEN 7-31-18.

DESCRIPTION:

U.S.BAYONET (1917).

ISSUED: C NOTES:

Fig. 94.
U.S. National Archives
National Archives Identifi-
er: 45522506
Local Identifier:
165-WW-379B-1
Creator(s): War Depart-
ment. 1789-9/18/1947
(Most Recent)
From: File Unit: Ordnance
- Types - Artillery - Bayo-
nets, 1917 - 1918
Series: American Unofficial
Collection of World War I
Photographs, 1917 - 1918
Record Group 165: Records
of the War Department
General and Special Staffs,
1860 - 1952

The Great Depression (1929–1939)

The Great Depression was not an event that was simply confined within US borders; it was a global economic depression that began in countries like Germany in the interwar period. This event was the worst economic collapse in the industrialized world, which lasted about eight years for some countries, but for others went on until about 1939. In the United States, it began with the stock market crash of October 1929, which cleaned out the pockets of millions of people. What ensued after the crash was complete pandemonium, where countless were laid off, companies crumbled, and industrial output sank to an all-time low. In 1933, the Great Depression had bottomed out, with an estimated 12–15 million Americans unemployed.

Fig. 95. U.S. National Archives
National Archives Identifier: 196261
Creator(s): Roosevelt, Franklin D. (Franklin Delano), 1882-1945 (Most Recent)
From: Series: Franklin D. Roosevelt Library Public Domain Photographs, 1882 - 1962
Collection: Franklin D. Roosevelt Library Public Domain Photographs, 1882 - 1962
Level of Description: Item, Type(s) of Archival Materials:, Photographs and other Graphic Materials
This item was produced or created: ca. 2/1936, The creator compiled or maintained the series between: 1882 - 1962
Access Restriction(s): Unrestricted, Use Restriction(s): Unrestricted
Subjects Represented in the Archival Material(s): Department of Agriculture. Farm Security Administration. 9/1/1937-1/1/1947, Depressions, New Deal, 1933-1939

World War II (1939–1945)

A lunatic who served as a war messenger in World War I on the Western Front rose from the fires of hell to formally become dictator of Germany on August 19, 1934. Adolf Hitler may have been formally declared *Fuhrer,* or leader, of Germany in 1934, but he had already sunk his teeth deep into the soul of the nation well before then. The National Socialist movement, or National Socialist Workers' Party (*Nationalsozialistische Deutsche Arbeiterpartei*), spread like wildfire and was colloquially known as the Nazi Party. Hitler was the sadistic spark that ignited World War II, a conflict that led to the deaths of roughly 75 million people, equating to about three percent of the world's population, in the mid-1940s.

The chief Allied Powers fought heroically, not accepting defeat under any circumstance. Night skies were lit up by anti-aircraft gun fire, the beaches were left tainted with blood, and the distinguishable clamor of tanks that left villages, towns, and cities in ruins were heard miles away. Hitler's onslaught shattered Europe and filled the streets with complete and utter carnage. A pungent stench of sulfur and decomposing flesh permeated the air. Cities were completely ravaged by Hitler's minions, who powered their way through countries and dismantled armies across Europe. Clouds of heavy, dense fog covered cities and the uncanny sense that death was approaching, engulfed people's souls.

In those times of desperation, a sign of hope emerged from the scorching furnaces of bladesmiths. An iconic combat knife was born. In a collaboration between USMC Captain Howard America, USMC Colonel John Davis, and Union Cutlery, they designed a prototype knife known as 1219C2. After rigorous trials the knife was finally adopted in 1943 by the United States Marine Corps. This knife would later be known as the famous combat knife, Mark 2. Several companies manufactured the Mark 2, such as Camillus, Colonial, Geneva Forge, PAL, Robeson, and Kinfolks. But none were better than Union Cutlery Company, which stamped all their Mark 2s with the name "KA-BAR." The Mark 2 combat knife replaced the combat stiletto/trench knife (the Mark 1), which served a single purpose—taking out enemies in close combat. The Mark 2 combat knife also served as a multi-purpose tool that could be used as a pry bar, can opener, hammer, and even in light bushcraft/woodcraft. The blade had a clip point and was 7 inches in length with an overall length of 12 inches. After the War, Union Cutlery changed its company name to KA-BAR Knives.

The Ka-Bar combat knife was not the only important knife in the war, as British commandos used the Fairbairn–Sykes. William Ewart Fairbairn and Eric Anthony Sykes created this famous commando knife just before World War II. British commandos, elite forces who were trained to disrupt the enemy by using the element of surprise, used the knife more as stabber, rather than a slasher. The commandos would grab sentries and then stab them in the jugular, or pull their bodies toward the knife, letting the knife do the work. The Fairbairn–Sykes dagger-like knife was designed to be a used as a silent killing weapon, but not a total fighting knife *per se.* The Fairbairn–Sykes had a double-edged blade made of high carbon steel with a needle-sharp tip.

The Shift in the War, the Fight Between Good and Evil:

Humanity did not allow Hitler to take over the world with his psychopathic ideologies and selective veil of death. The Allied Forces would prevail, without surrender, under any circumstance. The attack on Pearl Harbor by Japanese military awoke a sleeping giant. Once the United States had to defend itself in the war, Hitler's chances of world dominance diminished dramatically. America's lionhearted soldiers stormed the beaches of Normandy and unleashed hellfire on Nazi troops, breaking the Nazi empire's spine. Fearless US Marines island-hopped through the Pacific, annihilating the Japanese military that stood in the way of capturing Iwo Jima. The Soviet Union invaded Manchuria and obliterated Japanese forces. The British Pacific Fleet aided in the Battle of Okinawa, unleashing devastating naval strikes on Japan. The American 82nd AB were the first US paratroopers to launch a European air assault in Sicily, which was subsequently followed by a series of air assaults throughout

Europe. British paratroopers of the 1st Airborne Division took part in the same air assault over Sicily, known as Operation Husk, in July 1943. Nearly a year later, on June 6, 1944, Operation Overlord and the D-Day landings were aided by the largest air assault in history. The night skies were covered by paratroopers from the US 101st and 82nd Airborne Divisions, the British 6th Airborne Division, and the 1st Canadian Parachute Battalion. The air assault took place a few hours before the famous coastal landings. Brigadier General Theodore Roosevelt Jr. took part in the first wave of assaults in the beaches of Normandy. There he led troops from the beach over to the seawall to establish cover and begin their move inland. General George S. Patton led the US 7th Army, landing on the southern coast of Sicily on June 10, 1944. General Bernard Montgomery led the British forces and Canadian 8th Army, landing on the island's southeastern coast.

The Battle of Stalingrad (August 1942 to February 1943) was an important turning point for the Soviet Union. Although two million people died in the brutal battle, the Soviet Union regained control of the Eastern Front. The invasion of Sicily by Western Allies brought down dictator Benito Mussolini's army in July 1943. The marvelous, amphibious landing in Normandy on June 6, 1944, aided in the future liberation of Paris on August 25, 1944. Germany's loss at the Battle of the Bulge in the Ardennes region of Belgium was the final nail in the coffin for Hitler. The Nazis were being crushed by the chief Allies on the Eastern and Western Fronts; their looming defeat was palpable. Cowardly, Hitler could not accept defeat and committed suicide in a bunker below the Reich Chancellery on April 30, 1945. On May 7, 1945, Germany surrendered, and by August 14, 1945, Japan was defeated, finally bringing World War II to a much-needed end.

Fig. 96. U.S. National Archives: Pearl Harbor December 7th 1941
National Archives Identifier: 12008991
Local Identifier: 80-G-32424
Creator(s): Department of Defense. Department of the Navy. Naval Photographic Center.
(12/1/1959 - ca. 1998) (Most Recent)
From: Series: General Photographic Files, 1943 - 1968
Record Group 80: General Records of the Department of the Navy, 1804 - 1983

113062

Fig. 97. U.S. National Archives: Victory over Iwo Jima
National Archives Identifier: 74250597
Local Identifier: 127-GR-90-113062
Creator(s): Department of Defense. Department of the Navy. U.S. Marine Corps. 9/18/1947- (Most Recent)
From: File Unit: World War II – Iwo Jima, ca. 1940 - ca. 1958
Series: Photographic Reference File, ca. 1940 - ca. 1958

Fig. 98. U.S. National Archives: Sky is lit up by antiaircraft artillery in Okinawa.
National Archives Identifier: 74251486
Local Identifier: 127-GR-95-118775
Creator(s): Department of Defense. Department of the Navy. U.S. Marine Corps. 9/18/1947- (Most Recent)

From: File Unit: World War II – Okinawa, ca. 1940 - ca. 1958
Series: Photographic Reference File, ca. 1940 - ca. 1958
Record Group 127: Records of the U.S. Marine Corps, 1775 -

Fig. 99. U.S. National Archives: Normandy - "Into the Jaws of Death"
National Archives Identifier: 195515
Creator(s):   Roosevelt, Franklin D. (Franklin Delano), 1882-1945 (Most Recent)
From: Series: Franklin D. Roosevelt Library Public Domain Photographs, 1882 - 1962
Collection: Franklin D. Roosevelt Library Public Domain Photographs, 1882 - 1962

Photograph taken by A.J. depicts a modern KABAR Combat Knife.

KNIVES OF THE INDIGENOUS PEOPLE

The Ulu

The *ulu* (pronounced "ooloo") is a unique half-moon shaped knife used by the Inuit people of Alaska. This traditional Inuit knife dates back to 3500 BC, and is said to have ancestral secrets, handed down from generation to generation among the indigenous people of Alaska. The Inuit have used the *ulu* for thousands of years to accomplish a multitude of tasks, including processing game, cleaning skins, filleting fish, chopping food, and making clothing. This knife has evolved over time. Originally blades were produced out of slate, shale, or quartzite, and now are often made from modern-day carbon steel. Handles were traditionally made of either bone, ivory, or wood, and were attached to the blades using cordage, sinew, rawhide, or pine root. Today these handles are typically attached using rivets or pins. Modern chefs use this knife specifically for its chopping and mincing capabilities, as the blade's shape allows the chef to use a rocking motion to quickly dice up ingredients.

Fig. 101. U.S. National Archives
National Archives Identifier: 42197751
Creator(s): Department of the Interior. National Park Service. Alaska Region. (12/2/1980 - 5/1995) (Most Recent)
Department of the Interior. National Park Service. Pacific Northwest Region. (8/17/1970 - 5/1995) (Predecessor)
From: File Unit: Cape Krusenstern, 1972 - 1976
Series: Alaska Task Force Photographs, 1972 - 1976
Record Group 79: Records of the National Park Service, 1785 - 2006

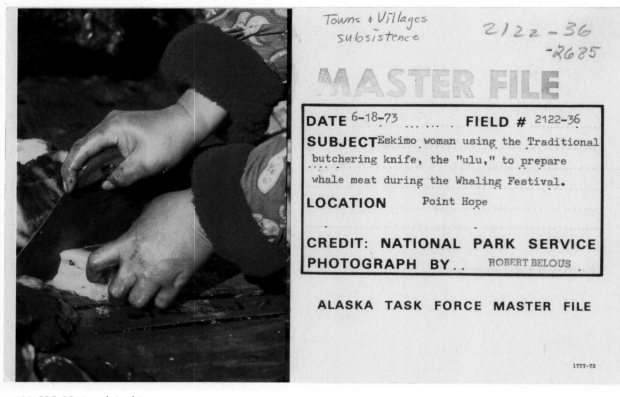

Fig. 102. U.S. National Archives

National Archives Identifier: 42217138

Creator(s): Department of the Interior. National Park Service. Alaska Region. (12/2/1980 - 5/1995) (Most Recent)

Department of the Interior. National Park Service. Pacific Northwest Region. (8/17/1970 - 5/1995) (Predecessor)

From: File Unit: Towns Villages, 1972 - 1976

Series: Alaska Task Force Photographs, 1972 - 1976

Record Group 79: Records of the National Park Service, 1785 - 2006

Fig. 103. Image taken by A.J. depicts two modern style Ulu knives, the one on the left was made by Ezina Designs. It has a damascus steel blade, with a stag handle. The one on the right was made by Knives of Alaska, and has a D2 steel blade.

The Karambit, Indonesia

The modern *karambit* is typically used as a fighting knife, but when it was first developed by the Minangkabau people in West Sumatra long ago, it was used a multipurpose knife. The date of the knife's origin is still up for debate, as there is no historical documentation to support it. Over time, it gained popularity in Asia due to its unique crescent moon shape, slowly making its way to Indonesia. The Indonesian variation differed slightly in design and was used primarily as a farming tool and utility knife. As other countries like Malaysia, Thailand, Cambodia, Laos, Philippines, and Myanmar adopted the *karambit*, versions of the knife took on different shapes and designs, though all were created with the intention of multipurpose use. As some countries used it for farming, others used it as a self-defense weapon. Due to the impact of foreign trade, the knife eventually gained global popularity and reached countries in Europe and North America.

Today, the *karamit's* claw-like design has stood the test of time, unchanged and favored as a self-defense weapon among Filipino martial artists. The famous safety ring was incorporated into the design somewhere between the late 1200s and the early 1500s. The addition of the safety ring, which is essentially the pommel, provides the user with an additional layer of security from an opponent attempting to disarm them. This feature also has an additional safety purpose, meant to prevent the user from injury when thrusting forward or stabbing their opponent. Other countries chose to incorporate an additional blade instead of the safety ring. A design like this would typically have both blades either facing the same direction, or one blade facing forward while the other faced backward. There are also designs where the blade is double-edged, which means it can cut and slice more freely, enabling the use of additional angles of attack. A double-edged *karamit* is illegal to own in several countries, due to its highly lethal capabilities.

Naturally, as in any industry, things tend to evolve as far as designs are concerned in order to make them more practical. In the knife community, *karambits* can be found as fixed blades or foldable pocketknives. The foldable version is a fairly recent development which allows for a more efficient way to carry the knife. The issue with the foldable *karambit* is that it contains several required moving parts to function correctly in order to expose the blade. The multipart system is prone to unexpected malfunctions, making it not as sturdy as the fixed blade. Due to the shape of the knife, the fixed blade version is stronger and can be quite inconvenient to carry. The user needs to consider both options and select the version that best suits their needs.

Fig. 104. Image taken by A.J. depicts two modern style Karambits. The one on top was made by TOPS Knives and has a blade made of 1095 steel, with G10 hande scales. The one on the bottom was made by Bastinelli and is made of N690Co steel.

Parang—Jungle Knife: Malaysia (18th–19th c.)

The parang originated around the eighteenth century in Malaysia. There is no real record of this machete-style knife ever being used for military conflict, rather, it was more of a jungle traversing multi-purpose tool. The ideal bushcraft knife for the Malay Archipelago region, the parang's strong versatile properties could be used to carve, chop, and slash with little strain on the wrist. The knife was perfectly balanced with a concave spine, curving toward the edge at the point. It was made of carbon steel and had a convex edge for additional edge strength. Typically made with a wooden scabbard/handle, composed of two pieces of wood held together by rattan strips or rope. The blade would measure anywhere from 11 inches to just over 36 inches and weigh about 2 pounds.

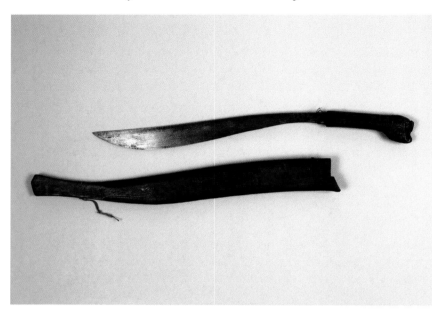

Fig. 105.
Object: Jungle Knife (Parang) with Sheath
Date: 18th–19th century
Culture: Malayan
Medium: Wood
Dimensions: L. with sheath 19 5/8 in. (49.8 cm); L. without sheath 16 1/4 in. (41.3 cm); W. 1 3/4 in. (4.5 cm); Wt. 8.2 oz. (232.5 g); Wt. of sheath 2.3 oz. (65.2 g)
Classification: Knives
Credit Line: Bequest of George C. Stone, 1935
Accession Number: 36.25.801a, b

Met Museum

Fig. 106.
Object: Knife (Parang) with Sheath
Date: 18th–19th century
Culture: Malayan
Medium: Horn, wood
Dimensions: L. with sheath 17 3/4 in. (45.1 cm); L. without sheath 15 3/4 in. (40 cm); L. of blade 12 3/4 in. (32.3 cm); W. 4 in. (10.2 cm); Wt. 15.8 oz. (447.9 g); Wt. of sheath 4.7 oz. (133.2 g)
Classification: Knives
Credit Line: Bequest of George C. Stone, 1935
Accession Number: 36.25.840a, b

Golok—Indonesian (18th–19th c.)

The golok is a machete-style sword that originated from Southeast Asia. While its exact origins are unknown, some historians say it originated in Indonesia, while others trace it to the Philippines. Goloks were slightly heavier than traditional machetes and also shorter in size. The blade was between 9.8 inches (25 cm) to 19.7 inches (50 cm) in length, and made of carbon steel with a convex edge. The knife was mostly used for clearing vegetation from an area, which is why having an edgewise taper or primary grind would avoid the likelihood of the blade jamming or getting stuck in green wood. The carbon steel used for the golok is of softer temper, meaning it can be resharpened easier in the field. The golok's handle was traditionally made of wood, with a flared pommel, to avoid slipping away from the hand. The handles could be either simple in design or with more ornate wood cravings at the pommel.

The British, the French, and the Dutch began colonizing Southeast Asia around the nineteenth century. During the British colonization of Southeast Asia, the British Army noticed the effectiveness of this machete-like tool and in the 1950s, adopted it as a British military standard issue knife.

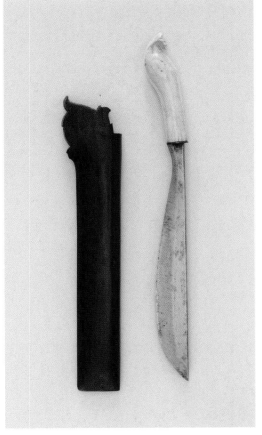

Fig. 108.
Object: Knife (Golok) with Sheath
Date: 18th–19th century
Culture: Malayan
Medium: Ivory, wood
Dimensions: L. with sheath 9 1/2 in. (24.1 cm); L. without sheath 8 13/16 in. (22.4 cm); L. of blade 6 in. (15.2 cm); W. 7/8 in. (2.2 cm); Wt. 2.1 oz. (59.5 g); Wt. of sheath 1.3 oz. (36.9 g)
Classification: Knives
Credit Line: Bequest of George C. Stone, 1935
Accession Number: 36.25.851a, b
Met Museum

Fig. 109., Object: Dagger (Golok or Pedang) with Sheath, Date: 16th–19th century, Geography: Sumatra, Culture: Sumatran, Medium: Steel, silver, ivory, Dimensions: H. with sheath 18 5/16 in. (46.5 cm); H. without sheath 14 5/8 in. (37.1 cm); W. 3 1/2 in. (8.9 cm); Wt. 7.8 oz. (221.1 g); Wt. of sheath 10.2 oz. (289.2 g), Classification: Knives, Credit Line: Bequest of George C. Stone, 1935 Accession Number: 36.25.822a, b, Met Museum

The Dayak Mandau Sword (Early to Mid-20th c.)

A traditional machete-style sword, developed by the Dayak people of Borneo in the early twentieth century, was known as the Dayak *mandau* Sword. This sword is primarily known as a general purpose/utility jungle knife. It is also associated with what has historically been known as the headhunting tradition of the Dayak people. This single-edged sword measured about 18.5 inches (470 mm) in length, had a razor-sharp convex edge with a beautiful handle traditionally made of antler or bone. The uniquely designed handle at times contained tufts of pig bristle. The sword's scabbard was often made of wood and decorated with ornate carvings. This sword is also known as *parang ilang* among the Iban and Penan people of Sarawak and Brunei.

The Dayak people are an indigenous tribe who live along the outer banks of large rivers. It is said that they live in the "lungs of the world" within the lush rainforests of Indonesia, East Kalimantan, and the Island of Borneo. They live by an ancient code, whereby they have taken the responsibility to protect the forest and its resources from foreign intruders. For the most part, they are a harmonious tribe that live as one with nature away from advanced, modern societies.

Bolo Knife

The bolo knife was created in Philippines for the purpose of clearing brush and harvesting crops. It had a blade length that varied from 10 to 15 inches and was made of carbon steel. During the Philippine Revolution of 1896, this machete-style knife was used by revolutionaries as a combat weapon to fight Spanish colonial authorities. Three years later during the Philippine-American War, Filipino revolutionaries used the bolo knife once again, this time, to fight against American troops. Filipinos were outgunned in both battles and had to use what they had to the best of their abilities. These guerilla warriors, or *bolomen*, used the broad-bladed knife to hack off the limbs of their opponents in the grisliest fashion. These revolutionaries took pleasure in lopping off the heads of their opponents with a single blow. As the bolo knife gained widespread popularity, several countries began issuing a bolo-style knife to their troops when engaging in jungle warfare. In World War II, the United States Marine Corps issued their troops bolo knives, such as the Boyt Co. Corpsman Bolo Knife. The knife measured 17 inches overall, with an 11.5-inch blade. This knife was standard issue in the jungles of the Pacific.

There are several variations of the bolo, or machete-style knife, which emerged in the Philippines or Southeast Asia, such as: the *barong*, the *batangas*, the *guna*, the *kampilan*, the *pinuti*, the *pirah*, the *punyal*, and the *sundang*. Each has a specific function, whether used primarily for agricultural purposes or self-defense, and they all vary in size and shape with different handle materials and handle designs.

Fig. 110.
U.S. National Archives: Bolo knife being sharpened on rock during U.S. Navy Jungle Survival Training.
National Archives Identifier: 6389932
Local Identifier: 330-CFD-DF-ST-85-12458.jpeg
Creator(s): Department of Defense. American Forces Information Service. Defense Visual Information Center. (1994 - 10/26/2007) (Most Recent)
Department of Defense. Defense Audiovisual Agency. 6/21/1979-9/30/1985 (Predecessor)
Department of Defense. Department of the Navy. Naval Imaging Command. 1988-ca. 1993 (Predecessor)
From: Series: Combined Military Service Digital Photographic Files, 1982 - 2007
Record Group 330: Records of the Office of the Secretary of Defense, 1921 - 2008

The Puukko

The *puukko* style knife is not a modern-day invention, as their designs have existed for thousands of years. There have even been archaeological discoveries which suggest this knife design was already being used during the Stone Age. Some archaeological excavations have unearthed evidence of the *puukko* being used during the Dark Ages as well. In the eighteenth century, the design gained popularity among the Sami, an indigenous people of Finland. It is said that the Sami are responsible for developing the Finnish-style *puukko* design. The name *puukko* itself means "knife" in Finnish. By the nineteenth century, the knife was being mass produced in Finland at Fiskars Ironworks. Due to its multi-purpose utility, it quickly became a traditional belt knife in Finland. The *puukko* was, and still is, used for carving wood, hunting, processing game, and performing several bushcraft tasks. Traditionally, the dimensions of the knife blade range between 2.75 to 4.0 inches. However, there have been instances where *puukkos*, such as the *vakipuukko*, which resembles a short sword or seax, had a blade that measured as much as 18 inches.

Originally, the blade material of the *puukko* was a high carbon steel, but over the years, knifemakers began to produce them in a stainless or laminated steel. The *puukko* blade is a hidden tang, where the continuation of the blade is hidden within the handle. The blade's tang style is also referred to as a narrowing tang because it is wide at the blade's shoulder and tapers toward the end. Most of the time, the tail end is not visible at the handle butt. The *puukko* that has a visible tail end at the handle butt is referred to as a stick tang. If the tang is longer than the handle, it is referred to an extended or protruding, exposed tang. Extended tangs sometimes have an end plate. The blade finish is either polished, ground, or has black foraging scales. The black foraged scales help protect the carbon blade from corrosion. The blade is single-edged and typically has a 90-degree spine. The edge curves as it begins approaching the tip. The primary bevel is ground as flat as possible, referred to as a Scandinavian grind, or "Scandi" for short. The edge angle is typically ground at a higher angle, and zeros at the end, giving it a very thin effect. The *puukko* has different blade shapes depending on its origin or maker. Blade types include: Curved Back (Drop Point), Straight Back, Dropped Straight Back, Clip Point, Upswept, Clipped Upswept, Ricasso, Groove or Wave Back. The handle is typically made of wood, particularly curly birch, stacked birch bark, or even antler. The handle cross section shape can be identified as having a round, drop, cut drop, lens, oval, cut oval, or double-cut oval profile. The traditional *puukko* did not have a finger guard, because they were primarily intended as cutting, slicing, and carving multi-purpose tools, not as a stabbing weapon. The knife was either simple in design or very ornately decorated with beautiful handle engravings and precious metal inlays.

Lastly, another unique characteristic of the *puukko* is the sheath. There are three basic types of *puukko* sheaths such as the friction, hat, and click (snap). Typically, the sheaths are made so that they dangle from the belt and move liberally, not preventing the person from walking or sitting. As far as design, it is truly a work of art. The more elaborate sheaths have metal (nickel or silver) fittings, engravings, and high-quality leather, horn, or wood. The simpler designs are made of leather and have a wooden piece on the inside to reinforce the sheath, so the blade doesn't pierce through.

A popular Finnish *puukko* design is the Tommi *puukko*, which originated in Kainuu. There have been many amazing Tommi *puukko* makers in Finland, one of the most notable was Kalle Keränen. Kalle learned the art of knifemaking from Thomas Woodward. In 1870, Kalle began making new *puukko* designs with cast fittings and ornate sheaths. Because of his mentor Thomas Woodward, Kalle began referring to his knives as "Tommi" *puukko*. His straight back *puukko* designs have lovely brass end caps; the handle itself is made of either sallow root or masur birch with an oval handle cross section profile. The blade usually had a diamond-shaped cross section. Another group of gentlemen that later emerged as master Tommi *puukko* makers are the Kempainen brothers from Kuhmo, Finland. Mauri Heikkinen, Jukka Hankala, Pentti Kaartinen, and Veijo Käpylä are also counted among exceptional

Tommi *puukko* makers.

In 1879, the Iisakki Järvenpää knife company was founded by Iisakki Järvenpää in Kauhava, Finland. In 1884, Iisakki created the first *puukko* handle using birchbark. In 1888, Iisakki is famously known for making the "crown prince *puukko*" for Russian Tsar Nicholas II (the last of Russia's tsars). Today, the Iisakki Järvenpää knife company is known as the largest manufacturer of knives in Kauhava, Finland. They produce traditional-style *puukkos* made with curly birch handles and blades that are individually ground featuring a scandi grind with no secondary bevel. Typically, their blades are a stainless steel hardened to 57-58 rockwell, or a high carbon steel hardened to 57–58 rockwell. They also make specialty knives for the avid outdoorsman that can be used for skinning game, filleting fish, or whittling. https://www.iisakkijarvenpaa.fi

Morakniv (a.k.a. Frosts Mora, initially a timber sledge company), is a Swedish company, founded by Frost-Erik Erson, that began manufacturing knives as early as 1891 in Ostnor, Sweden. Initially, the knives they produced resembled a Finnish style *puukko*. In 1988, the Frosts Mora knife company merged with the KJ Erikson knife factory, and both companies became what we know today as Morakniv. Today they produce traditional and modern *puukko* designs. https://morakniv.se

Marttiini is a Finnish knife company, founded by Janne Marttiini (also known as Johan Henrik), that began production in 1928 in Lapland, Finland. With its subarctic climate, harsh winters, and unforgiving wilderness, the region is not suitable for most people. Its small population is sporadically spread throughout the area. Janne Marttiini had a goal in mind of producing the toughest knives possible, capable of withstanding the harshest environments imaginable. Marttiini produces knives made of high carbon steel and stainless steel and beautiful *puukko* knives with handles made of all sorts of material like curly birch, reindeer antler, and leather. They produce a knife for every type of outdoorsman—from hunting knives to kitchen knives. https://www.marttiini.fi

Helle (A/S Helle Fabrikker) is a Norwegian knife company that was founded by two brothers, Steinar and Sigmund Helle, in 1932. The Helle factory is situated in Holmedal, a small village located in the western region of Norway. They have been producing great quality outdoor knives for almost 100 years now. They, too, produce traditional style *puukko* knives, in addition to modern foldable *puukko*-style knives with finger guards. The materials they use for their blades range from a non-laminated stainless steel (Sandvik 12C27), to a triple-laminated stainless steel (one version with a stainless core and another version with a carbon core). The triple-laminated steel is made proprietary for Helle, and is known as H3LS (stainless version) and H3LC (carbon version). Their scandi grind knives have a grinding angle between 22 -23 degrees. Helle produces top-notch outdoor knives that are not only highly functional, but are absolutely beautiful. https://helle.com

The lamination process for knives strictly depends on the knife maker's formula. The lamination process could entail the encasement of a hard steel, like a carbon steel core, infused with a softer alloyed steel. By laminating the blade of a knife, the properties are improved, thereby decreasing the chances of rusting or breaking. Durability and strength can also be increased by laminating steels. Lamination could be performed using a couple or several different steels in the process. There are knifemakers who choose to laminate a softer steel core with a harder steel. The combination used in the lamination process all depends on what the knifemaker is trying to achieve. Another detail to consider is the Rockwell hardening and whether they are hardening the steel/steels at 57-58 HRC or 58-60 HRC.

The knifemakers described in this section are just a handful of those who are producing great quality *puukko* knives today.

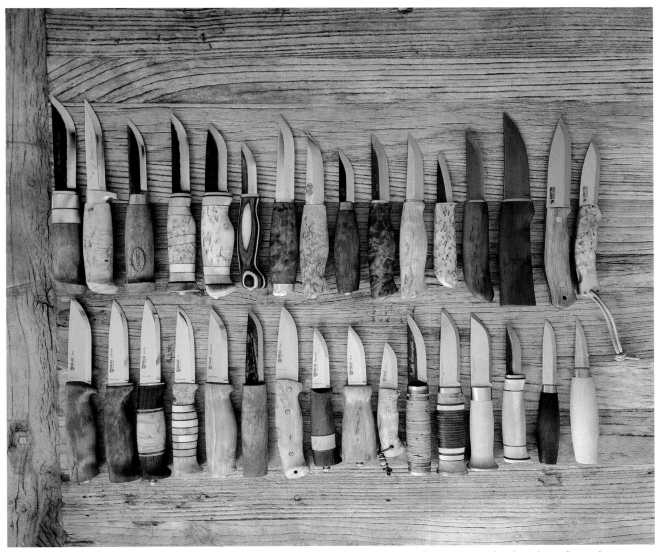

Fig. 111. Image taken by A.J. depicts several different styles of the Puukko, made by various knifemakers throughout Scandinavian and Nordic countries.

Fig. 112. Image taken by A.J. depicts a traditional style puukko made by Marttiini from Finland.

Leuku

The *leuku* is another traditional knife produced by the indigenous Sami people of Finland. Considered the "older brother" of the *puukko*, the *leuku* is also called *stuorra niibi* or *stourniibi*, which is Finnish for "big knife." The exact time frame in which this knife may have been initially developed is unknown. Some historians estimate it was over 500 years ago, while others believe it may have been over 1,000 years ago. These knives were originally produced with the purpose of chopping down small trees, clearing brush, splitting firewood, and processing game. Because of its indigenous origins with the Sami, the *leuku* is sometimes referred to as "the Sami knife." The blade typically measures 7.5 to 10 inches in length and is made of a carbon steel. The handle is usually made of curly birch, has a wide flat pommel, and has nicely fitted brass bolsters which aid in strengthening critical areas of the knife, such as the handle/blade junction. These bolsters also help prevent any chipping or breakage often attributed to heavy use. Brass itself has always been deemed "sacred" by the Sami people since pre-Christian times. The *leuku* carries legendary "spiritual powers" meant to protect the owner from evil. According to Sami folk medicine, the knife holds special healing powers, as it is sometimes used to stop bleeding or take away pain. Sami children are often gifted their first knife between the ages of eight and ten.

The Norwegian Special Forces use a nontraditional *leuku* style knife, which also has a brass finger guard. The guard is an important component, as its placement between the blade and handle protects the user's hand from accidentally slipping onto the blade. In the event the knife may have to be used as a stabbing weapon, the guard will provide enough security to avoid unwanted injury. The Norwegian Special Forces use the Stromeng Samekniv 8-inch knife, KS8, with the added finger guard.

Fig. 113. Image taken by A.J. depicts two Leuku. The one above is made by Helle, and the one below is made by Stromeng.

Fig. 114. Image taken by A.J. depicts a modern Scandinavian knife design made by Helle, the Sylvsteinen, that has a 5.5"
triple laminated stainless steel blade with a satin finish and curly birch handles. The handle also features a beautiful antler
inlay with black fiber spacers. The knife has an overall length of 9.375".

Photograph was provided by Fallkniven, the Gentleman's Folder, with stag scales.

MODERN KNIVES

INFLUENTIAL PEOPLE IN THE KNIFE COMMUNITY
(PAST & PRESENT)

A.G. Russell (August 27, 1933–October 12, 2018): Knifemaker, designer, and founder of A.G. Russell Knives, Inc., in 1964. Co-Founder and Honorary President of the Knifemakers' Guild, (1970). First Honoree of the Knife Digest Cutlery Hall of Fame in 1974. Honoree of *Blade Magazine* Cutlery Hall of Fame in 1988. Founded the *Knife Collectors Club*. His passion was designing custom knives and had several famous models, like the A.G. Russell One Hand Knife, and the A.G. Russell Signature Sting3. https://www.agrussell.com

Allen Elishewitz: former U.S. Marine Recon, renowned knifemaker, and he operates Elishewitz Custom Knives and Tactical Concepts along with his wife Valerie. He has been making knives since 1988 and has been member of the American Knifemaker's Guild since 1994. His amazing unique knife designs have earned him several awards over the years. He is also famously known for designing the Hogue Deka.

Andrey Biryukov: Famous Russian blacksmith and custom knifemaker who works a great deal with steels like S125V, M398, 20CV, and CPM 15V. Makes beautiful, fixed blade and folding knives, with a signature style. Became a blacksmith in 2004, mastering his craft under the supervision of a Master Smith. Released an array of amazing knives that won him several awards and earned him recognition, around the world. His knives typically sell for 8000 (108 USD) to 15000 (203 USD) rubles and are well priced considering the steel and quality.

Andrew Jordan: Bladesmith with over twenty years of experience. Studied under a Japanese swordsmith/bladesmith for two years, where he learned medieval sword smithing techniques. Makes incredible unique blades using traditional techniques, hand forging, and hand skills. Continues to make beautifully designed kitchen and hunting knives. https://www.jordanknives.com

Anthony Marfione: Well-respected, custom knifemaker and founder of Microtech Knives. He has designed several knives used by the United States Military. Some of his more popular models include the Halo, UDT, Socom, and Ultratech. https://www.microtechknives.com

Antti Makinen: Grandson of Yrjo Puronvarsi, famous bladesmith from Kauhava, Finland. Antti was taught how to forge by his grandfather. He now honors his late grandfather by forging all the blades under YP Taonta. These blades are recognized as some of the best in the Kauhava region. They are forged from C75, a European version of 1075. The blades are perfect for a puukko style knife and can be found at http://www.brisa.fi/

Ben Abbot: Bladesmith and Founder of Ashgrove Forge. He is a two-time champion of *"Forged in Fire,"* a show on the History Channel. Creates some fascinating knives with incredibly unique designs. https://www.ashgroveforge.com

Bill Duff (August 24, 1942–March 2, 2019): Worked for Buck Knives for some time after being honorably discharged from the Marine Corps in the early 1960s. In the 1970s, Bill Duff, Don Collum, and Dean Parks founded Rigid Knives out of his garage in Santee, CA. When he sold Rigid Knives in 1976, he continued to be passionate about making custom knives and began using his own name on the knives he produced. Known for his unique knife designs and superb hollow grinds. A member of the Knifemakers' Guild since 1978. He, no doubt, was a "renaissance man" for the knife industry.

Bill Harsey Jr.: Award-winning knifemaker and designer, who creates exceptional folding and fixed blade knives. Has a stellar reputation among the knife community. Worked on collaborations with several knife companies (Gerber Legendary Blades, Lone Wolf Knives, Spartan Blades, Ruger/ CRKT, Fantoni, and Chris Reeve), designing truly special, one-of-a-kind pieces. One of his most popular designs was the Yarborough Knife, named after Lt. Gen. William P. Yarborough, "father" of the Special Forces. Another popular design is his Applegate/Fairbairn Combat Fighting Knife.

Walter Wells "Blackie" Collins (1939–July 20, 2011): An internationally recognized knifemaker and designer. Known for a great deal of contributions to the knife community, which include the assisted opener on folding knives, introducing thermoplastic knife handles, and sheath devices for the diving knife industry. He was one of the founding members of the Knifemakers' Guild. Was the first editor for *Blade Magazine* and inducted into the *Blade Magazine* Hall of Fame. He wrote several books on knifemaking, scrimshaw, knife throwing, and personal defense.

Bo Randell (WD Randell, September 27, 1909–December 25, 1989): Founder of Randall Knives and world-renowned knifemaker and designer. His knives became famous during the late 1940s and remained so throughout the late 1980s. He made knives for military members during WWII and the Vietnam war, pilots, astronauts, and outdoorsmen. Some of his famous models include the Model 1 All Purpose Fighter, Model 2 Fighting Stiletto, Model 3 Hunter, Big Game Skinner, Camper, Carver, Fisherman, Alaskan Skinner, Raymond Thorp, Model 17 Astro, Model 18 Survival, Gamemaster, and all his unique Bowie designs. https://www.randallknives.com

Bob Dozier: Famous knifemaker and designer, who began his career working for A.G. Russell, trying to restore life into the Morseth Knife Company. Eventually founded Dozier Knives and Arkansas Made Dozier. Specializes in D2 steel, known for its superlative qualities, as a high carbon, high chromium tool steel. His knives portray a unique elegance, designed not only for hunters & outdoorsmen, but also for knife enthusiasts to enjoy. They are fully functional, powerful blades, made to be used, and not just for display. http://www.dozierknives.com

Bob Kramer: Bladesmith with extraordinary forging talents. He produces some of the best kitchen knives on the market. His beautiful damascus steel blades are truly a work of art. His knives are built to last and are perfectly balanced. Kramer knives are lucrative and expensive gems that are not for everyone but can absolutely fill a void for those who can afford them. https://www.kramerknives. com

Brad Southard: Owner of Southard Knives and Tools, LLC. He creates 100 percent handmade custom knives. His folding knives are incredibly produced using only the finest, modern manufacturing techniques. Collaborated on a project with Spyderco, where he has a line of production knives, created expertly and with the absolute best materials. https://www.southardknives.com

Brian Tighe: Founder of Brian Tighe Knives, with over thirty years of experience as a knife maker. Specializes in custom folding knives that merge high-tech, premium materials with sophisticated styling. All his knives are unequaled displays of art and are functional multi-purpose cutting tools. He won "Most Innovative Design" in the 2010 and 2012 BLADE show. Tighe has worked on additional collaborations with Columbia River Knife and Tool (CRKT) and Spyderco Knives. http:// www.briantighe.com

Buster Warenski (June 5, 1942–July 31, 2005): Famous knifemaker, world-renowned for his "art" knives. His knives are literally so beautiful, they are gilded art pieces, known as his "Legacy Knives." Used some of the finest precious metals and gems to create his masterpieces. A couple of his more famous creations was the recreation of the King Tut gold dagger and his "Gem of the Orient" (containing 153 emeralds and 9 diamonds, with gold filigree, overlaid on a jade handle), which sold for over $2 million. He was president of the Knifemakers' Guild and a member of the *Blade Magazine* Cutlery Hall of Fame. http://www.warenskiknives.com

Charles Allen: Alaskan Master Guide and Owner of Knives of Alaska. In 1994, his skinner/cleaver, the "Alaska Brown Bear," won *Blade Magazine's* Award for "Most Innovative American Made Design." He teamed with Hobie Smith of Smith International, Inc., to form DiamondBlade, LLC, which builds innovative Friction Forged® blades, known as "super blades." These special blades stay sharp longer, have fine-grain structure, are hardened differently, and are highly corrosion and rust resistant. These innovative blades were developed with the support of MegaDiamond, Advanced Metal Products, DiamondBlade, Knives of Alaska, universities, and other organizations. https://www.diamondbladeknives.com; https://www.knivesofalaska.com

Chris Reeve: He is the founder of Chris Reeve Knives, a manufacturing company which he built alongside his partner, Anne Reeve. He introduced the Reeve Integral Lock™, known as the "framelock." He also worked closely with Dick Barber from Crucible Industries, where he played an essential role in developing the first blade specific steels, CPM S30V and CPM S35VN, the predecessors to CPM S45VN. His pocketknives are astonishingly made to absolute perfection. One of his most popular knives is the Sebenza, featuring a Reeve Integral Lock™. The newest generation, the Sebenza 31, features the addition of a Ceramic Ball Interface to the lock-bar, a stonewashed drop point blade, made of CPM S45VN, hardened at 60-62 HRC. The handles are made from an 6AL4V sandblasted titanium, featuring an off-set clip design. Though it may look simple in design, it is extremely well engineered using only the highest quality materials, which is why it is known as one of the best pocketknives in the world. Chris is known in the knife community for going "above and beyond" in everything he does, as shown in his top-notch knife designs. Chris Reeve was inducted into the Cutlery Hall of Fame, in June 2015.

Daniel Edward Henry (1924–1993): Possibly one of the best Bowie knifemakers in history. He embraced a classic design and enhanced it 10-fold. His iconic Bowies were geometrically perfect, with exceptional beveling, symmetry, and balance. Daniel Edward Henry was decades ahead of the competition, as far as grinding, polishing, fitting, and finishing are concerned.

Daniel Winkler: Founder of Winkler Knives and a Master Bladesmith since 1993. He gained widespread fame for his specialty in Early American weaponry. Winkler's knives and axes were featured in the movie "The Last of the Mohicans." He worked with Special Operation Forces (SOF) teams from around the globe, making combat axes, which led to formation of Winkler Knives. https://www.winklerknives.com

David Broadwell: Knifemaker, designer, and founder of Broadwell Studios. He started his career making fine writing instruments and moved on to become a collector of grade knives. He is a true artist, which is clear when you hold one of his knives in your hands. Broadwell makes sub hilt fighting knives, daggers, swords, Bowies, Persian style knives, tactical knives, and kitchen cutlery, as well. Has collaborated in projects with Boker Knife Company and designed two incredible knives for Boker's Magnum Collection. https://www.broadwellstudios.com

Dean Russell: In 1958, he collaborated with Grohmann Cutlery to make his famous "Russell Canadian Belt knife." His knife design became immensely popular due to the ergonomics and unique style, which allowed for great game processing without sacrificing comfort in the handle. The Russell Canadian Belt knife is still categorized as one of the best hunting knives.

Dmitry Sinkevich: Knifemaker and designer, who has collaborated with Zero Tolerance to produce elegant, functional, multi-purpose pocketknives. The knives are built with premium materials such as titanium and carbon fiber handles. They feature a CPM S35VN or a CTS 204P blade. Also teamed up with Shirogorov Knives to produce the famous "Pero knife," which is exceptionally crafted, with its amazing angular profile and sleek lines. The Pero knife features a drop point blade, with a stone-washed finish. It also has a multi-row bearing system (MRBS) bearing pivot, with hardened steel washers for effortless movement and smooth operation. https://www.sinkevichdesign.ru

Doug Ritter: Award-winning journalist and founder of Equipped To Survive. He has several decades of experience reviewing survival and outdoor equipment. He is also the founder and Chairman of Knife Rights (www.kniferights.org). Knife Rights has been fighting for people's knife rights for over a decade, responsible for the enactment of 32 bills repealing knife bans throughout the United States. Doug is also a very reputable knife designer, responsible for the creation of the RSK series of knives, manufactured by Hogue, Inc. https://www.dougritter.com; https://www.hogueinc.com

Edmund Davidson: Knifemaker and designer, with decades of experience, who has created over 100 unique integral patterns, some of which have been patented. Extremely knowledgeable in knifemaking from nearly unbreakable combat knives to investment pieces, with fine engravings, scrimshaw, gold, and jewels. He continues to push the envelope and test the limits of what is possible as far as knifemaking. He followed the works of R.W. Loveless and learned a great deal from T.M. Dowell and Billy Mace Imel. https://www,edmunddavidson.com

Eero Kovanen: Bladesmith and knife designer that produces a variety of puukko style knives, from traditional to embellished, with beautiful bolsters and Damascus steel. He is a Finnish Master Guild Qualified Master Bladesmith. http://en.eerokovanen.com

Enrique Peña: Founder of Peña Knives, knifemaker & designer specialized in folding knives. Makes genuinely wonderful folding knives, from balisongs to Front Flippers. Only uses premium materials such as M390 for his blades and titanium for the handle scales, along with ceramic bearings. https://www.penaknives.com

Eric Anthony Sykes: A captain in the British Army and firearms expert. Partnered with William E. Fairbairn (British Royal Marine and expert in hand-to-hand combat) to develop the legendary combat dagger known as the "Fairbairn-Sykes Fighting Knife." The same knife handed to British Commandos, Airborne Forces, and SAS during WWII.

Ernest Emerson: Founder of Emerson Knives, knifemaker & designer, who offers utterly unique designs for pocketknives and fixed blades. His knives are highly sought after by elite military and law enforcement. The one-of-a-kind design lends itself to quick access and deployment of the blade when necessary. Began making knives out of his garage in 1979, and quickly became the "go-to" for tactical knives. His knives have been used by elite forces from all over the world, including those in some of the most covert operations in modern history. His Emerson CQC-7 was used in the raid that killed Osama Bin Laden and was sold at auction for over $35,000. Not only is he a renowned knifemaker, but he is also an expert martial artist, inducted into the Martial Arts Hall of Fame. https://www.emersonknives.com

Ethan Becker: World renowned knife designer, responsible for several contributions to the knife community. Has been designing knives for several decades. Founded Becker Knife and Tool in the early 1980s and focused on designing strong tactical and survival knives. He dedicates a great deal of his time testing knives in the outdoors and perfecting designs, so they outperform industry standards. Ethan has collaborated with several companies over the years, but his most popular project was with KA-BAR. He designed the Becker Champion BK2, known as one of the best survival knives on the planet. Also responsible for bringing us the Becker Kephart BK62, known as the closest reproduction of the Horace Kephart knife. Ethan Becker owns the only Horace Kephart knife in existence and based his model on that design. He brought us the Becker Combat Bowie BK9, which is an absolute beast at chopping and batoning wood. The BK9 is virtually indestructible and a superb survival knife, made of 1095 Cro-Van steel, with a 9.25-inch blade and Ultramid handle. Becker is also famously known for his Kukri style knives.

Gawie Herbst: South African knifemaker and designer. Transitioned his knifemaking hobby into an all-out career in 1998. Founded the Herbst Knifemaking Academy in Pretoria, South-Africa, alongside his son, Thinus Herbst. Award-winning member of the Knifemakers' Guild in Southern Africa. Gawie Herbst is famously known for his beautiful designs and iconic traditional style. http://www.herbst.co.za

George Herron (passed 2007): Famous, award-winning knifemaker & designer, inducted into the Blade Cutlery Hall of Fame in 1987. Founded the South Carolina Knifemakers' Guild. Focused primarily on hunting knives and skinners and was known by many as one of the greatest custom knife makers of all time. George Herron was a pioneer and, most importantly, a mentor to several knifemakers in the community.

Harvey King: Renowned knifemaker, designer, and member of the Professional Knifemakers Association and the American Bladesmith Society. Makes spectacular knives crafted of premium tool steels with beautifully finished bone or wood handles. He sold his first knife in 1988. Not long after, Harvey King's reputation catapulted for making stellar knives. http://www.harveykingknives.com

Hideao Kitaoka: Third-generation Master Bladesmith from Japan. He is the only bladesmith in Takefu who specializes in single-bevel knives. Forges his blades from high carbon steel for superior edge retention. Hideao Kitaoka focuses on sushi chef knives.

Isamu Takamura: Japanese bladesmith and founder of Takamura Cutlery in Echiezen City, Fukui Perfecture, Japan. His cutlery became the first in the region to utilize High Speed Powdered Steel (HSPS) for kitchen knives. Isamu Takamura forges R2/SG2 steel, which provides improved sharpness and superior edge retention.

J. Neilson: An American Bladesmith Society mastersmith who crafts custom fixed blade knives from northeastern Pennsylvania. He works Damascus in a way only few can, to produce true works of art. He forges his blades out of high carbon steel (1080, 1084, 1095, W1, W2, 5160, 52100, 15N20 and Cru-forge V). These blades are not just for looks, as they are made to perform as intended. His blades are typically flat ground with a convex edge. Neilson's scandi bushcraft knives are of superb quality. https://www.mountainhollow.net

Jake Hoback: Knifemaker and designer, with over twenty years of experience. Founder of Jake Hoback Knives in northern Idaho. Known for producing knives with high-tech, innovative features, such as his Hoback Roller Detent (HRD), internal lightening pockets, hardened stainless lock inserts, hardened bearing races, and clean blade movement. Jake Hoback produces folding knives as well as fixed blades but enjoys the science behind the folding pocketknife the most. There is no doubt he produces dependable, rugged, and tough knives. https://www.jakehobackknives.com

James Black (May 1, 1800–June 22, 1872): Knifemaker and designer who is responsible for developing the infamous Bowie knife, used by James Bowie.

James Glisson: Knifemaker and designer who has been producing and selling knives since 2003. Creates gorgeous knives with different handle materials, such as: iron wood, merino sheep horn, buffalo horn, giraffe bone, walrus tusk, and wooly mammoth tooth. James Glisson has gained recognition around the world and is a member of the Arkansas Knifemakers Association.

Jason Brous: Knifemaker, designer, and founder of Brous Blades. Has been making knives since 2010 and is famously known for his remarkable stout neck knives with dual-finger-hole grips. Jason Brous typically works with D2 tool steel.

Jason Knight: Award-winning Master Bladesmith and designer, who joined Winkler Knives, in 2017. Began making knives, through a process known as "stock removal." In 2001, he attended the Bill Moran School of Bladesmithing and from that point forward, his skills began reaching levels unattainable by many in the knife community. Was mentored by George Herron and Daniel Winkler, who also provided the support needed to pursue greatness, while remaining true to his creative niche. In 2007, he received his ABS Mastersmith rating, and was given the B.R. Hughes Award, for "Best Knife by a Mastersmith Candidate." Jason Knight is also a host on the show "Forged in Fire," on the History Channel. https://www.winklerknives.com

Jeff Randall: President of TransEquatorial Solutions, Inc., and co-owner of ESEE Knives/Randall's Adventure & Training. He spent over twenty years exploring the darkest jungles of South America, as well as traversing the earth managing international projects. Jeff is a certified NASAR SAR TECH 1 Evaluator, certified Wilderness First Responder (WFR), certified Rope Rescue and Swiftwater Rescue, and a graduate of the Peruvian Air Force's ESSEL. He and Mike Perrin are passionate about teaching survival training to those with the necessity or desire to learn. It didn't take long for Jeff and Mike to embark on another journey: reinventing dependability in the woods by creating ESEE Knives. He understood what the avid outdoorsman yearned for… what that adventure-seeking wild man needed when out venturing into the unknown wilderness. Jeff and Mike are the driving force behind ESEE, a lineup of dependable knives and survival products, which guarantee functionality and dependability when you need it most. Their products have brought satisfaction to many soldiers, sailors, marines, airmen, firefighters, law enforcement, outdoorsmen, and among others. https://www.eseeknives.com

Jens Anso: Knifemaker, designer & Founder of Anso of Denmark, and a founding member of GiantMouse. Makes both kitchen and folding knives, which are perfectly crafted works of art. He uses premium material for both blade and handle, as seen with his HADDOCK knife, featuring an RWL-34 steel (Super Stainless Steel) blade with titanium handle scales, clip, and spacer. The HADDOCK also has a titanium pivot, pivot-ring, and screws, with the option for micarta inlays on the handle scales. Some of his handmade kitchen knives feature a 33-layered VG10 San Mai steel and beautiful wood handles, made to fit comfortably in your hand. *"Don't make something unless it is both necessary and useful, but if it is necessary and useful, don't hesitate to make it beautiful."* (Jens Anso) https://www.anso-of-denmark.com; https://www.giantmouse.com

Jeremy Marsh: Knifemaker and designer who offers collector grade folding knives. Has been producing folding knives since 2003, displaying distinctive designs not seen before in the knife community. His knives offer great geometry, ergonomics, balance, and functionality. Jeremy Marsh was mentored by David Broadwell.

Jerry Fisk: Master bladesmith and designer recognized as a "National Living Treasure" by the University of North Carolina. Was elected vice president of American Bladesmith Society in 1999 and served in that position until 2008. Was part of the Board of Directors for the American Blade Smith Society from 1994 to 2008. He has won countless awards in the knife community and is considered a legend for many. Some of his knives are curated art pieces held at the New York State Museum, the Private Owned Swiss Museum, and the Historic Arkansas Museum. Has mentored many and taught full classes around the world, such as Sao Paolo, Brazil; Paris, France; and St. Petersburg, Russia. Renowned for blending old knifemaking techniques with modern methods to produce collector grade knives. To this day, Jerry Fisk's skills are extraordinary and unmatched. http://www.jerryfisk.com

Jesper Voxnaes: Knifemaker, designer, and founder of Vox Knives and founding member of Giant-Mouse. Has been making and designing knives for over twenty years. Over the years, he has partnered with several leading knife manufactures to produce innovative knife designs. His Boker SAGA knife won the 2013 iF Product Design Award. He has collaborated on projects with Lucas Burnley and Spyderco. The collaboration with Viper Knives produced some breathtaking knives. https://www.voxknives.com; https://www.giantmouse.com

Jess Horn (Passed 2016): A knifemaking legend, when it comes to his top-quality custom folding knives. His knives are investment pieces, built with premium materials, and stellar craftmanship. Horn first began making knives, in 1968. The knives were made with ATS-34 and 154CM steels and featured natural handle materials. Jess Horn was also a longtime member of the Knifemakers' Guild.

Jimmy Lile (August 22, 1933–May 5, 1991): Famous knifemaker and designer, responsible for producing the legendary "First Blood Knife," the *Rambo* knife. No doubt, an iconic creation which remains popular today among collectors and knife enthusiasts. https://jimmylile.com

Jody Samson (Passed 2008): Knifemaker/bladesmith and designer. Famous for his butterfly knives and swords, which have been featured in movies such as *Conon the Destroyer, First Knight, The Mask of Zorro, Blade, Blind Fury, Batman and Robin, Batman Forever,* and *Streets of Fire.* Jody Samson was mentored by John Nelson Cooper, one of the most inventive knifemakers of his day. http://jodysamson.com

Joe Flowers: An extremely popular knifemaker and designer, avid outdoorsman, and survival instructor. He is the owner of Bushcraft Global, a company that specializes in wilderness expeditions, teaching self-reliance, and survival skills. He has designed several knives in collaboration with Condor Tool and Knife. He is an extremely motivated knife designer, always seeking to create knives that can outlast or outperform the knives currently found in the market. He is highly respected in the knife community and has an incredible future ahead of him. https://www.bushcraftglobal.com; https://www.condortk.com

John Nelson Cooper (November 1, 1906–September 24, 1987): Famous knifemaker, designer & founding member of the Knifemakers' Guild. Began making knives in 1924 in Pennsylvania, by using the "stock removal" process. His handles were pinned using traditional knifemaking methods. He realized that the old way of making knives was subpar there were too many inconsistencies in the final product. After some careful research, he created a method which he later patented in 1967. The idea was to make the blade and the handle a singular unit by bonding, welding, brazing, and finally applying epoxy. An incredible mentor who taught Jody Samson and Vic Anslemo how to make knives in 1969. He sold knives to John Wayne, Sammy Davis Jr., and Lee Marvin. He also made several knives featured in popular movies, such as *The Sacketts* and *Jeremiah Johnson.*

Jukka Hankala: Award-winning Finnish bladesmith and designer. His specialty is traditional Finnish knives that are beautifully decorated with ornate ferrules and superb facet grindings. Was awarded in Gembloux Belgium in 2008, 2009, and 2010. Jukka Hankala was also awarded the 2010 *Coup de Coeur* at S.I.C.A.C. in Paris.

Katsushige Anryu: Fourth-generation Japanese Master Bladesmith. Has been forging for over fifty years. His specialty are kitchen knives with a one-of-a-kind style. If there is someone who utterly understands the art of traditional Japanese knifemaking, it is him. Katsushige Anryu combines old school methods with modern technique to produce blades that are tough and razor sharp.

Ken Onion: Famous knifemaker, designer, Marine Corps veteran & member of the Blade Cutlery Hall of Fame. Has contributed immensely to the knife community with his innovative "SpeedSafe" assisted opening mechanism for Kershaw Knives, along with his ingenious knife sharpeners with Work Sharp. Was mentored by Stanley Fujisaka and built his first knife in 1991. He holds thirty-six design patents, including some for locks, mechanisms, and knife designs. He has collaborated on projects with several companies over the years, such as Kershaw Knives, Spyderco, and CRKT. Ken Onion is extremely talented and very well respected with in the knife community.

Kit Carson (Passed in 2014): Retired master sergeant of the US Army, knifemaker, designer, and member of the Knifemakers' Guild. He was inducted into the Blade Cutlery Hall of Fame in 2012 and mentor to Ken Onion. Has made knives for over thirty years and left several contributions to the knife community, as seen with the popularization of the flipper style folding knife. Kit Carson developed the famous M16, M4, and M21 knives, produced by CRKT.

Kurt Swearingen: Bladesmith and designer who began making knives in 2007. Swearingen makes wonderful Loveless style hunting knives, made from CPM154 steel, a particle metallurgic version of 154CM. Typically, the handle material is made of micarta, but he does make handles in other material as well. Studied techniques from the likes of none other than Mastersmith Lin Rhea and Mastersmith Dickie Robinson. https://www.swearingenknife.com

L.T. Wright: Knifemaker and designer, famously known for his outdoor knives. Without a doubt, L.T. Wright, is one of the best knifemakers of his time. In addition to his amazing knifemaking skills, he is a wonderful mentor, who is greatly loved in the knife community. L.T. was mentored by renowned knifemaker R.W. Wilson, who showed him a few tricks of the trade and helped him hone his skill. What started out as an idea in 2003, soon became a career for L.T., when he founded L.T. Wright Knives (LTWK) in 2005. Several of his handcrafted knives have been used by wilderness survivalists around the globe, including contestants from the hit show "Alone." He produces camping, fishing, hunting, bushcraft, survival, and EDC knives. He makes knives using all sorts of steels, such as O1, A2, D2, 3V, AEB-L, and 1075. L.T. uses a variety of knife handle materials, such as exotic woods, micarta, G10, and bone. Some of his popular models include: the Genesis, the GNS, the Next Gen, the Bushcrafter, and the Small Work Horse. These knives are not made for display, as they are fully functional cutting tools and heirloom pieces that will last several lifetimes. https://www.ltwrightknives.com

Lars Falt: Founded the Swedish Armed Forces Survival School and is a living legend in Sweden. He is a trained survival instructor at the English SAS and US Special Forces. Fault collaborated on a project with Casstrom to design a strong bushcraft knife. The knife is known as the Casstrom Lars Falt Knife, made with a high carbon tool steel Uddeholm Sleipner scandi grind and curly birch with black liner handles. The blade steel is hardened to 58-60 HRC. https://www.casstrom.com

Les George: Knifemaker and designer who began making knives in 1992. Mentored by Stan Fujisaka, famous knifemaker in Keneohe, Hawaii. Served ten years in the US Marine Corps, where he worked as a Senior Explosives Ordinance Disposal Technician. Collaborated on projects with Kershaw, ProTech, Zero Tolerance, and Spartan Blades. Some of the models he designed for Kershaw include: the Boilermaker, the Innuendo, the Seguin, the XCOM, the Spline, the Pico, the Westin, and the Valmara. George also designed the V14 Dagger for Spartan Blades. http://georgeknives.net

Makoto Kurosaki: Famous bladesmith and designer in Japan. Creates beautiful chef knives made from premium steel, such as White Steel, R2/SG2, VG10 Damascus, Ryusei Blue Super, and SG2.

Marty Jelinek: Knifemaker and designer from Australia. Created several popular models, though his most popular is the 4-inch drop point hunter and his 3-inch drop point EDC.

Mel Pardue: (Passed away on January 23, 2022) Renowned master knifemaker, with over forty years of experience. Mentored by Frank Centofante. Member of the Knifemakers' Guild since 1976. Inducted into the Knifemakers Hall of Fame in 2019. Designed several popular knives, including the Griptilian and the Pardu Stimulu, for Benchmade Knives. Founded Mel Pardue Knives, where he produces jaw-dropping works of art. Few can work Damascus steel as Mel Pardue. Teaches knifemaking classes at the American Bladesmith School in Arkansas. https://www.melpardueknives.com

Michael Walker: Renowned custom knifemaker, designer, and sculptor. His innovations had huge impacts in the knife community over the years. Invented over twenty different knife mechanisms, including the popular Walker Linerlock, which he patented in 1980. Began making "collector grade" art knives and later transitioned to folding knives. Had a limited partnership with Ron Lake in 1981, which led to the development of several great knife designs. In 1985, he became a member of the Knifemakers' Guild. Michael Walker has collaborated on projects with Spyderco, CRKT, Schrade, Boker, and Klotzli.

Michael Zieba: Award-winning knifemaker, designer, and founder of Zieba Knives in New York. The first and only knifemaker who is part of the Brooklyn Made Chamber of Commerce. Specializes in folding knives, balisongs, and kitchen knives. All premium materials used to make his knives are sourced from American-owned companies, then handcrafted and assembled in Brooklyn, NY, by Michael Zeiba. https://www.ziebaknives.com

Mick Strider: Bladesmith/knifemaker, designer, US Army veteran (ranger), and founder of Mick Strider Custom Knives. Began making knives in 1988 for use by military. Because of his experience in the military, he had a great understanding of what soldiers needed in combat zones. Creates specialized fixed-blade knives with nearly indestructible, full tang blades. These blades are also subdued to avoid detection. Creates some of the strongest folding knives in the industry, as seen with his SJ75 series of folders. Released in 2012 and made of premium steel with subdued blades and 45-degree angle, these knives are a Mick Strider staple. https://www.mickstridercustomknives.com

Mike Perrin: Co-Owner of ESEE Knives and Randall's Adventure & Training. Mike, alongside Jeff Randall, are the creative souls behind many of ESEE's knife designs. Mike is the lifeblood of the company, inspiring a flow of innovative designs that cemented the company and gave them the edge in the knife community. He is also the Vice-President of TransEquatorial Solutions, Inc. He is a certified Wilderness First Responder (WFR) and NASAR SARTECH. He has travelled throughout Central and South America teaching wilderness survival skills, along with the staff of Randall's Adventure & Training. He is an avid outdoorsman and wilderness expert, with extensive knowledge which he is always willing to share. Mike is a prolific product designer and has a strong grasp on what ESEE customers need from their products, and what they don't need. He is a pragmatic designer calling on years of personal experience in the field.

As a big ESEE fan, I owe a huge level of gratitude to Mike Perrin for being one of the creative souls behind some of the knife models I enjoy the most. https://www.eseeknives.com

Mike Snody: Knifemaker and designer. Renowned for his use of premium exotic materials in his custom knives. Began making Japanese-style fixed-blade knives in 1998, and by 2004, had delved into other knife designs and styles. Has created kitchen knives, machetes, fighting knives, and pocketknives. Most of Snody's knives focus on self-defense. Uses excellent quality steels in his blades, such as A2, S35VN, 154CM, 440C, and Damascus. Also collaborated on projects with Benchmade, Spyderco, H&K Knives, and KA-BAR. In 2005, Mike Snody's design, the Model 425 Gravitator for Benchmade, won the "Knife of the Year" Award from Shooting Industry Academy of Excellence. https://www.mikesnody.com

Minosuke Matsuzawa: Bladesmith, designer, and founder of Masamoto Sohonten Company in Japan. Began making knives in 1866, with the goal of becoming a master at his craft, such that he would be remembered for generations. He remained consistent at producing high quality chef knives throughout his life. Developed new crafting techniques over the years, which took his skills to a whole new level. The knives produced by this first-generation bladesmith have yet to be matched. His knives bear an engraving as proof that he made them himself. First maker in the Kanto region to develop Honyaki kitchen knives. Minosuke Matsuzawa left a legacy that continues to produce high quality knives six generations later; Masamoto Sohonten, family owned.

Mitsuo Nagao: Knifemaker and designer from Japan. The only remaining knifemaker producing the famous Higonokami Kanekoma knife. This knife was first produced in Miki, Hyogo Prefecture, over 100 years ago in 1894 by Komataro Nagao. The skill was handed down for five generations. Today, all knives are still hand-forged by Mistuo Nagao in Japan. https://www.higonokami.jp

Nao Yamamoto: Famous award-winning knifemaker and designer from Japan. First learned the craft during his apprenticeship under Masami Asai (Echizen Marukatsu). Later became an apprentice under Kamotou Hamono in Takefu, Japan. Once completed, returned to work with Masami Asai, for several years where he inherited techniques, to include the inscription, "Eschizen Marukatsu." Yamamoto is recognized for his work with VG10 Damascus, Shirogami, and Aogami steel. His chef knives are some of the best in the region.

Peter Carey: Knifemaker and designer since 1997. Specializes in custom Tactical Folders and Dress Tactical Folders. Uses premium material for his blades, such as CPM154, S35VN, Stainless Steel Damascus, and Satellite 6K. His handle materials are typically carbon fiber, titanium, zirconium, and G10. For his dress tactical knives, he uses exotic woods, pearl, mammoth ivory, mokuTI, and timascus. Developed a custom pivot design known as "The Original Carey Pivot." All of Peter Carey's knives are handmade and of superb quality. http://www.careyblade.com

Phill Hartsfield (1932–May 20, 2010): Renowned knifemaker and designer who began making knives in 1977 and is famously known for his chisel ground blades. He used a high-speed tool steel that was ground and stropped until razor sharp. All of his blades are typically bead blasted and non-reflective. Phil Hartsfield's Extra Long Aikuchi and Extra Long Kozuka are amazing.

Ramon Chaves: Knifemaker and designer. Produces exceptionally tough folding knives, made to last a lifetime. In 2010, his hobby of making knives transitioned to a noteworthy career. Typically uses M390 for the blade and titanium for handle. Ramon Chaves is famously known for his ULTRA-MAR series of heavy-duty folders. https://www.chavesknives.com

Rex Applegate (June 21, 1914–July 14, 1998): Colonel in the American military who worked for OSS and trained Special Forces personnel in close combat. Was also the coordinator for all clandestine agent close combat training for the most covert operations of his time. In the 1980s, released a knife design called the Applegate-Fairbairn fighting knife, which was a modified version of the World War II Fairbairn-Sykes fighting knife (dagger). Different variations of this knife are available through Boker. He collaborated on a project with Bill Harsey Jr., to develop a series of tactical folding knives, produced by Gerber Legendary Blades. Rex Applegate was inducted into the Blade Cutlery Hall of Fame in 1994.

Rick Hinderer: Knifemaker, designer, and founder of Rick Hinderer Knives who focused on hard use folding and fixed blade knives. First began making knives in the 1980s, as collector grade art knives. Later transitioned to dependable hard-use tactical folders. His attention to detail and keen insight on knife design led to the development of several amazing knives, gaining him worldwide recognition as a superb knifemaker. He has collaborated on projects with Gerber, KA-BAR, Kershaw, Viper Knives, and Zero Tolerance. Works with some of the best steels (CPM20CV, S35VN, and O-1) available in the market. Some of his popular folding knives are the Eklipse, the Full Track, the Halftrack, the FireTac, the Maximus, the MP-1, and the XM-Slippy. Rick Hinderer's more popular fixed blade knives are the Fieldtac, the FlashPoint, the FXM 3.5, and the LP-1. https://www.rickhindererknives.com

Rob Ratliff: Knifemaker and designer, famous for making custom gemstone handles for his spectacular, Damascus steel blades. Works with great steels, such as D2 and CPM, which offer good edge retention and nice corrosion resistance. Rob Ratcliff preferred blade grinds are hollow, flat, or convex, while the handles are made of various exotic materials from around the world.

Robert Carter: Knifemaker, designer, and grandson of legendary Mel Pardue. Learned how to make knifes from the absolute best, Mel Pardue (grandfather) and Joe Pardue (father). Robert Carter's folding knives are jaw-dropping works of art, which are not only beautiful but made to be used.

Robert Terzuola: Famous knifemaker and designer who began making knives in 1979 and became a member of the Knifemakers' Guild in 1981, with an endorsement by Bob Loveless. His journey began with fixed blade knife designs and later transitioned to tactical folding knives. Famously known as "the father of the tactical folding knife," with the release of the very first folding knife, the ATCF. Created a series of popular knives, such as the 3A, the TT-1, the Model 7, the Eagle Rock 514, the TTF3A, the Model 26, the Starmate, the TTF3B, the Pathfinder, the Century Starfighter, the Battle Guard, the TTF6 and countless more. Robert Terzuola has also collaborated with Spyderco, in designing the popular SLIPIT. https://www.terzuola.net

Robert Wilson Loveless (R.W. Loveless, January 2, 1929–September 2, 2010): Legendary bladesmith and designer who began making knives in 1954. Military veteran who served during WWII. At the age of twenty-five, he sold knives to Abercrombie & Fitch (originally an outdoor and sporting goods store, before becoming the clothing brand we know today). Sold "A&F," hunters, sub-hilt Bowies, and fighting knives, along with 1,000 knives, called "Delaware Maids," becoming their best-selling item. In addition to being a huge contributor to the knife community, he was also a wonderful mentor to new knifemakers. Partnered with several incredibly talented knifemakers over time, such as Steve Johnson (1971–1974) and Jim Merrit (1982–2010). A founding member of the Knifemakers' Guild in the 1970s, where he served two terms as president (1973–1976). Loveless developed and popularized several knife designs, such as the full-tapered tang method (blade was a single piece of steel running to the end of the butt versus being cut to half the length). The tang was pinned down in place to the handles or glued, and then tapered the butt-end, as he did with the point of the blade. This resulted in a balance of weight of the blade, so that it was centered. Loveless introduced two steels to the knife community: 154CM steel and ATS-34. Known as the "father of micarta," as he pioneered the using it for knife handles. Loveless made specialized knives for the CIA and the US Army Special Forces. These were the first tactical knives produced by a knifemaker during, his time. Collaborated on projects with companies, such as Gerber, Lone Wolf Knives, Beretta, and Schrade Cutlery R.W. Loveless was inducted into the Blade Cutlery Hall of Fame in 1985.

R.W. Wilson: Famous knifemaker and designer. Wilson was one of the first members of the Knifemakers' Guild. Famously known for his tomahawks and premium quality custom knives. His tomahawks have been featured in movies, such as "Jeremiah Johnson" featuring Robert Redford, for which he handmade sixteen tomahawks. Also handmade 500 tomahawks for the 150th Anniversary of the Texas Rangers, the nation's highest regarded law enforcement agency. An amazing mentor to L.T. Wright and has also taught other knifemakers this wonderful skills. https://www.rwwilsonknives.com

Roman Landes: German knifemaker, engineer, and member of the German Knifemakers' Guild. Author of *Messerklingen und Stahl*, in which he developed a basis for selecting and treating knife steels, depending on the intended use. The research captured in this book was indeed groundbreaking, though just the beginning for Roman. His contributions continue to pulsate throughout the knife community, inspiring knifemakers around the world.

Ron Lake: Renowned knifemaker and designer. Became a member of the Knifemakers' Guild in 1971 and inducted into the Cutlery Hall of Fame in 1998. Famously known as the "father of the modern-day folding knife." In 1970, he developed the first trail-lock "Interframe" folding knife, which he also patented. Collaborated on projects with several companies, such as Coast Cutlery, CRKT, and Schrade. Several of his knives are on display at the Smithsonian and the Metal Museum, in Memphis, TN. http://www.lakeknives.com

Saijiro Endo: Bladesmith, designer, and founder of Kai Cutlery (Kai Group) in 1908 Seki City, Japan. Famously known today as "Shun" in the US and Europe, it is the kitchen cutlery production side of Endo's cutlery. Shun remains true to its beginning, with its high quality and beautiful craftsmanship seen throughout their knives.

Sal Glesser: Knifemaker, designer, and founder of Spyderco Inc. Responsible for designing the iconic round hole opener and the famous Spyderco pocket clip. His portable hand creation in 1976, consisting of a series of angles, ball joints, and alligator clips, led to the creation of Spyderco knives. He and his wife, Gail, built the company from scratch. Today, Spyderco is one of the most innovative knife companies in the industry. Most of the knives produced by Spyderco are folding knives, although they do produce great fix blade knives too. Their first folding knife was produced in 1981, and was the C01 featuring their signature round hole. Since the release of first model, Gessler has designed several popular pocketknives. https://www.spyderco.com

Scot Matsuoka: Famous knifemaker and designer. Founder of Matsuoka Knives (Koloa Duck Knives) in Kauai, Hawaii. Mentored by Ken Onion, whom he first met at a Knife Show in Las Vegas, NV, in 1993. In 2003, began making knives professionally and was featured on the April 2006 cover of *Blade* magazine. He specializes in custom folding knives, with blades made from premium quality steel, such as CPM154, BG-42, Devin Thomas Damascus, and 440C. Handle scales are made from various beautiful materials, such as dyed box elder burl, satin finished titanium with anodized milling, giraffe bone, and even mammoth tooth. http://www.matsuokaknives.com

Serge Panchenko: Bladesmith, designer, and founder of Serge Panchencko Knives. He makes some of the most unique knives available in the market. Collaborated on projects with Spyderco, Blackfox, and Boker. A good example of his one-of-a-kind knife is the Serge Panchencko Coin Claw Folder. http://sergeknive.com

Sergey Shirogorov: Award-winning knifemaker and designer from Russia, known to be one of the best folding knifemakers in the country. Produces excellent quality premium steel, rare folding knives. The blades are typically made of ELMAX or M390 steel, with handles made of G10, Carbon Fiber, or stonewashed milled titanium. The folders run on a multi-row bearing system, displaying lightning-fast action. The design is clean, showcasing beautiful geometry and balance. Sergey Shirogorov's popular designs include models F95, F3, Neon Zero, and 111.

Shigeki Tanaka: Bladesmith and designer from Takefu, Fukui, Japan. Gained worldwide popularity for his beautiful chef knives, portraying exquisite balance between traditional styles and modern technique. Shigeki Tanaka forges his blades from super steels, such as Blue Steel, R2/SG2 Damascus, Silver Steel, and VG10 (17 Layer Damascus).

Takayuki Iwai: Bladesmith and designer from the Fukui prefecture, Takefu City, Japan. Was industry certified as the youngest traditional craftsman of cutlery in 2006. Took over his father's cutlery, IWAI Blacksmith Company, and produces top notch kitchen knives, made from excellent steel and handle material. Takayuki Iwai's blades are made from Aogami, Aogami Super Clad, Shirogami, and VG10 Damascus.

Takeshi Saji: Famous bladesmith and designer from Japan. Renowned for making some of the best chef knives in Japan, by combing old traditions with unique knife designs. One of the few in the region to produce a folding Santoku Japanese Knife, (Takeshi Saji, R2/SG2 Damascus Steel, with Carbon Fiber Handle Scales). He is also one of the few to produce a Japanese traditional chef knife with White Cow Bone, Chinese Quince, White Stone, Red Pakka Wood, and Black Micarta. Takeshi Saji's knives are one-of-a-kind, fully functional art pieces, made to cut and chop. These knives are not meant for mere display.

Tapio Syrjala: Award-winning Master Bladesmith and designer. Founder of Tapio Syrjala Custom Knives from Finland. He has been making knives since 2013. In 2018, was accepted as a Master Bladesmith by the Finnish National Agency of Education (EDUFI). In 2016, won the first prize in Finnish Hunting and Fishing Magazine for the "Big Puukko Competition." In 2019, won Best Folding Knife at the Helsinki Knife Show. He is also a member of the Finnish Knifemakers' Guild and Finnish Puukko Association. Some of his knives are Bob Loveless inspired but given a modern twist. Makes astonishing Damascus steel puukkos and spectacular Damascus steel daggers. He selects only the best premium steels and handle materials for his knives. Tapio Syrjala's folding knives are truly a work of art. They are perfectly crafted showcasing beautiful lines, stellar Damascus patterns, and superior handle materials. https://www.tsyrjalaknives.com

Tim Flack: Bladesmith and designer from South Africa, famously known for recreating unique knife designs, featured in video games. Forged a modern kukri style knife, featured in the video game "Far Cry 4." This sparked a new interest for knife collectors and opened a market for game knives, as collector grade pieces.

Todd Begg: Knifemaker and designer from Petaluma, California. Produced "collector grade" folding knives from top quality materials with innovative, modern designs. Begg's folding knives sell for remarkably high prices because of their rarity and superior craftsmanship. https://www.beggknives.com

Tom Mayo: Famous knifemaker and designer making custom knives since 1981. Inspired by Bob Loveless and his stellar creations. Mentored by Glen Hornby, popular knifemaker and designer from Glendale, CA. Over the years, he grew to liking a more traditional style of knife, inspired by Bo Randall, such as the clip point and trailing point. Knifemaking skills eventually evolved into a unique, well-bred design, combining all the styles and techniques from knifemakers that inspired him through the years. Today, you will find that he has mastered his skill to a point only few can reach. Tom Mayo makes spectacular folding and fixed blade knives, using premium steels such as ATS-34, BG-42, and 440V. http://www.mayoknives.com

Travis Wuertz: Award-winning bladesmith and designer. Delved into making knives at the young age of thirteen, when he began taking lessons from Master Bladesmith Tim Hancock. He skills grew over time, winning him "Best Fixed Blade" in 2017 at the International Custom Cutlery Exposition. His custom knifemaking skills funded his college education, where he earned a Bachelor's degree in Mechanical Engineering and a Master's degree in Agricultural & Biosystems Engineering from the University of Arizona. Travis Wuertz went on to win the competition in two different episodes of "Forged in Fire," a show on the History Channel. https://www.traviswuertz.com

Warren Osborne (Passed January 4, 2016): Famous knifemaker and designer. Began making knives in the 1980s. He was a member of the Knifemakers' Guild since 1985. Had a long-standing relationship with Benchmade and collaborated on many projects with them. Designed the famous 940 knife model for Benchmade, known as the 940 Osborne. Popularized CPM M4, as the first knifemaker to use it on the blades of his BSI competition cutters. Renowned for making exquisite knives with the best possible materials and ornate designs. His specialty was interframe folding knives with beautiful engravings, all typically fashioned with a 2,000 to 3,000 grit hand rubbed finish. Warren Osborne took great pride in his career as a knifemaker, showing meticulous care and dexterous crafting abilities in all his creations.

Wayne Meligan: Bladesmith and designer from Pensacola, Florida. Originally a nurse who later became an incredible bladesmith, with appearances on the History Channel's, "Forged in Fire." Makes several ornate choppers/fixed blade knives. Admired by those who desire a change of path in life by embracing what they love, while sheading masterful creations along the way. Anything is possible if you have the desire and motivation, and clearly, Wayne Meligan is a prime example.

William Ewart Fairbairn (February 28, 1885–June 20, 1960): British Royal Marine veteran, who reached rank of colonel and also served as a police officer. A master in combatives, who developed specialized methodologies for the Shanghai police during interwar time. Also taught allied Special Forces during WWII. He created a new fighting system known as Defendu. The martial art techniques he developed are still being used today in modern close combat training for military around the world. Fairbairn's impressive knife-fighting abilities led to the creation of the Fairbairn-Sykes fighting knife. Partnered with Eric Sykes to develop this style knife, also known as a stiletto-style fighting dagger. Later created the Smatchet (a short, but heavy, fighting sword, measuring about 16.5 inches in length). The Smatchet blade is coated to prevent detection and used particularly as a combat knife. It has a broad, leaf-like blade, that tapers at the ends. The Smatchet is a single edge weapon, with razor sharpness which can easily penetrate through flesh, and if needed, decapitate an opponent. This weapon was used by British and American Special Forces during WWII. William E. Fairbairn's contributions to the knife and martial arts community are unmatched.

William "Bill" F. Moran Jr. (May 1, 1925–February 12, 2006): World renowned, legendary Master Bladesmith, designer, and founder of the American Bladesmith Society. Known as the "Father of the Modern Knife Forging Movement," and the "Father of Modern Damascus." He made his first knife at the tender age of twelve, and not too long after, he began selling custom knives. His skills improved immensely over time. Popularized the dying skill (at the time) of forging Damascus steel, by reintroducing pattern welding into the mix. Became famously known for his astonishing Damascus steel knives. In 1972, became president of the Knifemakers' Guild. His knives were highly sought after by heads of state and celebrities worldwide. When he created the American Bladesmith Society (ABS), in 1976, he laid the foundation so that the art of forging blades would never be forgotten. He mentored many knifemakers over the years, with the hopes that it would inspire others to pursue knifemaking. Bill F. Moran Jr. will be remembered not only for his amazing knifemaking abilities, but also for saving ancient traditions that were almost forgotten in America. The William F. Moran Museum, located in Middletown, MD, maintains some of his creations on display to the public. The intent of the museum is to preserve his legacy and to continue to teach young, aspiring knifemakers to learn the skills of a bladesmith. https://williammoranmuseum.com

William "Bill" Scagel (William Wales Scagel, February 12, 1873–March 26, 1963): Pioneer custom knifemaker and designer. This man was at the forefront of modern custom knifemaking, paving a path for every other rising knifemaker to follow. Was inducted into the Blade Magazine Cutlery Hall of Fame in 1990. In 1996, he was inducted into the American Bladesmith Society Hall of Fame. His knives were truly special for the time, reaching the hands of American frontiersmen, mountain men, and avid outdoorsmen far and wide across our nation. Began his journey making knives in the early 1900s. Some of his knives were sold through Abercrombie & Fitch during the 1920s. Famously known for his stag and spacer handles. Scagel's signature design was a half stag and half stacked leather assembly as a handle. He made Bowies, hunters, fighters, folders, and hatchets, all of which were "collector grade" quality. Also made beautiful, highly sought after kitchen knives. All of his knives were made entirely by hand, without the use of modern grinders or buffers. Made knives for the early expeditions of the Smithsonian Institution. Bo Randell was Scagel's *protégé*, who learned as much as he could from this master bladesmith. There is no doubt that Bill Scagel's style and knife designs had a prolific impact on the knife community, influencing knifemakers for over a century. Today, the public can view some of his knives in Orlando, Florida, at the Randall Knife Museum, which showcases the largest Scagel knife collection.

Yoshimi Kato: Famous third-generation bladesmith and designer from Takefu, Fukui prefecture, Japan. He is the head of Kato Uchihamono, formerly Kintaro Knives (known as some of the best kitchen knives in Japan). Premium Japanese steel is used to forge the blades, such as Blue Super Steel, Silver Steel, R2/SG2 Damascus Steel, VG10, VG10 Damascus, and VG10 Nickel Damascus. The blades are perfectly fitted into spectacular handles, made from exotic woods.

Yrjo Puronvarsi: Famous bladesmith from Harma, a town 24 km south of Kauhava, Finland. Was known for forging high quality blades from C75, the European equivalent to 1075. Today, his grandson, Antti Makinen, manages the business, continuing the family tradition of forging their premium blades. It is important to note that Antti only forges the blades. Customers purchase the blades and fit them into their handle material of choice. Yrjo Puronvarsi blades can be found at https://www.brisa.fi or https://www.lamnia.com

Yu Kurosaki: Master bladesmith and designer from Japan. He was an apprentice of Hiroshi Kato, Yoshimi Kato's father-in-law. Strives to constantly produce something new and innovative when it comes to the design and style of his kitchen knives. Yu Kurosaki is a young and talented, up-and-coming bladesmith in Japan, producing high quality knives with premium Japanese steel. His kitchen knives are known to be razor sharp with wonderful edge retention.

Photograph provided by ESEE Knives.

KNIFE COMPANIES

Photograph provided by Chris Reeve Knives, the Sebenza 31 with Macassar Ebony Inlays.

CHRIS REEVE KNIVES

Chris Reeve Knives began operations on January 1, 1984. It emerged from a one-car garage in South Africa, to become not only a first-rate brand, but also a pioneer in the knife industry. Chris and Anne Reeve poured their hearts into the knife company and over time their determination drove them to unmatched heights in the knife manufacturing business. They built a reputation out of creating the finest tools, with the highest quality materials. Over the years Chris has worked closely with Crucible Industries, to develop CPM S30V and CPM S35VN, the predecessors to CPM S45VN stainless steel. These steels are now a staple in the knife industry, used by countless knifemakers worldwide. Chris Reeve Knives produces highly sought-after knife models such as the Sebenza 31 and Inkosi. Their models have now moved over from CPM S35VN to CPM S45VN. The handle materials vary from a 6AL4V titanium handle scales, to others which have elegant, polished box elder burl inlays. All of their models come with the famous Reeve Integral Lock™ with ceramic ball interface, with the exception of their Impinda model and their highly desired fixed-blade models. Chris Reeve Knives has also collaborated with renowned Bill Harsey, to develop some of the most sophisticated tactical fixed blades in the industry, such as the Yarborough knife, which is issued to the US Army Special Forces.

Today, Chris Reeve Knives runs their operations from Boise, ID, where they continue their trailblazing journey inspiring us all with their innovative, awe-striking designs. Chris Reeve Knives is most known for their dedication to quality as shown with their products, customer service, and business practices. The company has won 16 Manufacturing Quality Awards, plus countless other notable industry awards. See https://chrisreeve.com/pages/press-kit for more info. (https://www.chrisreeve.com)

I am a proud owner of their limited run small Sebenza 31 in CPM S35VN blade steel with a tanto blade, sandblasted 6AL4V titanium handle scales, and silver hardware. I cannot speak highly enough of this knife, the design is literally perfection in every facet, and measurement.

Photograph provided by Chris Reeve Knives, the Green Beret, a Chris Reeve and Bill Harsey collaboration.

Q&A with Anne Reeve, *Owner of Chris Reeve Knives*

Chris Reeve knives are exceptionally well-made works of art, that are carefully engineered to perform beyond expectations. What was the knife model that started it all, the model that kick-started the company?

Our One-Piece Range of fixed blades had a good solid following, but it was really the Sebenza that kick-started CRK in the early 1990s.

What is your most popular knife model?

They are all very popular evidenced by our 9–12-month backlog but the single most popular is the Large Sebenza 31 with plain sandblasted handles. The same knife in the smaller size is next.

Knives typically require some form of maintenance, to make sure they continue to perform well and extend the life of the knife. What maintenance would you say your knives require if any? This question refers to oil/lubricant, cleaning, etc...

As is the case with any product, the frequency of maintenance is directly related to the amount of use, so a knife carried and used daily will require more attention than a "safe queen". Unlike many other knives, ours are designed to be disassembled for cleaning and maintenance. Each knife is supplied with appropriate wrenches and a container of fluorinated grease that is made specifically for us.

There is a great deal of knife sharpening options available today, such as electric belt sharpener, pull-through sharpener, whetstone, diamond stone, ceramic, leather strop, etc... What would you say is the best for Chris Reeve Knives?

We recommend regular maintenance of the cutting edge and have found the Spyderco Tri-Angle Sharpmaker to be the most convenient and effective method of doing this. We will sharpen any of our knives at no charge other than return postage.

If you were stuck in a wilderness survival situation and had the option to select only one knife, from the entire Chris Reeve Knives line-up, which would it be and why?

We have always said the best survival knife is the one you have on you all the time. This means you would have it when the survival situation occurred and you would be completely familiar with the knife. In a wilderness situation, probably a 7" Green Beret or Pacific would fit the bill best because they can both do heavy work but can also be used for food prep, etc.

Are there any intentions to add more fixed-blade styles to the line-up?

Yes, we have plans to introduce additional fixed blades in the not-too-distant future.

Are there any other knife-makers or designers you admire?

It's difficult to focus on just one or two because there is abundant talent in our industry. We have worked with Bill Harsey, who has been a friend for over 30 years and collaborator for nearly 20. We have also worked with Grant and Gavin Hawk whom Chris considered among the most innovative minds in the industry.

What would you like to say to the fans?

Thank you - we would be nowhere without you! But in all seriousness, it is very humbling to have our knives so highly sought after and to receive such wonderful compliments. We have become friends with so many of our customers – I am still trying to make a single word out of customer-become-friend!

Photograph provided by Chris Reeve Knives, the Inkosi with Micarta Inlay

ESEE KNIVES

There are few knife companies that have been able to achieve what ESEE Knives has accomplished. They are an incredible brand who stands by their products 100 percent. They offer a variety of knives, from multi-purpose utility knives to heavy duty survival knives. The company is co-owned by Jeff Randall and Mike Perrin and was built on the floor of the Amazon Jungle, designing products out of a needs-based philosophy. Their designs are simple, functional, and pragmatic like the founders of the company.

"Beginning in 1997, Jeff Randall and Mike Perrin started down the path of reshaping the manner in which the survival and wilderness industry carried out business. Having become frustrated with the endless amount of exaggeration and hype often associated with "survival" gear and training, they launched Randall's Adventure & Training to bring realistic tools and knowledge to the consumer market.

Working under contract with the Peruvian Air Force's "Escuela De Supervivencia En La Selva" (School of Jungle Survival), also known by the acronym ESSEL, they introduced many clients to the art of jungle survival in the vast Peruvian Amazon jungle.

After a number of years operating in South America, they relocated their training stateside and launched a sister company to produce high quality field grade knives and gear – ESEE Knives.

Their first design was the RTAK made by Wicked Knife Company in Arkansas, and later produced by Ontario Knife Company (OKC). They also developed the TOPS Knives made Laser Strike. After spending five years developing the RAT line for OKC, they launched ESEE Knives." (https://www.eseeknives.com)

At ESEE, knives are not just good-looking products, they are also rigorously tested by avid outdoorsmen on a regular basis before they reach the hands of the general public. Most of their knives are made of 1095 high carbon steel, which is versatile, remarkably tough, and has moderate edge retention. Given the composition and heat-treat of 1095, it can be resharpened to a razor-sharp edge, with little effort. ESEE is proud of the "tried-and-true" knives they manufacture and offer to their customers.

ESEE has an all-star team of avid wilderness explorers, certified Wilderness First Responders (WFR), certified NASAR SARTECH, certified Search & Rescue (SAR), Swiftwater Rescue Technicians, Rope Rescue Technicians, and former Law Enforcement Officers.

I am proud to say that I own over sixteen ESEE knives. I use them extensively outdoors when going on day hikes, camping, or fishing. I enjoy using the Izula, the ESEE 3, and the ESSE 6, the most. Personally, I feel that the ESEE 6 is the most versatile of their line-up. This knife is great at performing a plethora of small camp tasks as well as heavier tasks, such as chopping and batoning through hardwoods. The ESEE 6 is also a good knife for kitchen tasks such as food prep, as it produces nice, clean cuts with little effort. The Izula and Izula II are fantastic EDC fixed blades, which I have carried through all my wilderness adventures from the arid Mojave desert, to the frigid mountains of the Pacific Northwest.

Q&A with Shane Adams, *ESEE Knives Marketing Director/Utility Player*

ESEE has a wonderful reputation for producing great knives that have gained a huge, loyal following in the knife community. What knife would you say is the most popular, and why?

If you are going by sheer numbers the Izula is our most produced knife. It just checks a lot of boxes for folks and hits a great price point.

If you were stuck in a wilderness survival situation and had the opportunity to pick only one knife from the entire ESEE lineup, what knife would that be, and why?

For me it would be the Laser Strike. It is a 5" blade that is thick enough to easily baton wood if needed and also has the capability to make fire in the handle.

ESEE produces the majority of their knives using 1095 steel, due to its toughness and ease to sharpen. Will ESEE ever produce knives using other steels like A2, O1, CPM3V, or M390?

In the last year we have added S35VN to our line up for the ESEE3, and soon the CR3.0, ESEE-AGK, Izula, and ESEE 4. WE do not jump on the "super steel bandwagon" as quick as most. We evaluate and test for a long time before bringing something to market. Carbon steel has its place in the hard use knife market and always will for people that put their blades in hard use situations. My crystal ball says we will, at some point, but only when we are ready and we have fully tested the steels and they meet our criteria.

Shane, you are an avid outdoorsman, mountain climber, and fisherman, what style knife do you typically carry, and why? This question refers to knife grinds, steels, and handle material.

I carry our CR2.5 more than any knife we make. Rarely do I need a larger knife. On most days I will have a folder in my pocket and that is normally a Spyderco PM2 in M390. I have all kinds of folders but that PM2 is the one that tends to find it's way into my pocket.

Aside from ESEE knives, are there any other knife-makers you admire?

Plenty. Our industry is full of great people. From the guys at LT Wright Knives, to Russel Reese of Cohutta Knvies, to our very own James Gibson. All craftsman in their own right but also just great people.

Do you have something you would like to tell ESEE fans?

THANK YOU. Seriously….. Thank. You. This company has been built on the word of mouth by our customers. We spend little to no money on advertising in common channels, instead, we try to make sure we take care of our folks when they need us most. We would not be here were it not for the efforts of our customers that are out there actively shaking the trees and introducing people to our products. We are eternally grateful for them.

What many don't know is that we started as a training company first in the early 90s and kind of backed into the knife industry. Training remains a key focus for us, and Randall's Adventure & Training remains our proving ground for all our products.

Photograph provided by ESEE Knives.

Photograph provided by Fallkniven, the Embla.

FALLKNIVEN

Fallkniven was founded in 1984 by Peter Hjortberger, with the intention of making superb knives for people of all walks of life. Fallkniven is a family-owned business, nestled in Norrbotten, Sweden. The Hjortberger family have been hunters and fishermen for decades and understand from personal experience how an outdoors knife should be. Over the years, the company has collected many accolades, and today is acknowledged as one of Sweden's foremost knife specialists. Their knives are made using a lamination process that takes an excellent steel and folds it over another excellent steel, to make a superior blade steel that can withstand all sorts of weather and impact. Their knives are so highly regarded that their F1 model is used as the official survival knife of the Swedish Air Force. Their knives have great ergonomics, blade geometry, toughness, and strength. In 1999, Fallkniven acquired the prestigious title of "Purveyor to the Royal Court of Sweden," a title held by only a select few in the country.

I am a proud owner of several Fallkniven knives, such as the F1, F1x, F1xb, S1, S1x, and A1. These knives are made with premium materials and are of the highest quality. I cannot speak highly enough of these multipurpose tools… they perform exceptionally well at every task. (https://fallkniven.se)

Photograph provided by Fallkniven, the S1x and F1x.

Q&A with Peter Hjortberger, *Owner of Fallkniven:*

Fallkniven is known for producing excellent knives, used for bushcraft, wilderness survival, and even tactical environments. What would you say is Fallkniven's most popular knife?

By far the F1 Pilot Survival Knife https://fallkniven.se/en/knife/f1/ sold in several hundreds of thousands pieces and used worldwide by amateurs and professionals. Since 1995 the official survival knife for pilots in the Swedish Air Force. Originally a knife meant for hunting purposes but as such, good for almost any task. The idea and philosophy behind the F1 knife revolutionized the survival knife concept in 1995 and our company has kept that advantage since then. No company, small or large, is close to our technology and we are sure about that since we test our knives at the Technical University of Lulea. And our competitors'...

If you were in a wilderness survival situation and had the opportunity to select only one knife from Fallkniven's lineup, which knife would that be and why?

For sure I would choose the A1xb https://fallkniven.se/en/knife/a1xb/ since that knife is the strongest, sharpest, safest knife in the world, at least for the moment. It's our most modern knife and the best we are able to make, at least for now. The sheath is just as smart and intelligent as the knife is strong and sharp.

What grind and steel would you recommend for bushcraft / woodcraft?

I would go for the new F1xb https://fallkniven.se/en/knife/f1xb/ which is handy enough to always follow you. The laminated cobalt steel blade is extremely tough and the entire construction is breathing safety. The convex edge is both thin and strong and very well prepared for any task in the woods. The sheath is strong and smart and will allow you to wear the knife upside down.

What Fallkniven knife is the most versatile?

Many of our models are very versatile but the S1xb https://fallkniven.se/en/knife/s1xb/ is very useful and will fit in many situations. In much our knives offer the same qualities but are made in different sizes in order to meet the market demand. No matter what, some like small knives, others like large ones and still the task is the same - to survive. Yet we always state: It's NOT the equipment that will make you survive, it's your experience and knowledge. The knife is just a tool.

What are your recommendations for long-term storage of a knife? Keep the knife clean and dry, that enough. And leave it sharp.

Do you admire any other knife-makers? The late R W Loveless, USA.

What is your favorite Fallkniven knife?

Erik and I are always testing many models and often swap from one to another from one weekend to another. Erik started to use the A1z https://fallkniven.se/en/knife/a1-2/ twenty years ago and it seems like he still likes larger knives. Right now it is the A1x https://fallkniven.se/en/knife/a1x/. Myself, being a hunter since 1974, I enjoy the straight, clean swedish design in the SK1 https://fallkniven.se/en/knife/sk11-2/, that knife is always on my side when I'm in the woods.

What would you like to say to your fans?

Much! They are intelligent knife nerds just like we are and we like being within this family. We really like to receive feedback from people who actually know something about living in the woods. We also enjoy receiving positive comments from elite soldiers from all over the world, much often they state that their Fallky knife has helped them stay alive. Such statements warm our hearts.

Photograph provided by Fallkniven, the A1x.

Gransfors Bruk, Photographer: Emelie Torstensson.

GRANSFORS BRUK

Founded by Anders Pettersson in Gransfors, Sweden, Gransfors Bruk's rich, long history of making traditional axes began in 1902. The forge never truly turns off at Gransfors… it merely cools at the end of the day and heats back up the following day. It resembles a human heart; in that it slows down when it's time to rest and begins to beat faster when it is time to forge new experiences. At Gransfors they care about the functionality, efficiency, and balance of their products. Forged by hand with keen eyes and attention to detail, they embrace the traditional way of making axes. Their axes are razor-sharp, have fantastic ergonomics, and are made to be used.

They are an environmentally conscious company that truly cares about the wellbeing of the planet. All their materials are carefully and sustainably sourced. Owning dependable tools is important, because a day may arrive when your life depends on their performance.

I trust all my Gransfors Bruk products because I have used them extensively for multiple outdoor tasks and know that they perform better than any axe currently available in the market. I own twelve Gransfors axes, ranging from the mini hatchet to the large splitting axe. My favorite is their Small Forest Axe, Model 420, because it is large enough to fell a small tree, but small enough to use for bushcraft tasks.

Gransfors Bruk, Photographer: Samuel Uneus.

Q&A with Emelie Torstensson, *Gransfors Bruk Marketing Manager*

Gransfors Bruk is known for producing the best axes in the industry. What axe would you say is the most popular and why?

Our most popular ones among our customers are the Wildlife hatchet and the Small forest axe. Most customers says it's related to their all-round capabilities as axes and their suitable size for backpacks and bags.

If you were in a wilderness survival situation and had the opportunity to select only one axe from Gransfors Bruk's entire lineup which would it be and why?

It depends on the situation. Do I have to hike with it or am I on a base camp? I would probably choose the Wildlife hatchet. It's easy to carry, suits in a backpack and not too small for making up fire and taking care of the basics at a camp. But if I would be "stuck" in the same place, it would be the Scandinavian Forest Axe. It is big and works perfect to cut down trees to make a shelter and cut wood.

Emelie, roughly how much time does it take to produce a single axe, from beginning to end?

That's a tricky question to answer, there's many steps in the production. Usually around a couple of hours, but divided into parts in a process spread out during a couple of days. The axe models also differs, some of them are more time demanding than others.

Have there been any alterations to the design of the axe heads over time, or have they maintained their original design?

In general, they have kept their shape since their original design.

Is there a Gransfors Bruk axe that is pretty much capable of doing every task successfully, such as felling, chopping, splitting, and carving?

One axe can't do all tasks great, but we have capable allrounders, like for example the Outdoor hatchet, Small Forest Axe, and Scandinavian Forest Axe. It's almost impossible to for example do carving with a splitting maul and it takes a lot of time to fell a large tree with our small hatchet. But we have axes to basically every task.

Which is the best light weight axe you produce at Gransfors Bruk?

If it's weight your trying to limit, the Small Hatchet is the lightest. My favorite when travelling or hiking light is the Outdoor Axe, which it's also light, but a bit more capable and sturdy. But ask anyone here and you will get probably 30 different answers.

Is boiled linseed oil the best oil to use on the axe handles or are there alternatives that are just as good?

We recommend raw linseed oil, not boiled. Boiled linseed oil is mainly used for indoor use and paint. From 2021 we will have our own oil that is extracted linseed oil by means of a unique refining process. It consists of 100 percent of unsaturated, i.e. dried fatty acids from linseed oil.

Do you have anything you would like to say to your fans?

In times characterized by the Covid-19 virus we mainly want everyone to take care of each other and our mutual environment. For decades this has been an important part of how we work, there's more information on our homepage: www.gransforsbruk.com

Gransfors Bruk, Photographer: Samuel Uneus.

Photograph taken by A.J., the LionSTEEL M1

LIONSTEEL

The year was 1969 and humanity had reached new heights physically, technologically, and artistically. We landed on the moon, the internet was born, and Led Zeppelin released their debut album "Black Mountain Side." Most importantly, in that year, Gino Pauletta and his family decided to embark on their own journey, into the world of knifemaking. They did what they could with the little they had and made the best of it. What makes or breaks a company is the brand and the image it portrays. Gino knew this, and he also knew his journey would require the courage of a lion to be successful, thus "LionSTEEL," was born. Gino made knives with every ounce of passion and dedication he could muster, and it paid off. His little workshop in the small town of Maniago, Italy, grew into a very successful operation. He created classy, unique knives that could easily be identifiable by the beautiful design and the iconic lion logo.

I own several LionSTEEL knives (B35, B41, M1, and M4) and I couldn't be more pleased with their performance, comfort level, and aesthetics. LionSTEEL uses premium blade steels for most of their knives, such as M390, Niolox, and Chad Nichols Damascus.

Photograph provided by LionSTEEL, Andrea Mazzoli, the LionSTEEL M4.

Q&A with Gianni Pauletta, *Owner & CEO of LionSTEEL*

LionSTEEL is a very reputable knife company that produces some of the best knives available in the market for survival, bushcraft, and EDC. What model would you say is the most popular of your line-up?

The SR1 was the knife that changed the LionSTEEL's life. The introduction of this knife was the breakout point for us, after that moment we started to be recognized as a company able to produce good knives.

I can say the best-selling folding knife was the TRE and the Myto. In regards to the fixed blade the M4 is the top seller followed by our T5 and M5.

Your knives typically come in two steels, which are M390 and Sleipner. What are your thoughts about Sleipner steel, as far as performance and maintenance?

In my opinion Sleipner is the top steel we have used, that does not mean that it is the one that has top performance but only that it has the right balance of a top steel and good price. You can reach 61/62 HRC, guarantee a good wear-resistant edge, and it is easy to re-sharpen too. This last point is very important, especially if you need to do it with no tools. At the end of 2021 we decided to add other steels like CPM MagnaCUT, CPM 3V and Bohler K490 to our knife production, also.

If you were in a wilderness survival situation, and only had the opportunity to choose one knife from your line-up, which would it be, and why?

Personally, I prefer to stay in front of the beach with a glass of wine, anyway. But in a survival situation, M5 Sleipner would be my knife. Right size with good performance for heavy work or light, finer detailed work.

What are your thoughts on the new steel MagnaCut?

Good question… currently we are leaving for the Shot Show 2022 and we will introduce the new knife L.E. One. It is a Collaboration with Ernest Emerson. It is a SOLID Karambit with CPM MagnaCut blade. What I can say to you at this moment is that I like its datasheet and for this reason we introduce it. We do not yet have enough experience with MagnaCut to confirm the same thing as the M390 or Sleipner, but I am sure that I will have a lot of satisfaction with it.

Is there anything you would like to tell your fans?

Only a promise, despite that time is running very fast I can confirm that I still have the same passion for knives as the beginning, like a baby in front of a candy. Only with this passion can you study, work and build a new knife better than the old one.

Photograph provided by LionSTEEL, Andrea Mazzoli, the LionSTEEL M5.

Photograph taken by A.J., the Next Gen, Genesis, and Gen 3.

L. T. WRIGHT KNIVES

Occasionally, there are those whose talents are so brilliant that they unknowingly influence their trade for years to come. As they hone their skills, they create masterpieces along the way and share them with the world. There is a man who goes by the name L. T. Wright, who realized he had a radiance early on and honed that skillset without delay. When he saw his creations, he noticed that his talent was special because it enabled his hands to grind, heat-treat, temper, and sharpen steel into spectacular blades. Performing the steps to create a knife can be done by many, however, not many can do it right. L. T. Wright easily does it better than most.

L. T. Wright produces simple knife designs that are highly effective and efficient in any environment. He is an experienced knife designer and maker who has been producing blades for over a decade. He mastered his skillset under the supervision of R. W. Wilson, a well-known bladesmith and one of the first members of the Knifemakers' Guild. When the time was right, L. T. spread his wings and showed the world what he was capable of. L. T. put together an extraordinarily talented team of knifemakers, which he oversees and takes much pride in helping refine their skills. He strives in pushing his team to someday become better knifemakers than he is.

I have tremendous respect for L. T. Wright. Personally, I own several of his knives and cannot speak highly enough of them. I use them for every task that requires a knife… which is nearly everything. L. T. is a person who is tremendously passionate about knives and knifemaking. Invest in an L. T. Wright knife and you feel the radiance that L. T. harnessed years ago.

I own the following knife models produced by L. T. Wright: GNS, Genesis, Bushbaby, Bushcrafter, and Frontier First. I have these models in a variety of steels and grinds. They are all great multipurpose tools, from bushcraft to kitchen, they excel beyond expectations.

Photograph provided by L.T. Wright.

Photograph taken by A.J., the Frontier First.

Q&A with L.T. Wright, *President of L.T. Wright Knives (a.k.a L.T. Wright Handcrafted Knife Company)*

L.T., at what point did you realize that you had a special gift, as a knife-maker?

After I made a knife from a kit and gave it to my Dad for Christmas I was surprised to see how many of his friends wanted to order one. I wasn't expecting so many people to like it and want one. Then when I started making my own knives to take to knife shows, people really responded to them. The knives were selling themselves. I'm still surprised when I come in the shop in the morning to see that we sold knives overnight. So, it was really that realization that people appreciated what I was making and were responding to them.

In a wilderness survival situation, where your life depends on it, if you were allowed to only pick one knife from your entire lineup, what knife would that be, and why?

I would choose the Genesis scandi in A2 steel and a micarta handle. This is the knife that I carry. I have put a lot of time behind the knife so I know its strengths and limitations. I know it well and I've used it a lot so I can make this knife do what I need to do. I can complete major tasks with this knife and have them done well. I know I can rely on it to get the job done reliably and well.

Your knives are beautifully designed, extremely well made, functional, balanced, and have fantastic ergonomics. I would like to focus on your very first design, the one you made for your father. What purpose could that knife serve today, whether it is bushcraft/woodcraft, wilderness survival, basic carry, camping chores, combat, or simply utility? What grind and steel was that knife?

The very first knife was a kit knife, not a knife of my design. It was in 440c stainless steel and hollow grind. The intention for the knife was field dressing game because my Dad is an avid hunter. The first knife I feel like I designed would have been something I called The Whitetail Classic. It had a brass guard, I used 440 c and hollow ground the blade. It was intended to be a hunting knife.

The Bushcrafter and Genesis knives in scandi grind, 3V steel, are undeniably the absolute best bushcraft knives ever introduced to the bushcraft community. Some people would say that is just my opinion, however, when taking into consideration what a bushcraft knife is intended to do, your knives check all the boxes and beyond. How much time did you dedicate in developing the designs of the Bushcrafter and Genesis?

The Bushcrafter was designed by our good friend Tim Stetzer. He is a police officer, outdoor enthusiast, and a writer for many outdoor magazines. For the Genesis, it was based on me looking for a spear point blade with a broomstick style handle and kephart design. I settled on the standard Genesis being 4.25–4.5 inches in sharpened edge. I thought that would be a good length for woodcrafting. All of the years I had been making knives had gone into the Genesis. From working with knives, working on knives, talking about knives, and looking at knives, all of that went into the Genesis. I start with what's the intention for the knife and then add to it.

What recommendation would you give a new knife-maker today, who is looking to leave his day job and dedicate all his efforts into knife making?

I would recommend keeping it as your part time gig or hobby until you're sure that when you make a knife it will sell or that you have a backlog of orders. You also need to make sure that you love making knives. You need to love it more than anything because it will take all of your time. Be ready for the work of running a business, all of it. The shipping, paperwork, customer service, etc. It also helps to have a spouse that is an accountant. My wife Elaine makes so much about the business easier for me.

Is there a special message you would like to share with the knife community? This can be anything you want to say to your fans.

Thank you. Having the fan base we have has allowed us to grow and experiment. Since our fans like to see new things we can try new things. Thank you for the feedback and continued support. I am so grateful for that and the relationship we've built with our customers over the years. I get to make knives every day because of our fan base, and I thank them so much for that.

If you had the opportunity to give kudos to another knife-maker, who would that be? And why?

This could be any knife-maker you admire.

First and foremost, R.W. Wilson (https://www.rwwilsonknives.com) He let me come over to his house and taught me how to make knives. He took me to knife shows with him and taught me how to sell knives and talk to customers. He built my first grinder that I still have. I can't say enough about all that he's taught me and what a great guy he is.

Another knifemaker would be Greg Gottschalk (http://www.gottschalkknives.com) He helped me early on teaching me how to forge and make damascus. He is a machinist so he makes parts for our machines here in the shop. He has helped us with the folder side of the company and is the reason we'll be coming out with one soon.

Bruce Godlesky (http://birdogforge.com) was instrumental in teaching me how to hand forge, especially tomahawks. I would encourage everyone to check out what these three are working on and what they have to offer. They are knowledgeable, talented, and generous people.

Photograph provided by L.T. Wright.

Photograph provided by L.T. Wright.

Photograph taken by A.J., the GNS.

Photograph taken by A.J., the Bushbaby.

Photograph provided by Opinel, Photographer: Thierry Vallier.

OPINEL

In 1890, out of the small forge shop of Daniel Opinel in Albiez le Vieux, in the heart of the French Alps, and the creative mind of Joseph Opinel, emerged an iconic knife that would forever change the landscape of the pocketknife. Joseph Opinel, son of Daniel, embarked on a journey to create a small, lightweight, multi-purpose pocketknife, at which point Opinel was born. Word of this spectacular pocketknife spread throughout France, followed by the rest of Europe. Popularity of the knife increased rapidly, pushing manufacturing to new, unforeseen levels. Joseph began producing the knife in multiple sizes to accommodate for the needs of people from different walks of life and industries. In 1901, the Pont de Gevoudaz Factory was established, where Joseph streamlined production and created machines to produce handles at faster speeds. As of 1909, all the knives were produced with the famous Crowned Hand emblem, which was a symbolistic move, because the "blessing hand" was that of Saint John the Baptist, extracted from the coat of arms of Saint-Jean-de-Maurienne, the closest town in Albiez-le-Vieux, the birthplace of the Opinel family. In 1915, Joseph made the bold move of relocating his operations to Chambery, in Cognin, with the intention of expanding his knife making business. In 1917, out of an old tannery, Joseph, with his two sons Marcel and Leon, started the foundational framework and marketing of the Opinel brand. In 1926, a sudden fire in the factory destroyed nearly everything. The Opinel family persevered from the tragic event, and in 1927, established a new factory. In 1955, Marcel invented the Virobloc© system, also known as the ring lock. His revolutionary invention was a fantastic addition to the pocketknives, as it improved the safety of the knife. The ring lock prevented the blade from accidentally closing on your fingers. On January 29, 1960, Joseph Opinel passed away at the age of eighty-eight. His son Marcel passed away exactly thirty years to the day after Joseph's passing. Today, the company is managed by Marcel's great-grandchildren Francois and Denis. The current factory is located in Chambery, at a place called La Reveriaz. The Opinel pocketknife has been included in the Museum of Modern Art's list of iconic objects, and was displayed amongst the 100 most beautiful objects in the world at the Victoria & Albert Museum.

I own several Opinel knives and enjoy them immensely. They are beautiful, simple, lightweight, practical, and very functional knives. The knives are multipurpose and can be used for bushcraft, culinary tasks, and foraging, to name a few. Nowadays, the knives come in a variety of wooden handles, stainless, or carbon steel blades, and all sorts of sizes, at an unbeatable price. (https://www.opinel.com)

Photograph provided by Opinel, Photographer: Thierry Vallier.

Q&A with Opinel

Opinel has been around since 1890, producing fantastic products for all sorts of tasks, such as whittling, bushcraft, foraging, and culinary arts; what Opinel knife would you say is the all-in-one, do-it-all knife for most situations?

Our classic No.08. It founded the company and carries our brand values and inspirations.

Which Opinel knife is your most popular, and why?

No.08 Carbon steel, it's the original knife that Joseph made in the Alps in 1890.

Opinel has maintained a unique design for all their knives, using either a stainless or carbon steel for the blades. Would Opinel ever release knives with other types of steel, such as O1, A2, D2, S30V, CP-M3V, or M390? And why?

Maybe! Our product team is always looking for the best materials to offer great quality knives at an affordable price point. We strongly believe in a product offering that's simple and speaks to the many.

Opinel's handles are beautifully made from all sorts of wood. Has Opinel ever considered making knife handles from woods like African Blackwood, Zebrawood, Desert Ironwood, Kingwood, or Snakewood? Why or why not?

We are consistently releasing limited edition knives with beautiful woods to elevate our product line. Recently, we released the limited-edition No.08 with Arizona Ironwood. In doing so, we are keeping the environment and sustainability at the top of our mind.

What do you recommend in regards to long-term storage of Opinel knives?

Avoid leaving your carbon blade knife in damp environments for too long. Place a little food grade mineral oil on all metal parts regularly. Dry the blade using a dry cloth after each use.

Should Opinel handles ever be retreated with oil over time? If so, which oil would you recommend?

If you feel that the wood needs to be nourished, you can apply an edible oil (sunflower oil works well). This oil is also good to put in the Virobloc© or on the blade to clean it and avoid rust.

Are there any other knife-makers you admire?

Any brand that contributes to the knife industry with smart designs that are respectful of the environment.

What would you like to say to your fans?

Thank you for the trust you've placed in us and our products for the last 130 years! We look forward to providing great knives for generations to come!

Photograph provided by TOPS Knives, the Brothers of Bushcraft (B.O.B.) Fieldcraft Knife.

TOPS KNIVES

There is no better way to capture the needs of those in harm's way, than actually being one of those individuals. From the experience of elite military members emerged a knife company that truly understands Operators and the gear they need when deployed to hostile environments throughout the world. TOPS Knives was founded in 1998 by a group of elite military members who wanted to produce high-quality knives that those in harm's way can depend on, regardless of the situation. The knives produced by TOPS are made to be used, abused, beaten, not stored away in a desk drawer gathering dust. They make knives for survivalists, military, law enforcement, and the avid outdoorsman. Their products are designed by people with an extensive background in military field operations, martial arts, wilderness survival, and Native American weapons.

"To create the highest-quality, rugged, unique, overbuilt, and functional tools for service members and outdoorsmen of all kinds through our superior manufacturing, finishing processes, and genuine field operators' testing." (TOPS Knives, Mission Statement).

The steels TOPS typically uses are 1095 HC, 5160 HC, 154CM, ATS-34, 440C, S35VN, and other high quality steels.

Their custom shop produces unique knife designs that are one-offs, custom projects, and limited runs. The shop is run by Leo Espinoza (TOPS President/Owner) as a creative outlet to produce top-notch, one-of-a-kind knives. (https://www.topscustomshop.com)

I am a proud owner of several of their knives and have used them extensively for bushcraft. They make very unique designs, some of which I have found to be very useful in the woods. Some of my favorites include the MSK 2.5, Fieldcraft by Brothers of Bushcraft, Tanimboca Puukko, Backpacker's Bowie, Trail Seeker, and their Grandpa's Ax. (https://www.topsknives.com)

Photograph provided by TOPS Knives, the Mini Tanimboca Puukko.

Q&A with Craig Powell, *TOPS Knives General Manager*

TOPS knives are very well known for producing high quality knives. Which knife would you say is the most popular one and why?

Tough to answer because it changes over time. TOPS got it's start with tactical knives and we still sell a lot in that category, but the most popular model is the Fieldcraft knife. The reason is it fits that mid-size, do most things knife spot. A 4.5" blade can do small tasks easily and handle a lot of larger tasks. Since it's not huge, it's more likely to be carried than a bigger knife might. It's got a great handle and blade shape that make it versatile for a lot of different types of uses. Works well for hunting, camping, and field use. We've had everyone from bushcrafters, to hunters, to special forces, to weekend warriors buying this knife.

The TOPS Brother of Bushcraft (BOB) Fieldcraft knife has gained a huge fan base in the bushcraft / woodcraft community. This knife is made of 1095 high carbon steel, will TOPS produce this knife in other steels, such as CPM3V, M390, A2 in future?

We make it in 1095 and in 154CM currently. We may make a run in CPM S35VN sometime soon, but don't really have plans to make it in a bunch of other steels.

If you were stuck in a wilderness survival situation, and had the opportunity to select only one knife from the entire TOPS lineup, which one would that be and why?

Whatever knife you have on you is the best knife for a survival situation may be a cliché, but it's true. If I ever do find myself in that situation, most likely I'll have a knife about the size of the Fieldcraft on me. I have one of those that I carry. I have a Baja 4.5, and I have a Cochise, and I love the Brakimo also (among others). They're all roughly the same size and whenever I head out into the woods, that's probably what I'm carrying on my person. I'll have other tools in my vehicle or around camp, but that's the one most likely on my hip. So not necessarily a specific model, but more a size. It comes down to convenience. I'll carry a machete or a hatchet if I plan on using one a lot, but if I'm just out, it's most likely going to be smaller. Most people I think are the same. They're not carrying extra weight unless they need to, so a great survival knife is the one you're most likely to have on you when things go wrong.

TOPS has supported Military, Law Enforcement, and Outdoorsmen for nearly 30 years. What knife would you recommend to a young Infantry Soldier, Marine or Sailor, getting ready to deploy to a war zone?

Since the beginning, TOPS has been focused on our nation's military and first responders. This question is tough because what someone may be allowed to carry varies wildly between military branches. But if they are allowed and want something that will work for the daily stuff that can be hard on knives, but also for self-defense if needed, the C.U.T. 4.0 is a great option.

What TOPS knife is your personal favorite and why?

Probably the Mini Scandi Knife. It's the one that I have carried more than any other knife we make. I have 2 of them I like it so much. It's easy to conceal, so I can take it places where a knife on my hip might otherwise be frowned upon. It's great outdoors for gutting/cleaning fish, cutting small veggies, whittling, etc. They are super sharp, have a great tip, a comfortable handle. It's easy to wear as a neck knife or just toss in your pocket. So it finds itself with me a lot of the time.

Craig, are there any other knife-makers that you admire?

I admire a lot of different makers for different reasons. I admire people that preserve the old ways of doing things; the ones that use coal forges, use traditional heat-treating methods, and appreciate the process to create one of a kind pieces. I also admire the guys that use current technologies to make knives that are as close to perfect as they can with precision machines and come up with new ways to improve knives. I also admire the guys that make items to go along with knives. I love seeing a leather sheath that is wearable art. I admire seeing Kydex makers find a way of attaching a knife to something that is specific to what their customer is looking for. So yeah, I would say there are others that I admire.

Is there anything you would like to say to your fans?

TOPS' fans are the best. They are supportive and always eager to see what we have coming out. We are proud to continue making knives in the USA for people that love knives and love quality gear. We will continue to do so until we are no longer able.

Photograph provided by TOPS Knives, the Poker.

Photograph provided by Victorinox, Leah Pepper and Nina Poosikian, the Swiss Champ.

VICTORINOX

There is a name that resonates deeply with many people, the name "Swiss Army." From childhood to adulthood, even today, we still reach into our pockets and pull out our small dependable multitool, the Swiss Army pocketknife. Victorinox has a rich history, dating back to 1884, when the first knives were developed by Karl Elsener I. In 1897, Karl patented the "Swiss Officer's and Sports Knife," also known as the "Swiss Army Knife." In 1909, Karl registered his mother's name Victoria as the brand name, and today it is a registered trademark in over 120 countries worldwide. The year 1921 was significant because the invention of stainless steel (Inox) changed the cutlery industry forever and influenced the name of the company. Thus was born "Victorinox," the name of the company is a combination of "Victoria" and "Inox." Victorinox has always been about elegance, functionality, and most important, consistency. In order to keep up with the massive demand for his stellar pocket-knives and maintain consistent high quality, Carl Elsener II introduced automation in 1931. He commissioned Brown, Boveri, & Cie., a Swiss company of electrical engineers, to setup the world's first all-electric hardening plant in Ibach, Switzerland. In 1945, the pocketknife became a hot commodity among US soldiers stationed in Europe during WWII. The iconic Swiss Army knife quickly gained popularity in the US shortly after the war and the rest is history.

I have nothing but sincere admiration for Victorinox Swiss Army, because their beautiful pocketknife was a big part of my childhood and adulthood. This little bugger never leaves my pocket... recalling my first knife injury at the age of six, to slicing open my Meal Ready Eat (MREs), while in the United States Army. Even today, holding a Swiss Army pocketknife in the palm of my hand gives me butterflies in my stomach because of all the memories. I own several Victorinox products and use them every single day... they are indispensable. (https://www.victorinox.com)

Photograph provided by Victorinox, Leah Pepper and Nina Poosikian.

Q&A with Felix Immler, *Victorinox Swiss Army Carving Expert, Educator and Author*

Victorinox has a long history making knives, dating back to 1884. In 1891 the company began supplying / producing knives for the Swiss Army, hence the name Swiss Army Knives. What would you say is the most iconic knife model, in the Swiss Army Knife lineup?

It's definitely the Victorinox Swiss Champ. It's the ultimate pocketknife, packing no less than 33 functions, including a large and a small blade, a wood and a metal saw, a magnifying glass, a pressurized ballpoint pen, and countless possibilities. Wherever you are and whatever happens, if it can be fixed, it can be fixed with the Swiss Champ.

If you were in a wilderness survival situation and the opportunity to select only one knife from the entire Swiss Army knife lineup, which would that be and why?

I would select the Victorinox Work Champ. Robust, rugged and ready for anything, the Work Champ is the ultimate portable tool chest. The 21 functions include a large blade, reamer, punch, wood saw, metal saw, metal file, scissors, pliers and many more.

Victorinox produces some of the best stainless steel blades in the market, will knives ever be made in other steels, like O1, D2, A2, CPM3V, S30V, or M390?

Victorinox guarantees all knives and tools to be of first-class stainless steel underlining the top quality of our products.

Most of the knives produced by Swiss Army are a flat grind, with a small secondary bevel, will knives be made with other grinds in the future, such as saber, scandi, or convex?

As a carving expert I'm more involved in the daily usage of the knives, and not so much in its development. As far as I know, there is nothing planned, but never say never.

Is there any recommendation you would give a knife owner, as far as the maintenance, in long-term knife storage?

Do not clean the knife in the dishwasher, treat your knife with a drop of oil from time to time and never let the cutting tools become completely dull.

What is your favorite Swiss Army knife?

It's the Victorinox Huntsman. In my opinion this knife has a very good price-performance ratio. In 95% of all situations I have everything I need on the knife. In terms of size, this knife can be carried comfortably in a trouser pocket.

Is there anything you would like to say to the fans?

The tools in the Swiss Army Knife are of high quality. In most cases, the tools in the Swiss Army Knife are significantly smaller than the respective special tools with the same functions. If you use the tools incorrectly or with all your strength the functions can be damaged. Use the Swiss Army Knife responsibly, then you will enjoy this product for a long time. Further, you can find tips and tricks for using the Victorinox pocketknife on the YouTube channel "Felix Immler". Further, please find here "The Nine Key Rules for Carving Safely with Kids." Enjoy the outdoors with your Swiss Army Knife.

Photograph provided by Victorinox, Leah Pepper and Nina Poosikian, the Hiker with wood scales.

Note: *There are many more great knife companies out there that produce excellent products but were not highlighted. This is primarily a reference book meant to educate people on knife history, steels, grinds, blade types, knife maintenance, and/or activities performed with knives (culinary arts, bushcraft, and carving). The "extras" are sections which cover knife community influencers, modern knife companies, grip exercises, and knife superstitions. Highlighting every knife company in existence would be superfluous and would reach beyond the scope of this book. I will provide a list of company names that deserve to be at least mentioned, because they produce fantastic, good quality products. This list can be found at the end of the book.*

Photograph provided by LionSTEEL, Andrea Mazzoli, the LionSTEEL M5.

Photograph provided by TOPS Knives, the Heat-Treat Process.

STEEL

The experimentation with steel over the years—trying to improve its properties to make it harder, more wear resistant, and more corrosion resistant to perform certain tasks—has brought us where we are today. There are many people throughout human history we have to thank for helping us reach the point where we are now, who have helped give us access to a multitude of different steels for use in a plethora of applications. These modern steels helped us achieve tasks we thought were impossible to accomplish and they continue to help us reach new heights in every industry. In the following sections we will dive deep into the different steels that are available but focus more on those related to the knife industry.

BLADE STEELS AND THEIR PERFORMANCE LEVELS

There are basically two types of blade steels: stainless and carbon. One may say that the structural foundation of steel is simply iron and carbon. However, that is not entirely the case, because things are a little more complex than that today. There are several other types of steels available, such as tool steels, atypical steels, and laminated steels. We will cover the different types of steel in the Knife Steels section. In the steel industry, metallurgists experiment with different steels by melting and alloying them with a mixture of metallic/nonmetallic elements. A process is then followed by applying specific heat-treat and cooling methods, known as annealing, to produce a substance that is suitable for several applications. The steel making process does have additional steps, such as descaling and cutting blanks, but I will not be covering those steps because that delves more into industrial steel versus specialty steel.

New steels are being produced nearly every year, capable of handling pressures and temperatures we never thought possible. That said, not all steels are suitable as knife blades. Those steels that are suitable, though typically have a purpose, such as: combat, fighting, survival, bushcraft, woodcarving, hunting, foraging, and culinary. When the purpose of a blade is defined, then there are few things one must consider. Selecting the right steel, designing the blade geometry, heat-treat methods, and choosing the appropriate blade grind, are just a few factors to take into consideration. Those are some of the topics that will be covered throughout this section of the book.

Today, there are a plethora of different blade steels available for choosing. Some share similar properties while others are completely different, but all have a specific purpose, or intended use. In this section, we will explore the various blade steels available in the knife industry, so that you can better understand when choosing the one best suited for your needs.

A knife blade's performance is not simply measured by the type of steel used; there are additional factors to consider. The first consideration is the type of steel used to make the blade and what metallic/nonmetallic elements were added to improve the blade's overall properties and capabilities. The next factor to consider would be the normalization process. Normalization is a sort of reset button for the steel, meant to correct any internal stresses it may have by altering the microstructure, and in turn, reducing hardness and increasing ductility. After the normalization process, blades will typically go through a cooling process, meant to allow the steel's new lattice bonds to settle. The next step is reheating the steel to where it reaches a critical temperature, at which point it will be rendered nonmagnetic. The steel is taken off the heat, tested with a magnet, then depending on the steel, quenched in either oil, water, or brine. Steels which show proper hardenability will not be cut by a file when performing a file test. The file will just slide off without cutting the steel. The final step in the heat-treat process is tempering, which is typically done after a blade has been fully profiled.

A blade's hardness shows users the ability of a blade to resist deformation when subject to pressure/tension when applying grades of force. Hardenability, though, should not be mistaken for hardness (material property). When describing the hardenability of a blade, we are often looking at the structure achieved from cooling. Hardenability refers to how much more a material can harden using thermal/heat treatment. There are visual aids one may use to better understand this steel transformation, such as the *Continuous Cooling Transformation* and *Time Temperature Transformation* diagrams. These visuals help in the determination of structures at a variation of cooling rates. Hardenability levels are related to the thermal/heat treatment process, whereas a steel's hardness relates to material properties, (due to elements added during the alloying process, such as carbon, chromium, vanadium, cobalt, molybdenum, and tungsten).

Elements added during the alloying process will also influence hardenability. A steel's chemical structure will impact how deeply it will transform to martensite during a quenching method. Hardenability alludes to how deep into the steel we can achieve hardening upon quenching from high temperature. The hardenability of a steel can be measured using the Jominy End Quench Test. Here, one end of the steel is heated to the point of austenitizing and then quenched in a controlled and standardized flow of water. The surface of the steel is then grinded until there is no visible decarburization. Then it is measured at predefined, fixed intervals from the quenched end of the steel, along the length. This is a "rough depiction" of the Jominy End Quench Test and of how the hardenability of a steel is calculated.

When discussing structural hardness related to the measure of resistance to deformation/penetration, there are two different Rockwell tests that can be performed. The Rockwell B Scale uses a ball indenter, and the Rockwell C Scale (RC/HRC), uses a diamond indenter. The Rockwell C Scale (RC/HRC) seems to be the most common of the two. When used as a reference, it can help individuals understand the blade's resistance to penetration and irreparable deformation from another material. The higher the number on the HRC scale, the harder the steel. Hardness can also be correlated to a knife's strength. A steel that has an HRC above 55 on the Rockwell Scale is considered hard. Tensile strength increases or decreases on par with hardness. Therefore, the harder the steel, the greater the tensile strength. More information on the Rockwell C Scale can be viewed on page 434.

Toughness is yet another characteristic to consider, as it shows how resistant a blade will be to chipping or cracking. You want a blade to be somewhat malleable/ductile in order to prevent chipping or cracking. A good blade should be able to absorb impact without succumbing to either. In general, the harder the steel, the less tough or likely, to absorb impacts without chipping. Higher amounts of carbon, chromium, or tungsten will make a blade less tough, by increasing hardness, whereby making the blade more brittle. It is a give and take relationship, which is why metallurgy is a science. Achieving a balance between elements is crucial to the steel's final performance. Chromium aids in making blades harder, more wear resistant, and corrosion resistant, although, high amounts make it more brittle. This can be adjusted by adding nickel into the blend/mix. Nickel can help increase a steel's toughness and hardenability. Nickel is also extremely well at withstanding extreme cold temperatures.

Wear resistance is always an important consideration because a blade that wears easily means it will require a great deal of pampering over the course of the blade's lifetime. Wear can take several forms, such as abrasion, adhesion, galling, erosion, and spalling. The blade design can have a huge impact here, as well as exposure to certain temperatures and fluid environments. Wear can be measured by the levels of mass lost at a given time. The more you rub on a particular surface at a particular speed will eventually determine how much material is removed. At microscopic levels, metals are made up of an array of neatly packed atoms and molecules that create the lattice geometry. Controlling the atom's ability to move within the lattice aids in managing the strength, ductility, and wear properties. Naturally, metals are not perfect because they contain tiny irregularities, or defects, within the lattice. These irregularities/defects are generally referred to as dislocations, which are lines within the lattice that are damaged. These damaged points allow for additional movement to occur within the atoms and molecules. A dislocation means the bonding has defects. There are also voids within the lattice, known as vacancies, which allow for additional movement between the atoms and molecules within the lattice. These vacancies and irregularities, which contribute to a metal's weak point(s), can be prevented by altering its chemistry. A metal's chemistry is altered by alloying. Alloying means atoms of other elements are added, either larger or smaller than the current ones, to help fill the vacancies and thus restrict movement. Heat treat comes into play, as well, because this is where extreme heat temperatures rearrange atoms in the material, causing new, improved bonds. By reducing, or eliminating these dislocations and vacancies, a steel becomes stronger and harder, equating to less wear, overall.

Another factor to consider when choosing the right blade is corrosion resistance. Consider asking yourself the following questions: Where will most of your tasks and adventures take place? What will humidity levels be like? Will it be raining or is it a persistently wet environment in general? The level of corrosion resistance dictates the amount of resistance to rust an object has. Exposure to external elements, such as humidity, moisture, and salt can cause a blade to rust. It is important to understand that the natural elements that prevent corrosion on a blade will impact the blade's performance, such as its edge. Remember the "give and take" relationship. Higher levels of chromium increase the level of corrosion resistance. Typically, a steel must contain over 10.5% chromium to be considered stainless and at least 14% to be considered a true stainless. Usually, stainless steels contain between 10.5% to 30% chromium. Chromium forms a protective film that protects against rust. This does not mean it is impervious to rust and corrosion, rather, it will "resist" a little longer. Adding nickel to the mix can enhance the corrosion resistance of a blade. Silicon is another element to consider because it acts as a deoxidizer and also degasifies by helping to increase tensile strength, hardness, and forgeability.

Edge retention constitutes the amount of sharpness a blade's edge will retain after periods of use. This goes hand in glove with wear resistance, as well. Good edge retention is achieved by performing a balancing act between choosing the right steel alloy, the heat-treat process, and overall geometry. Yes, a blade's overall geometry and design play a significant role here. The style of blade, angle of the edge, as well as the type of grind, define the overall blade geometry, and are important when thinking about edge retention. Additional considerations would include whether there is a secondary bevel or not. Is it a convex grind versus a saber grind? You get the point.

As far as the types of steels go, well… that is an entirely different topic, and one that is covered under the knife steels section.

STEELS VS. LOW TEMPERATURES

Temperature, especially extreme temperatures, can have a huge impact on how blade steels perform. Extreme cold temperatures can easily bring about certain metals used in knife blades to chip or break. Temperatures colder than -40°C can begin to impact a blade's performance, depending on the material. Aluminum and titanium alloys are suitable choices when dealing with temperatures colder than -40°C. In fact, titanium alloys continue to perform well in temperatures between -75° to -100°C but are a little less reliable than a low carbon steel. Carbon steels are truly a better option for temperatures colder than -40°C. Low carbon steels can perform extremely well at temperatures colder than -75° to -100°C. It is important to note that the more carbon content, the harder and more brittle the material may become. Low carbon steels containing 3.5% nickel or higher is preferable. This is because nickel performs exceptionally well in freezing temperatures. Temperatures colder than -190°C require a high nickel content to prevent the material from breaking. Although it is highly unlikely that you will be recreationally using a knife outdoors in temperatures colder than -190°C. As a matter of fact, most people will not be using their knives outdoors in temperatures below -40°C. The way in which blade metals react to cold temperatures also depends on the Rockwell Hardness (HRC), and what alloys/elements are present in the blade material. PH stainless steels, (i.e., precipitation hardened stainless steels) are not suitable for temperatures below -25°C because they become brittle and may crack. Blade geometry, grind, and secondary beveling also play an important role in whether the material will roll, chip, or completely break.

Austenitic stainless steels perform well in colder temperatures because they typically contain 16%–26% chromium and up to 35% nickel. These stainless steels have high corrosion resistance and are also nonmagnetic. The most common type is the 18/8, or 304 grades, which contain 18% chromium and 8% nickel. *Helle* knives uses stainless steel 18/8 in order to protect blades from breakage in cold settings. *Helle* also adds a high carbon core to these blades, supporting their strong cutting edge, as a result of their triple lamination process. Austenitic stainless steels of the 300 series are suitable for temperatures down to -196°C.

Martensitic stainless steels are rather good candidates for low temperatures, (about -75°C), because they typically contain various amounts of manganese, nickel, chromium, molybdenum, and vanadium.

When considering low temperatures, the ideal material should have a low "Ductile-to-Brittle" temperature (DBTT). Metals such as aluminum, gold, silver, nickel, and copper have a Face-Centered Cubic (FCC) or alternatively called cubic close-packed, crystal lattice structure. Therefore, they do not undergo significant shifts from ductile to brittle. Metals such as iron, tungsten, and certain steels have a Body-Centered Cubic (BCC) crystal lattice structure, which tend to undergo a drastic shift, nearly linear, from ductile to brittle. Titanium is a hexagonal close-packed crystal (HCP), meaning it can experience changes in composition, referred to as lattice distortion, at certain temperatures. However, this refers to pure titanium (Grade 1–4), **not** a titanium alloy (Grade 5–38). When unalloyed titanium is heated to over 880°C, the atoms begin to rearrange, therefore transforming the lattice structure to a BCC. If you want a strong, durable titanium, then you need to change its chemistry to meet your intended goals. Heat treating and combining it with other elements can optimize titanium's performance. A titanium alloy can easily withstand extreme temperatures without any significant change due to the heat treat process and the additional elements added. Titanium Alloy – Grade 5 (Ti 6AL-4V) is the most widely used titanium alloy in the world.

In general, metallic crystals are not perfect. At times they may have voids, or empty spaces, known as vacancies, where atoms are missing. Metallic crystals may also have defects known as dislocations, which are lines of defective bonding. These imperfections can be corrected and altered by heat-treating and alloying. When steel is heated to certain temperatures the atoms rearrange. Combining or alloying the steel with other elements creates new bonds, where it can enhance its properties. Therefore, these two processes can create stronger steel alloys prepared to withstand extreme pressure and temperature.

Gransfors Bruk, Photographer: Emelie Torstensson.

KNIFE STEELS

All knife steels have iron (Fe); it is what you alloy the iron with that creates the type of steel-alloy and determines whether it is considered a carbon steel or stainless steel. There are additional steels to consider than just the typical carbon and stainless steels in the knife industry. There are tool steels and atypical steels that exist and are in current use for blade steels. I will try not to go too deep into the woods here and just give a list of the steels in use and a short description about the steel. I will also try to give an example of one or two knifemakers that are currently using the mentioned steel.

Alloying Elements:

A

Aluminum (Al): This element is used for deoxidizing steel, whereby making it more corrosion resistant. It also aids in grain refining, which produces increased hardness and overall strength.

C

Carbon (C): This element is the reason why there is life on earth. For the purposes of knifemaking, it increases the overall hardness of steel but too much can increase the brittleness.

Chromium (Cr): Increases toughness and corrosion resistance of steel. There must be more than 10.5% chromium in the steel to be considered a stainless, but most knifemakers consider the threshold to be at least 14% to be categorized a true stainless. High levels of chromium increase tensile strength, but can also reduce ductility.

Cobalt (Co): Increases the overall strength of steel.

Copper (Cu): Increases corrosion resistance and durability in steel.

M

Manganese (Mn): Increases the overall hardness but adding too much can also cause brittleness in the steel.

Molybdenum (Mo): Increases the overall hardness but adding too much can also reduce durability.

N

Nickel (Ni): Increases the overall toughness and corrosion resistance in steel.

Niobium (Nb): Increases strength and toughness in steel.

Nitrogen (N): This element is wonderful at improving wear resistance, strength, hardening rate, and corrosion resistance in steel. Too much of this element can have an adverse effect in the overall performance of the steel. The quantity that is added to steel needs to be carefully measured to prevent negative effects, such as inconsistent properties and some embrittlement of heat affected areas. Nitrogen does not react well with sulfur and oxygen, whereby limiting its absorption into the steel. This element does very well when paired with aluminum, to produce fine-grain size and improve the overall corrosion resistance.

P

Phosphorus (P): Increases the strength but adding too much also can cause brittleness in steel.

S

Silicon (Si): Increases overall strength in steel.

Sulfur (S): This element is seen sometimes seen as an impurity in the steel. Some knifemakers like to have small quantities of the element in the steel because it increases machinability. The downside is that it lowers the overall toughness of the steel.

T

Tantalum (Ta): This element is nearly immune to chemical degradation and shows very high levels of corrosion resistance. Adding this element to steel increases its overall ductility, rust resistance, wear resistance, and strength.

Tungsten (W): This is the hardest element on planet earth. It increases the durability of steel but adding too much of this element can also reduce ductility.

Titanium (Ti): Increases the overall strength and corrosion resistance in steel. It also helps reduce the density of steel objects, while also increasing the durability.

V

Vanadium (V): Increases the overall hardness and durability in steel.

Carbon Steels:

Very High Carbon Steel: 0.96%–2.1% carbon

High Carbon Steel: 0.55%–0.95% carbon

Medium Carbon Steel: 0.3%–0.54% carbon

Low Carbon Steel: 0.05%–0.25% carbon

The maximum carbon content a steel can have is 2.1%, anything over that amount will change its classification.

1095: A form of carbon steel with 0.95% carbon. It is typically used for survival and combat knives. This is a hard steel that can be easily sharpened in the field. This steel is highly favored by several knifemakers. The high carbon content means it can rust easily, therefore maintaining a light coat of oil on your blade is necessary. It can reach a HRC of about 55, potentially even higher to 59 HRC, while still maintaining the integrity. Going beyond 59 HRC introduces the possibility of the steel becoming too brittle, enabling it to easily chip during impact with other materials. It contains **0.90%–1.03% carbon, 0.30%–0.50% manganese, 0.040% phosphorus**, and **0.050% sulfur**.

Knifemakers such as ESEE, KA-BAR, and TOPS use it for their knives.

1095 CroVan (a.k.a Sharon Steel): This steel is a step up from the standard 1095, offering slightly better toughness and edge retention. It contains **0.95%–1.10% carbon, 0.40%–0.60% chromium, 0.5% manganese, 0.06% molybdenum, 0.25% nitrogen, 0.025% phosphorus, 0.25% silicon, 0.025 sulfur**, and **0.25% vanadium**.

This steel is used by KA-BAR knives on their Becker (BK) series.

1084: Known as the "beginner's steel" for forging. It is a great steel, with 0.80% (.80/.93) carbon content. When heat treated properly, it is suitable for large knives, due to its strength. This steel can rust if left, carelessly, in humid environments without a light coat of oil. It is also important to wipe down the blade after use to prevent rust. It has an HRC of 60. It contains **0.80%–0.93% carbon, 0.60–0.90% manganese, 0.050% phosphorus,** and **0.040% sulfur.**

Feder Knives uses this steel for some of their kitchen knives.

1075: Another high carbon steel, like 1095 and 1084, with the exception that it has less probability of chipping or breaking, due to the lower amounts of carbon. 1075 steel is a great option for large chopping knives, like parangs or goloks. It can reach 57 HRC, after suitable heat treat, without affecting the integrity of the steel. It contains **0.72%–0.80% carbon, 0.40%–0.70% manganese, 0.04% phosphorus,** and **0.05% sulfur.**

Condor Tool & Knife uses this steel for their large choppers, like the Argyll Scottish Machete, German Aviator Machete, King Kukri Machete (designed by Joe Flowers), Bolo Machete, Mini Duku Machete, and Parang Machete.

1070: Contains 0.65%–0.72% carbon. Another great option for machetes. This steel can take a real beating due to its toughness while still performing beyond expectations. It can be hardened to about 60 HRC. It contains **0.65%–0.75% carbon, 0.60%–0.90% manganese, 0.04% phosphorous,** and **0.050% sulfur.**

Schrade uses this steel for several of their knives.

1060: Has a carbon content of 0.55%–0.65%. A particularly good steel for swords and axes. The fact that it contains less carbon means that it can absorb more impact than the other higher carbon steels and not break. If heat treated properly, 1060 become extremely resilient. It also offers good hardness and pliability. It contains **0.55%–0.66% carbon, 0.60%–0.90% manganese, 0.040% phosphorus,** and **0.050% sulfur.**

Katanas can be made of this steel.

1055: Used in swords and some machetes, though needs to be heat treated properly to avoid breakage. It contains **0.48%–0.58% carbon, 0.60%–0.90% manganese, 0.040% phosphorus,** and **0.050% sulfur.**

Cold Steel uses this steel for several of their knives, such as their Kukri Machete, GI Tanto, Black Bear Bowie Machete, and their Jungle Machete. Gerber also uses this steel for their Gator Bolo Machete and Gator Kukri Machete.

1045: Used in axe heads, due to its low carbon content (**0.45%**), and high ductility, making it ideal for processing wood. This steel can withstand high levels of impact without chipping or breaking. It is also used when making multi-layered Damascus and when combined with other steels to produce, certain European swords. It is a great steel for traditional axe heads due to the dimensions/thickness of the head.

5160: Like 1060 in carbon content but mixed with more chromium. A very tough steel, with less chance of rusting than the other carbon steels. It has a hardening capability of 57-58 HRC. It contains **0.56%–1% carbon, 0.7%–0.9% chromium, 0.75%–1% manganese, 0.035% phosphorus, 0.15%–0.3% silicon,** and **0.04% sulfur.**

Winkler Knives and TOPS uses this steel for some of their knives.

Aogami/Blue Steel: A Japanese high carbon steel. Aogami Super is considered the best Japanese, high carbon steel for blades, developed by Hitachi Metals. This steel has great edge retention and hardness. Contains **1.40%–1.50% carbon, 0.3%–0.5% chromium, 0.30%–0.50% molybdenum,** and **2.0%–2.5% tungsten**.

Miura Knives uses this steel for their kitchen knives.

Shirogami/White Steel: This steel is known as the purest of carbon steels. It contains up to 2.7% carbon. This steel can achieve amazing hardness and good edge retention. It is highly recommended to patina the knives, so they may not rust as quickly. This steel is seen a great deal in Japanese kitchen knives. It contains **1.2%–1.4% carbon, 0.25% manganese**, and a hardness of 61 to 64 HRC.

This steel is used by Naoki Mazaki San, a Japanese bladesmith, who specializes in kitchen knives.

Tool Steels:

Tool steels contain high levels of carbon between 0.50%–1.50%. Considered carbon steel but developed mostly for industrial tooling. These are also high-speed steels and high wear resistant steels. Tool steels can be considered carbon steels, but not all carbon steels can be considered tool steels.

A-Grades (Air hardend, medium-alloy, cold work tool steels):

A2: An extremely tough steel, with fine wear resistance, and nice edge retention. Consists of a low chromium content, around 5%, meaning it will need to be maintained properly to avoid rust build-up. Carbon content is around 0.95%–1.05%, which means it has a lower wear resistance, than other tool steels. It has hardening "sweet spot" between 57–62 HRC. It contains **1% carbon, 5% chromium, 1% molybdenum**, and **0.4% vanadium**.

This steel is used by Bark River Knives, Winkler Knives (WKII), and L.T. Wright Knives. The steel was also used by Ron Lake in the late 1960s. George Herron began using it around the same time as Ron Lake.

A4: Air hardened, medium-alloy tool steel, with excellent toughness and good wear resistence. It contains **0.95% - 1.05% carbon, 0.90% - 2.20% chromium, 0.25% copper, 1.80% - 2.20% manganese, 0.90% - 1.40% molybdenum, 0.30% nickel, 0.50% silicon**, and **0.03 sulfur**.

A6: Air hardened, medium-alloy tool steel, exhibiting exceptional toughness. Contains a wear resistance between an O1 and a D2. It has a hardness range between 61–62 HRC. It has **0.70% carbon, 1% chromium, 2% magnesium, 1.25% molybdenum, 0.30% nickel**, and **0.50% silicon**.

A10 (Graph-Air): Graphitic, medium-alloy tool steel, that is air hardened. This steel contains graphite particles, enabling self-lubrication in dry environments, which aid with oil retention. Can be hardened to over 60 HRC, at a low hardening temperature, reducing size change and deformation during heat treatment. A10 exhibits great wear resistance, high toughness, and excellent machinability. The steel contains **1.35% carbon, 1.80% manganese, 1.50% molybdenum, 1.85% nickel**, and **1.20% silicon**.

D-Grades (D-Type):

D2: An air hardened tool steel with a high chromium content, though not high enough to consider it a true stainless steel (14% chromium or above). Carbon content ranges between 1.50%–1.60%. Has great edge retention and good wear resistance. Due to the high chromium content, it has a moderately good rust resistance. Can be a fairly hard steel to sharpen, depending on the sharpening method used. Although, if using a belt sharpener (i.e., Work Sharp, Ken Onion), it may not take much effort to give it a nice working edge. It has a hardness in the range of 55–62 HRC. It contains **1.50%–1.60% carbon, 11.00%–13.00% chromium, 0.25% copper, 0.60% manganese, 0.70%–1.20% molybdenum, 0.30% nickel, 0.60% silicon, 0.03% phosphorus, 0.03% sulfur,** and **0.90%–1.10% vanadium.**

D2 is a popular knife steel, used by Benchmade (Adamas), ESEE (Zancudo, Avispa), Medford Knives (Praetorian), L.T. Wright Knives, Ontario Knife Company (RAT 1), KA-BAR (D2 Extreme). Famous knifemaker Bob Dozier used D2 for some of his knives, as seen with his Bob Dozier Chute Knife.

O-Grades (Oil hardened tool steels):

O1: A forgiving steel, both easy to work with and heat treat. It is also an oil-hardened tool steel. Has exceptional edge retention and toughness. Can be rough on grinding belts due to its overall toughness. O1 was developed by the Halcomb Steel Company in 1905, (which was later acquired by Crucible Steel). O6 is the tougher steel "brother" of O1, though not typically used for knives. Has a hardness in the range of 57 - 62 HRC. It contains **0.90% carbon, 0.50% chromium, 1.20% manganese, 0.30% nickel, 0.30% silicon, 0.50% tungsten,** and **0.20% vanadium.**

O1 steel is used by several knifemakers, such as L. T. Wright, Randall Knives (W.D. "Bo" Randall— RIP), Battle Horse Knives, Tree Man Knives, and Behring Made Knives.

Uddeholm produced a version of O1, called UHB-46.

O2: An oil-hardening tool steel with excellent wear resistance and good edge retention. Equivalent to K720, and similar to 90MnCrV8. It has hardness in the range of 63–65 HRC, which is acceptable for light/medium use knives. It contains **0.85% carbon, 1.40% manganese, 0.03% phosphorus,** and **0.03% sulfur.**

M-Grades (High-speed tool steels with Molybdenum between 3.5% to 10%):

M2: A strong steel that can hold an edge slightly longer than D2, although rather brittle. Not recommended for knives with large blades. It has about 0.85%–1.05% carbon, but only about 4% chromium, meaning it has low rust resistance, though better than O1. It contains **1.05% carbon, 4.5% chromium, 0.25% copper, 0.40% manganese, 5.5% molybdenum, 0.30% nickel, 0.03% phosphorus, 0.45% silicon, 0.03% sulfur, 6.75% tungsten** and **2.2% vanadium.**

This steel has been used by Benchmade for some of their knife models. Spyderco has also used this steel for a couple of their models, such as the Paramilitary 2 and the Spyderco Military.

M3: A high-speed tool steel that contains high amounts of carbon and tungsten. This steel is also referred to as REX M3-1 or PM M3. It contains **1.05% carbon, 4.15% chromium, 5.75% molybdenum, 6.15% tungsten,** and **2.5% vanadium.**

M4: A super versatile high-speed tool steel with high amounts of carbon, vanadium, and tungsten. It has a hardness of 61 HRC. It contains **1.30% carbon, 4.25% chromium, 4.75% molybdenum, 5.85% tungsten,** and **4.1% vanadium.**

M7: A high-speed tool steel with great edge toughness and wear resistance. This steel has very high amounts of molybdenum. It contains **1.02% carbon, 3.8% chromium, 8.6% molybdenum, 1.8% tungsten**, and **1.9% vanadium**.

S-Grades (Shock resisting tool steels):

S1: Shock resistant tool steel, that contains **0.40%–0.55% carbon** and **0.15%–1.20% silicon**.

Used by Roman Landes, famous German knifemaker and metallurgist.

S7: Strong shock resistant tool steel either air or oil hardened. This steel has a high impact toughness. It contains **0.45%–0.55% carbon, 3.00%–3.50% chromium, 0.25% copper, 1.30%–1.80%, 0.20%–1.00% manganese, molybdenum, 0.03% phosphorus, 0.20%–1.00% silicon, 0.03% sulfur,** and **0.20%–0.30% vanadium**.

Used by Roman Landes, famous German knifemaker and metallurgist.

W-Grades (Water hardened tool steels):

W1: A water hardening tool steel with high percentage of carbon content. A small amount of chromium is added to increase rust resistance and hardenability. It can achieve a hardness of 50–51 HRC. It contains. **0.70%–1.50% carbon, 0.15% chromium, 0.2% copper, 0.10%–0.40% manganese, 0.1% molybdenum, 0.2% nickel, 0.10%–0.40% silicon,** and **0.15% tungsten**.

W2: Water hardening tool steel, like W1, and without vanadium or chromium. Prone to rust, due to the lack of chromium. This steel is not very tough compared to other carbon steels. Can reach a maximum hardness of 65 HRC. It contains **1.15% carbon, 0.15% chromium, 0.25% manganese, 0.10% molybdenum, 0.20% nickel,** and **0.25% silicon**.

SK Series:

SK3: A Hitachi-produced tool steel with the lowest carbon content, compared to SK4 and SK5. Has high amounts of phosphorus and sulfur compared to other Japanese steels. Easy to sharpen and polish and is particularly tough (just not ideal), for kitchen knives, due to its impurities. SK3 has good wear resistance, helping to balance out the knife with its other characteristics. A good choice for beginner chefs on a budget wanting to experiment with carbon steel. Once a patina sets in, it becomes less reactive and more tolerable to maintain. How this steel performs also depends on who produced it, as there is also SK3 (Sanyo), SK3 (Nisshin) and SK3 (Aichi). It contains **1.00% carbon, 0.15%–0.50% manganese, 0.030% phosphorus, 0.15%–0.35% silicon,** and **0.030% sulfur**.

SK4: A carbon tool steel that is tougher than SK3 and contains chromium, molybdenum, and vanadium. Known for its high hardenability and toughness. It contains **1.04% carbon, 0.40% manganese, 0.35% phosphorus, 0.035% silicon,** and **0.030% sulfur**.

Used in Japanese kitchen knives.

SK5: Tougher than SK3 and SK4. Known as a mid-range Japanese carbon tool steel. The maximum hardness level of SK5 is about 65 HRC. Shares similar properties to other steels, such as W2 and 1084. It has **0.9% carbon, 0.3% chromium, 0.25% copper, 0.50% manganese, 0.25% nickel, 0.03% phosphorus, 0.35% silicon,** and **0.03% sulfur**.

This steel is mostly used in Japanese kitchen knives.

K series (developed by Bohler-Uddeholm):

K340: A non-stainless, cold work steel. It has outstanding toughness, excellent strength, good wear resistance, and moderate corrosion resistance. It has **1.10% carbon, 8.30% chromium, 0.40% manganese, 2.10% molybdenum, 0.90% silicon,** and **0.50% vanadium.**

K390: A non-stainless, cold work tool steel. An exceptionally tough steel with similar edge hold to A11. This steel is difficult to grind and sharpen; patience and consistency are key when trying to resharpen the edge. It has more durability, strength, and wear resistance than CPM M4. M390 has a higher edge retention than K390. It has **2.47% carbon, 4.25% chromium, 2% cobalt, 0.4% manganese, 3.8% molybdenum, 0.55% silicon, 1% tungsten,** and **9% vanadium.**

Used by Spyderco, on their Spyderco Police 4.

K980: Low alloy tool steel.

K990: Water hardend tool steel. This steel is similar to W1 tool steel. It contains **1.03% carbon, 0.07% chromium, 0.14% copper, 0.22% manganese, 0.01% molybdenum, 0.10% nickel, 0.014% phosphorus, 0.17% silicon,** and **0.012% sulfur.**

Crucible Particle Metallurgy (CPM) Tool Steel:

CPM 1V: High alloy, medium carbon tool steel, with extremely high toughness and heat resistance. It has moderate wear resistance; much better than an A2 tool steel. It has higher toughness than most shock-resistant tool steels, as well as CPM 3V. It has **0.55% carbon, 4.50% chromium, 2.75% molybdenum, 2.15% tungsten,** and **1% vanadium.**

CPM 3V: This is the ideal knife steel due to its high toughness, wear resistance, and structural composition. By many avid outdoorsmen and knifemakers it is considered the "Holy Grail" of knife steels for bushcraft. Can handle high levels of stress and impact and has maximum resistance to chipping, or breaking. It handles impact better than A2, D2, Cru-Wear, or CPM M4. Because it has high levels of carbon, it *can* rust, just not as easily as 1095, D2, or even A2. Due to it being alloyed with moderate levels of chromium, vanadium, and molybdenum, any rust formed can easily be wiped off with a steel wool and repolished. The rust will not cause heavy penetration like in other steels. It contains **0.80% carbon, 7.50% chromium, 1.30% molybdenum,** and **2.75% vanadium.**

CPM 3V is used by L. T. Wright, Bark River, Benchmade, and many others. It is a great steel to use on hunting, survival, and bushcraft knives.

CPM 4V: A powder metal tool steel with a higher wear resistance than CPM 3V but just not as tough. Due to its extremely high carbon content it can rust, so make sure to care for it properly. It has **1.35% carbon, 5% chromium, 0.40% manganese, 2.95% molybdenum, 0.80% silicon,** and **3.85% vanadium.**

Used by Bark River, Spyderco, and Kizlyar.

CPM 9V: Has excellent wear resistance, greater than CPM 10V and D2. It has low strength because it can only be hardened to about 56 HRC or lower. It has a high carbon content, and so it should be maintained properly to avoid corrosion. It has **1.80% carbon, 5.25% chromium, 0.50% manganese, 1.30% molybdenum, 0.90% silicon,** and **9% vanadium.**

CPM 10V: An exceptional wear resistance steel, with extremely high carbon and vanadium. Due to the high carbon content, it is important to exercise good maintenance by wiping down after use and adding some oil on the blade before storage. Even though it has a high vanadium content helping to resist rust, it is always good to exercise good maintenance on any high carbon steel. It has **2.45% carbon, 5.25% chromium, 0.50% manganese, 1.30% molybdenum, 0.90% silicon, 0.07% sulfur**, and **9.75% vanadium.**

This steel is used by Spyderco in their K2 model.

CPM 15V: This is crucible's highest abrasion resistant steel on the market. It has an extremely high carbon and vanadium content. It has more vanadium than any other crucible tool steel. This is a remarkably high wear resistant tool steel. Because of its high carbon content, make sure to maintain the blade properly to prevent rust buildup. It has **3.40% carbon, 5.25% chromium, 0.50% manganese, 1.30% molybdenum, 0.90% silicon, 0.07% sulfur**, and **14.50% vanadium**.

This steel is used by Andrey Biryukov on a couple of his skinner knives.

CPM CRU-WEAR: An air-hardened tool steel with superior properties related to wear resistance and toughness. It has greater toughness and wear resistance than the conventional Cru-Wear. It has more vanadium carbides than D2, making it a harder steel with superior wear resistance. It has enough tungsten and molybdenum content, which provide additional hardness capabilities. It has more impact toughness than A2, D2, and M2. It contains **1.1% carbon, 7.5% chromium, 1.6% molybdenum, 1.14% tungsten**, and **2.4% vanadium**.

This steel is used by Spyderco and Bark River.

CPM M4: A tough steel with excellent wear resistance and has around **1.42% carbon**. It has better wear resistance then M2 and M3.

This steel is used by Bark River.

Other Tool Steels:

Sleipner: A high-carbon tool steel developed by Bohler-Uddeholm. Its chemical composition enables it to be tempered to a high hardness with great ductility and strength. Easy to grind and capable of obtaining a razor-sharp edge with good edge retention. It has a decent amount of chromium, meaning it will have moderate corrosion resistance. It has **0.9% carbon, 7.8% chromium, 0.5% manganese, 2.5% molybdenum, 0.9% silicon**, and **0.5% vanadium.**

S390: A Bohler-Uddeholm powder metallurgy steel. This steel has good hardness, strength, and wear resistance. Offers good toughness, but not as tough as M390. S390 is not a stainless steel like M390. It is a stronger steel than M390, though more brittle. It contains **1.64% carbon, 4.80% chromium, 8% cobalt, 0.30 manganese, 2% molybdenum, 0.60% silicon, 10.40% tungsten**, and **4.80% vanadium.**

Vascowear: An air-hardend tool steel that contains a high vanadium content. It is an extremely hard steel to come by, because of the very low production amount. It has higher wear resistance than D2 and greater toughness than M2. This steel is like CPM CRU-WEAR. It contains **1.12% carbon, 7.75% chromium, 0.30% manganese, 1.60% molybdenum, 1.20% silicon, 1.10% tungsten**, and **2.40% vanadium.**

K3 (Nippon Koshuha): Water hardend Japanese tool steel, with great wear resistance and toughness.

Daido YK3: Water hardend Japanese tool steel, exhibiting good wear resistance and toughness. It contains **1.10%–1.30% carbon, 0.30% chromium, 0.25% copper, 0.10%–0.50% manganese, 0.25% nickel, 0.03% phosphorus, 0.35% silicon,** and **0.030% sulfur.**

YC3 (Hitachi): Water hardening Japanese tool steel that has good wear resistance and impact toughness. It contains **1.10%–1.30% carbon, 0.30% chromium, 0.25% copper, 0.50% manganese, 0.25% nickel, 0.03% phosphorus, 0.30% silicon,** and **0.030% sulfur.**

T70 (Trinec): Low alloy tool steel produced in the Czech Republic. It contains **0.70%–0.80% carbon, 0.15% chromium, 0.20% copper, 0.40% manganese, 0.10% molybdenum, 0.20% nickel, 0.025% phosphorus, 0.40% silicon, 0.025% sulfur, 0.15% tungsten,** and **0.10% vanadium.**

T100 (Trinec): Water hardend tool steel produced in the Czech Republic. It contains **1.10% carbon, 0.15% chromium, 0.20% copper, 0.40% manganese, 0.10% molybdenum, 0.20% nickel, 0.025% phosphorus, 0.40% silicon, 0.025% sulfur, 0.15% tungsten,** and **0.10% vanadium.**

OC70 (Metal Ravne): Low alloy tool steel produced in Slovenia. It contains **0.70% carbon, 0.25% manganese,** and **0.20% silicon.**

MAXAMET: Made by Carpenter Technology, a non-stainless, high-speed, powder tool steel with remarkably high hardness and great edge retention. Due to its non-stainless quality (about 4% chromium), it *can* rust. Always remember to wipe it down after use and add a drop of mineral oil or Tsubaki knife oil, on both sides of the blade. A fairly hard steel to sharpen, so be patient and consistent when trying to resharpen the edge. High amounts of vanadium and tungsten make it an extremely hard alloy, with particularly good wear resistance. MAXAMET contains **2.1% carbon, 4.75% chromium, 6% cobalt, 0.3% manganese, 0.25% silicon, 0.07% sulfur, 13% tungsten,** and **6% vanadium.**

Spyderco uses this steel on some of their folding knives.

Stainless Steels:

In order to be considered a stainless steel there must be a chromium content higher than 10.5%, although, most knifemakers consider a true stainless to be of 14% chromium or higher.

154CM: A steel first introduced by Bob Loveless (R. W. Loveless) in the early 1970s. Created by Crucible Materials Corporation (Crucible Industries). New 154CM batches, however, are not being produced to the same standards as the earlier stock. It is still a great steel, just not as good as those produced in the 1970s. It is like 440C, but tougher and harder. It can be hardened between 59 - 61 HRC. It contains **1.05% carbon, 13.50%–14% chromium, 0.50% manganese, 4% molybdenum, 0.03% phosphorus, 0.70% silicon, 0.03% sulfur, 0.00%–0.40% tungsten,** and **0.00%–0.40% vanadium.**

AEB-L: A strong stainless steel, which seemingly holds up under high levels of stress and pressure. It has a similar hardness to that of ELMAX. It has higher toughness than ELMAX, CPM-154, M390, and D2, though a lower edge retention. Similar qualities to Sandvik 12c27. Makes a great steel for bushcraft and kitchen knives. It contains **0.68% carbon, 13% chromium, 0.6% manganese, 0.025% phosphorus, 0.4% silicon,** and **0.014% sulfur.**

This steel is being used by L. T. Wright (Genesis, Jessmuk, Northern Hunter, NextGen, and GNS), and Ken Avery Knives (Kitchen Knives).

ATS-34: A steel first introduced by Bob Loveless (R. W. Loveless) to the knife community. Is a Japanese steel developed by Hitachi Metals, Ltd. Similar to 154CM, with its wonderful stainless steel and great qualities. Tough, with great edge retention, and rust resistance. The usual Rockwell hardness is 59-61 HRC. It contains **1.05% carbon, 14% chromium, 0.40% manganese, 4.0% molybdenum, 0.03% phosphorus, 0.35% silicon,** and **0.02% sulfur.**

This steel is used by A. G. Russell for several of his knives.

410: A **12% chromium** martensitic steel, which can be hardened to reach great strength and wonderful edge retention.

Kershaw uses this steel for some of their knife handles.

416: A martensitic steel, great for knife guards, bolsters, pommels, butt caps, liners, and spacers. It contains **0.15% carbon, 12.0%–14.0% chromium, 1.25% manganese, 1.0% silicon, 0.06% phosphorus,** and **0.15% silicon.**

420 & 440 Series (420HC, 420B, 440A, 440B, 440C):

420HC: is used a great deal in the knife community. This steel has good strength, wear resistance, durability, and great corrosion resistance. It can be hardened between 56 - 58 HRC. It contains **0.40%–0.50% carbon, 13.0% chromium,** and **0.60% molybdenum.**

Buck Knives uses 420HC for several of their knives, and in their iconic Buck 110 Folding Hunter. They also use it on their current version of the classic Buck 119 Special Hunter. The original 119 gained major popularity upon its release in the 1940s. The knife was designed by Hoyt Buck himself, the founder of Buck Knives.

Gerber uses 420HC on their LMF II Infantry knife.

440A: contains **0.65%–0.75% carbon, 16.00%–18.00% chromium,** and **0.75% molybdenum.**

440B: contains **0.75%–0.95% carbon, 16.00%–18.00% chromium,** and **0.75% molybdenum.**

440C: contains **0.95%–1.20% carbon, 16.0%–18.0% chromium,** and **0.75% molybdenum.**

440C is used by A. G. Russel for some of their knives, one being the A. G. Russell Signature Sting3.

AUS Series:

AUS-6: A low-cost steel with about **0.65% carbon**, comparable to 440A. It can be hardened between 55 - 57 HRC. It contains **0.55%–0.65% carbon,** and **13.0%–14.5% chromium.**

AUS-8: A better steel than AUS-6, with **0.75% carbon**. It is a strong steel, comparable to 440B. It can be hardened between 57 - 59 HRC. It contains **0.70%–0.75% carbon, 13.0%–14.5% chromium,** and **0.10%–0.30% molybdenum,**

SOG knives uses this steel for several of their knives. Cold Steel and CRKT also use this steel for several of their knives.

AUS-10: A top quality, hard steel, comparable to 440C, with **1.10% carbon** content. Is the strongest of the AUS series of steels, produced by Aichi Steel, in Japan. This steel also contains trace amounts of nickel, manganese, and silicon to enhance the ductility and elasticity. It can be hardened between 58 - 60 HRC.It contains **0.95%–1.10% carbon, 13.0%–14.5% chromium,** and **0.10%–0.31% molybdenum.**

AUS - 10 has been used by Spyderco for some of their knives. Cold Steel uses AUS-10 as well. It is also used in Japanese kitchen knives.

CPM SxxV Series (Crucible Industries):

CPM S30V: Chris Reeve worked closely with Dick Barber from Crucible Industries, to develop this steel. This steel has excellent edge retention, moderate toughness, amazing corrosion resistance, and is quite easy to sharpen. Much tougher than 440C and D2, with better corrosion resistance than 440C. It can be hardened between 59 - 61 HRC. This is a martensitic stainless steel that contains **1.45% carbon**, **14% chromium**, **2% molybdenum**, and **4% vanadium**.

This steel is used by Benchmade, Chris Reeve, and Spartan Blades.

CPM S35VN: Chris Reeve worked closely with Dick Barber from Crucible Industries, to develop this steel. The main difference between S30V and S35VN is the addition of niobium, hence the "N" at the end of the name. This steel is slightly tougher than S30V, offering pretty much the same great edge retention and corrosion resistance. The addition of niobium carbides, in replacement of vanadium, makes S35VN 15% tougher, than S30V. It can be hardened between 59 - 61 HRC. A martensitic stainless steel that contains **1.40% carbon**, **14% chromium**, **2% molybdenum**, **0.50% niobium**, and **3% vanadium**.

This steel is used by Chris Reeve and Spartan Blades.

CPM S45VN: First introduced by Frank Cox, Knife Steel Specialist at Niagara Specialty Metal. The final refinement of the chemistry was performed by Bob Skibitski of Crucible Industries. S45VN offers improved corrosion and wear resistance over CPM S35VN. It has more chromium than S35VN, making it a high-grade stainless steel. Nitrogen was also added into the mix, meaning it has a higher edge retention by about 5%. It is not as tough as S35VN, though tougher than S30V. It can be hardened between 59 - 61 HRC. This is a martensitic stainless steel that contains **1.48% carbon, 16% chromium, 2% molybdenum, 0.50% niobium, 0.15% nitrogen** and **3% vanadium**.

This steel is used by Bark River, Chris Reeve, and Spartan Blades.

CPM S90V: A martensitic stainless steel made by the Crucible Particle Metallurgy process. This steel offers better corrosion and wear resistance over 440C and D2. This is an excellent tool steel that can be used for EDC knife blades, without having to worry too much about rusting. Even though this steel has high carbon content, it is alloyed with high amounts of chromium which balances out the corrosion resistance. It can be hardened between 56 - 59 HRC. This steel contains **2.30% carbon**, **14% chromium**, **1% molybdenum**, and **9% vanadium**.

This steel is used by Benchmade, Spyderco, Fox Knives, and Maxace Knives.

CPM S110V: A martensitic stainless steel made through the Crucible Particle Metallurgy process. This steel has a higher carbon, chromium, and molybdenum content than S90V, with the addition of niobium and cobalt, for improved toughness. It can be hardened between 58 - 61 HRC. This steel is far superior to S90V, in corrosion and wear resistance. It contains **2.8% carbon, 15.25% chromium, 2.50% cobalt, 2.25% molybdenum, 3% niobium**, and **9% vanadium**.

This steel is used by Spyderco, Zero Tolerance, and DireWare.

CPM S125V: This is a rare, martensitic stainless steel that is not widely available, or used, for that matter. It offers the highest edge retention on the market as far as stainless steels are considered. Due to its extremely high wear resistance, it is exceedingly difficult to machine and sharpen. Contains **3.25% carbon, 14% chromium, 0.50% manganese, 2.50% molybdenum, 0.03% phosphorus, 0.90% silicon, 0.03% sulfur, 0.40% tungsten,** and **12% vanadium**.

This steel is used by Fantoni in Italy.

VG (V Gold) Series:

VG-1: A high carbon, Japanese stainless steel manufactured by Takefu Special Steel Co., LTD. This steel has better edge retention than 440C, VG-10, or ATS 34. It contains **1% carbon, 15% chromium**, and **0.4% molybdenum**.

This steel is used by Cold Steel as well as Japanese kitchen knifemakers.

VG-2: A high carbon, Japanese stainless steel, manufactured by Takefu Special Steel Co., LTD. This steel is a strong, semi-alloy stainless steel with particularly good edge retention and in addition to strength. The steel is very ductile and resilient, making it tough. It can be hardened to about 57–58 HRC. It contains **0.70% carbon, 15% chromium**, and **0.20% molybdenum**.

This steel is used by Japanese knifemakers, particularly for kitchen knives. It is also used by Fallkniven.

VG-5: A high carbon, Japanese stainless steel manufactured by Takefu Special Steel Co., LTD. Provides good hardenability, toughness, corrosion resistance, and wear resistance. Can be hardened to about 59 HRC. It contains **0.80% carbon, 15% chromium, 0.40% molybdenum**, and **0.20% vanadium**.

VG-10: A high carbon, Japanese stainless steel manufactured by Takefu Special Steel, Co., LTD. This is a high alloy stainless steel developed over sixty years ago. Widely used in knife blades by knifemakers around the world. This steel has great edge retention, good corrosion resistance, and can be hardened to about 60 HRC. Although it is a hard steel, it is not difficult to sharpen. VG-10 is a great option for kitchen knives, bushcraft knives and EDC pocketknives. It contains **1.05% carbon, 15.5% chromium, 1.5% cobalt, 0.5% manganese, 1.2% molybdenum, 0.03% phosphorous**, and **0.3% vanadium**.

This steel is used by Spyderco, Fallkniven, Boker, and Zwilling J. A. Henckels.

CTS Series (Carpenter Technology Corporation):

CTS-BD1: A budget friendly, entry level, vacuum-melted stainless steel developed by Carpenter Technology Corporation. CTS -BD1 has decent edge retention and wear resistance. This steel contains **0.9% carbon, 15.75% chromium, 0.6% manganese, 0.30% molybdenum, 0.10% vanadium**, and **0.35% silicon**.

This steel is used by Spyderco.

CTS-40CP: Produced by Carpenter Technology Corporation, this steel alloy is a powder metallurgy, high carbon, and chromium stainless steel. Can be hardened to about 61.5 HRC and has similar properties to 440C. It is a good stainless steel with great corrosion resistance, and toughness. It contains **1.20% carbon, 16%–18% chromium, 1% manganese, 0.75% molybdenum, 0.04% phosphorus, 1% silicon**, and **0.03% sulfur**.

This steel is used by Bob Dozier.

CTS-204P: A nearly identical steel to M390. This is a premium US-made steel that uses tungsten as an alloy, which equates to high strength and wear resistance. The high amounts of chromium make it a great corrosion resistant steel. It contains **1.90% carbon, 20% chromium, 0.35% manganese, 1% molybdenum, 0.60% silicon, 0.65% tungsten, and 4% vanadium.**

This steel is used by Microtech.

CTS-XHP: An exceptionally good steel for EDC, surgical instruments, and kitchen knives. Its high carbon and chromium content make it a strong, corrosion-resistant stainless steel. This steel has high amounts of niobium, which increases hardness and wear resistance. It has **1.6% carbon, 16% chromium, 0.5% manganese, 0.8% molybdenum, 0.35% niobium, 0.4% silicon, and 0.45% vanadium.**

This steel is used by Spyderco, SOG, Jason Clark, CRKT, and Cold Steel.

CrMo/CrMoV Series:

14-4CrMo (Latrobe): A martensitic stainless steel with good wear resistance and better corrosion resistance than 440C. The molybdenum in the steel provides the high wear resistance and edge retention. This steel is nearly identical to ATS-34 and 154CM. It contains **1.05% carbon, 14% chromium, 0.50% manganese, 4% molybdenum, and 0.30% silicon.**

2Cr13: A martensitic stainless steel with good corrosion resistance and hardness produced in China. Typically used for precision tools, such as surgical blades or other fine cutting tools. It contains **0.16%–0.25% carbon, 12%–14% chromium, 1% manganese, 0.60% nickel, 0.040% phosphorus, 1% silicon, and 0.030% sulfur.**

3Cr13: A martensitic stainless steel with low carbon and high chromium content produced in China. Aside from iron, the main ingredient in this steel is chromium, with about 13%. Though it has a low carbon amount, it has just enough manganese and silicon to increase its strength slightly. It is a decent steel to use for EDC knives and comes at an affordable price. It shares similar properties with 420js. It has **0.35% carbon, 13% chromium, 1% manganese, 0.6% nickel, 0.04% phosphorus, 1% silicon, and 0.03% sulfur.**

4Cr13: A martensitic steel with a low carbon and high chromium content produced in China. It has a higher hardness than 3Cr13 after quenching. It can be hardened to about 50 HRC, has good corrosion resistance, and decent wear resistance. It contains **0.40% carbon, 13.5% chromium, 0.80% manganese, 0.60% nickel, 0.040% phosphorus, 0.60% silicon, and 0.030% sulfur.**

This steel is typically used for kitchen knives or small EDC knives.

4Cr14MoV: A low carbon and high chromium stainless steel produced in China. This is a low-end, budget friendly steel, and can be compared to 420 steel with slight improvements in the properties as far as corrosion resistance. It contains **0.48% carbon, 14.50% chromium, 1% manganese, 0.50% molybdenum, 0.035% phosphorus, 1% silicon, 0.03% sulfur, and 0.15% vanadium.**

5Cr15MoV: A low-end stainless steel produced in China, with low carbon and high chromium content. This steel is typically used in budget-friendly kitchen knives. It can reach a hardness of 54 HRC. It contains **0.5% carbon, 15% chromium, 0.40% manganese, 0.60% molybdenum, and 0.10% vanadium.**

6Cr16MoV: This steel is an improvement in strength and corrosion resistance from 4Cr14MoV and 5Cr15MoV. It is produced in China and typically found in kitchen knives or small EDC knives. It contains **0.60% carbon**, and **16% chromium** which translates to decent strength, with good corrosion and wear resistance.

7Cr17MoV: This is a budget-friendly stainless steel that is produced in China. This is a good option for small, fixed blades or EDC folding knives. It is affordable and a great option steel to practice bushcraft and sharpening techniques, without having to worry about losing serious cash should you damage it. It also has high amounts of chromium, making it a good choice for an affordable fishing knife. The steel contains **0.75% carbon, 17%–18% chromium, 1% manganese, 0.75% molybdenum, 0.60% nitrogen, 0.04% phosphorus, 1% silicon**, and **0.04% sulfur.**

8Cr13MoV: Stainless steel produced in China with high carbon and chromium content. It has similar properties to AUS-8. This steel is quite popular in the knife community and is budget friendly as well. Offers good edge retention, corrosion resistance, hardness, and wear resistance. The steel contains **0.80% carbon, 14.5% chromium, 1% manganese, 0.30% molybdenum, 0.20% nickel, 0.04% phosphorus, 1% silicon, 0.04% sulfur**, and **0.25% vanadium.**

This steel is used by Spyderco.

9Cr13MoVCo: Martensitic stainless steel part of the Cr13 family, produced in China. Has similar properties to AUS-10, and can be hardened to about 59 HRC, making it a pretty hard steel. Contains **0.85% carbon, 13.50% chromium, 1% cobalt, 1% manganese, 0.20% molybdenum, 0.035% phosphorus, 1% silicon, 0.30% sulfur**, and **0.20% vanadium.**

9Cr18MoV: Martensitic stainless steel with high chromium and high carbon content produced in China. Can be hardened to about 60 HRC, making it a hard steel and good option for bushcraft and survival knives. This steel compares to 440C, as they share a similar chemical composition. Contains **0.95% carbon, 18% chromium, 0.80% manganese, 1.30% molybdenum, 0.60% nitrogen, 0.04% phosphorus, 0.80% silicon, 0.03% sulfur**, and **0.12% vanadium.**

This steel is used by Civivi for their EDC knives.

Sandvik Series:

Sandvik steels have small/fine carbines distributed throughout the steel, ensuring high toughness (ductility) and sharpening ease. Sandvik steels can be easily sharpened to razor-sharp standard with little effort. Due to Sandvik's amazing cutting performance it can be used for razor blades, kitchen knives, and even wood carving knives.

6C27: This is a low carbon martensitic stainless steel with generous amounts of chromium, making it corrosion-resistant tough steel. This steel it typically found in butter knives and potato peelers, where the need for wear resistance is low. It contains **0.32% carbon, 13.7% chromium, 0.3% manganese, 0.25% phosphorous, 0.2% silicon**, and **0.010% sulfur.**

7C27Mo2: A particularly good, overall steel for knives. It is a martensitic stainless steel with generous amounts of chromium. If heat treated and hardened properly, it can offer good corrosion resistance, high toughness, and decent wear resistance. This steel can be found in the cutters for electric shavers. It contains **0.38% carbon, 13.5% chromium, 0.6% manganese, 1% molybdenum, 0.025% phosphorous, 0.4% silicon**, and **0.010% sulfur.**

This steel is used by Kershaw.

12C27: Developed in Sweden by Sandvik AB, this is an excellent steel for bushcraft, or any other outdoor activity. It also performs very well as a steel for kitchen knives. One of my personal favorite knife steels, due to its toughness and corrosion resistance. It is quite easy to sharpen and a great steel for a bushcraft beginner on a low-to-mid budget range. It contains **0.60% carbon, 13.5% chromium, 0.40% manganese, 0.025% phosphorus, 0.40% silicon,** and **0.010% sulfur.**

This steel is used by Boker, Spyderco, CRKT, Opinel, Bastinelli, Fred Perrin, Casstrom, Karesuando, Telkut, Stedemon, RUIKE, EKA, Brisa/EnZo, and Morakniv.

12C27M: First developed in Sweden by Sandvik AB. Some would place this steel under the tool steel category, as it was first produced with the intention of using it for kitchen tools. Can easily out-perform various other steels in the kitchen and the outdoors. Has excellent edge retention, hardness, toughness, and great corrosion resistance. This steel is quite easy to sharpen; minimal effort will get this steel razor sharp. It has more corrosion resistance than the standard 12C27. It has **0.50% carbon, 14.5% chromium, 0.60% manganese,** and **0.40% silicon.**

This steel is used by Bear and Son, Buck, and Opinel.

13C26: If searching for a steel that can be easily sharpened to a razor-sharp edge, then 13C26 should be your first choice. This Sandvik Steel was specifically designed for razor blades. It is a hard stainless steel with great corrosion resistance and edge stability. It contains **0.68% carbon, 12.9% chromium, 0.60% manganese,** and **0.40% silicon.**

Typically found in razor blades or surgical blades. This steel is used by MCM, Buck Bond Arms, and Kershaw.

14C28N: This Sandvik steel is tough, and the high amounts of chromium make it a good corrosion-resistant steel. This steel is a high alloy stainless steel, containing an interesting mixture of manganese, silicon, and phosphorus. This steel makes a good choice for kitchen and EDC knives. It contains **0.62% carbon, 14% chromium, 0.6% manganese, 0.11% nitrogen, 0.25% phosphorus, 0.2% silicon,** and **0.01% sulfur.**

This steel is used by Kershaw.

19C27: The most wear resistant knife steel in the Sandvik Series line-up. The carbides are more on the coarse side, meaning edge angles and stability are therefore limited. This steel is intended for box cutter blades where a high level of toughness and wear resistance is needed. The steel contains **0.95% carbon, 13.5% chromium, 0.65% manganese,** and **0.40% silicon.**

This steel is typically used for box cutter blades but can also be found in kitchen knives.

Super Stainless Steel:

H1: This steel offers the highest corrosion resistance currently in the knife industry. It simply will not rust on you. It can be left at the bottom of the sea floor for days, possibly months, and will show little to no rust. This is the best steel for those who enjoy aquatic sports and live near humid environments. When I go deep sea fishing, this is knife steel is first on my list. In addition to its incredible corrosion resistance, it offers good edge retention and strength. H1 is a precipitation-hardened stainless steel, developed in Japan. It contains **0.15% carbon, 16% chromium, 0.1% copper, 2.0% manganese, 1.5% molybdenum, 8.0% nickel, 0.1% nitrogen, 4.5% silicon, 0.04% phosphorus,** and **0.03% sulfur.**

This steel is used by Spyderco in their "Salt Series."

N680: This is probably the most inexpensive nitrogen-alloyed stainless steel available. The edge retention is not great, more on the low-to-mid level, but still a little better than 420. N680 is easy to grind and heat treat; that, paired with cost, make it a good choice for those beginning their journey as a knifemaker. Do not kid yourself, even though this steel has subpar edge retention, it is still a very tough cookie and can handle a beating. This steel is also a great choice for those who enjoy aquatic sports and reside in humid environments. The steel contains **0.54% carbon, 17.30% chromium, 0.40% manganese, 1.10% molybdenum, 0.20% nitrogen, 0.45% silicon,** and **0.10% vanadium**.

This steel is used by Benchmade, Hogue, and Lone Wolf.

N690: This steel is a step up from N680 because it has higher carbon, manganese content, with the addition of cobalt. Although not considered a high-end steel anymore, it is still a great steel and a wonderful option for those who reside in wet or highly humid environments. This steel falls in third place, as far as the best steel for aquatic sports; H1 would be first and LC200N as second. This is still strong and offers great wear and corrosion resistance. N690 contains **1.07% carbon, 17% chromium, 1.5% cobalt, 0.40% manganese, 1.10% molybdenum, 0.40% silicon,** and **0.10% vanadium**.

This steel is used by Boker, Fox, Bastinelli, GiantMouse, and Andre De Villiers.

LC200N: This steel offers high corrosion resistance and great edge retention. This steel is great for those looking for a high corrosion resistant steel for an aquatic lifestyle, the "Salt Life," for lack of a better term. This steel is perfect for the kind of person who needs a good knife while fishing or spending the day kayaking. This knife is perfect for humid or wet environments. It would also perform very well in the kitchen. This steel contains **1.0% carbon, 15% chromium, 1.0% manganese, 1.0% molybdenum, 0.5% nickel,** and **0.5% nitrogen**.

This steel is used by Spyderco in their "Salt Series."

CPM-20CV: A nearly identical steel to M390. This is a martensitic stainless steel with high amounts of vanadium and chromium. This steel contains the highest amount of chromium than any other stainless steel, making it a super stainless steel. The corrosion resistance of this steel is nearly unmatched, except for M390. It is remarkably like M390, some even may say it is the same steel, but 20CV has micro amounts higher phosphorus and sulfur than M390. The difference between 20CV and M390 is practically unnoticeable. It contains **1.9% carbon, 20.00% chromium, 1.0% molybdenum, 0.6% tungsten,** and **4.0% vanadium**. Note: CPM 20CV is produced by Crucible, whereas M390 is produced by Bohler.

This steel is used by Zero Tolerance, Kershaw, Benchmade, and Spyderco.

M390: Developed and produced by Bohler-Uddeholm. A martensitic super steel, exhibiting superior corrosion and wear resistance, with high hardness. This steel contains exceptionally large amounts of chromium, molybdenum, vanadium, and tungsten. Widely used by knifemakers due to its superior properties. It can be a bit hard to sharpen, just remember to be patient and consistent. This steel contains **1.90% carbon, 20.00% chromium, 0.30% manganese, 1.00% molybdenum, 0.70% silicon,** and **0.60% tungsten,** and **4.00% vanadium**.

Knife companies such as Mircotech, LionSTEEL, Fox Knives, MKM, GiantMouse, and Viper Knives use this steel for some of their knife blades.

M398: Developed and produced by Bohler-Uddeholm. It has better edge retention and corrosion resistance than M390, with the drawback being that it is harder to sharpen due to its high HRC. It contains **2.70% carbon, 20.00% chromium, 0.50% manganese, 1.00% molybdenum, 0.50 % silicon, 0.70% tungsten,** and **7.20% vanadium**.

Other Stainless:

ZDP-189: High-end Japanese stainless steel developed via Powder Metallurgy. It varies in percentages of carbon and chromium, therefore providing great hardness and corrosion resistance. Typically, this steel will be found mostly in kitchen knives, but it can be found in EDC knives too. Because the steel has high hardness levels, with a maximum hardness of 67 HRC, one can expect excellent edge retention. The remarkably high levels of chromium make it an incredible stainless steel, where corrosion is not a major concern. The downside, though, is that it is awfully hard steel, making sharpening difficult, especially for beginners. It contains **3% carbon, 20% chromium, 0.5% manganese, 1.4% molybdenum, 0.4% silicon, 0.60% tungsten,** and **0.1% vanadium.**

This steel is used by Spyderco.

R2: A powdered stainless steel that shares remarkably similar properties to SG-2. It has similar edge retention to ZDP-189, although lacks the wear resistance, which does make it easier to sharpen. This steel is mostly found in Japanese kitchen knives but can also be found in survival or hunting knives. It contains **1.35% carbon, 16.00% chromium, 0.40% manganese, 3.00% molybdenum, 0.03% phosphorus, 0.03% sulfur, 0.50% silicon,** and **2.00% vanadium.**

This steel is used by Shun and Fallkniven.

BG-42: A martensitic stainless high-speed steel. Is double vacuum melted to assure a high level of cleanliness and top-notch properties. This is an excellent knife steel with great wear and corrosion resistance. Blades made with this steel show wonderful edge retention. BG-42 is typically hardened to 61-61 HRC. Showcases similar hardness to M50, but with the corrosion and oxidation resistance of 440C. This steel is remains popular with custom knifemakers. It contains **1.15% carbon, 14.5% chromium, 0.5% manganese, 4% molybdenum, 0.3% silicon,** and **1.2% vanadium.**

RWL34: A martensitic, rapid solidified powder (RPS) steel that was given the name "RWL," after R. W. Loveless. Has superior corrosion resistance, hardness, and strength. This steel, which closely resembles 154CM, was produced by Damasteel, in Sweden, as a powder metallurgy version of ATS34. It contains **1.05% carbon, 13.5% chromium, 0.50% manganese, 4% molybdenum, 0.50% silicon,** and **0.2% vanadium.**

This steel is used by Brisa for some of their knives, as in the Brisa Scara 60 neck knife.

Cowry-X: A powder metallury "super steel" developed by renowned knifemaker Mr. Ichiro Hattori in Seki, Japan. Contains **3.00% carbon, 20.00% chromium, 1.00% molybdenum,** and **0.3% vanadium.**

Used by Fallkniven in their HK9cx and NL5cx.

ELMAX: Developed by Bohler-Uddeholm. As far as toughness and edge retention is concerned, this steel can take a beating and still perform remarkably well. Has exceptional corrosion resistance and great dimensional stability. Contains **1.7% carbon, 18.0% chromium, 0.30% manganese, 1.0% molybdenum, 0.80% silicon,** and **3.0% vanadium.**

This steel is used by Spyderco, Bradford Knives, LionSTEEL, Bark River, Dew Hara, Heretic, Fox, Shirogorov, Fallkniven, Bastinelli, Microtech, Enzo, GiantMouse, and Moorhaus.

SPY27: A Crucible steel, produced exclusively for Spyderco. Great corrosion resistance, hardness, and edge retention. Contains **1.25% carbon, 14% chromium, 1.5% cobalt, 2% molybdenum, 1% niobium, 0.1% nitrogen,** and **2% vanadium.**

This steel is currently used exclusively by Spyderco.

Atypical Steels:

4116 Krupp: German steel offering high stain resistance though poor edge retention.

Used by Henkels in some of their kitchen knives. Boker also uses this steel for their fillet knives. Boker's blades (with this steel) typically have a 56-58 Rockwell hardness and undergo a sub-zero quench process.

80CRv2: An extraordinarily strong steel containing low amounts of chromium and vanadium. This steel is tough and a great option for survival and bushcraft knives, including tomahawks and swords. This is not a stainless steel, so it tends to rust easily if not cared for properly. It is high in carbon, but still very tough, and capable of taking on heavy tasks. The steel contains **0.85% carbon, 0.60% chromium, 0.50% manganese, 0.10% molybdenum, 0.40% nickel, 0.025% phosphorus, 0.30% silicon, 0.30% sulfur** and **0.25% vanadium**.

Used by Daniel Winkler, Master Bladesmith and owner of Winkler Knives.

X55CrMo14 or 1.4110: A martensitic steel that contains **15% chromium, 0.5%–0.8% molybdenum, 0.48%–0.60% carbon, 1.0% manganese, 1.0% silicon, 0.15% vanadium, 0.040% phosphorus,** and **0.015% sulfur.** This steel exhibits great corrosion resistance.

Used by Swiss Army/Victorinox in some of their pocketknives.

Vanax: An atypical stainless steel produced by Bohler-Uddeholm containing extremely high amounts of nitrogen and chromium. This steel is tougher than ELMAX, exhibiting amazing corrosion resistance while easy to sharpen. It contains **0.36% carbon, 18.20% chromium, 0.30% manganese, 1.10% molybdenum, 1.55% nitrogen, 0.30% silicon,** and **3.50% vanadium**.

Vanax 37/Vanax SuperClean: Developed and produced by Bohler-Uddeholm. It is a third-generation powder metallurgy nitrogen steel. This is a super, corrosion resistant, stainless steel, with good wear resistance and a fine-grain microstructure. Because of its high HRC, around 60–62 HRC, a cryo or deep freeze is needed in the heat treatment process to go beyond the 60 HRC limit. This steel is a massive concoction of alloys, containing **0.005% aluminum, 0.36% carbon, 18.20% chromium, 0.05% cobalt, 0.09% copper, 0.30% manganese, 1.10% molybdenum, 1.55% nitrogen, 0.18% nickel, 0.187% phosphorus, 0.30% silicon, 0.009% sulfur, 0.06% tungsten,** and **3.50% vanadium.**

K490: A Bohler-Uddeholm, niobium-alloyed high carbon steel. Niobium centric steels, (or niobium-alloyed steels), focus on niobium as the "special component" to improve the steel's overall properties, such as with the formation of harder carbides which contribute to grain size refinement and wear resistance. Normally, this steel would fit in the same categories as S35VN, or S110V, but because it has a lower chromium and contains 3.7% tungsten, it is more of an atypical steel. Contains **1.4% carbon, 6.4% chromium, 1.5% molybdenum, 0.5% niobium, 3.7% tungsten,** and **3.7% vanadium.**

Niolox: A niobium-alloyed stainless steel. The addition of niobium aids in wear resistance and grain refinement. Better grain refinement equates to a tougher, stronger steel. Contains **0.8% carbon, 12.7% chromium, 1.1% molybdenum, 0.7% niobium,** and **0.9% vanadium.**

This steel is used by Kizlyar and LionSTEEL.

Nitrobe77: A remarkably interesting steel because it includes niobium and nitrogen. This is a stainless steel with extreme toughness. It contains **0.1% carbon, 14.5% chromium, 3.0% molybdenum, 0.5% niobium, 0.9% nitrogen,** and **0.1% vanadium.**

Nitrobe77 steel is used by Des Horn.

3V Mod: This steel has the second highest niobium content of all the niobium-alloyed steels and also contains tungsten and nitrogen. A special steel, with extremely high toughness and strength. Contains **0.8% carbon, 7.5% chromium, 1.3% molybdenum, 2.5% niobium, 0.1% nitrogen, 1.5% tungsten,** and **0.75% vanadium.**

RN15X: This steel is produced by Dorrenberg–Edelstahl from Germany. This martensitic steel has the highest niobium content of all the niobium-alloyed steels by far. Could easily fall under the stainless steel category, but due to the extremely high amounts of niobium, it falls in the atypical category. High amounts of niobium equate to great wear resistance, toughness, and strength. This steel has **1.4% carbon, 15% chromium, 2.0% molybdenum,** and **4.5% niobium.**

CPM REX 45: A cobalt centric, super high-speed steel. The high cobalt content enables this steel to have good wear resistance and toughness. Contains **1.30% carbon, 4.05% chromium, 8.0% cobalt, 0.30% manganese, 5.00% molybdenum, 0.50% silicon, 0.06% sulfur, 6.25% tungsten,** and **3.05% vanadium.**

This steel is used by Spyderco.

CPM MagnaCut: An extraordinary steel created by Larrin Thomas, author of knifesteelnerds.com. A niobium and nitrogen alloyed steel. This steel contains properties to fall under a high carbon steel category, yet almost enough chromium to be considered a stainless steel. It has the same capabilities (toughness and edge retention) as CPM Cru Wear or CPM 4V, but with more corrosion resistance. A great knife steel, making it useful in several knife styles such as survival, bushcraft, combat, and even EDC. CPM MagnaCut has an exceptionally fine microstructure which translates in toughness, strength, and sharpening ease. This steel contains **1.15% carbon, 10.7% chromium, 2.0% molybdenum, 2.0% niobium, 0.2% nitrogen,** and **4.0% vanadium.**

In its infancy, this steel was tested and is used by Shawn Houston, Phil Wilson, Darrin Thomas, Devon Thomas, and Matthew Gregory. Now several knifemakers use it, such as Bark River Knives, Dawson Knives, Demko Knives, and Spyderco.

Laminate Steels:

3G: Produced in Japan as a powder laminate steel and used to reinforce other steels to make the blades stronger. Typically, a laminate steel would be about 20% stronger than a stainless steel. The layering for a 3G laminate steel would be VG2-SGS-VG2.

Used by Fallkniven in their SK1 (Jarl), SK3 (Juni), HK9, FH9, FH9s, TK1, TK2, TK3, TK4, TK5, TK6, U1, P/36, PXL, and a few other knives.

Laminated CoS: Contents 420J2-CoS-420J2

Used by Fallkniven in their SK6 (Krut), V1, GP, FH9bh, PXLwh, Alpha, Delta, Sierra, Zulu, KK, F1, F1 Pro, S1 Pro, SK2 (Embla), and several other knives.

Laminated SGPS (Super Gold Powder Steel): Contents 420J2-SGPS-420J2

Used by Fallkniven in their U2 and U4 knives.

Laminated VG10: 420J2-VG10-420J2

Used by Fallkniven in their NL1 (Tori), NL2 (Odin), NL3 (Njord), NL4 (Frej), NL5 (Idun), F1, F2, F3, F4, K1, K2, WM1, H1, S1, A1, and A2 knives.

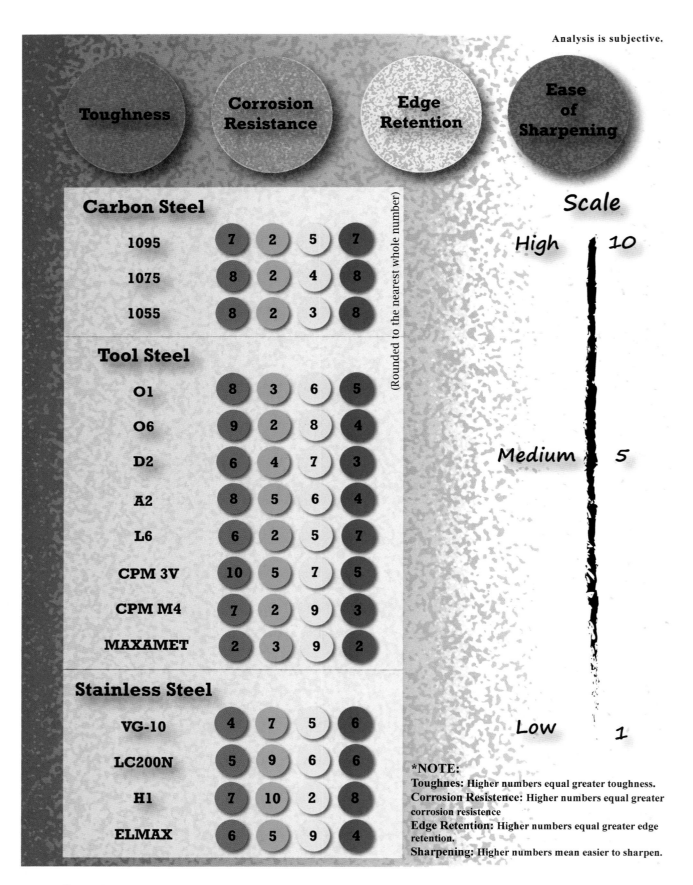

Analysis is subjective.

Toughness

Corrosion Resistance

Edge Retention

Ease of Sharpening

(Rounded to the nearest whole number)

Carbon Steel

	Toughness	Corrosion Resistance	Edge Retention	Ease of Sharpening
1095	7	2	5	7
1075	8	2	4	8
1055	8	2	3	8

Tool Steel

	Toughness	Corrosion Resistance	Edge Retention	Ease of Sharpening
O1	8	3	6	5
O6	9	2	8	4
D2	6	4	7	3
A2	8	5	6	4
L6	6	2	5	7
CPM 3V	10	5	7	5
CPM M4	7	2	9	3
MAXAMET	2	3	9	2

Stainless Steel

	Toughness	Corrosion Resistance	Edge Retention	Ease of Sharpening
VG-10	4	7	5	6
LC200N	5	9	6	6
H1	7	10	2	8
ELMAX	6	5	9	4

Scale

High 10

Medium 5

Low 1

*NOTE:
Toughnes: Higher numbers equal greater toughness.
Corrosion Resistence: Higher numbers equal greater corrosion resistence
Edge Retention: Higher numbers equal greater edge retention.
Sharpening: Higher numbers mean easier to sharpen.

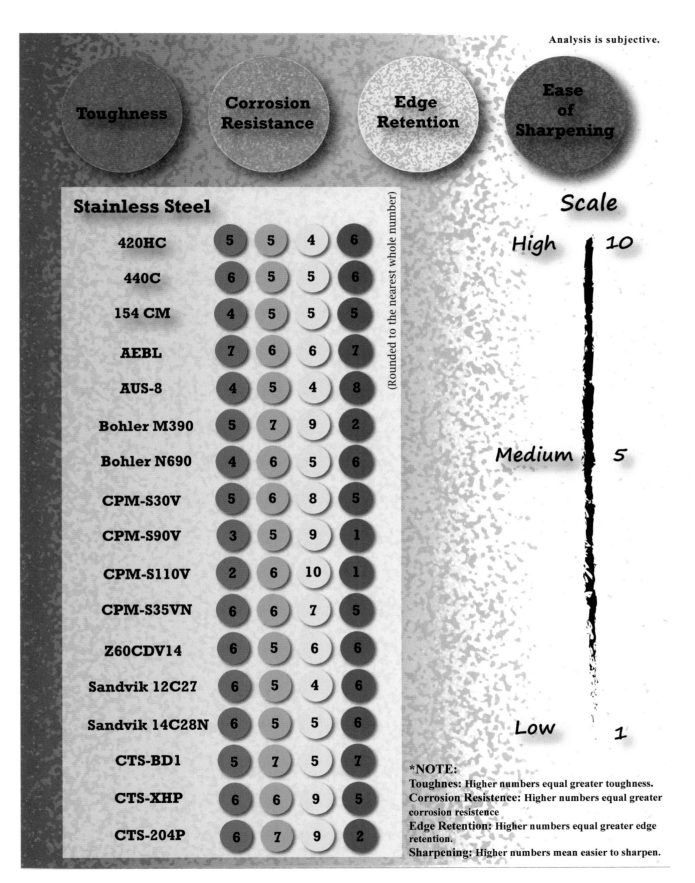

Analysis is subjective.

Stainless Steel	Toughness	Corrosion Resistance	Edge Retention	Ease of Sharpening
420HC	5	5	4	6
440C	6	5	5	6
154 CM	4	5	5	5
AEBL	7	6	6	7
AUS-8	4	5	4	8
Bohler M390	5	7	9	2
Bohler N690	4	6	5	6
CPM-S30V	5	6	8	5
CPM-S90V	3	5	9	1
CPM-S110V	2	6	10	1
CPM-S35VN	6	6	7	5
Z60CDV14	6	5	6	6
Sandvik 12C27	6	5	4	6
Sandvik 14C28N	6	5	5	6
CTS-BD1	5	7	5	7
CTS-XHP	6	6	9	5
CTS-204P	6	7	9	2

(Rounded to the nearest whole number)

Scale

High 10

Medium 5

Low 1

*NOTE:
Toughnes: Higher numbers equal greater toughness.
Corrosion Resistence: Higher numbers equal greater corrosion resistence
Edge Retention: Higher numbers equal greater edge retention.
Sharpening: Higher numbers mean easier to sharpen.

BLADE COATING VERSUS NO COATING

If you are interested in a knife made with a steel that is highly corrosive in humid environments or simply rusts easily if not cared for properly, then a blade coating might be a good option. Coatings found in outdoor, bushcraft, or survival knives can sometimes be too thick and have gritty surfaces. Do not remove them; instead, take high grit sandpaper like 1,500 or above and gently sand down the coating to smooth it out. The coating is there for a reason, which is to protect the blade steel from corrosion. Sometimes these hard use steels can corrode easily and require a lot of maintenance. If you are in the wilderness or a survival situation, it might be too cumbersome to always be rubbing your blade with a little oil or making sure it is always dry. Another reason knifemakers add coatings is to reduce the amount of time you are dedicated to caring for your knife blade. Knives are made to be used and enjoyed, not to be a chore or pain to deal with. Blade coatings are good and are there for a reason, so do not remove them entirely—simply adjust the surface texture to your liking with high grit sandpaper.

Either way, the more you use your knife, the more you will inevitably remove parts of the coating. If you would like to recoat your blade, ask the knifemaker if they provide this service, either for free or a fee. If your knife blade would benefit from a coating and the knifemaker cannot restore the coating, then adding a forced patina is a good option. There are also some circumstances where certain coatings are not an option because they can create unwanted surface friction when chopping or slicing objects, making chopping or slicing gritty and rough. In a situation like one presented in a kitchen, where we need razor-sharp cutlery and smooth, frictionless slicing, then adding a patina to the blade is more appropriate than a coating. The forced patina process can be accomplished by heating up some apple cider vinegar in a pot to a boiling point. Once the vinegar begins to boil, remove it from the heat. If your knife blade is anywhere from 3 to 6.5 inches in height, then you can use a mason jar as your vessel to patina your blade. Pour the hot apple cider vinegar into the correct size mason jar and then place your knife blade into the mason jar. Make sure you boiled enough vinegar to reach the bolster or cover the entire blade. Do not stick the handle into the hot vinegar or you will damage it. To protect the handle before putting the knife blade into the mason jar, use some painters' tape and plastic wrap to protect the handle. You only want to put the blade into the hot vinegar. Another option is to remove the handle scales, if possible. Once the blade is in the mason jar with the hot vinegar, it should take about thirty minutes to one hour for it to patina. Pull the knife/blade out of the mason jar, and DO NOT WIPE IT DOWN. Oxygen plays an important role in the oxidation process too, therefore, let it air dry for a few minutes. Once air dried, add oil the blade, then gently wipe it off. Re-oil the blade if you are going to store it away; otherwise it is ready for use. The abovementioned forced patina process creates what is known as black oxide on the blade. Black oxide provides corrosion protection, but it is more on the mild to moderate protection. We will cover a little more about black oxide in the Knife Storage section, on page 276.

Some people like to use mustard to add a patina to their blades. To do this, remove the handles, if possible, or tape them up. Lay the knife on a tray and cover one side of the blade with mustard, then flip the knife and cover the other side as well. Wait about thirty minutes to one hour, then gently remove the mustard with a damp cloth. If you are not happy with the design, then add a little more mustard and reconfigure, as necessary. The areas not covered with mustard will typically not patina. Once the knife blade achieves a patina you are happy with, wipe it down with a clean, damp rag and add a little oil to it.

Any substance that contains the right amount of acidity (low pH Level) should work to patina your blades, just be careful not to use toxic chemicals. It is quite easy to patina your blade using natural ingredients (orange, lemon, apple, potato, onion, vinegar, etc..), without having to use something that is potentially toxic.

Photograph taken by A.J.

Blade Grinds

Full Flat   Scandi   Double Bevel   Saber   Chisel   Convex   Hollow

Graphics created by A.J. - Blade Grinds
Background Photo - Gransfors Bruk, Photographer: Emelie Torstensson.

Blade Types

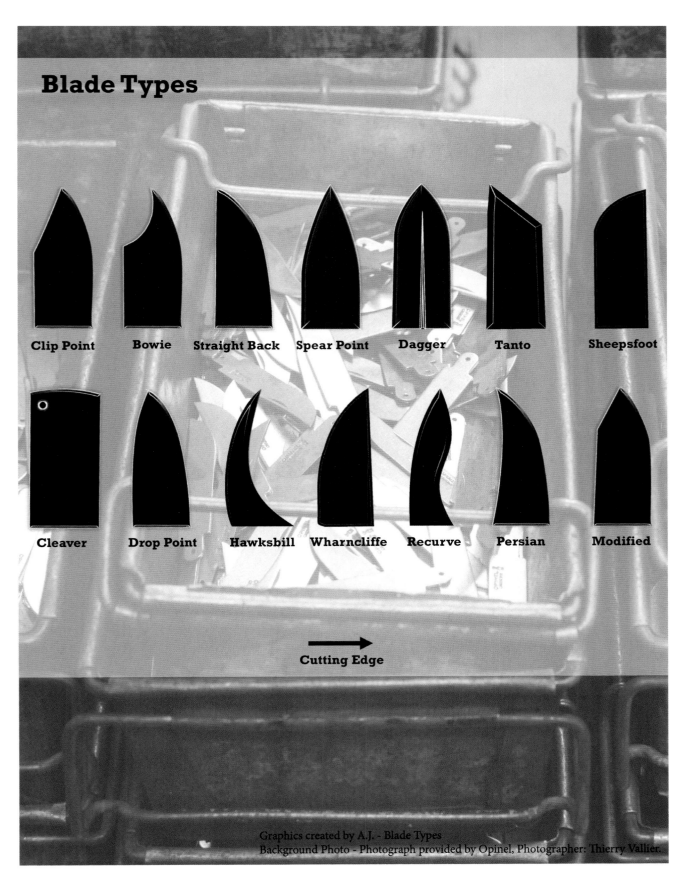

Clip Point   Bowie   Straight Back   Spear Point   Dagger   Tanto   Sheepsfoot

Cleaver   Drop Point   Hawksbill   Wharncliffe   Recurve   Persian   Modified

Cutting Edge

Graphics created by A.J. - Blade Types
Background Photo - Photograph provided by Opinel, Photographer: Thierry Vallier.

Knife Tangs

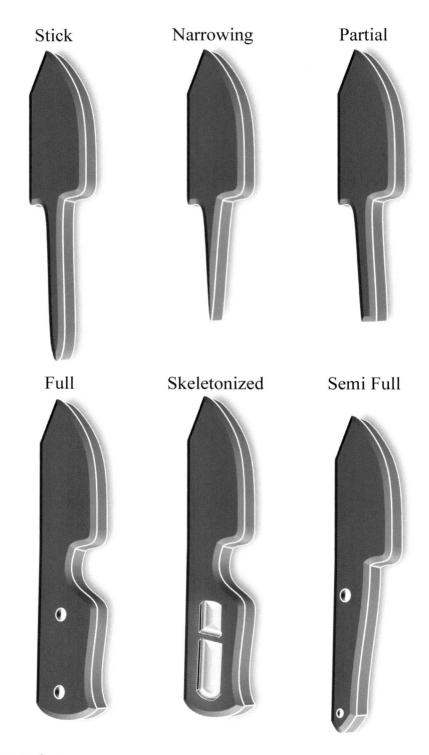

Stick   Narrowing   Partial

Full   Skeletonized   Semi Full

Graphics created by A.J. - Knife Tangs

Edge Types

PLAIN

PARTIALLY SERRATED

FULLY SERRATED

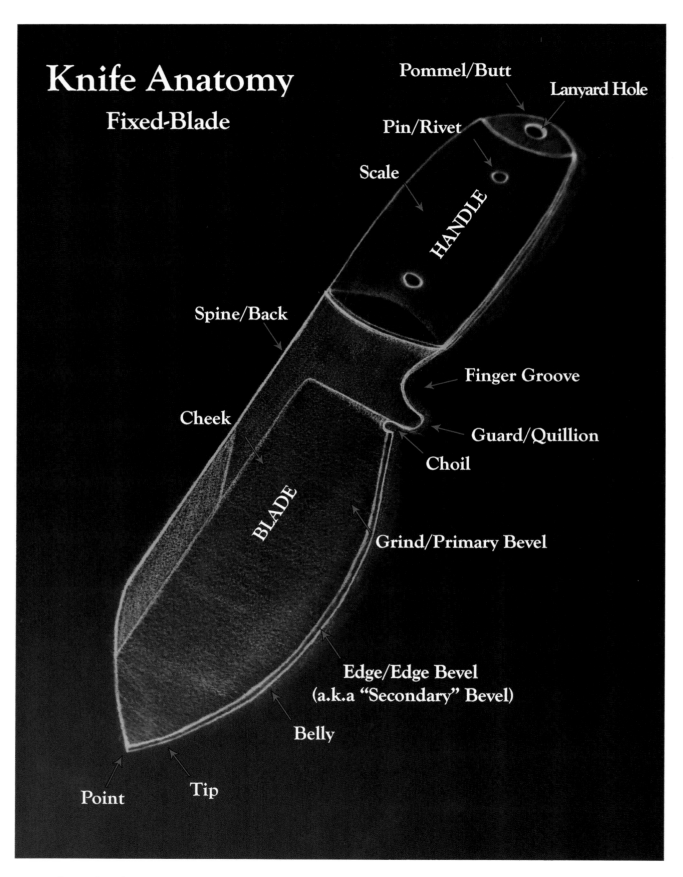

Knife Anatomy
Fixed-Blade

Pommel/Butt

Lanyard Hole

Pin/Rivet

Scale

HANDLE

Spine/Back

Finger Groove

Cheek

Guard/Quillion

Choil

BLADE

Grind/Primary Bevel

Edge/Edge Bevel
(a.k.a "Secondary" Bevel)

Belly

Point

Tip

Knife Anatomy
Folding Knife

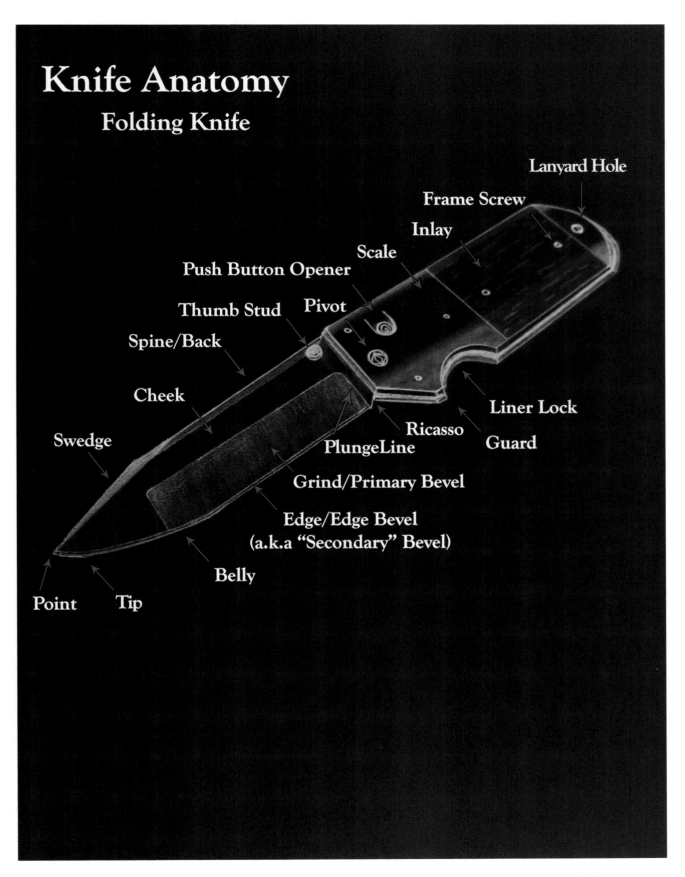

Lanyard Hole

Frame Screw

Inlay

Scale

Push Button Opener

Thumb Stud

Pivot

Spine/Back

Cheek

Liner Lock

Swedge

Ricasso

Guard

PlungeLine

Grind/Primary Bevel

Edge/Edge Bevel
(a.k.a "Secondary" Bevel)

Belly

Point   Tip

Straight Razor Grinds

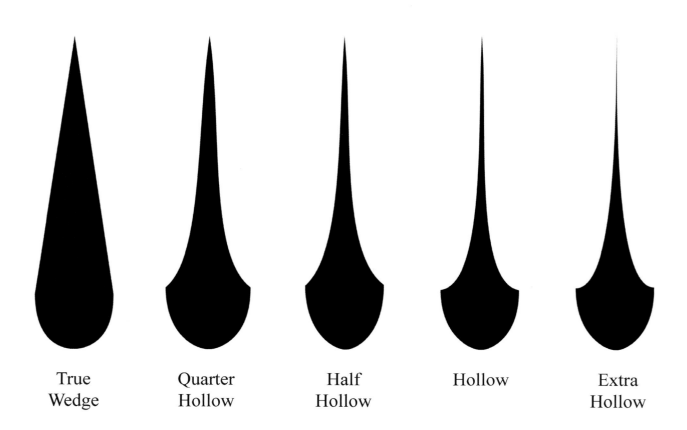

True
Wedge

Quarter
Hollow

Half
Hollow

Hollow

Extra
Hollow

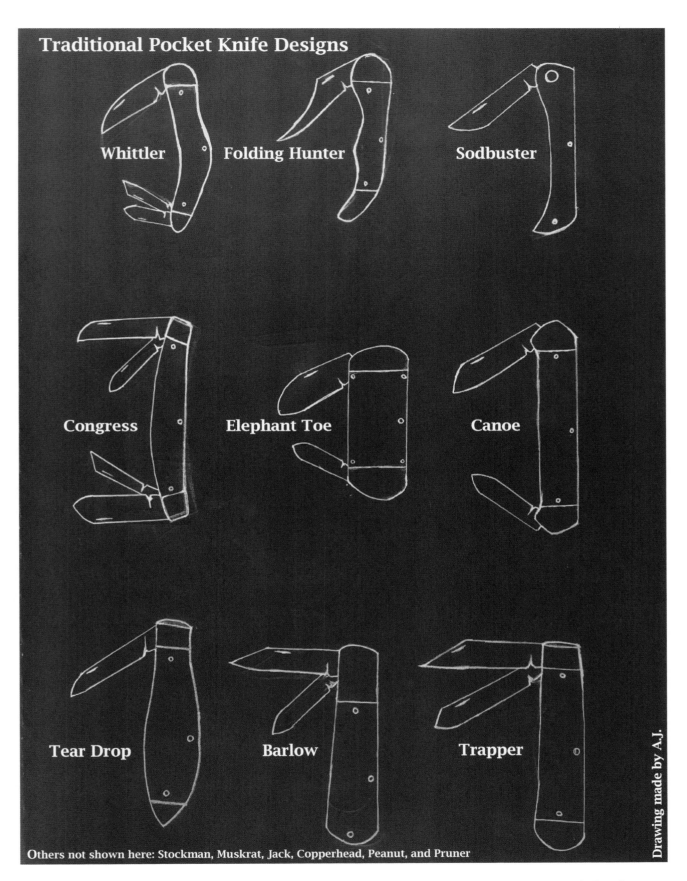

Traditional Pocket Knife Designs

Whittler

Folding Hunter

Sodbuster

Congress

Elephant Toe

Canoe

Tear Drop

Barlow

Trapper

Others not shown here: Stockman, Muskrat, Jack, Copperhead, Peanut, and Pruner

Drawing made by A.J.

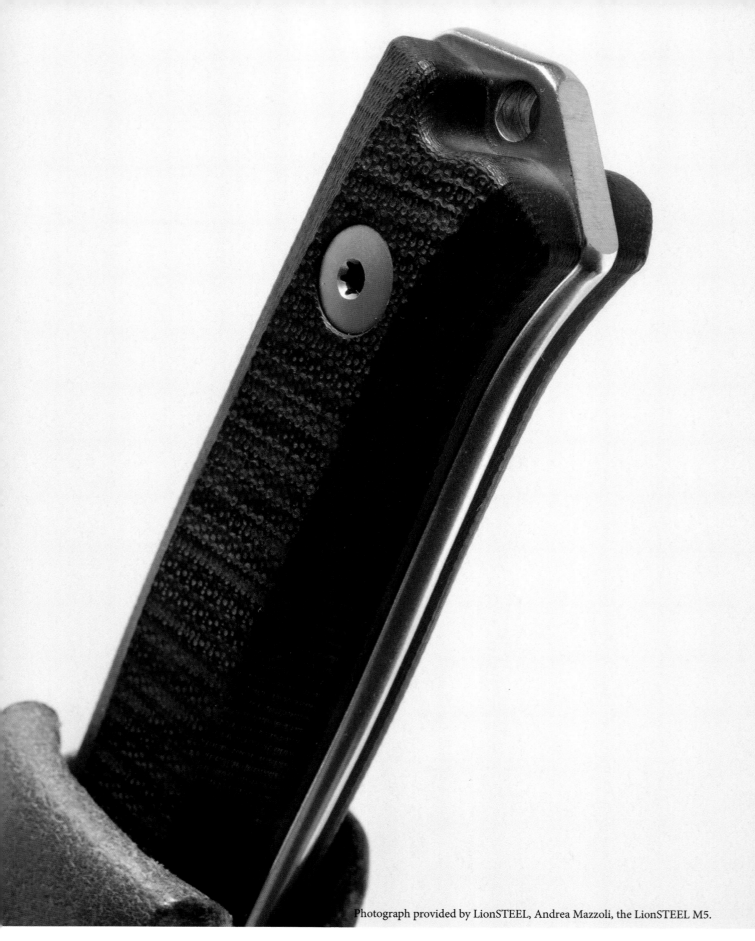

Photograph provided by LionSTEEL, Andrea Mazzoli, the LionSTEEL M5.

KNIFE HANDLE MATERIAL

There is a plethora of different types of handle material available today to choose from. In this section, I cover a list of the most common materials one would find on the market.

Natural

Bone

Bone has been used as handle material for thousands of years. Bone from deceased animals is used as handle material. Due to its dense characteristics, legbones of cattle are the most commonly used. Bone needs to be stabilized, because it is porous and can shrink, crack, or break over time. Even with good stabilization procedures, it can still deform overtime, even break. Stabilized bone is hard and pretty tough, but not as tough as other materials, like G-10 or Micarta. It can get very slippery when wet, in addition, temperature, light, and moisture can have a huge impact on its characteristics overtime.

Horn

Horn is strong material, typically derived from buffalo, ram, or impala. Horn is a two-part structure, composed of a hard core and a keratin outer layer. It is basically the same material found in human hair and nails. Horns are lasting features, which, in some animal species, grow continuously. It is very beautiful material with unique characteristics. The downside is that is prone to natural expansion and contraction and is less durable than other natural materials. It can break under high levels of stress or impact. This is definitely not the right material for heavy duty tasks. That is not to say it is unsuitable material; on the contrary, it is suitable, it just depends on the user's overall intentions with the knife. Identifying what your primary intentions are with your knife should help you decide the type of handle you need.

Leather

Leather has been used for an exceptionally long time as handle material. It can be wrapped or stacked using leather washers on the tang. Leather as handle material is amazingly comfortable, but it lacks durability, and with extremely hard use can start to fall apart over the years. It is rarely used today as a primary material; instead, it is used as more of an accent piece.

Mammoth Fossil

This material is rare, but not as rare as other exotic materials. Mammoth tusks, molars, and bones are found in Siberia, and they are unearthed more frequently than you think. There are millions of mammoths still buried in Siberia's permafrost, and due to this, a new gold rush has emerged. Mammoth ivory is legal, which is pretty good news for elephants. The majority of the world's mammoth ivory is derived from Yakutia, located in Eastern Siberia, within Russian territory. Mammoth fossil needs to be stabilized before use as knife handles. This material is best suited for fine pocketknives or small fixed-blade knives that will not be used for heavy duty tasks.

Natural Wood

Natural wood is absolutely beautiful but does require some care. If not maintained properly, it can fade, crack, break, chip, or split. It can also rot if left in wet, humid environments for long periods of time. Not all wood is the same; it can range in stability, toughness, and strength. Desert Ironwood, or Ipe (Brazilian Ebony) are very strong woods that are naturally stable and can handle fairly heavy abuse. Maple is strong, but not as strong as Ironwood. Dogwood is dense, just not as dense as a Sugar Maple. How the wood handle will react over time depends on the level of use and the type of wood. All wood requires some degree of care, where periodic application of natural oils can help prevent degradation and improve its performance in extreme environments. Natural materials will always require more care than synthetic materials. A great way to determine the durability/hardness of wood is to review the Janka Hardness Rating Bar Chart on page 430. The Janka hardness test was created by Gabriel Janka, an American Researcher. The test calculates the resistance of wood to denting, by measuring the amount of force required to embed a 0.44" steel ball into the wood to about half of its diameter. The woods with higher ratings are harder than those with lower rating. For example, Buckeye Burl has a low rating of 350, whereas Lignum Vitae (Genuine) has a rating of 4,380, making it one of the hardest woods available.

Stabilized Wood/Hybrid Wood

Stabilized wood has higher durability than traditional wood. Wood stabilization is achieved by performing a series of steps, which involve pressure, a vacuum, and heat to impregnate wood cellular structure with certain resins or phenolics. The wood is first dried to remove any moisture content. Then the wood and stabilizing agents are loaded to a chamber under a vacuum. What this will do, is remove any air from the wood's pores and fill any gaps within the wood. It is then placed under huge amounts of pressure to enable the agent to fully penetrate the wood. Lastly, it is heat-treated, so that the liquid agent transforms to a solid and bonds tightly with the wood. Different dyes can be added during the process to give the wood a pop of color. Once it is ready, it can be easily shaped, drilled, sanded, and polished. Stabilized wood is much tougher than traditional wood and can also withstand extreme environments better. Any type of wood can be stabilized, but the most common are maple, oak, elm, burl, prickly pear, and desert cactus.

Stag

This material is derived from naturally shed deer antlers. It is a popular choice for handle material because it is unique, as no antler is identical to another. It is dense, durable, and feels smooth in the hand. Using antlers can be a sustainable way to produce handle material. Deer shed their antlers once a year, typically in the late winter. People scavenge for this natural material mid-March, and sell them in bulk to interested parties.

Sambar stag is a popular choice among knifemakers because it is more dense than typical antlers and has less marrow. It also has nice rich colors, versus the usual dulled out color scheme.

The downside is that stag handles do require a certain degree of care, otherwise they can break or deform over time. Handle material that has not been properly stabilized can be quite brittle. Stag handles are not stabilized in the same fashion as wood, because it does not involve resin. The antlers are dipped in a solution that will help them retain their form and size when exposed to outdoor elements. Not all antlers need a solution, but it is better to be safe than sorry. Stag can be quite slippery when wet; in addition, may not be an ideal material in humid environments, because over time it can warp. Stag is also a natural material that cannot sustain heavy abuse.

Metals

Aluminum

Aluminum is lightweight, has high corrosion resistance, durability, and moderate toughness. It is a less expensive alternative to titanium. Temperature and moisture can affect the overall feel, whereas moisture can make it slippery and low temperatures can make it quite cold. It can chip or break with heavy use. It is also prone to scratches and dents over time.

Brass

Brass is an alloy of copper, zinc, and other elements. It will form a beautiful patina overtime, but it will not rust or corrode. Brass is tougher than copper but can still scratch or dent if put under certain level of stress or pressure. Even though brass is stronger than copper, it can form stress cracks. Brass is also more malleable than bronze. This material is great for handle pins on fixed blade knives. Be careful when considering this material for rivets or screws on a foldable knife; because it is pretty soft material, the screws can damage easily.

Bronze

Bronze shares similarities in its overall composition with brass, in that it is also an alloy of copper and zinc with other elements, like tin. Bronze will oxidize but will not rust, however, over time it can acquire a bronze disease, which is a form of corrosion. It is a powdery green substance that forms on the surface and begins eating away at the metal. It is a fairly good choice for knife scales if maintained accordingly and wiped down to prevent corrosion. It makes a good choice for knife handle pins or rivets (although nickel is by far better) because it is highly corrosion resistant. Nickel can develop rust over time, but it takes certain extreme conditions for that to happen.

Copper

Copper is a nice material for EDC knives because it will form a nice patina over time and also has antibacterial properties. Keep in mind that copper is a soft metal, which can bend given the right amount of force. It can also scratch pretty easy. It can be quite slippery when wet, but it will not corrode. Note that copper, like brass and bronze, does react with oxygen. Copper oxidizes over time to form a protective green patina, that prevents the metal from corrosion. There is also a brown patina that can form over time, and acts like a protective film. If the film, known as reddish-brown cuprous oxide, is ever damaged, it can cause the copper to lose its anti-corrosion properties.

Stainless Steel

Stainless steel is stronger than copper, aluminum, and brass. It is also more corrosion resistant than bronze. The downfall is the weight; it is a heavy steel alloy. It is affordable compared to titanium, and also scratches less over time than other metals. It will not oxidize, but some stainless steels do need maintenance because they can rust under certain conditions. It is a great option for an EDC knife handle.

Titanium

Titanium is an excellent choice for handle material, but more so for pocketknives. It will not corrode like other metallic materials. It is extraordinarily strong, lightweight, and durable. It can be costly, but expect premium quality with low density and high strength. Titanium can also be colored during the anodizing process to almost any color in the rainbow. Titanium does get scratches and dents over time and may require a bit of maintenance.

Hybrid/Synthetic

Acrylic

Acrylic is a nice material, but it can break or chip under high levels of stress. It is moderately strong and durable but does require some level of care. Acrylic can develop scratches over time and may not be the best choice for handles that will be exposed to heavy abuse. It is a decent choice for pocketknives, but not adequate for fixed blade knives that are intended for heavy duty use.

Carbon Fiber

Carbon fiber is quite possibly the strongest of all the synthetic handle materials, but it comes at a hefty price. It is remarkably ultra-lightweight and shows a great level of single direction super strength. The reason for the single direction is because of how the carbon fiber is woven and set in the resin. It can break or fall apart if pressure is applied in a specific direction. It is also slightly brittle and can break with heavy amounts of sharp impact. Do not let its brittleness deter you, it is still a tremendously strong material. Remember that strength correlates with brittleness, whereas toughness correlates with ductility. This is definitely not a handle material I would consider for bushcraft or tasks that require high impact. If the knife handle were to be struck improperly, it can break, or if the knife were to fall on a hard surface it may damage the handle. This is excellent material for pocketknives or small self-defense knives.

Celluloid

Overall, Celluloid is poor handle material. Over time it will break down, crack, discolor, and eventually, crumble. Celluloid also releases a substance that can rust the knife. It is made from an unnatural concoction of chemicals, such as nitrocellulose, camphor, alcohol, colorants, and fillers. This synthetic material was developed in the late 1800s. It was very popular handle material during the mid-twentieth century, used on straight razor handles and pocketknives. Out of all the handle materials available today, Celluloid is the worst. Do not waste your money on this material.

C-TEK

C-TEK is resin-infused aircraft aluminum honeycomb handle material. It can be used on its own or combined with other material to enhance colors or patterns. It is similar to wood in that it can be sanded, sawed, and polished as desired. It is tougher than acrylic, but not has tough as G-10. There are several colors available for choosing, even gradient style patterns. If you are interested in this material, look into Wireworks by Ankrom.

FRN

Unlike other materials, Fiberglass Reinforced Nylon (FRN) requires zero maintenance and is quite inexpensive. This material can be injection molded into nearly any shape without affecting its overall integrity. It is a thermoplastic material that is super strong and can resist some levels of bending without breaking. If the handle material does not contain some form of texture, it can be more slippery than G-10 when wet. It is a great option for mass production operations. FRN is a decent alternative to G-10, but it has a cheap plastic feel, and many people will never warm up to that. Spyderco is a great example of a company who has really taken FRN to the next level and found ways to take advantage of its unique properties.

G-10

G-10 is a premium laminate composite made of fiberglass with similar characteristics to carbon fiber, just slightly inferior in some respects. It is much cheaper than carbon fiber and very tough, hard, and ultra-lightweight material. It can endure heavy amounts of abuse related to temperature, moisture, impact, chemical, etc. It is grippier than other material when wet and will not expand or contract under extreme temperatures like micarta. It is available in a plethora of colors and color combinations.

Gemstone Composite

This material is made from a mixture of fine, crushed natural stone and resin. Every piece is different in pattern with unique characteristics. Like most resin-infused materials, gemstone composite offers better resistance to chipping and breaking than acrylic. It also offers more stability than natural material. It is available in colors such as pink rose, dark coral red, light green with gold crystals, black and many more. It can easily be drilled, sanded, and polished as needed.

Kirinite

Kirinite is not as brittle as standard acrylic and resists chipping and cracking. It can be sanded, shaped, and drilled, and buffed easily. The benefit of this material over natural materials is that it won't shrink, warp, or crack. It is very stable material with high toughness. It is available in numerous colors and patterns. It is created using a single-batch process, therefore, every piece is unique in pattern. This material does not feel as slippery as other materials when wet.

Micarta

Thin layers of linen, canvas, burlap, or paper are soaked in phenolic resin and hardened. It is an extraordinarily strong synthetic material that is less slippery than G-10 if left with a matte finish versus glossy. Depending on the finish, it can absorb fluids under certain conditions, causing it to stain over time. Micarta is also very tough and can sustain moderate to high levels of impact very well. Micarta tolerates extreme temperatures well with little change to its shape. It does expand and contract a little under certain temperatures, but that is nothing to worry about. Micarta is also resistant to solvents, grease, and other chemical substances. It does not become brittle over time and is a highly regarded material for survival and bushcraft knives. It is available in nearly any color imaginable and can also be combined with multiple colors to produce multi-color patterns. Micarta is not indestructible, and a lot of its characteristics are derived from the resin/epoxy it is made with. Not all micarta is created equal; therefore, be mindful about who is manufacturing it and what materials they are using to make it. Micarta does offer a great amount of scratch resistance too.

Pinecone

Pinecones are caste in resin to make exotic, unique knife handles. Resins can be dyed in several different colors, including blue, green, yellow, gold, orange, white, red, black, and brown. This material is pretty hard and tolerates moderate abuse. It is tougher than acrylic and more stable than natural materials. This material can be sanded and polished very easily.

Richlite

Richlite is a common material used for kitchen countertops. It is extraordinarily strong and can take moderate levels of impact without breaking or chipping. It is composed of about 65% FSC-certified or recycled paper content and 35% phenolic resin. In other words, it is resin-infused paper. It can be easily sanded and molded to one's liking, similar to wood.

Suretouch

Suretouch is material made from a combination of G-10 and rubber. It has the same strength and durability as G-10 with the nice grippy feel of rubber. It is available in same color combinations that you would typically find in G-10.

VaporRez

VaporRez is a resin-based material, similar to composite phenolic-based materials. It is available in an array of colors and patterns. It is tougher than acrylic, in that it will not chip or break as easily. It is better than natural material in that it will not warp, shrink, or crack. It can handle moderate levels of heat without affecting its shape. It will not be as slippery when wet as other handle materials.

XGrip

XGrip is a very strong, high performance, phenolic material that can be easily shaped, drilled, sanded, and polished. It comes in unique patterns that are not found in natural materials, G-10, or Micarta. This material is much stronger than acrylic in that is will not chip or break as easily. It is also better than most natural materials in that it will not warp, crack, or shrink.

Exotic Material

Aside from the more common material, there are also exotic materials that are harder to come across, such giraffe bone, animal tusk, tortoise shell, peach tree wood, hippo tooth, dinosaur bone, coprolite, meteorite, oosic, armadillo tail, porcupine quills, and believe it or not, human bone. Some of these materials carry a hefty price tag and are very rare. It is also illegal to produce items out of some of these materials, such as tortoise shell. The owner of tortoise shell items needs to have a certificate demonstrating that it was acquired before 1973.

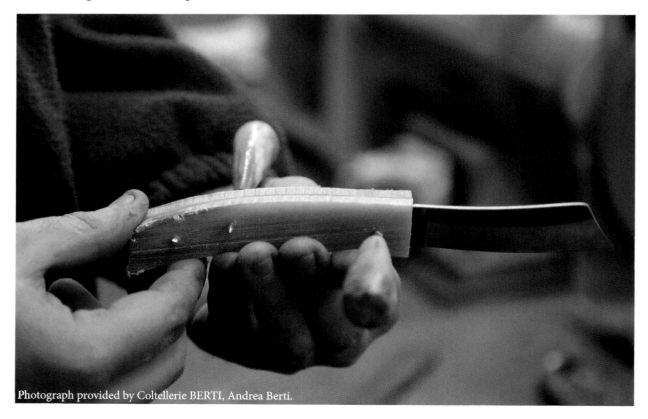

Photograph provided by Coltellerie BERTI, Andrea Berti.

KNIFEMAKING

There are several ways to make a knife. These are just two methods: forging and stock removal, or reductive process.

Forging:

Forging requires a great deal of practice & training to master. I recommend taking lessons prior to attempting this process on your own. The forging method described below is simply one way of doing it. Not everyone follows the same process or uses entirely the same tools.

The following items are required for forging:

Hammer

Anvil

Tongs

Vise

Chisels, Punches, and Drifts

Forge

High Carbon Steel or Damascus

Sandpaper

Magnet

Quenching oil

Metal Storage Container

Gloves, Protective Clothing, Goggles, Facemask, and Ear Protection

Fire Extinguisher

Grasp the steel object with tongs and heat it in the forge until the color reaches the ideal sought after, tone of bright yellow. This is achieved when the steel is heated to just over 2,000° F. Once the steel has reached the desired color, remove it from the forge (using your tongs of course), and set it on an anvil. Then, grab your hammer and begin to hammer the corners into the shape of a knife point. The idea here is to focus on equally tapering both sides of the steel. How the sides are tapered ultimately depends on the shape you are trying to achieve. The steel will cool at a point during the forging process, so it will need to be reheated to continuing shaping the blade. Beveling is the first stage in creating the cutting edge of the blade. Hammer the flat sides of the steel, to begin beveling it out. The same action must be performed on the opposite side of the blade, until both sides are equal and symmetrical. Once the desired shape is established, you then want to "normalize it." Normalization requires reheating of the steel until it reaches its critical temperature, typically around 1400° F. At this temperature, the steel will not be magnetic, giving you to opportunity to test the steel on your magnet. Once this critical temperature is reached, let the steel air cool, until it reaches about 400° F. Make sure all the red color has gone away and repeat the reheat process a couple more times. After it has cooled, sand down the blade to smooth out any rough edges. Now, you must reheat the steel again, prior to dipping it in oil, until it cools down to room temperature. This process is known as quenching, which hardens the steel. Timing is crucial in the quenching process, because if the steel is not dipped in the oil quickly after heating, it may not harden. Once properly quenched, you want to reheat the blade again, to just a little over 400° F, to relax the steel from any internal stress caused during the quenching process. This process is called tempering. The final steps after the tempering process are attaching a handle and sharpening your blade.

Gransfors Bruk, Photographer: Emelie Torstensson.

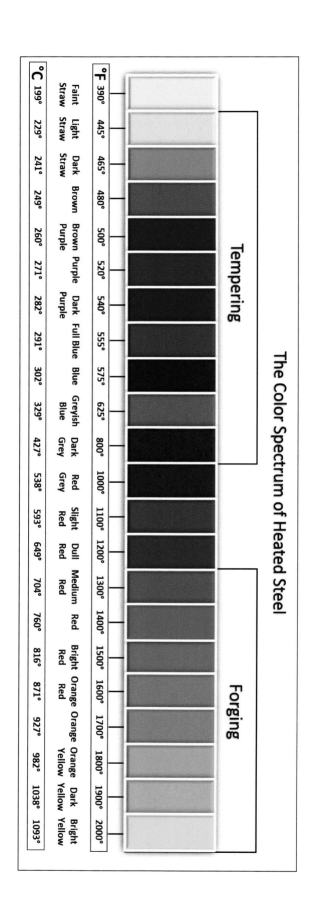

The Color Spectrum of Heated Steel

Tempering

Forging

°F			°C
390°	Faint Straw		199°
445°	Light Straw		229°
465°	Dark Straw		241°
480°	Brown		249°
500°	Brown Purple		260°
520°	Purple		271°
540°	Dark Purple		282°
555°	Full Blue		291°
575°	Blue		302°
625°	Greyish Blue		329°
800°	Dark Grey		427°
1000°	Grey	Red	538°
1100°	Slight Red		593°
1200°	Dull Red		649°
1300°	Medium Red		704°
1400°	Red		760°
1500°	Bright Red		816°
1600°	Orange Red		871°
1700°	Orange Yellow		927°
1800°	Orange Yellow		982°
1900°	Dark Yellow		1038°
2000°	Bright Yellow		1093°

Gransfors Bruk, Photographer: Emelie Torstensson.

Stock Removal (a.k.a. Reductive Process):

The stock removal process, or reductive process, can be as equally intensive as forging and requires additional attention to detail and practice to master. There are many ways to perform the stock removal process, the method below is simply one way of doing it.

The following items are required to perform the stock removal process:

Permanent Marker

Manila Paper

Sandpaper

Ruler

Rasps

Clamps

Pliers

Tongs

Kitchen Oven

Forge (if not mailing the knife blank to a shop, for heat treatment)

Steel Cutting Bandsaw (one powerful enough to do the job)

Tabletop Sander with Enough Belts with Different Grits

Drill Press with Various Bits

Angle Grinder

Steel

Epoxy

Pins/Rivets

Gloves, Protective Clothing, Goggles, Facemask, and Ear Protection

Before you get started, make sure you are wearing all of your protective gear. Your knife design should be drawn onto manila paper and already cut out. This is what will be laid on top of the steel blank and used to draw the same shape onto the steel blank. Use your permanent marker to trace out the shape of the design onto the steel blank. Then, using the angle grinder with cut-off wheel attachment, rough cut the clamped steel blank and slowly cut out the shape of your knife. The result at this stage will not be perfect because the cut-off wheel can only perform straight cuts versus curved. Typically, you will do general cuts around the steel areas you do not need. Then, after clamping down the premature knife blank to the work bench, begin cutting the additional material that is not needed. (It is possible to use a drill press to drill holes along the general shape of the knife and use a hack saw to finish cutting it out).

Once the knife shape has reached as close to the desired shape as possible, you can use the belt sander (or hand file) to finish profiling the knife. If using a belt sander, you will begin by using the coarser grit to remove enough material until you reach the final shape. This is the point where you will get closer to the final design by grinding down the knife until you can no longer see the sharpie marks. Be cautious not to overdo this part as you risk altering the original design. Finally, use a drill press to drill holes where your pins will go. Make sure that these holes are evenly spaced and placed in a straight line (if needed, use a ruler to ensure accuracy).

Now we get to the best part, making the bevel/edge type. Using your belt sander, remove 65% to 85% of material toward the final bevel. This task will be done freehand. To the best of your ability, make consistent strokes, as evenly as possible, across the belt sander. The remaining material will be removed after hardening and tempering the steel. This would be a good time to grab some sandpaper to sand down the knife and even things out so as to make it look nice and shiny. Remember, once the steel has hardened, performing this task will be more cumbersome, so take a moment to sand it down and make it look nice.

The next step in the process is heat treatment. Be aware that different steels require different heat treatments. This phase will enable the steel to reach maximum hardness, which is necessary when considering edge retention and sharpness. Now, you could always mail your knife blank to a shop that performs this process for a fee, or you can attempt to take on the challenge of doing it yourself at home. Should you choose the latter, make sure you have the proper equipment and preferably, experience. Grab tongs and place the knife blank into a forge. Heat the steel until it reaches a critical temperature, usually 1400° F, where it will no longer be magnetic. The point here is to transform the steel into martensite, essentially blade steel. Pull the knife out of the forge, testing the magnetism with a magnet, and if the steel is ready, meaning no longer magnetic, dip it into the oil (or water), to quench. After quenching, the blade will be extremely hard and brittle. **Do not drop it** because it can shatter.

To adjust the hardness and ease any internal stresses, you will now temper the knife. This can be done by placing the knife in a conventional oven, preheated to 400° F, for about three to four hours. What happens during the tempering process is a nice tradeoff between hardness and toughness levels. If done properly, the internal structures of the steel will reach their peak, showing superior toughness and strength when removed from the oven.

Assuming that the heat-treat process and the quenching process have been performed successfully, you will now want to let the steel cool before moving to finish off the edge or attaching the handle. Once the knife has cooled, work on your edge using a belt grinder and polish out the blade. Make sure that while working on your edge you do not overheat the blade or you will ruin the temper. Finally, add your desired handle material. Do this by using a drill press to match the holes on your handles with the ones previously added to the knife blank. Add epoxy to the knife (where the handles will be placed), lightly hammer in the pins, and clamp it all down. Once your handle is fixed, profile the handle (assuring that everything is flush) using a belt sander. Give the knife one final polish, making sure everything is as smooth and beautiful, as expected.

Photograph provided by TOPS Knives.

BLADE MAINTENANCE

Owning a knife comes with a level of responsibility. It is the owner's responsibility to maintain the knife to a working standard. This means maintaining a sharp edge on your knife and wiping down the blade after use, before storage. Unless you are taking the extra time to ensure that your knives are dry after cleaning and lightly oiled, **do not store your knives in their sheath**. Sheaths will acquire/retain moisture over time, ultimately aiding in corroding the blade. Should a sheath be your best option for storage, then Kydex sheaths might be a better option than leather, though none are still good enough at preventing corrosion. In addition, it is important to add a drop of oil on both sides of the blade, evenly spreading it throughout the blade's body. Proper maintenance procedures should be performed regardless of the type of steel. All steels rust, including stainless steels. Stainless steel is corrosion resistant to a certain point, but it is not 100% anti-corrosive. I suggest using a food grade oil on your blades, such as a mineral oil or Tsubaki knife oil. Keep in mind that culinary knives are not the only style of knife used in food processing and preparation. All knives in general serve a multi-purpose. It is in those unanticipated moments that you will find the need to use your tactical knife, to slice an apple or skin a deer. Use food grade oils to avoid consuming a substance that can make you sick.

Proper maintenance always needs to be considered in regard to the knife handle as well. If the handle is made of wood, then apply a food grade oil from time to time. This will help maintain it in good shape, while preventing cracking or breaking. Rubbing a couple drops of raw linseed oil or food grade cutting board oil, to the handle should suffice. A few drops of pure vitamin E oil would work too, should you have nothing else. These couple of drops will be enough to maintain the handle in good shape. Handle maintenance will not be as frequent as that of your blade. Axe handle maintenance, though, is a little different and it will be discussed later in the book.

Knife Sharpening

Sharpening a knife is a commitment to your investment. To do this process properly, you must be prepared to allocate enough time to conduct knife maintenance. The sharpening process, for the most part, should never be rushed. Keep in mind that what works for me might not work for you. There is a certain level of personal satisfaction that comes with sharpening your knives. That said, some may see sharpening a knife as more of an onerous task, rather than gratifying. Either way, make sure you take the proper steps to maintain your blade. A dull knife is more dangerous than a sharp one. Knives are tools, expected to perform when needed. A lack of maintenance will eventually lead your tool to fail. Maintenance will keep your investment in top shape and protect you from danger, so don't skip this part. Nothing lasts forever and everything requires some form of maintenance, including us (mind, body, and soul).

Practice and Patience

Sharpening your knives requires practice and a great deal of patience. In order to master the basic techniques of sharpening, developing muscle memory is important. The only way to develop muscle memory is to practice, practice, practice. During the process of developing your muscle memory, it is completely normal to see the first several attempts result in failure. That is why it takes a great deal of patience, because in life, we do not learn to walk before we learn to crawl. Failure is a part of life; we must learn from it and keep moving forward until we succeed. Just be sure you are not using an expensive knife the first few attempts until you get the hang of it, otherwise it will be a costly mistake.

There are several methods to sharpen knives, which include copious amounts of materials one can use. That is why it is important to learn about the steels you have in your possession and determine what are the best methods to sharpen those steels. Not all steels are alike, and some sharpen easier with certain materials. For example, premium steels, like M390, can be sharpened with waterstones, but will require a little more effort. It is easier to sharpen using a diamond stone, which can remove material faster and more effectively. Both materials work, it's just one may require more skill and/or patience than the other. Another thing to consider is the edge angle and grind. Not all edges are created equal, which is why it is also important to educate yourself on edge types and blade grinds. Some edges sharpen a bit easier, while others will require more work—but even that statement is relative because the steel type, edge angle, and the material you are using to sharpen matters.

The Dull Road

Do not panic—we've all been on Dull Road with one of our knives at some point or other. It is important to perform routine inspections on your knives. Always inspect the edge of your knife for defects and deformations, such as chips, nicks, dull spots, and a bent or broken tip. When inspecting your knife's edge, make sure you are in a properly lit area. To function as expected the edge of a knife must be continuous and uninterrupted by defects. The dull edge will **not** have an apex (think of a really narrow triangle), meaning the point of intersection between the bevels will be rounded versus pointy. Using your fingertips, very carefully and very gently, brush your thumb across the edge at a perpendicular angle to the blade. If your knife's edge lacks some form of toothiness or bite, then it is time to take it on a trip down Strop Lane or Ceramic Street (ok I will stop with the metaphors now). The "point" is, (sorry, had to throw that out there too), keep the edge sharp by performing periodic maintenance. A quick and easy solution is to simply strop your knife after each use. This will avoid your edge from becoming dull. Remember, a dull edge is more dangerous than a sharp one.

That said, stick to what works for you or what is appropriate for your knives. If you are keeping your knife's edge sharp, then you are exercising good knife maintenance, regardless of whether you prefer a razor-sharp edge or a simpler working edge.

Is it Razor Sharp?

Knives do not always have to be "razor-sharp" to be functional. In reality, not all steels can have thin razor-sharp edges, because depending on the steel, a thin edge is more susceptible to chipping, breaking, bending, rolling, etc. There is a plethora of different types of steels available in the knife community, as discussed previously. They do not all contain the same molecular structure, nor the same composition. In addition, they were not all made by the same supplier, nor heat treated by the same knifemaker. What that means is, a knife in CPM-3V steel from Bark River Knives may not perform in the same manner as a knife in CPM-3V from L.T. Wright Knives, because each manufacturer heat treats its knives differently. Every knifemaker has their own workflow and that is typically what they stick to because it is what works best for them.

When giving a knife *that* razor-sharp edge, consider the abovementioned information. Another thing to consider is the purpose of the knife. Will the knife serve a tactical purpose? Will it be used for self-defense? Will it be used for bushcraft? Are you looking to shave your hair with it? What are you looking to do with it? Do you really need a razor-sharp edge or simply "working edge" instead?

Harder steels will typically retain an edge for longer periods of use. Softer steels typically dull faster but are generally tougher. The "toughness" I am referring to is the ability to withstand high levels of impact without chipping or breaking. Tougher steels are usually a bit easier to sharpen and acquire a razor-sharp edge but will not retain that edge for very long. This is why it is important to know the differences between a carbon steel, stainless steel, tool steel, and an atypical steel.

Balance in the molecular structure of steel is important, which is why we alloy and heat treat. The ideal steel will be hard enough to exhibit good wear resistance, edge retention, and ease of sharpening. It will also be tough enough to have high levels of impact resistance. Finally, it would need to have some form of corrosion resistance. Currently, it is not possible for a steel to have the best of everything, but there are steels that come close. The entire process of making premium steels, including the final stages of knifemaking, such as heat treat, is a balancing act. When working with different steels, we must understand what style grind or edge works best for each of them. Not all steels perform well with a traditional Scandi grind or a convex edge. The geometry of a blade does matter because it should typically coincide with the general purpose of the knife. Remember, optimal performance is the goal. The goal is to produce a knife that performs great at most tasks, but good at all of them. In addition, maybe a working edge might be more appropriate versus a razor-sharp edge under certain circumstances. Just something to think about.

The Apex and Burr

A knife's "apex" is the triangular shape a knife's edge forms when sharpened properly. The blade's bevels meet at the center, forming a narrow, fine V-shape, known as the cutting edge. This cutting edge has an apex, which wears over time. The apex needs to be geometrically proportionate on both sides, so that it looks like a well-shaped V, evenly tapering to the point, forming a sharp cutting edge. Going down the apex, it begins to widen until it reaches the base, or non-sharpened sides.

When a knife's edge is dull or has small deformations, the edge needs to be sharpened until it forms a burr. A "*burr*" is a small fold of metal that builds up on the opposite side of the edge you are currently sharpening. Some people refer to the burr as a "wire-edge," because it feels like a wire when you brush your fingertips across the knife's edge. The burr will slightly tug or bite, as you gently brush your fingertips across the edge. It will be noticeable as it begins to buildup, which is a clear indication that an edge is being sharpened. Make sure the burr has formed throughout the cutting edge, not just a section. If a burr is not forming after several attempts, pay attention to the angle of the edge bevel and how you are placing it on the whetstone. The edge bevel must connect properly with the whetstone, to sharpen the surface of the edge accordingly. There should not be any gaps between the edge bevel and the whetstone. Perform long, gentle strokes, with the edge facing you. Work your way from the heel/bottom of the blade's cutting edge to the tip. Light pressure is the key here. Apply the same amount of pressure as if you were shaving your face. A good way to ensure you are sharpening the edge properly, is to paint the edge bevel with a marker (black *Sharpie*®), that way you can confirm it is being sharpened correctly. As you sharpen the edge, the paint from the marker will start to wear off. When the burr finally forms, rotate the knife to the other side and sharpen the edge, maintaining the same number of strokes and pressure you used on the first side. So do not forget to count your strokes. You will notice a small burr begin to form on the opposite side as well. Use a finer stone, higher grit sandpaper, or leather strop to remove the burr.

Test your knife using a piece of magazine or printer paper, placing the edge at the proper angle, try to slice pieces off the page. If your knife's edge is still a little dull, try to use an ultra-fine ceramic stone or rod to hone the edge a little more. Remember to be consistent maintaining the angle and applying the same number of strokes on both sides. Test the knife's edge again. If it is still dull and not cutting smoothly, try to sharpen it a little more using the first product you were using, until a small burr forms along the cutting edge. Perform the same method on the opposite side. Use a ceramic stone or leather strop to remove the burr and finetune the edge. Test the knife's edge again on a thin piece of paper. If it cuts the paper smoothly, then you are finished, unless you plan on also polishing the edge bevel. If the knife does not slice the paper properly, then try to perform the steps again, be patient, find the knife's edge bevel, place it properly on the whetstone, and sharpen the edge on both sides. Depending on the knife's steel, it can take a long time to acquire a burr and a good apex. Take your time, be patient, and maintain angle consistency throughout the process. You want to be sure to form a burr along the entire cutting edge of the blade, not just a section.

If you fail at acquiring a good apex, then try again, or consider another sharpening method. Consider using a belt sharpener or taking your knife to a professional to be sharpened. Sometimes it is better to pay a professional a few dollars and have them sharpen your knife, versus failing miserably and permanently damaging your knife.

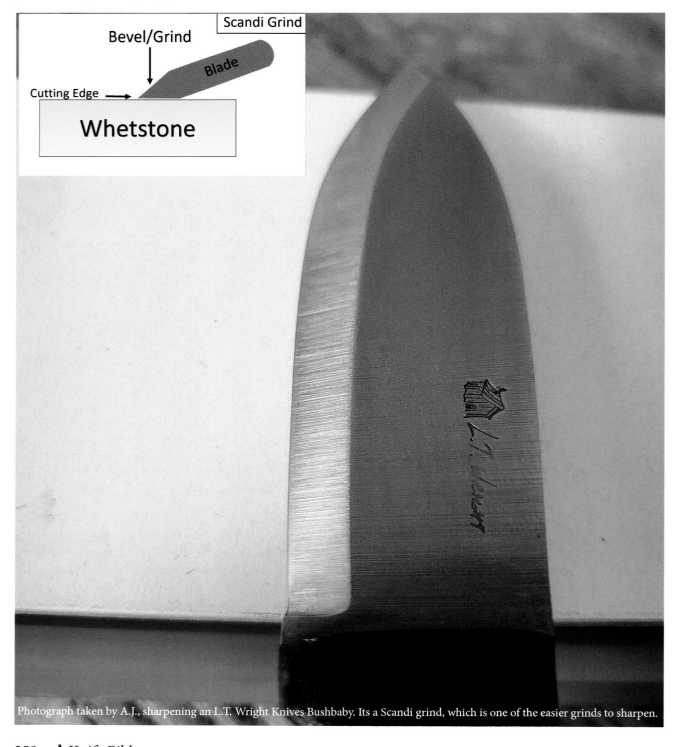

Photograph taken by A.J., sharpening an L.T. Wright Knives Bushbaby. Its a Scandi grind, which is one of the easier grinds to sharpen.

Difference between Whetstone and Waterstone

Whetstone is another term for "sharpening stone." The meaning of the word "whet" is to sharpen the blade (tool or weapon), per the Oxford dictionary. "Whet" is a dated term, but still used in the knife community when referring to sharpening stones. When referring to whetstones/sharpening stones, we could be talking about ceramic stones, diamond stones, waterstones, Arkansas stones (oil stones), etc... Waterstone is a type/sub-category of whetstone, originally produced in Japan, where the best water stones are derived. Waterstones are not exclusive to Japan; several other countries produce their own variations made from different materials. The stones are to be used in combination with water, hence the name "waterstones." As you sharpen your knife, you will notice the build-up of "slurry," which is developed by the mixing of water and loose sharpening particles. It is important to clean and rewater the stones frequently as you sharpen to prevent loose particles that remain on the surface from scratching the knife blade. Not all water stones are built the same; some need to be submerged in water for several minutes for them to fill up/saturate, while others are simply "splash-and-go."

It is important to take note of the "feedback" a whetstone provides, when sharpening. That is why it is important to pay attention... listen and watch what happens when you sharpen your knife on the whetstone. What is the stone telling you about itself or your sharpening method? Take note of that feedback and determine if the stone is doing the right job at sharpening your edge. You may need to either fix your method or change the stone to achieve the results you want.

Hopefully, this shed a little light as far as the difference between whetstone and water stone.

What is the best product to sharpen my knife?

There is a plethora of great products one can use to sharpen a knife. It is important to use what works best for you and your knife. In this section we will cover some of the sharpening products and systems that are currently available.

Waterstone

Waterstones are fantastic for sharpening knife blades, but they are not for everyone. They demand a certain level of skill, not had by everyone due to the time and patience required to master. Over time, as your sharpening skills improve, it will get easier to find the edge angles on a knife and maintaining angle consistency while sharpening. In my opinion, water stones fall within an expert level of sharpening, as do most freehand sharpening methods. Most waterstones will need to be submerged in water for a period of time. The reason is because the stone will soak-in some of that water and perform much better. There are also some waterstones that are "splash-n-go," which means they do not need to be submerged, simply splash, or spray some water on them and start sharpening. Higher grit waterstones, like 1,000 or above, are more forgiving on your blade's edge, in the event you make a couple mistakes while sharpening. For those who have mastered sharpening on waterstones, I recommend the brands like Naniwa (Japanese made waterstones of extremely high quality that offer excellent feedback). Naniwa has a series called "Professional Stones," which is some of their highest-grade stones. The Professional Stones replaced their popular "Chosera," stones. They are color-coded, and offer the following grits: 400, 600, 800, 1,000, 2,000, 3,000, 5,000, and 10,000. The Professional Stones are bonded with magnesium and have more continuous, uniformly sized cutting particles per unit of surface area than the typical resin-bonded stones. These are not meant to be submerged in water, only splash-n-go. If they are submerged in water for long periods of time, they will eventually start to crack and leach out bonding material. Keep a water source nearby and add water during the sharpening process as necessary. When finished, clean the surface off with some lukewarm water and a cloth. DO NOT USE WARM OR HOT WATER or you will eventually damage the stone. You may also use a Nagura Dressing Stone, while the water stone is still wet. Lightly wipe them down and let air dry.

Photograph taken by A.J., two Naniwa Stones.

The Shapton GlassStones Series are some of the best Japanese whetstones currently available. The GlassStones come in a High Carbon (HC) set, which are specifically for high carbon steels. They also produce a HR series that are designed to sharpen hard steels and modern steel alloys, like CPM-3V, M390, S45VN, to name a few. The HR series comes in several grits/microns, such as 120 grit (122.5 micron approx.), 220 grit (66.82 micron approx.), 320 grit (45.94 micron approx.), 500 grit (29.4 micron approx.) 1000 grit (14.7 micron approx.), 2000 grit (7.35 micron approx.), 3000 grit (4.9 micron approx.), 4000 grit (3.68 micron approx.), 6000 grit (2.45 micron approx.), 8000 grit (1.84 micron approx.), 10000 grit (1.47 micron approx.), 16000 grit (0.92 micron approx.), and 30000 grit (0.49 micron approx.). These stones are capable of faster cutting and have longer wear resistance than traditional waterstones. These GlassStones are NOT made of glass. The glass is simply the base that supports the white ceramic waterstone. All the stones are backed with 5 mm of glass, which helps provide a solid, flat base to support the ceramic waterstones. The abrasive particles in these stones are continuous and uniformly sized throughout the stones, which enables enhanced feedback and cutting capability. These stones can be used wet or dry, but wet is the preferred method. In fact, these can be referred to as "splash-n-go" style, which means they require a bit of water to function at their best. They do not need to be submerged in water for a given amount of time. Simply spray water on them and start sharpening. These GlassStones can be purchased at Sharpening Supplies, https://www.sharpeningsupplies.com.

Shapton has a series called "*Kuromaku*" and they are a set of ceramic color-coded waterstones. Each color will represent a different grade of coarseness. They have them color-coded as follows:

White (120 grit), Moss (220 grit), Blue Black (320 grit), Orange (1000 grit), Blue (1500 grit), Green (2000 grit), Wine (5000 grit), Melon (8000 grit), Yellow (12000 grit), and Purple (30000 grit).

Typically, these stones are meant to be used with water, but can also be used with oil. These come in a plastic case that can also be used as a stone holder. If you are a fan of free hand sharpening and enjoy the GlassStones, then these are also a fantastic option.

Suehiro is another Japanese brand, with nice extra-long and wide Debado MD Stones. Although if you're looking for an excellent 8,000-grit stone, then I would recommend that you consider Norton.

Waterstones will wear over time and require lapping/flattening. It is best to get a flattening stone, which Naniwa also offers, or like the DMT Dia-Flat 95 Lapping plate, to flatten your stone when it begins to show a worn surface. In addition, when using these stones, they will need to be placed in a stone holder or base, where they can remain stable during sharpening. The brands I mention above produce excellent quality stones. They produce nice slurries, good feedback, and stellar final results. Water stones can be purchased at Sharpening Supplies https://www.sharpeningsupplies.com, Knifeworks at https://knifeworks.com, or Bernal Cutlery at https://www.bernalcutlery.com.

Photograph taken by A.J., two Shapton GlassStones

Ceramic Stone

Ceramic stones are a great option for those who know how to maintain angle consistency throughout the sharpening process. It is important to understand that not all ceramic stones are waterstones. The reason is because there are ceramic sharpening products that do not require a drop of water. They are meant to be used dry. Spyderco, in my opinion, wins this category. Spyderco's ceramic bench stones are wonderful. They are made of "high alumina ceramic," which can cut most metals without a problem and are offered in medium, fine, and ultra-fine grits. Grit typically refers to abrasive particle size in sandpaper, but to give an approximation, the ultra-fine stone is about 2,000 grit. The fine is about 1,800 grit, and medium is about 600 grit. The stones measure 8" x 2" X ½. None of their stones require lubricant, such as oil or water. Spyderco also produces pocket ceramic stones that can easily sharpen or hone your knives in the field, or on the go. After use, simply use a plastic brush or abrasive pad, with powdered abrasive cleanser. This will remove metallic particles, keep the surface looking clean and feeling smooth. These ceramic stones can be found on Spyderco's website at https://www.spyderco.com or DLT Trading at https://www.dlttrading.com.

Photograph taken by A.J., two Spyderco Ceramic Stones

Ceramic Rod

Ceramic Rods are a good option to hone your knife edge. IOXIO manufactures a great ceramic rod made of aluminum oxide ceramics. The white rod is rated at 1,000 grit on the FEPA Scale and 3,000 on the JIS Scale. This is good product to maintain a nice edge. After using the knife, just run it through a few times and it will leave a fine edge on your blade. The rod can be purchased at Sharpening Supplies.com, https://www.sharpeningsupplies.com. Spyderco also offers a ceramic rod variation, called Galley-V, which is a double ceramic rod combo attached to a plastic base, forming a V-shape at 20-degree angles. The Galley-V shape system is great at touching up blades to keep them looking nice and sharp. The rods on this system are 12 inches in length. The base can be clamped or permanently attached on to a work bench or countertop. They also offer a good ceramic rod style sharpener, known as the Triangle Sharpmaker, which is highly regarded by Chris Reeve Knives, as their preferred sharpener for their pocketknives. The system comes with an ABS Plastic Base, 2 White Fine Ceramic Triangle Rods, 2 Gray Medium Ceramic Triangle Rods, and 2 Brass Hand Guards. Their ceramic products can be purchase on Spyderco's website https://www.spyderco.com.

Diamond Stone

Diamond stones are fantastic sharpening products, and if you can maintain angle consistency while sharpening, they can get your edge sharp pretty fast. These stones are great for tool steels or those harder to sharpen modern steels. Something to consider is that diamond stones are one of the least forgiving stones on the market. Mistakes on diamond stone can result in unintentional reprofiling of your edge, if not careful. Diamond stones remove a generous amount of material very easily; therefore, it is important to pay close attention. If you feel comfortable with these stones, then I recommend the brand DMT for their diamond stones. DMT has phenomenal sharpeners if diamond is your sharpening medium of choice. I recommend the DMT 8" Dia-Sharp diamond stones. In the Dia-Sharp diamond stones range they offer extra coarse (220 grit equivalent), coarse (325 grit equivalent), fine (600 grit equivalent), and extra fine (1200 grit equivalent). I suggest purchasing a universal stone holder, as it will raise the stone off the ground, enough to make knife sharpening easier. Stone holders usually come with non-slip, rubber feet to keep the stone from sliding when sharpening. Holders are usually adjustable from 6.5 to 8.5 inches. DMT diamond stones can be found in a number of places, such as Knifeworks (https://knifeworks.com), DLT Trading (https://www.dlttrading.com), Smoky Mountain Knife Works (https://www.smkw.com), or directly on DMT (https://www.dmtsharp.com).

Fallkniven also makes great diamond stones, such as the DC3 and DC4 whetstones. Both options combine two surfaces, diamond on one side and the ceramic on the other. The diamond side is about approx. 25 microns, which is equivalent to about 600 grit. The ceramic side is composed of synthetic sapphires. The surfaces will wear over time but will always maintain their shape. These stones do not require lubrication (water or oil), simply clean them from time to time with lukewarm water, a soft brush, and common cleanser. Both the DC3 and DC4 are fantastic pocket-sized sharpeners. They are built to even sharpen the toughest of steels, such as powder steels/modern steel alloys. Fallkniven also offers a larger version, the DC521 Benchstone, which measures 8.25" x 2.25".

Photograph taken by A.J., DMT Diamond Stone on stone holder.

Diamond Rod

Diamond rods are a good option to quickly hone and re-align your knife's edge. DMT offers 12" diamond steel rods, with a total length of nearly 17 inches. They offer a "fine" and "extra fine" grit. The fine grit (red) is 25 microns, about 600 micro-mesh diamond, and the extra fine (green) is 9 microns, about 1200 micro-mesh diamond. These rods can be purchased at Sharpening Supplies at https://www.sharpeningsupplies.com

Fallkniven also makes a diamond rod, the D12 Diamond Steel. It has micro-teeth that enable a fast-sharpening experience. It is about 12" inches in length.

Sandpaper

Sandpaper is one of my go-to products for knife sharpening. I really enjoy using it due to its affordability and availability. Sandpaper can also be cut to a specific size, making it extra convenient. When I am in the field/outdoors, I am not always on the search for the "razor-sharp" edge, but more of a "working edge." Especially if time is of the essence and I need a sharp edge quick. However, I have found that it is quite easy to achieve *that* razor-sharp edge using high grit sandpaper. I typically prefer the brand 3M™. If I am just looking to touch-up my knife's edge, then I will start with a 1,000 grit and work my way up to a 3,000 grit. Any grit beyond 3,000 is mostly for polishing the edge. If you have an edge with defects, then starting with a grit size between 400 to 800 will work better to restore the edge faster. When using sandpaper, place it over a flat surface, lay the knife's edge bevel at the correct angle, where it will be completely flat on the sandpaper. Sharpen the edge using a backward motion, away from the cutting edge. If you sharpen toward the cutting edge, you will likely cut through the sandpaper. Maintaining angle consistency is important. Keep the same backward motion and work your way upward from heel/bottom to the tip, along the edge. Remember to count your strokes on the initial side, so that you repeat the same number of strokes on the other side. I sharpen all my Scandi grind knives using the abovementioned method.

For convex grinds, lay the sandpaper flat on a mouse pad and gently sharpen the knife's edge. What the mouse pad does is allow the sandpaper to connect with the convex edge better, because a convex edge is not flat, it is convex, hence the name. After capturing the correct angle, work your way backwards, away from the cutting edge. Remember to not cut the sandpaper. Both methods will use gentle backward strokes, using only the weight of the knife. No additional pressure is needed, and as previously mentioned, start with the 1,000 grit, and work your way up to the 3,000 grit. If you seek to achieve a mirror finish on your edge bevel, then using grits that go as high as 8,000 will be needed.

Sandpaper can be purchased at your local hardware store (Lowes, Homedepot, etc.), Amazon, or at DLT Trading (https://www.dlttrading.com).

Photograph taken by A.J., set of 3M™ Sandpaper

Polishing Tape

Polishing tapes are great for touching up blades, with the additional benefit of giving a mirror finish. I buy polishing tapes at https://www.dlttrading.com and prefer the Edge Pro Polish Tapes. DLT has polishing tapes in 2,000, 3,000, and 6,000 grit, all of which can be attached to the Edge Pro Polish Tape Blank, which sells for roughly $10. Realistically, though, you do not need to purchase the entire sharpening system, as all you really need are these tapes and a tape blank. Once acquired, you can easily lay the blank flat on any flat surface, stick any of the polishing tapes to the blank, and then begin polishing. You could also hold the blank at eye level while gripping the ends of the blank with one hand, and correctly place the knife edge bevel on the blank with the other hand and begin polishing. Again, the 1 inch by 5 inch dimension should give you a greater surface area to grip. Personally, I specifically use these to touch up and polish the edge on my Scandinavian grind knives. I use these mostly for my Morakniv, Marttiini, and Helle knives. The Edge Pro polish tapes sell for about $10 for a pack of 15 tapes. Each tape can be used approximately five times each. Replacement is simple as well, as the tape easily peels off the blank. As mentioned above, these polishing tapes can be purchased on the DLT Trading website: https://www.dlttrading.com.

Guided Sharpener

Guided sharpeners are wonderful systems to sharpen your knives. Personally, I use the Work Sharp guided sharpeners to maintain the fine edge on my kitchen knives. I have their Guided Field Sharpener, their Guided Sharpening System with Pivot-Response, and their Whetstone Knife Sharpener. All of Work Sharp's guided sharpeners work well at restoring the working edge of your knife with little effort. All of their guided sharpeners are available on their website: https://worksharptools.com.

Photograph provided by WorkSharp/Darex, LLC, Josh Warren.

Photograph provided by WorkSharp/Darex, LLC, Josh Warren.

Photograph provided by WorkSharp/Darex, LLC, Josh Warren.

Precision Adjust Sharpener

The Work Sharp Precision Adjust Knife Sharpener is a great sharpening system. This three-sided, abrasive, "jig-and-clamp" style sharpener performs very well. It offers adjustable sharpening angles, from 15 to 30 degrees, in one-degree increments. It is extremely easy to transition between coarse, fine diamond, and fine ceramic stone. Sharpening your knives correctly involves consistency, precision, and repeatability; all easily attainable with the Precision Adjust Knife Sharpener. Other companies produce similar sharpening systems, but they are more expensive. But if you are willing to invest the extra money in a system, then I suggest you take a look at these next few companies who offer great options, such as the Iki Ruixin Pro Sharpener, the Wicked Edge Pro, the Edge Pro Professional, the DMT Aligner Pro, and the GATCO Ultimate Diamond Hone Sharpening System. Work Sharp does a wonderful job at producing amazing sharpening systems at an affordable price. Their Precision Adjust Sharpener can be purchased on their website: https://www.worksharptools.com.

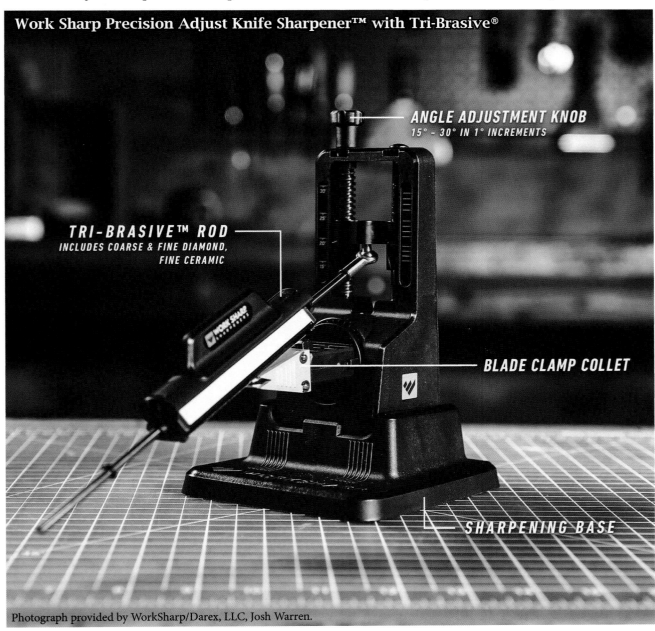

Work Sharp Precision Adjust Knife Sharpener™ with Tri-Brasive®

ANGLE ADJUSTMENT KNOB
15° - 30° IN 1° INCREMENTS

TRI-BRASIVE™ ROD
INCLUDES COARSE & FINE DIAMOND,
FINE CERAMIC

BLADE CLAMP COLLET

SHARPENING BASE

Photograph provided by WorkSharp/Darex, LLC, Josh Warren.

Q&A with Josh Warren from WorkSharp/Darex, LLC

Work Sharp is known for producing the best knife sharpening products on the market. You also produce products that can be used in the outdoors, while camping, fishing, hiking, or hunting. What would you say is your best outdoor sharpening product?

As an all-in-one solution our Guided Field Sharpener is hard to beat. It is an excellent tool for touching up an edge, and for restoring a totally dull blade while on-the-go. It uses a coarse and medium diamond abrasive for setting the edge and sharpening, and then a ceramic rod and leather strop for honing and refining the edge even further. It even has a broadhead wrench and a special groove in the ceramic rod for sharpening fishhooks.

What is your most popular knife sharpener?

Our Original Knife and Tool Sharpener is still our most popular. The versatility of this sharpener to sharpen kitchen knives, pocket knives, lawn mower blades and scissors and shears is unmatched. Users can expect that with light practice they can achieve sharp results on all of their cutting tools!

Which sharpener would you select, as the do-it-all / all-in-one sharpener?

This is almost impossible to answer. If I had to choose one it would be the Elite Knife Sharpener. This sharpener is a free-hand belt sharpening system. The freehand nature allows more belt to be exposed which allows for even more versatility. A wide variety of angle adjustments and use beyond just knife sharpening will keep me coming back to this tool as the one, if I could only choose one.

What Work Sharp product can be used to sharpen a Bark River knife, which is are known for their convex edge?

Any Work Sharp belt sharpeners can be used to sharpen a knife with a convex edge. The abrasive belt only makes contact at the bevel and does not impact the primary grind. A tip for sharpening a knife for the first time on any sharpener. Color the bevel of the knife with a sharpie. Then make a few passes over the finest belt or stone at a set angle. Then inspect the blade. Did the sharpie come off evenly on the whole bevel or did it come off more at the very edge or closer to the primary grind? Adjust your angle from there. Using this method will help show what angle the knife was sharpened at and how to best repeat the angle from the maker or manufacturer.

Can the Ken Onion Knife & Tool Sharpener be used on a scandi grind knife? if not, what would you recommend?

Yes, the Ken Onion can be used on a scandi grind knife, and it will create a convex micro bevel. If you want to maintain a full scandi grind without a micro bevel use a flat diamond stone or whetstone sharpener. The Work Sharp Guided Sharpening system is an excellent tool for the workbench and the Field Sharpener is excellent when on the go.

Joshua, what is your EDC and why?

Like most who EDC, my rotation changes slightly from day to day or week to week. Most often you'll find a Benchmade Mini Crooked River in my pocket. I like the classic style of the blade and it reminds me of the knives I used as a kid. I've always been attracted to clip point blade shapes and with S30v steel, I can keep the edge sharp n

Are there any knife-makers you admire?

Most knife makers are inspiring to me. The level of detail and ability to work with multiple materials to create a beautiful piece of art that also holds up to heavy use… its equally art and technical skill to create the tools I just carry around in my pocket. Ken Onion clearly rises to the top in my view. Ken has focused on the design aspects of knife making as much or more as he has spent time building knives. He is probably most well-known for his Speed Safe invention and patent which I was carrying in a few Kershaws long ago and long before I knew the name Ken Onion. Branching out of just knife making a design Ken has worked with us at Work Sharp to provide valuable insights and designs which have led to some incredible tools. I've used a handful of Ken's knives both production models and customs and each of them has a distinct feel and look that matches Ken.

Is there anything you would like to say to your fans?

Our customers inspire our innovation. This is a shared journey as we work together to learn about needs and rise to the challenge to meet those needs. If you are a Work Sharp customer, we would love to hear from you! Connect with us on social media, leave a comment on any of our YouTube videos, send our world-class customer service team a message, or stop by our office and meet the team that makes it happen! We learn more from our customers than we learn from anywhere else, and we want to build solutions for your real-world challenges. Thanks for following along and supporting us with your business. It means the world!

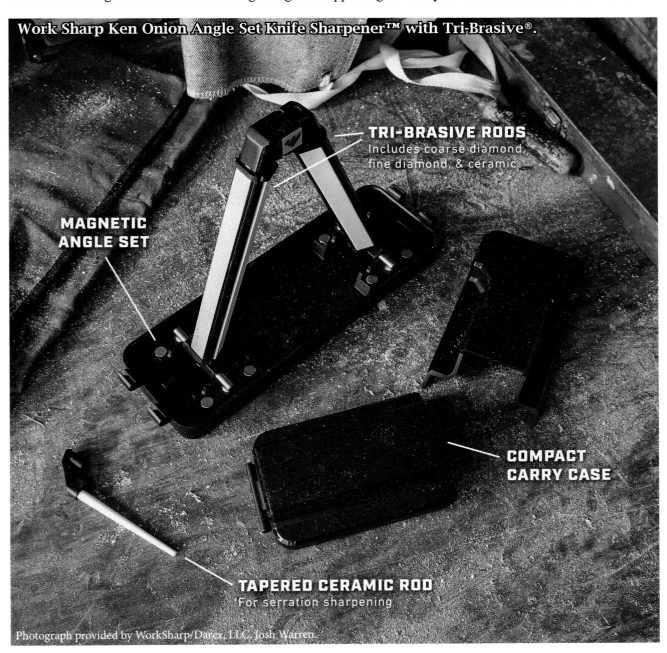

Work Sharp Ken Onion Angle Set Knife Sharpener™ with Tri-Brasive®.

TRI-BRASIVE RODS
Includes coarse diamond, fine diamond, & ceramic

MAGNETIC ANGLE SET

COMPACT CARRY CASE

TAPERED CERAMIC ROD
For serration sharpening

Photograph provided by WorkSharp/Darex, LLC, Josh Warren.

Leather Strop

Leather strops are another great product to consider, as the strop is a very forgiving sharpening product. Here, small mistakes will not do much damage to your knife's edge. When using a strop, use a similar workflow as if it was sandpaper. Sharpen the edge using a backward motion, away from the cutting edge, otherwise you will cut through the leather. I have purchased several strops through DLT trading and Amazon in different sizes and for different environments. Typically, I prefer to use a white compound (12,000 grit) on one side of the strop and a black compound on the other. The white stropping compound is defined as an "extra-fine" grain buffing compound, versus the black compound that is defined as a "fine" grain buffing compound (3,000 grit). There is also a green compound, defined as a "very fine" grain compound (6,000 grit). The green compound is quite popular, but I have found that the white and black are more than enough to get the job done.

Note: While out in the field/outdoors, I do take a small strop that is preloaded with black compound to reduce the amount of items I carry outdoors. At home, I prefer the white and black compounds.

Stropping paste is also a good option in replacement of compound bars. Herold-Solingen makes decent quality stropping pastes, with the red and green paste being the most popular to use on a leather strop.

Norton makes diamond paste, which is particularly good quality and rubs on easily to the strop. They have a 5-gram and 18-gram container (plastic syringe). The Norton Diamond Lapping Paste/Compound comes in 1-micron, 3-micron, 6-micron, up to as high as 90-micron. It is important to understand which Norton compound is oil soluble (OS) versus water soluble (WS) before using.

DMT offers Dia-Paste, with the some of the micron grades as Norton Lapping Paste such as 1-micron, 3-micron, and 6-micron.

Bark River offers a Cubic Boron Nitride (CBN) Emulsion that comes in 0.5-micron, 1-micron, 2-micron, 4-micron, 8-micron, and 16-micron. Bark River's Emulsion is a wonderful option that rubs on easily to a leather strop. According to KnivesShipFree, one drop should cover about six square inches in surface area. For people who do not understand how the micron measurements work, here is a small reference guide for a few of the available pastes/emulsions:

Bark River CBN Emulsion:

0.5 Micron = 35,000 Grit approx.

1 Micron = 16,000 Grit approx.

2 Micron = 8,000 Grit approx.

4 Micron = 4,000 Grit approx.

8 Micron = 2,000 Grit approx.

16 Micron = 1,000 Grit approx.

DMT Dia-Paste:

Copper Coded 6 Micron = 4,000 micro-mesh diamond approx.

Yellow Coded 3 Micron = 8,000 micro-mesh diamond approx.

Gray Coded 1 Micron = 15,000 micro-mesh diamond approx.

Norton Diamond Lapping Compound/Paste

Ultra-Fine 1 Micron (Ivory) = 14,000 micro-mesh diamond approx.

Super-Fine 3 Micron (Yellow) = 8,000 micro-mesh diamond approx.

Super-Fine 6 Micron (Orange) = 3,000 micro-mesh diamond approx.

Fine-Finish 15 Micron (Blue) = 1,200 micro-mesh diamond approx.

As seen above, depending on the manufacturer the micron to grit measurements can differ. Pay attention to this before purchasing, and most importantly, before using.

There are also sprays available that be added to leather strops to achieve exceptionally fine polished edges. DMT makes a Dia-Spray at 0.5-micron that is easy to spray on a leather strop and works very well. It is important to spray the leather strop evenly, otherwise it will not work as intended. The bottle is available in a 25ml size.

I purchase all my Leather Strops at DLT Trading, www.dlttrading.com, or I make them myself using wood purchased at my local hardware store and using genuine, good quality leather purchased at either at Amazon or Etsy.

Make sure, if you do decide to strop your knives, that you invest in good quality leather, one that is thick and not too spongy/springy. Ideally, the leather should be semi-hard, with a smooth even surface. If the leather is too spongy/springy, it can cause an overly aggressive convex edge that will not be as sharp. An aggressive convex edge will result in a rounded edge, versus a nice razor-sharp edge with a fine apex.

Photograph taken by A.J., DLT Trading Leather Strop and Bark River black and white compound.

Belt Sharpener

One of my favorite products for sharpening knives is the Work Sharp Ken Onion Knife and Tool Sharpener. This handheld belt sharpener features an adjustable angle guide for any angle between 15–30 degrees. The variable speed motor also provides good control for sharpening, allowing for consistency and efficiency. The system uses abrasive belts that are made specifically for sharpening all sorts of steels ranging from low to high-grade. Using the Ken Onion Sharpener does require a little practice though, so be patient in the beginning. Try the system out on your "cheaper" knives, those that are easily replaceable, versus going all-in and using your most expensive knife. Be careful, be patient... once you get the hang of it, and don't worry you will, I recommend you then acquire the grinding attachment. After having mastered the grinding attachment, you might not ever use any other sharpening system, or sharpening product, again. The Work Sharp Ken Onion Knife and Tool Sharpener is, by far, one of my preferred methods and system to give your knives a great working edge, nearly effortlessly. Not to mention that it takes less time to sharpen your knife with this sharpener than with any other system or product, without jumping into something meant for commercial/industrial use, like a Tormek, Grizzly, Dynabrade, Kalamazoo, or Knuth. Also keep in mind that any good commercial/industrial grinder can cost anywhere from several hundreds to thousands of dollars.

Frankly, unless you are a professional knifemaker, there is no reason to have a commercial or industrial belt grinder. An inexperienced individual will ultimately remove far too much steel, potentially reprofiling the edge. Untrained eyes could damage the edge permanently, or they might heat up the blade too much, potentially ruining the structure of the steel. When I touch up and sharpen my knife blades, I prefer products that are the least abrasive as possible but can still achieve a working edge on my knife blade. If you do not feel comfortable sharpening your knives, then have them professionally sharpened. Some knifemakers even offer to resharpen the knives you bought from them.

Recently, Work Sharp released their new and improved Knife and Tool Sharpener MK.2. Trust me when I say that it is fantastic. Offering the same capability as the original Ken Onion Edition Knife and Tool Sharpener, except now the sharpening angles are between 20 and 25 degrees. This new system works with the following abrasive belt grits: 80, 220, and 6000. Finally, it is possible to achieve a razor-sharp edge on this system, with little effort. There is also a new two speed motor, offering a low speed meant to enable greater control, as well as a new edge guide, supporting the blade's edge when sharpening through the tip.

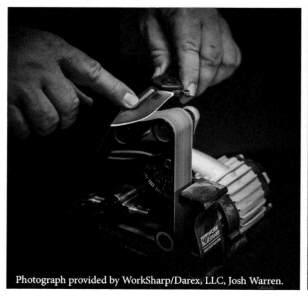

Photograph provided by WorkSharp/Darex, LLC, Josh Warren.

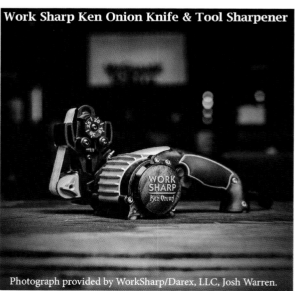

Work Sharp Ken Onion Knife & Tool Sharpener

Photograph provided by WorkSharp/Darex, LLC, Josh Warren.

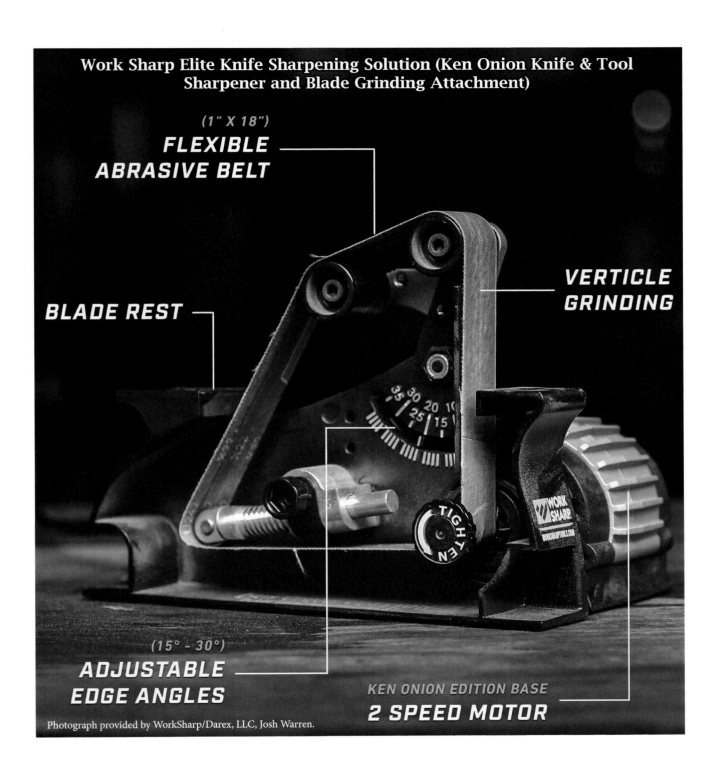

Work Sharp Elite Knife Sharpening Solution (Ken Onion Knife & Tool Sharpener and Blade Grinding Attachment)

(1" X 18")
FLEXIBLE ABRASIVE BELT

VERTICLE GRINDING

BLADE REST

(15° - 30°)
ADJUSTABLE EDGE ANGLES

KEN ONION EDITION BASE
2 SPEED MOTOR

Photograph provided by WorkSharp/Darex, LLC, Josh Warren.

Less Conventional Sharpening Methods:

Ceramic Cup/Mug: Not every ceramic cup/mug is created equal. Depending on the manufacturer, they may add extra material to the bottom to prevent it from damaging surfaces. The question is, can you sharpen you knife on a ceramic mug? The answer is yes, but it depends on the blade material and on the mug. Not all knife blade edges will easily sharpen or even hone on the bottom of a ceramic cup/mug. If the manufacturer did not add extra material to the bottom of the cup/mug and the knife blade material is not a super steel or even a high-end steel, then I would say yes, no doubt it can hone your knife. If your knife is very dull, then the answer is no, not even on the easiest steel to sharpen.

Photograph taken by A.J., sharpening knife on ceramic mug.

Car Window: The rough, top portion of a car window can be used to align an edge, hone it a little, but not really sharpen an edge. Obviously, this all depends on the window type, manufacturing process, knife steel, etc....

Photograph taken by A.J., sharpening knife on car window.

Brick: A brick can be used to sharpen a knife, if it is flattened properly and soaked in water for a few minutes. You may even need to add water periodically as you sharpen your edge. The possibility of sharpening the edge of you knife also depends on the type of brick, material, surface grit, and knife steel. Keep in mind, sharpening on a brick can seriously damage your knife.

Fingernail File: A fingernail file can absolutely be used to sharpen a knife edge. Usually, fingernail files are made of sandpaper or even gritty ceramic. There is no doubt that fingernail files are a good option if you happen to not have the typical sharpening items. Fingernail files are also a great pocket-sized sharpening option to put in a bugout bag, survival kit, or even take on your next adventure.

Cardboard: Using cardboard with some form of chromium oxide compound can work to maintain your knife's edge. It is important to consider that the cardboard must be as flat as possible, with no ridges, and accept the compound properly when applied. If the compound is too clumpy, then it will not work as a good edge maintenance backup system.

Belt: Using a belt as a strop is a particularly good backup option to finetune a knife edge. Obviously, the belt should be made of leather and have good grain consistency throughout the portion you will use. If needed, add compound if you do not mind getting the belt a little dirty and potentially dirtying your clothing when you put it back on.

Using any of the above "less conventional" methods require experience, consistency, and repeatable technique. Free-hand sharpening is difficult, as is using improvised methods, increase the difficulty level. Some of these methods/items can work to sharpen your knife's edge if you know what you are doing. For those people who are less experienced at sharpening knives, I suggest staying away from "less conventional" methods to avoid damaging your knife. However, if this is a last resort or an emergency, it might be your only option... just be careful.

As seen in this subsection, there are a great deal of options to choose from when sharpening your knife. I suggest you try a few of them, build a technique that works for you, and enjoy the sharpening process. Otherwise, you may need to send your knives to be professionally sharpened at a cost.

Photograph taken by A.J., Brommeland Strop in a Can.

Photograph taken by A.J., Bushcraft Supply Field Strop & Ceramic Rod

KNIFE STORAGE:

Store your knives in a cool, dry place with proper air ventilation. Should you choose to store your knives in a cabinet, make sure that they are skillfully placed in a knife storage tray with a large silica gel canister, to avoid humidity from finding its way onto the blades. If you decide to use silica gel canisters, remember to recharge them periodically, as indicated by the manufacturer. I recommend getting a digital hygrometer to monitor humidity levels in your storage area. Ideally you want this area to maintain a humidity level below 45 percent. Once humidity levels begin to crawl above the 50 percent humidity threshold, a redox reaction occurs, which is a combination of two reactions in one, "reduction" and "oxidation," which may start to affect your knife blades by forming rust. Rust is known as Hydrated Ferric Oxide (Fe_2O_3, H_2O), and it happens when iron returns to its natural state, because of the reaction it undergoes when exposed to oxygen and water. Iron will start to rust when relative humidity climbs above 50 percent, and steel will begin to rust when humidity reaches 80 percent. It is important to understand that Fe_2O_3, also known as **orange rust**, is NOT the same as Fe_3O_4, which is known as **black oxide**. Black oxide actually protects your steel from rust because it works as a protective coating. You can create black oxide on your steel by doing a forced patina on the blade. This can be done using several natural ingredients, like vinegar or citric acid. The forced patina process was covered in the **Blade Coating versus No Coating** section. Adding a drop of food grade neutral oil such as a mineral oil or camellia oil will also help prevent rust on your knives. Apply it on each side of the blade, spreading it evenly across the body and edge of the blade.

Note: There are companies that make and sell black oxide kits, but using these kits do require a certain level of experience, since these products/kits contain hazardous materials. If you are looking to use one of these kits for the first time, seek professional assistance/guidance before attempting to use it.

Remember to reapply oil on the knife blades periodically, as needed, depending on where you live and the environmental challenges you face. Tsubaki Japanese Knife Oil is essentially camellia oil, meaning it is food safe, and can be found on Amazon (www.amazon.com). A food grade oil (mineral or camellia) is always my first pick, because if ingested will not cause major health issues. Some food grade oils do expire and that is something to consider. Ballistol oil is another great option for knife and gun maintenance. In the Ballistol website (https://ballistol.com) the company says, *"Ballistol does not contain ingredients considered hazardous by the FDA. It does not contain any ingredients which may be harmful for warm-blooded organisms, reptiles, or aquatic organisms (if used as directed). If swallowed, DO NOT INDUCE VOMITING, ASPIRATION CAN OCCUR. CONSULT A PHYSICIAN IMMEDIATELY"* (05/05/2021).

Another option to protect against rust is using Sentry Solutions Tuf Cloth Dry Film Rust Inhibitor. You can also wrap your knife blades in "Volatile Corrosion Inhibitor (VCI)", or "Volatile Protective Inhibitor (VPI)" paper. VCI or VPI papers are treated with chemicals that safely prevent corrosion on metals. If you choose to use Sentry products or any other product that may have chemicals, remember, there may come a time when you need to use your knife to eat or process/prep food you plan to eat. Be mindful about what you put on your knife blades. There is more than one way to protect your knives from corrosion. Use what works best for you and the environment you live in. If you are outdoors in a humid environment, and do not have any of the above-mentioned products but happen to have beeswax, then consider rubbing beeswax on your knife's blade. Simply apply a light coat of beeswax on your blade and it will prevent rust.

At home, a dehumidifier is another product to consider, as it will absorb any unnecessary moisture from the air dripping it into its tank. Once the tank is full, just empty it out. It is as simple as that. Most of my knives are in my home office, giving me the liberty to plug in a dehumidifier without affecting the aesthetics my home's common areas. Additionally, I store my knives in a cabinet with proper ventilation containing several large silica gel canisters, and I also oil up my blades before storing them away.

These knife maintenance tips are simply suggestions based on what has worked for me over the years. I have lived in several different locations in the United States, such as Florida, Texas, Washington, and Virginia, as well as having lived abroad in Central America and Asia. Every location is unique and comes with its own environmental challenges. There are several methods to protect your knives from corrosion, but should you choose to follow the corrosion mitigation process mentioned, your knives should be fine pretty much anywhere.

Photograph taken by A.J., making feathers with the ESEE-3.

KNIFE
APPLICATIONS

CULINARY

Knives are for everyone. When did it become that only outdoorsy men who like to camp and wear flannel, while sipping away at black coffee and packing up their gear, were the main connoisseurs? Why is it that knives must be associated with "bad boys" and rough and tough guys or with dad's handy utility knife? Have we forgotten that, in general, most of us were introduced to this blade by some matriarchal presence in our life? In those tucked away memories of our childhood where maybe we tried whipping up mom her secret Mother's Day breakfast in bed, or standing atop of a chair next to your *nonna* while watching her magically dice away at onions for the perfect Sunday sauce without crying. Did we all seem to forget the days in which we used to watch grandma hack away at a chicken carcass to quarter it perfectly for the best braised legs, or when *maman* perfectly sliced our snack with her guillotine sharp knife? I have to say, it certainly seems so. The point that I am trying to make is that whether you have an *abuela*, a *bachan*, or a *mormor*, most of us were introduced to, and taught to use, what some would only consider a frowned upon weapon today. When, in fact, these matriarchal figures were always showing us the correct way to use the knife and wherein lies the true significance behind it…. survival.

If you haven't already noticed, the history of the knife is directly correlated to the history of humankind and our technological evolution in the world. Other than fire, I would dare say that it is the true item that allows us to trace our lineage as humans back to prehistoric times. Yes, you can follow the history of the first cutting utensil back to prehistoric dates, just as you can trace the steels back to their country of origin, but what you choose to tell the world with the blade you have at hand… THAT is how the history evolves and continues to unite humanity, whether obvious or not. And, if I may be even bolder, it is the one item that unites us all, regardless of race, sex, creed, religion, social/financial status, and language. We have all used it for survival, convenience, comfortability, and style and continue to further educate rising generations in this vein. Though many of us do not even think twice when using our blunt-tipped dinner knife to generously spread a thick layer of velvety butter onto a slice of finger scorching bread, the truth is that this very "unremarkable" daily utensil was purposely decreed to look blunt so as to appear less "aggressive" on the dinner table when dining amongst others. The point being, while many of us go on about our day understanding that "everything has a purpose," how many times do we really stop to consider not only the purpose, but how that reason came to fruition?

Knife Types

When regarding knives there is an East/West variety, a yin-yang balance, if you will. Here we share a few of the more popular options from within that balance.

Chef [ˈshef]—approx. 6"–11" long. This is the never-failing, honest extension of your arm. Never-failing because it can slice, dice, peel, chop, core, debone, fillet, cut, snip, rip… you name it, it can do it. Honest, because this intimidatingly shiny object will be brutally honest with you should you need more practice. It reveals if something is ready to serve and if something is nowhere near being prepped. Take for example, when carving that beautifully crisp chicken you made for Sunday dinner. If that bird isn't cooked properly, your knife will tell you by exposing the raw, gummy protein further causing your dinner to "bleed out," prior to serving. But should your succulent chicken be thoroughly cooked, then your knife will slice through and wiggle around the joints like butter. Yes, this knife could just smack right through the bird, but again, you must let it do its job… allow it to be a useful gauge for your meal. The chef knife is, furthermore, an "extension of your arm" because that is what it truly was designed to be. We have all heard this saying before, and have maybe even rolled our eyes at some of our pretentious friends who boast about the kitchen not knowing what they do yet still preach this phrase as if it were to earn them a culinary golden star. I am here to say, though, that when it comes to the "extension of your arm" description… the pretentious friend is right. Whether lefty or righty, the chef knife is meant to never leave your hand. Sure, certain actions within the kitchen might be achieved with your bare hands but, this intimidatingly sharp item fulfills your culinary needs with greater precision and style. This knife will never not be your most essential knife in the kitchen. Knives are so much a part of a chef's work, as seen through the name, that it would be difficult to consider their profession without one. While there are additional tools that a chef should learn to master, it is this knife that is responsible for their attachment to the craft. As a result, the beauty and allure of the chef knife has transcended commercial kitchens, finding comfort in residential ones, by appealing to novice home cooks to take on adventurous recipes in hopes of one day mastering technique.

Serrated [sə-ˈrāt] (a.k.a. Bread Knife)—approx. 8"–10" long. This hand driven saw is a necessary, toothy addition to your kitchen. It is a knife where pressure is applied and evenly distributed along the whole of the blade, encouraging your body to "work with it." I did previously mention that the chef knife can do it all, specifically slicing, and while that is true, certain jobs call for specific attention. Take for example, that extra crusty loaf of sourdough most of the world attempted to make during the Covid-19 quarantine, of 2020. Assuming that your loaf was one of the "greats," you would have yielded a wonderfully thick and crusty bread, one that if you dared to slice off a couple of pieces for your grilled cheese, your chef knife would dangerously slip and slide off towards your hand. These loaves request the attention of something that can really bite off equal slices of bread. So, this is where you would reach for your required bread knife. But wait! Now, you have decided to add thick and juicy slices of beefsteak tomatoes to your sammie. Yeah, sure… you could just run your chef knife through that too but consider this: what if your blade is not sharp enough and now you have let all the perfectly sweet juices run off onto your cutting board, turning that beefsteak into more of a tartar. No need to fret. Your bread knife could handle that, effortlessly, right from the start, as well. Finally, after layering up this masterpiece of a sandwich are you really going to attempt to slice it with your chef knife? Certainly, you could but you would also potentially rearrange your edible monument. Because of the individual characteristics of each ingredient, (the firm crusty bread weighing down on the thick-n-sticky bacon which slips on the tomato juices trying to find balance in the delicately crisp lettuce leaves), is this really the right decision to complete your hard effort? Pressing down on your towering work of art, watching the fillings seep from the sides before even making it onto the plate, let alone your mouth? I don't know about you, but I am salivating just thinking about writing that sandwich and certainly wouldn't want the wrong knife to alter that perfect initial bite. Therefore, save this mammoth of a treat from destruction by slicing it (diagonally, of course, but that will be a topic for a different book), with your trusty bread knife. That blade will saw away so perfectly, yet delicately aggressive, that you will finally savor every, crispy, chewy, juicy morsel.

This knife falls within the category of slicer, due to its long, narrow blade. Within the family of slicers, you will find various lengths and "teeth," all purposely designed to make smooth, neat slices with a single stroke. Some are more flexible than others and that is because delicate cuts of protein and flesh are considered, (i.e., smoked salmon or gravlax), to prevent tearing when slicing. Either way, these slicing knives are meat to facilitate your meal both texturally and visually.

Paring *['periNG]*—approx. 3" long. On several occasions I have witnessed people say that they find this to be the most underutilized knife in the kitchen. I certainly understand why. My grandmother used to grab a paring knife (when a steak knife wasn't available) to slice a tartly crisp apple right in her hand and then use the same knife to delicately raise the thinly, juicy slice up to her mouth. I remember that so clearly. I always wondered… how does she not cut herself? How does the apple not slip right off? How does the slice effortlessly make it into her mouth? When I was younger, and less trained, I tried many times to replicate this dance, realizing that it truly was an act mastered with time and practice. Maybe this is why it is sometimes lovingly referred to as the "granny knife." This knife doesn't get the recognition it deserves, I have to say. But maybe that is because some people don't really use it as much when compared to its older brother, the petty knife.

The paring knife is the blade you wish to have in your kitchen arsenal for those perfectly delicate cuts on much smaller ingredients. Again, your chef knife may be efficient enough for the task at hand, but to be exactly precise when slicing through your summer cherry tomatoes, expensive Japanese white strawberries, or even when prepping your toddlers snacking grapes, then certainly the best knife for the job is the "tiny" pairing knife.

Utility *[yoo 'tiləde]* (a.k.a. Petty Knife)—approx. 5"–6" long. The utility knife is quite useful as it is large enough to debone, filet, and complete various other jobs the traditional chef knife would. Yet, it is small enough to do the same jobs as a paring knife, though it might lack some of the favorable flexibility that many look for when using the smaller option. This "in between" kitchen knife is wonderful for those tasks which are not too big and not too small, therefore requiring a blade that is "just right." I have to say, personally, I am sometimes very surprised at how much my hand gravitates to a petty knife. Other than being less of a significant item to clean (size-wise), I think the fact that it is so light on the hand yet so sharp really appeals in those moments when you don't necessarily wish to use two different blades to complete one dish. Sometimes certain recipes don't require a lot of prep to where you really need to go "all in." The utility/petty knife is really a perfect balance between precision and function.

Santoku *[Sawn-TOE-koo]*—approx. 5"–8" long. Meaning "three virtues" in Japanese, this is a knife that gained popularity in kitchens, over the last few decades. Test one out and it is easy to see why, as it can slice through items with ease, especially those that tend to stick onto the side of a blade more due to additional juicy, sticky, or slimy factors. When compared to the size of a traditional chef knife, the santoku is clearly smaller, yet another aspect appealing to those who are more intimidated by a chef knife. The size difference is not without reason as it was designed to be a union of the utility and chef knife, resulting in a blade that is easier on the hand and arm, while still an effective slicer. That said, this knife is not a replacement for either of its inspirations. Though it may be appealing to the home cook as a simpler tool to use, upon closer observation the santoku knife may lead to a more cumbersome load on a professional. The lack of belly on the blade means that there isn't enough range of motion for overall comfort. So, if you prefer your knives to "rock" on the cutting board you certainly won't find that back-and-forth motion here. Cutting and slicing without fatigue and truthfully, accuracy, is difficult to manage with this knife. Would the santoku be a necessary knife to have in your kitchen collection? I would say this is certainly a preferential item as opposed to the previous ones mentioned. Check one out and consider how much you cook in general and then maybe this knife could take a place in your home, or not.

Cleaver *['klēvər]*—approx. 7"–8" long. These incredibly beautiful yet startling blades have been around for centuries with Japan, China, France, England, and countless other countries showcasing their version of this hefty knife. While some cleavers are surprisingly light, there is an undoubtful impression of confidence and control that these knives portray and that the holder, should have. The cleaver is certainly not the kind of item you wish to hold with a lack of self-confidence. If you are going to smack this knife down, then you better keep your eye on where this blade is going to land and remove any unnecessary joints from its direction because once this baby goes down it will take anything in its way too. Some countries (for example, Japan and China) designed their cleavers to be a replacement for the chef knife and therefore have been masterfully used for the same applications. This knife's function is essentially to cut through bone, tendons, meat… the whole animal! This is not an accuracy tool for finer cuts and it is also not a required tool for all to have either. The weighty cleaver undoubtedly gives you an immediate sense of power, where its weight and momentum will do most of the work for you.

Mezzaluna [met-*suh*-loo-n*uh*]/**Ulu** *[OO-loo]*—approx. 6"–20+" wide. A centuries-old tool, adopted by the Italians and indigenous tribes in Alaska, continues to be used today due to its remarkable efficacy. There is an extraordinary observation when holding onto the mezzaluna/ulu, as if one can almost trace back the primordial roots of the knife itself, and where each back-and-forth rock evolves closer to the modern tools of today. This knife has been used to concoct entire meals from beginning to end, literally. From skinning and butchering the caught game, to the processing and preparation for cooking. Then, this same "half-moon" blade would be wiggled into creating any additional side dishes, before finally dividing the meal at the table with your tribe. Today, the ulu is still traditionally used to perform these specific tasks further introducing it to younger generations. The mezzaluna version is highly popular with Italian nonnas who are looking to chop their herbs with rapid ease to mix into their *pomodoro* sauce while the rigatoni cooks away. The half-moon design is incredibly appealing to those who are intimated by a traditional knife as this design is meant to be used with both hands (the ulu, though, is a single-handed blade). Therefore, this knife is not only less daunting for some home cooks to pick up but can also relieve some of the pressure caused on one's hands and wrists from the traditional back-and-forth of a chef knife. Both versions hold wonderful cultural legacies. Though not popular in many kitchens, owning either one will appeal quickly to the hand while igniting wonderful conversations in the kitchen, guaranteed. Regardless of whether it has a single (ulu), double, or triple blade (mezzaluna), one thing is certain, this curved knife is beautifully elegant when dancing away on the board.

Tourné *[tour-nay]* (a.k.a. Bird's Beak) —approx. 2.5" long. Referred to as a "bird's beak" due to its curved design resembling exactly that, the tourné knife was in fact made to cut *towards* the hand. It is a knife designed with the vegetable in mind, as it can find its way through all its organic shapes. Classically, this knife was used to make symmetrical, seven-sided, oblong cuts. But either because people realized how tedious it was to make these delicate figures (not to mention dangerous), or because dining experiences changed and became more casual, the tourné knife has lost its presence in the kitchen.

KIKUICHI

Back in October 2020, when I first agreed to collaborate on this book, I decided that if I was going to do this, I was not only going to take the opportunity to get to know some of my favorite companies a bit better, but I was also going to "reach for the sky" and contact some of the more marvelous makers I had seen out there. I also knew, almost immediately, that I wanted to showcase as many makers as possible from around the globe. The more research I did, the more intrigued I was by what men and women alike were producing. Large, well-established companies offered beautiful items but there were also many unknown "mom and pops" competing for a fair chance at acclaim. It was abundantly clear that I wanted to make the effort to showcase brands that I could recommend while including lesser-known brands from all corners of the earth.

The following is a beautifully written introduction for the even more spectacular brand, known as Kikuichi, shared by Harry Rosenblum. As General Manager and Head of Operations in America, Mr. Rosenblum is also the man behind the Q&A that follows. Lastly, Ikuyo Yanagisawa, the wonderful female leader and president of the company shares her family legacy with us; a history which she has relentlessly strived to keep alive and honor.

"Kikuichi is the oldest knife company in the world, we trace our roots to the swordsmith, Shiro Kanenaga. The earliest known sword of his, was made in 1267. He made swords for the emperor and so was granted the chrysanthemum mark, which appears in our logo today. In Japan the chrysanthemum is a symbol usually reserved for items used by, or associated with, the emperor. Fast forward to the middle of the nineteenth century when the then-emperor outlawed the samurai, and suddenly there was no longer a market for swords. This is when the modern company was founded and when we started focusing on kitchen knives and other blades.

In much of our production the knives are made by a series of master craftsmen, each of whom focus on one part of the process and don't all work together in one factory. Each one is a small business, usually living above, or next to, their workshops.

First the blade is forged, often from two pieces of steel, with one becoming the blade edge, and the other becoming the spine and tang of the blade. The blade steel is harder and is called *hagane*. It is forge welded to the *jigane*, the softer steel. In ancient times it was discovered that by laminating the steel this way it was rendered easier to work and shape. Our highest quality and most precious blades are made entirely from the harder blade steel, these are called *honyaki*. It takes longer, and is much more difficult to forge these blades, and so their price can go into the thousands for a single knife.

After the blade is forged and pounded into shape it is heat treated before it leaves the first craftsman.

The second step is the grinding and sharpening phase. This is all done before the handle is put on. The blade is nailed to a board and then ground and sharpened, first on large spinning wheels and then on water stones.

Once sharpening is complete, the knife moves to our Master Knifesmith Mr. Akimasa Ohe. He sources handles from a shop that only makes handles and depending on the knife he chooses the proper size and shape (D-shaped or oval for most, octagonal for *honyaki* and special blades). These handles are most often made from Ho-Wood (Japanese Magnolia) with a water buffalo horn ferrule, but can also be made from walnut, ebony and ornamented with silver, bone, and other decorations as well.

Mr. Ohe then assembles the blade into the handle and makes sure the blade meets our quality standards. Only then does he do the final engraving of our chrysanthemum logo and name on the blade.

His hands are the last ones to touch our knives before the customer opens the box.

This is the process for all our single bevel, traditional Japanese knives and our double bevel, carbon steel knives with the *Wa* (or Japanese-style) handles. Our Western-style knives are made in partner factories to our specifications, and we work only with the best makers for each style and steel type."

Photograph provided by Kikuichi.

Q&A with Harry Rosenblum, *G.M. & Head of Operations (USA) for Kikuichi*

Which knife(s) is the most popular in your line, and what do you think makes it so appealing?

Our most popular knives are our Warikomi Gold Damascus Tsuchime knives. They are 17 layers of stainless steel sandwiched around a VG10 core for the blade edge. They are hand hammered giving each knife a unique pattern on the blade and the hammering helps release food that might stick to the blade.

What is your personal favorite knife and why?

I have to say that it depends on the usage, especially when it comes to Japanese knives, as there are specific shapes for specific uses. If I had to choose one type of knife to own it would probably be the Nakiri style, or what is often referred to as a Japanese vegetable knife, because I find it to be very versatile with its thin blade and flat profile.

What do you recommend for proper long-term storage knives?

Away from moisture, and away from things that might damage the blade. We recommend a cover, or saya, and storing in a drawer, or in a block. A magnet works well but you must be careful not to damage the blade when removing the knife from the magnet. For carbon steel we recommend a light coating of oil, such as Tsubaki or Camelia oil to keep the blade from rusting.

Are there any other knife-makers you admire?

Anyone making knives by hand, as it is very hard and a hard business to be in. In the United States, MKS knife, Bob Kramer, and Middleton Made Knives to name a few. Florentine Knives in Spain.

What is your earliest memory of using/being introduced to a knife?

My earliest memory of a knife is using a pocketknife for whittling sticks. In the kitchen I have memories of cutting vegetables with my mother when I was 7 or 8 years old.

Photograph provided by Kikuichi.

Today, after 750 years, Kikuichi remains a family business as seen with the remarkable and trail-blazing leadership of Ikuyo Yanagisawa. Having taken over after her father's fifty-year direction, Ikuyo fills a void in the industry, which is also finally becoming more normalized, rather that popular. This is a meaningful "full circle" moment that must be applauded as Ikuyo, who was raised in what is recognized as one of Japan's ancient cities, Nara, and under extremely traditional customs, is now on the forefront of this historically lush company. Without a doubt, Ikuyo Yanagisawa represents the evolution of women's rights, especially stemming from a country where their delicate and attentive natures were always glorified. Now, that same country, Japan, understands that a woman adds value both at home and in the workplace and as a result considers them a crucial component to the economic growth of the country. A businesswoman, philanthropist, humanitarian, wife, mother, and daughter, Ikuyo is now an emboldened woman seeking to change the how society views women while maintaining Kikuichi's traditional creative direction. Just like balance is ever important in Japanese culture, through the yin-yang, a perfectly balanced knife is also extremely necessary. Kikuichi's modern leader understands this not only through their designs but also as a symbolic representation of what a well-balanced society should be like, one in which both men and women also maintain an equal balance. This remarkable fourth-generation leader shared this personal family story with us; one that her father used to reflect on, at times.

"One story that has been related to me about Kikuchi is about how our store came to be where it is and what happened during and after WWII. My great grandparents started our store in Nara Park in the second half of the 19th century. Nara prefecture was at that time developing a national park in Nara, and the prefectural government suggested that Kikuichi place its headquarters in the newly designated park. Over the years my grandparents continued selling swords alongside the knives. Even though the swords were no longer being produced, we had a large collection of them from our family of makers over the centuries. Many Japanese military officers would arrive on horseback to purchase the swords before setting off for their assignments. It has always been a sign of rank to carry a sword, and only officers were allowed to have them. At the store we had a huge collection of swords until WWII. During WWII, the Japanese government was collecting all metal products for the war effort including the swords, so we hid many swords within our extended family at their residences. Today we have only 40 swords.

The US military police were stationed in Nara after WWII and when my grandfather returned from Manchuria where he served as a military officer, our business shifted more toward tourism with a focus on our fine cutlery. After the war the Japanese government made the sale and transport of traditional swords out of the country illegal, so today we do not sell our swords but keep them and display them as a part of our cultural heritage.

For our entire 750 years in business, our family has stayed in this area. As the current president of Kikuichi, we must protect our story and quality. This is one way we have lasted for so long and how we will survive for the next 750 years. Thank you."

Ikuyo Yanagisawa, 4th generation Owner & President of Kikuichi

What to Look for in a Knife

The most important component when seeking out a new knife is how it feels to *you*. If it feels good in the store, it will most certainly feel good in the kitchen. Once you have a better grasp of what you need then curating your own set, or collection, becomes quite an easier task. I'll be honest, 99.99% of us do not need to purchase a knife block. Sure, they come with a honing stick and shears, and hey, they sometimes throw in a few extra steak knives too… trust me, you don't need one. When these blocks first came out, makers were considering something that was fast and easy for the consumer to purchase, i.e., commercial. Finally, our parents felt like they had options in customizing their dining collection even further and would seek these knife blocks as a compliment to their heirloom china. It is quite possible that the driving factor was to show off on holidays and dinner parties when they would also bring out that classic olive-green Sears electric slicer, meant to elegantly hack away at the holiday turkey.

With time, though, I have seen that brands have become more aware of the fact that later generations finally discovered the secret they all hoped we wouldn't… which is that we don't need *all* those blades. In fact, now you can find incredibly made knives from renowned brands, which have decided to offer three to five of their knives as an essential kit… with a block! And man have these blocks evolved with their sleeker, sometimes magnetic, designs that would look great on any counter to showcase your modern kitchen knife selection.

You could always consider one of these newer blocks, but I would encourage you to pick and choose each knife you will use. Learn about the beautifully different companies out there. Support these businesses that have been doing this the "old-fashioned way" for centuries, or those "mom and pops" who started out a few years ago and produce some top-notch items. Play with textures and color, both in the blade (i.e., Damascus) and on the handle (wood, stone, horn, composite). Showcase your sense of adventure with a beautiful collection of knives from all over the globe. Frankly, whether you choose to go this route or if you simply prefer to purchase a block with a tap on your phone (and receive free two-day shipping, of course), or if you just have perfectly useful hand-me-downs… whatever you do, make sure it feels good to *you*.

Use

So, *what are you* going to be using the blade in question for: everyday cooking (chef's knife), slicing a couple of apples here and there (utility knife), chopping through large chunks of meat and bone (cleaver)? Are you going to be using this knife predominantly at home or in a professional setting? Are you a professional or a home cook with some experience or are you a novice who has no interest in cooking but needs to have *something* in the kitchen? These are all valid questions one should ask themselves prior to even searching for the "*Top 10 Best Knives of 2020*" (which honestly, that was a rough year, so I doubt anything "best" came out of that year, either way). Listen, as mentioned before, a traditional chef knife is never a bad idea. But depending on what your answer is to these questions, then you could be talking about the difference between a very high-end, customizable, and frankly expensive knife and a more affordable (dare I say, disposable) mediocre blade.

Length, Width, Weight

Because comfortability is key, these are three main factors to consider:

Length. Sure, everyone says that your kitchen knife should be an "extension of your arm," but what does that really mean? It means that it should feel so comfortably natural when used that you basically forget you're even holding a knife. It should not weigh you down, hurt your body, or make you feel insecure. This sharp object can make you feel like the most confident person in the room whether, or not, you have perfect knife cuts. But this confidence stems from an approachability and control over one of the main features of a kitchen knife. So, when considering length, "the bigger the better" is not always the way to go.

Width. Pretty much the same concept here as we are considering the width of the blade, and furthermore, does it have a bolster? The bolster signifies that you have a thicker blade in your grasp, whereas knives without a bolster are clearly thinner. Other than the personalization of a knife's design, I find this to be the most deciding factor when purchasing a chef knife. Think of how differently everyone holds a pencil. We have all adjusted how we write according to what feels good within our hand, as certain grips can hurt, bother, and even lead to blisters. This is the perfect example of how a bolster affects a person's decision when choosing a new knife. Now, let's flip our view on the knife from the center width and allow us to observe the flat side of the blade, taking into consideration the width of the "belly" of the knife. This is yet another reason I find that width *is* the deciding factor when choosing your knife, because the belly is what is going to ultimately accommodate to the "sway and rock" when used. Maybe you are looking for that specific motion on your cutting board to further give you ease and speed. Maybe you are looking for something with less movement, giving you more control over the blade itself. Neither is truly better than the other but, both options were designed to give the consumer the choice as to what feels best for them in the long run.

Weight. This characteristic takes a bit of a different approach than the previous two. Sure, you want to see how comfortable you feel with the actual weight of the item. Is it too heavy for your hands, or do you need something with more heft? While this is an important factor, you also need to consider balance and the relationship between the distribution of weight, between the tip and the handle. Does the tip tilt forward when held upright (i.e., heavier tip) or does it gravitate backward (i.e., heavier handle)? Remember, balance is key. Not just in the weight of the knife but how you hold your knife as well. When grabbing your blade, make sure it feels well balanced. This is to ensure that now your knife will work with you and not against you. Some knifemakers make knives which leave this preference open to their clientele upon commission, while others standout by crafting remarkably balanced pieces from the very beginning. The variety of design options today for handles (plastic, wood, metal, horn) along with the chosen steels used are all components that can, and will, affect the weight of a blade. There is no magic formula to consider when determining what feels comfortable to you.

Photograph provided by Cristina Martinez, Photographer: Neal Santos.

Photograph provided by Mike Pirolo, Photographer: Adam DelGiudice

Profile: Chef Mike Pirolo

Macchialina is the quaint, little spot continuously charming South Beach diners today. The moment you cross it's threshold, you realize that you have entered a place where the dining adventure will encompass the fantastic food and ambiance, as a welcoming familial experience awaits you. Macchialina is the type of place that will pull on your sensory heart strings, after your initial visit, reminding you why you have fallen in love with this spot in the first place.

Run by Chef Mike Pirolo, (who is also one-third owner), Macchialina is a place where the meticulous training of a chef who has worked and learned through the most rigidly refined of conditions is juxtaposed with a spontaneously comforting quality. This union of words best describes the relationship that Mike has had in his life and chooses to display both on and off the plate. A man completely influenced by technique and custom, it comes as no surprise that Mike Pirolo would find Japanese knives to be the chosen extension of his arm, when at the cutting board. Technique and custom, dare I say, are two of the largest driving factors in everything that is Japanese designed, and Italian made. Whether you have had the pleasure of befriending Mike or have only been introduced to him through his food, it is obvious that Mike's fingerprint is stylish and technical. His New York influence is depicted through his detailed precision while his casual Italian affect opens the door for this creative to play.

Where some chefs seem to have difficulty picking their "very favorite" knife, Chef Pirolo does not. While he does own a variety of knives from different places, he consciously chooses to not have different knives from different places for the same duties. Short and sweet, Japanese single-blade knives are his favorite style of knife and doesn't consider trading them in, any time soon.

While Mike does not describe himself as an outdoorsman, there *is* a curious twinkle in his eye encouraging him to eventually dabble in the world of foraging. Born in New York, raised in Italy, and claiming Miami as home, these cities' cultural influence are prevalent in Chef Mike Pirolo's personality and technique. For a man who finds it difficult to helm any city responsible for his "identity," Mike has certainly found a way to cohesively create his own persona through his magnificent embrace of all cultures who have welcomed him first.

Photograph provided by Mike Pirolo, Photographer: 52 Chefs

Q&A with Chef Mike Pirolo, *Macchialina*

What is your youngest memory with a knife, and do you happen to recall who introduced you to one?

My great-grandfather was a butcher, and my mom had all his knives and steels on display at the house growing up.

What do you look for when purchasing any of your kitchen knives?

I'm a huge fan of Japanese knives with one-sided blades. My personal favorite is the Nenox Gyuto, which I store in a wooden sleeve.

The food world has gone through so many facets and trends, but especially after this pandemic the hospitality world has been hit extremely hard. Where do you see the culinary world shifting to, and do you think that it will be a sustainable shift?

I think that restaurant people are by nature extremely adaptable. I see the return of "fine dining," now that people are starting to get back out there. I think they will be looking for elevated experiences.

What are some underutilized ingredients, or utensils, that you find make a significant difference when used? Do you have any non-negotiable "must-haves" in the kitchen?

Fresh herbs! There's not a sauce, pasta dish or entrée that doesn't have fresh herbs in it on any of my menus. Stainless steel sauté pans are always a must-have!

Any gnarly injuries you might have had or witnessed during your career?

Ooooof, too many to mention. The most common injuries are with the Mandolin. Please put three pairs of gloves on your slicing hand, so when your hand does slip it will hopefully only make it through the gloves and not break the skin!

If you could collaborate with a knife company to produce your ideal knife, what would that look like?

A heavy clever-style knife with a sharp edge to cut vegetables.

You are on a road trip to a remote area of the world… Where are you? Who are you with? What are you cooking?

In Alaska, with my family, catching salmon and grilling it over an open flame. I have never been and don't describe myself as an outdoorsman, but this would certainly be an adventure I look forward to experiencing in my life.

Favorite utensils

My Nenox chef knife

Favorite place to cook outside

In my back yard at my pizza oven

Favorite recipe to cook outside

Pizza and rotisserie chicken on an open flame

How much should you pay

Price: You don't really need me to tell you that you should always get something you can afford. Sure, there are times when we want to splurge by acquiring that one showstopping piece that *will be* used, or honestly, just showed off. But even during those gluttonous shopping experiences, we should recognize that everyone's budget is not equal. And that is perfectly fine. There are many wonderful knives out there within all budgets, but you must do your research and find them. Just remember, though, *you get what you pay for.* So, if you, frankly, just need something right now so that you can slice your grilled cheese sandwich in half, then go for it… do you. But if you are looking for a piece that is going to last you a very long time, feel comfortable in your hands, and dare I say, inspire you to cook, then I would certainly encourage you to adjust your budget by a few dollars. That said, if it's an heirloom piece that you're going after, you know... the ones that become prized possessions and get handed down generation to generation; then you need to understand that you are going to have to mentally prepare yourself for the number of zeros printed on your receipt.

Specialty knives can cost you a pretty penny and, quite frankly, if you are not going to use it daily then why would you want to go that route? There are all kinds of knives under the sun, each meant to perform specific, or various tasks, efficiently. Take into consideration the amount of time your hand will be grasping this blade. If it is not significant, then I recommend you consider purchasing an "upgrade" or "partner" for a design that already is accustomed to your grip.

At the end of the day, don't overthink your decision. Don't overwhelm yourself with options either. Everything that surrounds the world of cooking should be fascinating and fun, and this moment is no different. Just remember that this is an item that should last you for years, so choose something that suits your needs, feels great, and encourages you to get in the kitchen and cook up some great memories.

COLTELLEIRE BERTI

There is something that is innately synonymous with classic design, sleek curves, and timeless quality that has always been associated with Italian aesthetic. In the case of Coltelleire Berti, they not only encapsulate this, but they also harbor a deep-rooted family history into every facet of their company. Andrea Berti is the fourth-generation leader of this family-owned business. Although they have evolved in how they maneuver the business; their knives remain classic to their great-grandfather's vision. There is something inherently wonderful and beautiful when we get to witness the continued success of past ingenuity, during the modern, social media driven world of today.

Andrea was "born into" the knife world, shall we say. So much so, that he doesn't recall a particular moment in which he was methodologically introduced to "the knife." Instead, as he says, "the knife has always been a 'normal' object and has never had the appearance of inaccessibility that it has for children." By the age of twelve, he was already working in the family business, mounting the handles on the knives, or *bullette*. These are the nuances that breathe life into family businesses; passion that cannot be easily challenged by competitors. Berti, both Andrea and the brand, have cemented their presence in the industry through their craftsmanship and innovation.

Like other Italian brands, Berti leads their company aware of the "less is more…" You won't find any unnecessary frills here. Even their knife blocks are so stylishly and cleverly made, as they are designed to magnetically "attract" to each other. Meaning they have found the way to render the knife block completely customizable, according to the individual's needs. What a concept! Especially after noting how unnecessary and "better off" one is not purchasing a highly commercialized, "safe," knife block. Coltelleire Berti noticed the lack of life lasting quality in those blocks, while also recognizing that the consumer was indeed seeking out such a product for both design and functionality. So, they intentionally designed their kitchen knives to arrive with its own block, (although there is also the option to purchase without), allowing you to transform it into the personalized, modern version of your parents' bulky and dated knife block. If something is to reside on our kitchen counter, (which many would consider to be prized real estate), then it should certainly have both function and design embedded into every aspect. Berti has accomplished this.

Coltelleire Berti is beautifully Italian in every aspect of their business, from their fascinating family history to the intriguing anticipation of what they shall produce next. This is not a company that depends on any bells and whistles to appeal to the consumer. Their honest quality and timeless creations are meant to be the knives which transform into heirlooms. Berti has essentially romanticized the notion that their multi-generational company will hand create a product for you which will ultimately be passed down for generations to come, in your own family. In other words, when you bring a Berti knife home you are bringing home, family.

Photographs provided by Coltellerie BERTI, Andrea Berti.

Q&A with Andrea Berti, *4th Generation Owner, Coltelleire Berti*

Which knife(s) is the most popular in your line, and what do you think makes it so attractive?

There is no doubt that our most popular knife (and most copied by the competition) is the *Convivio Nuovo*—table knife. It was founded in 1997 with a process of retro-innovation applied to a knife of the 1930s, typical of Scarperia. Its success is given to the highly innovative "S" design, (until 1997 there were no others).

This blade geometry achieves two extraordinary results:

1. Comes out of the hand in a natural way as if it were an extension of the limb.

2. It lies naturally on the plate, greatly facilitating the cutting action. Now you can find it in some of the most prestigious restaurants in the world.

How important is the detail that goes into the design of the handle of a knife, compared to the attention that is placed on the blade?

The elements that characterize a knife are:

- Blade: must be produced with steels and processes that guarantee cutting effectiveness and durability, but its geometry cannot be neglected. Shape, thickness, dimensions, and type of sharpening are decisive in the success of a cut, at least as much as the quality of the material and the production process.

- Handle: geometry is fundamental, when holding a knife in your hand. It must be a pleasure, even if you use it for work many hours a day. There are very specific rules to be observed to make this as pleasant as possible. In addition, the handle contributes a lot to the overall aesthetics of the knife, which cannot be overlooked, since the knives end up on our tables and in our kitchens. So, it is good to offer different materials to meet the needs of everyone.

- Weight Distribution: this is a very delicate topic. Not everyone has the same tastes, some prefer heavier knives and others prefer lighter knives. Personally, I prefer a light knife that has the weight shifted on the blade in such a way as to help during cutting, without straining the wrist if you are working many hours in the kitchen.

Where do you see the future of kitchen knives, especially now that the world has returned to cooking at home or has begun its culinary "journey?"

I believe that the knife still has a great future in our world of modernity and automation. Taking care of ourselves, of our loved ones, and cooking with the appropriate tools that allow us to repeat ancient gestures, as in a ritual, is something indispensable.

What is your favorite knife (may or may not necessarily be of your brand) and why?

Among the knives we produce the one I prefer is the *Pontormo*, which is the reproduction of a knife which appears on the painting "*Dinner at Emmaus*," by Italian Renaissance painter, Pontormo, (located at the Uffizi, in Florence). I am fond of it both because it is a universal knife for the kitchen, with a multifaceted and fantastic use, but also because it's design and production represented the beginning of a new production path, which led me to propose several products that have now become icons of Italian cutlery.

Photograph provided by Coltellerie BERTI, Andrea Berti.

In addition to producing over 1500 different knives, I have a personal collection of a few thousand knives and among them, my favorite is a *mozzetta* made by my great-grandfather in 1935. It is a very simple knife, even "poor," but emotionally engaging. My great-grandfather produced exclusively mozzette all his life, until 1947. He made 60 pieces a week, starting them on Mondays so they may be ready to sell on Saturdays.

Photograph provided by Coltellerie BERTI, Andrea Berti.

How are the details of sharpening, grip, hardening, and use decided and how long does it take from concept to final production?

The design process always arises from a particular need for cutting… often felt by me, but also proposed by others such as chefs, designers, friends, etc.

The first thing to do is to define the geometry of the knife to better solve the cutting problem for which the knife is being born. Once a drawing has been defined, it is necessary to create a real model, normally not sharp, but with the chosen materials, to define volumes and weights. Finally, a first working prototype is created to verify its pleasantness and effectiveness.

The type of hardening and the geometry of the sharpening of the steel are the easiest things to establish, they are technical aspects which follow strict rules, knowing what the knife is intended for. These are obligatory choices. Of course, more choices are available depending on the quality (price!), that you want to obtain, but in our case, we never pose this problem: we always do the best we can do!

What do you look for when buying a new knife to add to your kitchen?

I don't want to be surprised by the "special effects" of shapes or materials, out of the ordinary. So, I prefer to focus on the correctness of the shape of the blade, the handle, the geometry of the sharpening, and the attention to the finish which allows you to understand how much of the design of the knife has been realized.

Unfortunately, no information is possible on the quality of the steel, just by looking at the knife. So, if it is declared by the manufacturer, we must trust that we will notice its quality later. There is a universal rule: at 10 € you cannot buy a good knife.

In 1.5 million years, since prehistoric man discovered the possibility of cutting with a chipped flint, there have been only 4 significant innovations from the point of view of the materials used: chipped flint until about 8000 years ago, then arrival of the first metals, and about 4000 years ago (with the discovery of the forging of iron) came the first knives with a sort of steel which was unable to control the composition, until the eighteenth century when the first blast furnace was introduced in England. From then, until the 1950s, all knives were made with carbon steel, of various qualities depending on the type of knife that was going to be produced. In those years, stainless steel was adopted and finally, since 1984 knives with ceramic blades have been produced. Of course, today there are infinite special steels (liquids, sintered, etc.), but it is good to leave them to the world of collecting, or for special occasions. For the kitchen, stay with a good steel knife.

Apart from the obvious, why do you think people are so intimidated by knives or are afraid to use them?

One cannot ignore the fact that the knife is also a weapon, and above all it was the only weapon until 800 years ago. For over a million and a half years, man has defended himself, and offended, with a sharp object, all this left a trace in our subconscious.

If you could build the knife kit of your dreams, what knives would you include and why?

For me, knives are not only objects that have the function of cutting; I prefer to consider them in the way a pair of shoes are considered by a lady who loves elegance: she will find the reason and the opportunity to wear thousands of different types. All shoes protect the foot but, on every occasion, there is the more suitable one.

So, we can circumscribe the ideal set of knives among those we produce:

2 sets of 12-piece table knives (one specifically for red meat w/bone, and the other for more transversal use)

7 knives for preparing food in the kitchen

7 knives for table service

4 knives for cutting sweets

4 knives for cutting cheeses

Photograph provided by Coltellerie BERTI, Andrea Berti.

Your Essentials

Ask almost any professional and they will tell you their favorite knife, prior to reminding you, as I have before, that you should always go with the knife that works best and feels best to you. If you haven't already noticed, I have not recommended a specific type of knife(s), as "Best of the Best." This is because choosing your knife is a very personalized decision. Each knife is unique to their owner's characteristics, need, price, comfortability, etc. The brands profiled in this section were chosen because of their history, authenticity, and reputation. Therefore, rather than telling you what specific brand to buy, I have recommended essential styles of knives to choose from when starting, or adding to, your essential kitchen set.

Setting Up Your Station

Many of us don't really consider having the proper workstation when cooking at home. While some take an immense amount of pride in their knife and cutting board selection, to the type of salt and olive oil showcased on their countertops, others just grab a knife and get to work. While I appreciate this fascinated foodie enthusiasm, considering where and how you will stand for a more efficient cooking experience *is crucial*. You should always set up your workstation so that you are not too far from where you will be cooking and can reach the food you will prepare. This area should also be comfortable, as this is the place where you will come to daily to prepare your nourishing meals and where you will probably test out adventurous recipes for memorable dinner parties. You should always look for a spot where your board can be placed squarely in front of you, further allowing you to stand in a comfortable, natural position. Just like you want your knife to feel great in your hands, you also want to make sure your cutting board is not too high, not too low, but *just right*. If Goldilocks taught us anything, it was that research is certainly key when seeking comfort.

General Safety Tips

Now that we have set up camp in the kitchen and figured out the best place to work, let's briefly go over some tips that will keep both you and others safe while in the kitchen.

- Always hold your knife by the handle.

- NEVER attempt to catch a falling knife!

- When passing a knife to someone, make sure it is either by the handle or lay it on a flat surface for the other person to grab a hold of the handle safely.

- Make sure your blade does not extend over the edge of your board, or any surface for that matter.

- **NEVER** use your knife to open doors, drawers, etc.

- **NEVER** leave knives loose where they are not easily seen.

- If you must carry your knife through an area, make sure you hold it straight down along the side of your body with the sharp edge facing behind you.

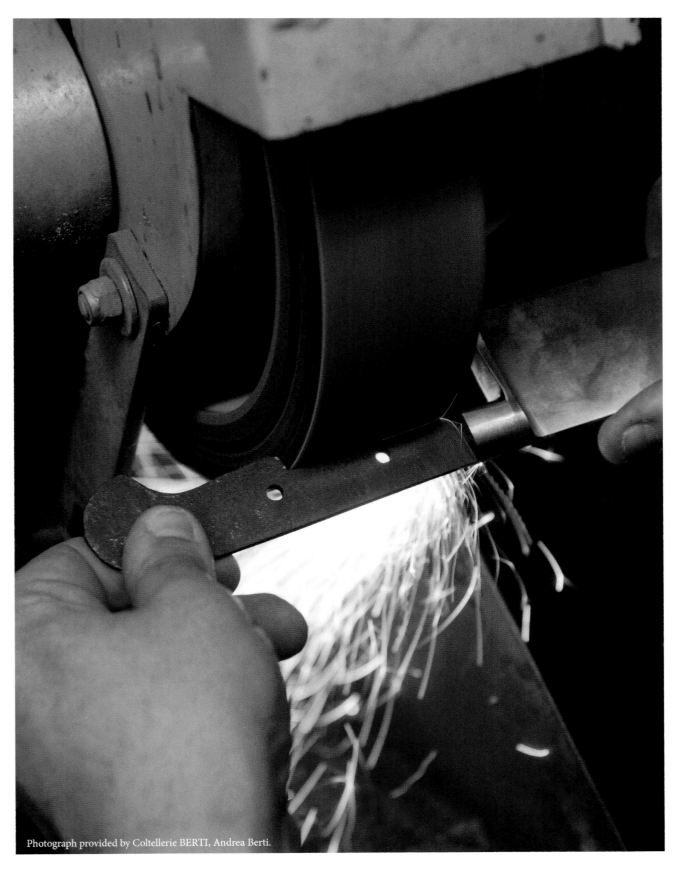

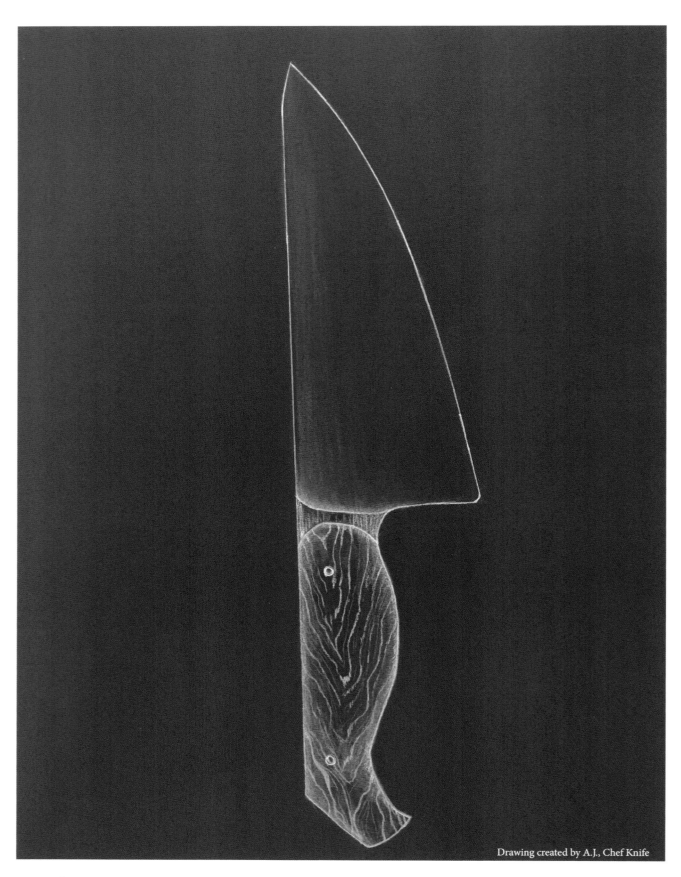

Drawing created by A.J., Chef Knife

Chef Knife

Classically French, though wonderfully translated into German, Italian, English, and Japanese styles. This is THE knife. If anyone were to ask me: what is the one knife they must have in their kitchen, I would certainly say a chef knife. Designed to be used for a wide range of tasks, this knife will not disappoint. That said, test out your knife prior to purchasing it (if you are not allowed to do so, then I would suggest you don't get it), as chef knives have evolved to accommodate various professions and more importantly, grips. A quality blade will always be well balanced, meaning the weight at the blade will be evenly distributed with the weight of the handle. Here again is another aspect that requires your personalization, as some people prefer their knife to be heavier at the tip while others opt for the opposite. When designed (or chosen) properly, your knuckles will never meet the cutting surface, further assisting your overall comfortability. While these characteristics may seem trivial to some, trust me when I say that the wrong knife (in terms of handle, weight, design, etc.,), will effectively scar you with pain, calluses, and blisters.

The blade of the chef's knife is divided into sections:

the tip	[meant to trim, peel, and any other precision work required.]
the cutting edge	[used for slicing, cutting, carving, and mincing.]
the heel	[best suited for cutting work which requires additional force and pressure. This is where the greatest force of the knife is concentrated. Think slicing through a hard squash or joint.]
the point	[used to make incisions, pierce, and cut delicate ingredients.]
the spine	[used for pounding or cracking, for example, lobster claws.]
the flat of the blade	[used for crushing garlic, then making a paste, and later lifting foods of the prep surface.]

Photograph provided by Messermeister, Custom Chef Knife.

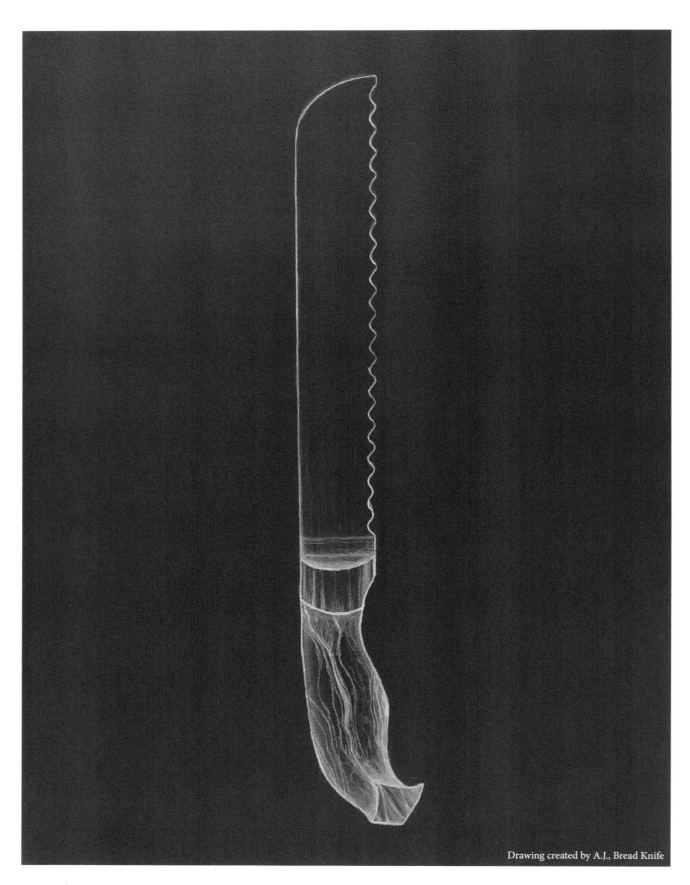

Drawing created by A.J., Bread Knife

Bread/Serrated/Slicer

At first glance, this is an "aggressive" knife. It has teeth, it has some weight to it, and it will saw through just about anything. I find this knife to be such a great, and necessary, addition to the kitchen. Crusty bread. Tomatoes. Pineapple. Frozen Bacon. Cakes. Towering Sandwiches. This knife can go through it all, and usually with little effort, while remarkably and minimally altering the end result. The bread/serrated knife does have a toothless close cousin, known as the slicer, and even that guy has some mega power as it delicately slivers through beautifully oily and tender proteins. Simply put, there would be no bagels (bread/serrated) with lox (slicer) if it weren't for these guys slicing their way through to make one of the most iconic breakfast sandwiches of all time.

Photograph provided by Messermeister, Bread Knife.

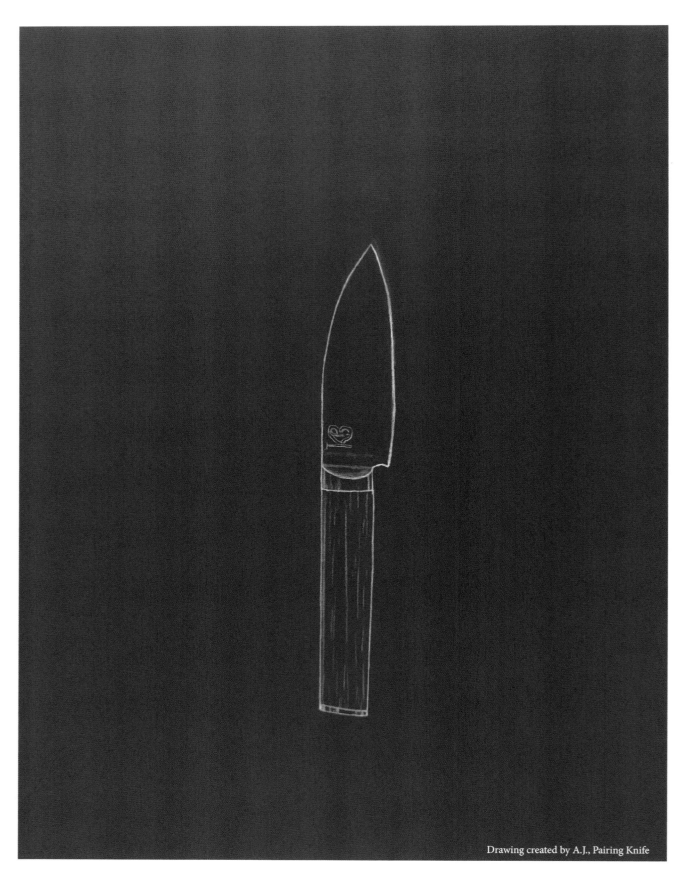

Drawing created by A.J., Pairing Knife

Paring Knife

The second most important knife to have, with the first being the chef knife. This is because, while your chef knife can basically "do it all," the paring knife gets into those additional nooks and crannies that the larger predecessor either cannot or would massacre. Interestingly enough, this knife is used more off the cutting board than on, as the lack of belly and very short handle deem it necessary to "hug" the majority of knife with your hand, while shimmying your wrist to carefully peel away at the surface of your culinary medium.

Photograph provided by Messermeister, Pairing Knife.

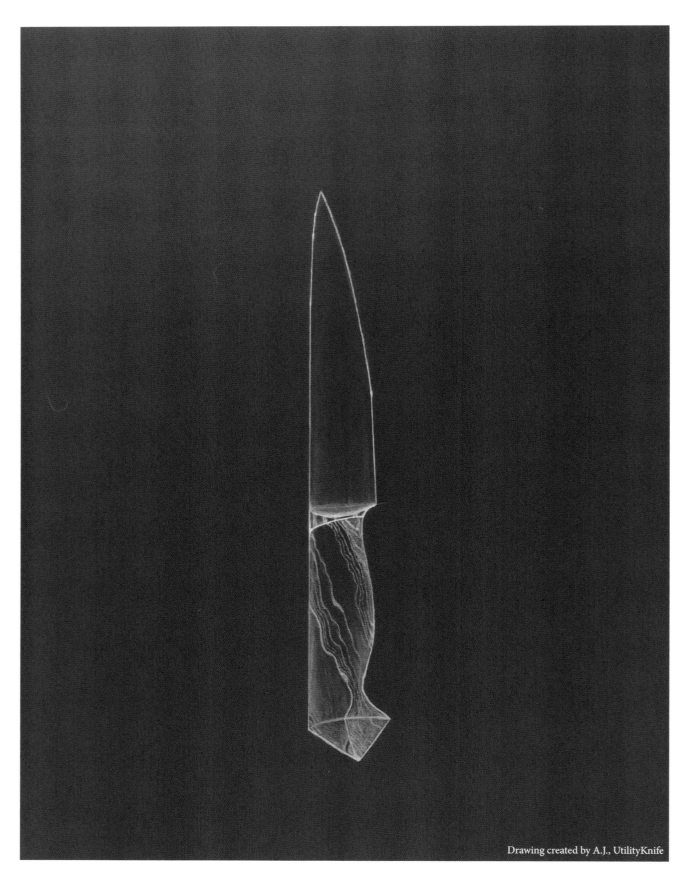

Utility Knife

It is assumed that the utility, or "petty," knife is used far less than the paring knife. But I would have to wholeheartedly disagree. As I mentioned before, this is certainly a knife that my hand unconsciously gravitates to when looking to accomplish those "in between tasks." Somehow it is always the best size for those quick hungry tasks that we need to complete efficiently and successfully to snack on something soon. Before, the utility knife would almost always be made with a fillet knife design but today these knives have evolved in design to resemble a look similar to the chef knife.

Photograph provided by Messermeister, Utility Knife.

Use/Profession

While some of us have the luxury of setting an entire mood prior to cooking… most of us are really just trying to get breakfast, lunch, (maybe some snacks), and dinner on the table—and fast! While yes, there may be days in which the jams are just blasting away in the background while you chiffon-ade your parsley so damn wonderfully it's about to snow green in your kitchen, most of the time, we are pressed for time either by our own grumbling stomachs or by the sound of hunger-laden, grumbling children. Whichever the scenario that most resounds with you one thing is very certain, your kitchen prep should not be a tedious chore. I subscribe to the notion that how you feel prior to and during cooking reflects itself into the final product. Meaning, if you don't want to do something, it will clearly shine through on your remarkably bland dish. But, when things are made with a purpose, they generally benefit us in the long run. The core of the problem lies in the fact that many of us do not know our way around a kitchen, let alone how to properly use knives. Yes, these tools can be extremely intimidating. From general knowledge, to use and care, to even their overall design; just because you don't know how to properly approach something doesn't mean you cannot learn. So, let's start by carving out some time to get a secure grip on your blade at home and take the first step. Learn not just how to use the knife but how to maintain it properly. Because let's face it, if you are going to be envious of your friends who know how whip around the kitchen with their chef knife, as it quite literally extends from their arm, then you might as well get even more flustered at the fact that your blade(s) are probably not as sharp as they should be—am I right or… am I right?

Photograph provided by Opinel

MESSERMEISTER

In this highly dense, male-dominated industry, Messermeister continues to solidify their future through the eyes of those who initially introduced many of us to knives… our mothers and grand-mothers. You may be surprised to learn that Messermeister is today a 100% female owned and operated company. Originally, the brand was established in 1981, under the name DAMCO (Dressler American Marketing Company) by Bern and Debra Dressler, who forged their presence in the knife community the old-fashioned way, through dedication and innovation. At the time, Bern Dressler witnessed a need for slight alterations in the traditional German knife design. Inspired by the no-tion that "you won't know until you try," he took a leap of faith and challenged what many told him could not be done. The outcome introduced his successful demi-bolster design which catapulted Messermeister to the revered German American brand it is today. After Bern Dressler's passing in 2002, Debra and her two daughters, Kirsten and Chelcea, now lead this second generation, fami-ly-owned business. This remarkable team of women are successfully transforming the brand, appeal-ing to younger generations, while remaining true to the classic technique and vision that established the company. The same sense of security shared by learning from the matriarchs of a family, is the same welcoming feeling which transcends into Messermeister's product line. This is a beautifully accessible line for anyone looking to feel comfortable purchasing and claiming a new kitchen knife, as their own.

Messermeister's quintessential Californian–German influence has attracted the attention of novice cooks to acclaimed chefs. It is visible to see the significant thought process placed on each item pro-duced, a decision which continues to set them apart from their competitors. The company remains cognizant of the fact that the most important detail will always be the trusted connection between the knife and its owner. As a result, the devoted fanfare has maintained their dedication to the brand, something which continues to humble everyone involved at Messermeister. They believe that the best knife out there is "the one that is cherished by its owner," and because of this they continue to purposefully design every element of their knives.

The following questionnaire was completed by Messermeister's Executive Vice President Marc Wade. Best known for his influential role in the development of the knife brand SHUN, Marc has been creating this path since the tender age of ten, when he first began making knives. His passion and experience are shared through his responses. He is well-respected in the community, which is not surprising considering his transformative twenty-plus-year career in the knife industry. He is a talented man who believes in the Messermeister name, the women behind the brand, and is excited for what is to come for the company.

From the very beginning, Messermeister sought to make "masters" out of everyone in the kitchen, (the name itself means *knife master* in German), an idea reflecting the same vision our prehistoric ancestors potentially had once they realized the weight this tool would have on the future of man-kind. As a result, the company understands the importance of adjusting and exploring the adventures and challenges life places forth. They recognize that consumers are beginning to seek out conscious-ly modernized tools, meant to take us through the next hundred years. Therefore, small, sustainable changes have been made, such as removing petrochemicals from their products and packaging, and even the development of a fully foldable kitchen knife meant to take *you* onto *any* adventure. Still, consumers continue to seek intentionality driven into designs. Messermeister has found balance in this relationship, producing hammer-forged knives in the traditional sense to develop their modern interpretation of where the kitchen knife *should* go. If we, in general, have become more mindful on how to live and sustain our future, then why shouldn't brands do the same? Messermeister "master-fully" agrees.

Q&A with Marc Wade, *Executive Vice President for Messermeister*

Which knife(s) is the most popular in your line, and what do you think makes it so appealing?

For Messermeister, the most popular range is our Oliva Elite line. The most popular shape is of course the 8" Chefs. We find that the popularity is driven by a combination of the uniqueness of the line and our use of natural wood materials. Besides its beauty, the tactile feedback that people get from the natural materials and a well-tuned featherweight knife is very satisfying.

Should culinary knife handles ever be retreated with oil over time? If so, which do you recommend?

Absolutely! Mineral oil is not only great for wood handles, but also creates a protective layer for the blade steel. It is totally food-safe too. You can drink it if you want to, but please keep in mind that it's a natural laxative.

Are there any other knife-makers you admire?

Personally, I have been incredibly lucky to work with some of the very best ever, many of them are no longer with us. They have all had an impact on my work in some way. My list starts with Bo Randall as he was most influential on getting me started. Ken Onion, Takeshi Ono, A.G. Russell, Bob Lum and Bob Loveless are also high on the list. There are other very talented guys out there who are only known inside the knife industry. I appreciate the guys who do production work over the custom crowd, because there is a special challenge to perfectly making 1,000 knives that are all the same, as opposed to one "really nice" piece. I do not appreciate brands that are more marketing companies than craftsmen knifemakers. There are plenty of them around.

Knife set vs. Individual knives. Which do you prefer/recommend, and why?

You can't beat a small set of 5 or 6 great knives. If they are made well, that's really all the diversity you need. Unless you are working in a commercial kitchen with a lot of specialized repetitive tasks, you want to look for versatility in a knife.

My set combination: a large knife for push-cuts on a cutting board (chef knife); a couple long, slim blades for pull-cuts; one fine edged and one with a low frequency serration; one very agile and flexible boning/fillet knife around 6" long; and a pointy paring knife for detail work. That's it!

Please explain why one should never place your knives in the dishwasher. Do you think there will ever be a time when a knife will be made to withstand the dishwasher?

If you have a wooden handle, that's where you can really see the negative affect of a dishwasher. Otherwise, there are plenty of knives that can withstand a dishwasher, just not good ones. Premium blade steels rely on elements like carbon in the alloy to give them hardness and edge retention. Carbon reacts poorly to corrosive elements like lye or citric acids that are in dishwasher detergents, causing them to break down the surface of the steel. People generally don't like rusty or pitted blades and knife makers don't like to get returns because someone didn't understand the nature of why shiny steel makes for dull knives. So, we all advise against the dishwasher. If someone tells you that the temperature of the dishwasher will affect the temper of a knife, then they really don't understand metallurgy.

What is your earliest memory of using/being introduced to a knife?

Like many knife makers, this is a generational business. The ladies at Messermeister grew up in the business so they really don't have memories that don't involve being around knives.

My brother and I were about 4 or 5 when our dad, a wood carver and hobby knifemaker, would hang around Bo Randall's shop in Orlando, Florida. Dad had us making our own knives by the time we were 10 or so. It kept us busy and out of trouble.

Why do you think some people so easily confuse/assume that sharpening and honing are the same thing?

Everyone has their own experience with knives and that leads to a lot of dubious advice on the subject. Honing and sharpening are totally different and both essential. Honing is preventative, just straightening the edge so it stays strong. It's comparable to an oil change in your car. Sharpening is when blade material is removed from the sides to reform the shape of the edge. That's more like an engine overhaul and not something you should have to do very often.

Where do you see the future of culinary knives, especially now that the world has either returned to cooking at home or begun their culinary "journey" ?

For both me and the Dressler family, our entire careers have been about innovating with one of the world's oldest tools. That would seem to be a fairly well trodden path with a small window for creativity. However, by listening well and constantly exploring with new materials, shapes or uses, we have been able to witness plenty of newness to get excited about.

At our core we are a "company of moms" and that drives much of how we connect with our audience. We are passionate about healthy food, entertaining with our friends and making beautiful, quality things for our kitchen. People have been connecting through food for a long time. We make the tools that make that easy and fun.

What is your favorite knife from your line and what is another favorite not from your line?

If I had to pick a single knife, I love our new Overland Utility knife. It's a kitchen knife that I can use as an everyday carry knife. It's not fancy, but very high quality.

Fox Italy makes some very elegant knives, particularly their folders. Although I don't spend hardly any time looking at other people's work, I can appreciate quality. They are some of the best blade grinders in the business.

If you could, please explain the design process that happens prior to producing a knife? How are the details of grind, handle, temper, and use decided and then how long does it take from concept to final production?

Our design options are almost limitless, so we first must decide what is worth chasing after. We call that, "defining the WHY" and it's basically a process of deciding if we *should* do a project. When we think we have a worthy idea, we then have an "intake meeting" to really flesh out the key concepts that are going to define the project. We have to sell it to ourselves before we can sell the idea to anyone else. This usually involves some preliminary market study, CAD sketches and material choices, along with a short list of manufacturing resources that we will enlist.

With all the criteria identified, we conduct a "go-no-go checklist" which is a decision-making tool we use to assess the feasibility of a project. In other words, *can we do it?* Sometimes we will get this far and decide that the juice is not worth the squeeze. The trick is to figure that out early on.

If a project is a go, then we go to work on fine tuning the computerized design, marketing plan, etc. We usually make several different versions of a concept in this phase hoping to whittle them down to a couple favorite designs. These meetings get pretty lively. We may have to make several 3D renderings (physical models) to completely understand how the design is going to perform in the real world.

As a designer, I normally push the limits of what I know our production team is capable of from a technical standpoint. They hate this because a factory's idea of innovation is making a process more efficient, not changing the process to make something new or unknown. A little internal sales job is usually required here too. We have a ton of collective experience to determine the appropriate performance specs, so the design, engineering and production teams will go online to walk through every detail. The Germans usually drink beer during the meeting, which is totally unfair because it's only 9 am here on the West Coast.

When we get to the prototype stage, we find out exactly what can or can't be achieved and it is at this point that we sometimes must modify our specifications to make the design manufacturable. For this, it is critical for us to have those well-defined criteria identified from our intake meeting. These key elements define the project, and we must know what our "non-negotiables" are. These criteria are all tied to the marketing plan and price target which define who is going to buy this knife, what are they going to use it for and what is important to that decision.

With a final prototype, we have costs and production schedules identified, so marketing and sales take over to create the package and tell the story. The whole process can take anywhere from 6 months to two years.

Photograph provided by Messermeister

Photograph provided by Messermeister

Photograph provided by Messermeister, Chelsea & Kirsten, daughters of Bernd & Debra Dressler.

Photograph provided by Messermeister.

Grip It Cut It

Slicing, chopping, dicing, mincing. These are not merely instructions on how something should look. These are dimensions created so that therein lies a sense of uniformity in the dish but also so that your food cooks simultaneously to a reasonable texture. Consider if you were going to braise a stew for hours, upon hours, and you decide to finely dice your carrots, celery, and onions (i.e., mirepoix) into *brunoise* size. After six hours you would not only be fascinated with your astoundingly tender meat, but you would also frantically attempt to recall if you even added the mirepoix into the pot as the vegetables would be so cooked down, they would've turned into a paste.

"The Claw"

The name directly implies the handle grip you should be forming with your "free hand;" a shape strictly meant to protect all the digits on that hand. Although the knife is only held by one hand during use, in cooking, both hands have a purpose. Your "free hand" is meant to help lead the blade on the board, while assuring that all the content is prepped.

Hammer Grip

Again, here the name implies how you should be grabbing your knife; in the same manner as you would a hammer. Certain knives require this handling for proper control, as in the case of a cleaver. Additionally, you might have to use this grip with your chef's knife if chopping through squash or cabbage, allowing for more clearance when moving the blade down. Here, gravity is your friend aiding through the momentum created by smashing the weight of your blade down onto the medium about to be hacked.

Pinch Grip

Herein lies your most traditional grip, for the most "traditional knife." The pinch grip is the best way to hold your chef knife, and any other possible knife, honestly. This grip allows you to have confident control over your movements. Holding a knife from the handle is completely wrong, as it does not allow you to have any true control over the knife. Rather than wrapping your entire hand around the handle, "pinch" the area where the blade and handle meet so that your thumb may kiss the knuckle of your index finger, and then wrap the remainder of your hand around the handle. At first, your index finger will want to naturally lie along the spine of the blade, but with further practice, a proper pinch grip hold will come.

Dagger Grip

This grip is essentially the hammer grip but held in the opposite direction. Whereas the hammer grip basically faces down towards the board, a proper dagger grip hold will face you. This is the customary grip for hunters, butchers, and some fishermen as they must make their way through a carcass, swinging their way though fibers and tissues of meats with enormous strength.

Toward-the-Thumb Grip

Similar to how one would hold a knife to whittle, this grip is portrayed by the knife resting on your palm while your thumb is the guide, and the remaining four fingers wrap around the knife and handle completely. Certainly, you have witnessed this grip before when someone has peeled an entire apple with their knife leaving behind a vibrant, fruity streamer.

Chop & Rocking Chop

When chopping, the entire knife will move up and then down with one swift movement. Whereas the rocking chop will keep the rounded tip of the blade on your board, in a similar fashion to a rocking chair, just like when you observe a professional mince herbs. Here your "free hand" will control the tip of the blade by acting as a cushion for it to "bounce back" in a see-saw type motion, while your main hand rapidly moves the handle up and down, to produce a fine mince.

Push Cut

This cut entails a forward moving motion where your body applies pressure downward while your wrist exerts into a forward push. Here the edge of the blade does most of the work, as this forward motion results in more of a slide down, as opposed to a push. This is only true, though, if your knives are sharpened well, because if dull, then you will be simultaneously sliding and pushing down, inevitably ruining your product. This is the classic cut that you will always use when working through a large cabbage, for example.

Rocking Push Cut

This cut is meant to be executed with a curved blade, as the tip never leaves the board. When the belly is lifted and replaced, it creates a rocking, circular action. Most effective when your "free hand" is securing the product down with the claw grip, guiding the direction of the push and pull. Most common when using the following cutting techniques: dicing, julienne, and chiffonade.

Saw Cut

The saw cut is another example where the name implies the correct motion of use for the knife. This will be the cut you will use when using a bread/serrated knife or slicer. Just as you would a saw, move your body back and forth with the blade, further creating that momentum that will motion the blade down. Depending on what the actual medium being sliced is, depends on the amount of pressure your body will exude onto the knife.

Horizontal Cut

Most common cut used when dicing onions and shallots or when slicing bread in half. When prepping your onions, for example, your secondary grip hand, or "free hand," will rest above the allium while the knife is rotated horizontally to carefully slice through the bulb in sections, prior to rotating your knife again to slice down vertical sections. The purpose of this cross sectioning is so that when dicing the onion perfectly even, jewels fall onto the cutting board. In the case of bread, your secondary hand will help keep the loaf in place as you saw your way through the center, hoping that the blade remains horizontally straight rather than meeting up towards your hand.

Photograph provided by Cristina Martinez, Photographer: Neal Santos.

Profile: Christina Martinez, South Philly Barbacoa

Cristina Martinez connected with my soul, from afar, in the same way I resonated with many of the influential women in my life… through their stories of resilience as expressed through their food. Some of you may know her as your local Philly neighbor, the city where she came to cement her presence—and influence—on both the taste and culture of the city. Others may know Cristina through her profiled episode, on Netflix's "*Chef's Table*." I, myself, only know her through the way her culinary presence connected with my soul. She is a true representation of what it means to care for your neighbor through food, and shared experiences.

As previously mentioned, this book was bred during the heart of the 2020 pandemic. A time that certainly left its scars on the hospitality industry, leaving many to reconfigure their business plan in a rushing bind. Cristina Martinez's path was not a comfortable or easy one. While it had its fair share of positive blessings, the fighting cry for something better, in her mind, gave her the strength to make decisions most of us would never even consider. Every move she makes in her life has been for the betterment of another. A child, a friend, a neighbor, a stranger. While she certainly has "won" the opportunity to give herself a break, this trailblazer of a woman knows no limits, as seen in her choice of knife. So, when the pandemic first collapsed our daily routine, Cristina decided that the food should still make its way to the people. Like countless other establishments, deliveries and takeout were the new normal, but she took it one step further. Packing up a truck with kilos, upon kilos, of barbacoa and tortillas, she navigated her way to nearby cities assuring the deliveries would arrive as fresh as possible. She made her way around D.C., NYC, and Philly, several times and guided by the salivating cry made by her followers on Instagram. Let us not forget that times of despair may be soothed, even if only temporarily, by the perfect bite of the most complicatedly simple of dishes. Cristina Martinez has always known this. Maybe it is her remarkable story of resilience, maybe it is her unwavering need to always lookout for her neighbor. Or maybe it is because she has experienced the magic such a bite can have on one's soul. Either way, we are all luckier to have someone like her in this world. After a year where hope seemed lost, Cristina Martinez is paving the way for future, caring neighbors.

Photograph provided by Cristina Martinez, Photographer: Neal Santos.

Q&A with Cristina Martinez, *South Philly Barbacoa*

What is your personal favorite knife, and why?

My machete! I use it for butchering the animals, and for serving the tacos at Barbacoa.

Are there any knife-makers you admire?

Alfredo Zarate

How focused do you think that someone should be on their knife cuts/skills?

When using a knife, you need to work fast, accurately, and focused. You cannot become distracted. You need to work with passion.

What is your earliest memory of using/being introduced to a knife?

Cutting cilantro and peeling nopales, around 6 or 7 years old, for my parents barbacoa business.

If you could host anyone for dinner (famous or not) who would they be and why?

Jay Fai and Abigail Mendoza Ruiz because it would be a dream to cook for them while chatting with them and getting to learn new things from them. It would be an amazing dinner that I would cherish forever.

Apart from the obvious, why do you think people are so intimidated by knives or scared to use them?

There is not much education in the home about knives, which causes a trauma or fear to approach them. As a child we are told "don't touch," but we must know it's dangerous and learn the correct method to utilize them.

After the last year, how would you change the industry?

We need to acknowledge undocumented workers in the food system and provide them basic human rights, including the right to work legally.

Favorite Utensil

My cazuela

Favorite Place to Cook

The "hoyo" (barbacoa pit)

Favorite Recipe to Cook

Barbacoa!

Photograph provided by Cristina Martinez, Photographer: Neal Santos.

Outdoor Living

Depending on where you were raised, picnics were probably more of an anticipated activity when compared to other places in the world. The truth is, though, that we have all been invited to participate in an outdoor event where some spontaneously preplanned lunch/snack situation was prepped into some form of transportable food vessel, along with cutlery, napkins, and a set of glasses accompanied by a refreshing drink. Whether planned to the very last detail or a simple lunchtime circumstance, we all share experiences on dining in the open. Picnics, birthday parties, beach days, hiking adventures, pit stops in the middle of nowhere, and even those valuable lunchtime cubicle escapes from the daily grind. All these examples prove that life leads us to shared experiences at one point or another, so wouldn't it be great if during those moments you had something to spread that wonderfully earthy, and expensive, cheese? Outdoor living isn't something that is always directed by conscious planning. Sometimes it is the result of spontaneous living. Yes, we can prepare our hiking packs and bug-out bags all we want, but again, what about those moments when life *just happens*? I was recently gifted my first Opinel No.8. It is beautiful. Classic. Chic. Wonderfully sharp. But I should admit that one of my initial afterthoughts, after admiring the obvious craftsmanship before me, was if I really needed one. Well, let's just say it proved me wrong... and quickly! Like the Opinel No.8, there are countless other wonderfully designed and equally beautiful knives which would be wonderful companions while outdoor dining. Look at Laguiole and Berti, for example. They have been designing these blades for centuries, and hold their own in both the chicest of indoor settings and in rugged outdoor rendezvous. It certainly is interesting to witness how far we have come with technology and yet how necessary these classic essentials remain, and assist, in one's life. Although their designs have evolved, the essential identity of the knife continues to be timeless.

Farming

If you want to know what a "real day's work" entails, then you don't have to search farther than your local farmer, forager, and overall land worker. These magnificent people have chosen a life that begins before the sun rises and, many would say, never "clocks out." There are some wonderful knives and accessories that make the day-to-day easier for these passionate men and women. Though, honestly, from the few that I have spoken with, their best and most dependable tools are their own bare hands. That said, they do always carry their trusted blade as their constant companion on, and off, the field.

Multi-Purpose Utility Knife: approx. 4"–8" long. Pocketknives have been coined "multipurpose" as that is exactly what they are meant for—a variety of uses. From cutting wire and twine, to opening boxes and bags of feed, to slicing through vegetables when checking quality... these knives have been quite literally by the side of these hardworking men and women, day by day. There is nothing this sharp little nugget can't do, which is why it will stand the test of time.

Foraging

Mushroom Knife: approx. 8" long. This little knife has the fascinating job of delicately harvesting all kinds of mycelium. Because mushrooms are delicate in and of themselves, you want something that will remove them with the least possible damage. Some designs come with brushes (as seen with the Opinel Sandvik 12C27), while others are classically traditional in design (take for example, the *puukko*). The mushroom knife certainly proves that it is small but mighty.

Butchering

Boning: approx. 6" long. Rigid, shorter, and thinner than your classic chef knife. This narrower design allows it to maneuver around the joints of a carcass, slithering away at the silverskin of meat protecting your overall product yield, while finding its way through the different muscle groups. Certainly not a knife that is required in many households, but for those who do need its help, it is recommended to look for a durable option when purchasing one.

Scimitar: approx. 12"–16" long. Along with the cleaver, this is the quintessential butcher's knife. The scimitar is the one that you envision when you picture your neighborhood butcher portioning out your holiday order. Its long, curved blade was designed so that it would meticulously slice through proteins without sacrificing portions.

Photograph taken by A.J., The Whole Ox.

Photograph taken by A.J., The Whole Ox.

Photograph taken by A.J., The Whole Ox.

Profile: The Whole Ox

Upon driving into Marshall, VA, you immediately notice the charm of this small-town depicted through the beautiful nuance of historic buildings, enlivened through the modern vision of recent generations. The Whole Ox also portrays this image. Identified as your local, neighborhood butcher, the store transports you to the classically rustic butcheries we have all romanticized of while maintaining the trustworthy element one should have with those curating the initial steps of your evening dinner, at home.

Owned and operated by husband-and-wife team, Derek & Amanda Luhowiak, The Whole Ox is a wonderful spot where you can go and greet your neighbors for lunch, adventurously pick-up nose to tail options to cook-up at home, or curiously wander into for a look and then leave with a bag full of wonderfully assorted pantry options.

There is an unspoken trustworthiness that we all require from those we gather our food from, when we are on the hunt for something new, delicious, or classically comforting. Usually, the main element that appeals us to return to these spots is the familial repertoire that they have with us. Having this level of trust with your butcher, for example, evolves into a relationship where they will ultimately know what cuts you will always look for and what your adventurous nature is in general. And, let's face it, if the shop is family owned and operated (as they usually are), well that certainly doesn't hurt in establishing this necessary relationship we seek.

In the case of The Whole Ox, Amanda "breaks down" the protein and produces sought-after cuts from local, quality farmers, while Derek turns these remarkable cuts of marbleized meat into savory dishes meant to satisfy their diners or nourish your household. Head butcher, Amanda, is approachable and comfortably warm as she shares memorable stories with patrons while also crediting her father for introducing her to the fascinating world of meat cutting, at a very young age. Derek is the head chef, of The Whole Ox, where he has seamlessly introduced locals to a variety of dishes which would never hide the quality of Amanda's work, but rather highlight them, through a perfect simplicity of flavor. This place was established by family and is managed as such, as Derek & Amanda share their united glory while applauding their individual successes.

Photograph taken by A.J., The Whole Ox.

Q&A with Amanda Luhowiak, *Butcher and Co-Owner of The Whole Ox*

What is your personal favorite knife and why?

My orange-handled Richmond chef knife because my husband, Derek, gave it to me for my birthday.

Who do you admire in your field and what knife brands do you really love?

I admire my husband who has worked in kitchens and as a Chef/butcher his entire life, without his teachings, support, and guidance I wouldn't be who I am professionally today. My favorite knife brands are Dexter Russell and R. Murphy (made in the USA).

What do you look for when purchasing a new knife to add to your kitchen?

Usually inexpensive (in case it needs replacing), then functionality, and comfort.

What is your preferred method of storage: block, drawer, magnet? And why?

Magnet even though this is not always the most convenient option, depending on space, then the drawer. I prefer to be able to see them and have very easy access.

What is your earliest memory of using/being introduced to a knife? Any gnarly injuries?

My earliest memory was as a very young child helping my dad skin squirrels and birds and clean fish. There was this one day at work that another butcher sharpened our knives, for us ladies out front, and not that it was so gnarly but 3 of us cut ourselves that day.

How did you fall in love with your craft and how did that influence your love of knives?

I owe the love of my craft to both my dad and my husband because for basically my entire life I have been learning to harvest and prepare, not only my own food but food for others.

Where do you see the future of your company?

The Whole Ox just turned 10 years old, and I hope that in the future my business will be a fixture in our community for a very long time to come.

What would you like people to know about your field that maybe they wouldn't normally know?

That even though I am a butcher I encourage eating smaller, cleaner amounts of protein that come as local as possible, and that I eat lots of veggies too!

Favorite utensils

Cutting board and a chef knife… with those two utensils you can do just about anything!

Favorite place and recipe to cook outside

The outdoor woodfired oven at my house!

Absolutely any meat, veg or pizza in the woodfired oven.

You are on a road trip to a remote area of the world…

Where are you? Who are you with? What are you cooking?

I'm on Prince Edward Island with my husband, Derek, and we are eating mussels, clams, oysters, and potatoes, over a campfire on the beach.

Photograph taken by A.J., The Whole Ox.

Fishermen & Oysters

Filleting Knife: approx. 6" –11" long. Sure, you could use a chef knife to prep your fish but consider the amount of delicate flesh you would inevitably lose to the blade. That is why filleting knives were designed, as they are so flexible they practically dance through the body of the fish so effortlessly, separating the flesh from the bone and ultimately yielding a greater delectable reward.

Oyster Knife: approx. 2.75"–4" long. Short knives with longer triangular blades and more rigid in comparison to a traditional knife; oyster knives were designed to wedge within the center crevice of these bivalves to shuck them open. This "shucker" is just one in the larger family of shuckers, to include clam and scallop knives too. Though basically they are the same to the naked eye, their sizes do vary according to the average proportions of the shells they are meant to open. Don't be fooled by their funny name and dainty size, as it is certainly not humorous when these smaller knives slip and meet your hand instead. Though blunt, they can still pack a punch. When they slide it is fast, and by the time you notice you're hurt, you are probably saying "oh shucks!"

Photograph taken by A.J.

Wine & Cheese

Wine Key: Like a pocketknife, the wine key is a sommelier's best friend... never leaving their side. These keys are always assisting in opening bottles of wine for a patron's best, and sometimes worst of times, too, respectively. An idea brought to life by German, Karl Wienke (pronounced "wine key"), this tool's original design became popular for the task it could complete, but also for its similarities to the foldable pocketknife. Eventually, the wine key was widely adopted through several patents in Germany, England, and America. Today, there are countless designs and variations accessible to the public from your general dollar store novelty to the most obscenely expensive adaptation imaginable.

Photograph taken by Sharon, at Neighbors

Photograph provided by Jacqueline Pirolo, Photographer: Adam DelGiudice

Profile: Jacqueline Pirolo

Sommelier Jacqueline Pirolo is one of the three managing partners at Macchialina in Miami Beach, FL. She is the younger sister to Head Chef Mike Pirolo, previously profiled in this book, too. Jacqueline is charmingly down-to-earth and her optimistically adventurous approach toward wine certainly makes her a force to watch. The Food & Beverage industry in general is harshly complicated in all its facets, yet even more needlessly abstruse for any lady in the field. Jacqueline Pirolo, though, has worked tirelessly to change that and in fact embrace such intricacies by establishing a name for herself in the local wine world.

> *"I think there is often a negative correlation that exists in our society for people that choose a career path in the restaurant industry. It is often looked at by many as a steppingstone until you figure out what you really want to do. I know I struggled with this. I loved working in the restaurant industry, studied marketing in college and upon returning felt the pressure to "do something with my degree." Two years in, and I was miserable, and went back to waiting tables. I was so much happier with my work life balance. I struggled telling people that I was a server, always feeling the need to have an explanation of my plan after. I have heard similar stories from many others. I think as a society we all need to do better to not fall into what we think the "norms" are. Everyone's path looks different, and we should celebrate that."*
>
> *-   Jacqueline Pirolo*

This same ideology is the driving factor which influences the selection of wine Jacqueline chooses to introduce to her patrons and wine-of-the-month club. There is an anticipated build-up which is noticeable through her wine pairing recommendations and through the identifiable notes each vintage encapsulates. She embraces the fact that just like everyone's path is different, so is the same for the vines and their individual characteristics; intriguing to the palette rather than immediately rejected. Classic and adventurous while approachable and welcoming, these words describe who Jacqueline is and the wines she has sought to share.

Where some would feel intimidatingly overshadowed at the family dinner table, by the successes of their siblings, this is certainly not the case, or at least does not seem to be so, within the Pirolo family. Each member applauds the other while lending their hand to further highlight their loved-one's talents. And so, Jacqueline shall continue travelling the globe seeking to introduce herself to new flavorful notes while toting one of her many wine-keys, which would ultimately be confiscated at the TSA. It is certainly reassuring to see where Sommeliers are gravitating towards and the greater influence they are having on both establishments and cities, as a whole. Jacqueline Pirolo is not just the *aperitivo* to the Pirolo family... she is the pairing, rather, which compliments all the facets within their kinship.

Photograph provided by Jacqueline Pirolo, Photographer: Adam DelGiudice, Wine Key.

Q&A with Jacqueline Pirolo, *Sommelier and Managing Partner of Macchialina*

Do you recall the moment that you fell in love with the world of wine?

I was 21, home from college during a holiday break. My brother, and wine mentor, Fabrizio, worked for a wine importer, selling wine to various restaurants around NYC. We went out for dinner to one of his accounts and he opened a bottle of Lambrusco with a salumi board that we had ordered. An iconic pairing: one that years later Macchialina has become well known for. Thinking back, that was the first time I experienced the conviviality that happens when sharing a bottle of wine around a table with friends. I did go back to the small college town of Oswego NY after that holiday break and searched everywhere for Lambrusco, which was impossible to find!

What do you look for when purchasing a wine opener, especially during a time when there are so many models available to the consumer?

For me it's got to be a double hinge, the simpler the better, especially when working service, the fancy ones tend to disappear quite often!

Talk to us a bit more about where you see the future of wine and how it has evolved in the past few years.

In Miami I see a rise in popularity in the lesser-known regions/varietals. I see a lot more interest within the consumer on experiencing these wines in the comfort of their own home. When I first moved to Miami, 6 years ago, there weren't many boutique wine shops; most people were purchasing wine from supermarkets. That has finally changed and now there are a ton of great spots to purchase wine. Macchialina has set up a mini retail shop in the front of the restaurant that caters to the neighborhood looking for the lesser-known Italian wines. Natural wines have gained popularity; 10 years ago, when we opened, we were one of a few places pouring natural wines. It's awesome to see our cities wine scene being mentioned along with NYC, LA & Chicago.

What are your go-to wines... the ones we will always find in your home?

BUBBLES, SHERRY & VERMOUTH! I wish I always found these in my home, but I always seem to be running out! My partner makes the perfect gin martini with amontillado sherry (instead of vermouth), finishes it with a Castelvetrano olive and it's my favorite!

In your opinion, what are some perfect wine pairings that many of us wouldn't immediately consider, but just work?

Champagne with our creamy polenta! Our polenta cooks for 3 hours every day, it's a very rich and decedent dish. The effervescence in the champagne helps to wipe your palate clean, the acidity makes you ready for the next bite, all while not overpowering the dish or getting lost in it.

Who would you love to curate a wine list for and what would you include?

My family – I would have all their favorites:

> A Chateaneuf du Pape for my love - Will, a Gewürztraminer for my brother John, an Aglianico for brother Mike, something from the Hatzidakis winery for my brother Fabrizio, a Montepulciano for my mamma, a soave for my sister Jen, a Pet-Nat for my sister Lizzie, a Lambrusco for Evelyn, and a Champagne for Andres! –And although he isn't old enough to drink yet, I would have an entire section devoted to the 2020 vintage, which is my nephew, Giacomo's, birth year.

For those of us who are looking to create the perfect little wine bar at home, what are some of the items that we should always have?

Tasty snacks! Wine is meant to be drunk while eating, as it will continue to change and evolve.

Cheese Knives:

Cheese. Queso. *Fromage*. It is the one thing that makes even the most devout vegan reminisce of the days when they used to devour this rich nibble with a single breathe. Wine and cheese are as marvelous a pairing as peanut butter and jelly, or chocolate and salt. So, it's of no surprise that in the wine & cheese coupling a shared interest in sharp objects is required to truly appreciate their value and charisma. The wine key is essential, for most wines. But the relationship between cheese and knife is essential and is completely relevant to the textural characteristics of the cheese itself. Therefore, there are various shapes and sizes of cheese knives and cutters, all meant to highlight the experience while consuming, ultimately making it less tedious to enjoy. Unless of course you are planning on inhaling this appetizing snack rather swiftly, in which case you just need any knife that will tear it apart.

Opinel

Opinel. A brand whose name can stand alone for many, it is the sleek, conversation starting design that is known worldwide. A brand so uniquely recognizable that the word itself has been correlated to the pocketknife. In 1989 the word "*opinel*" was officially added to the Larousse French dictionary to mean pocketknife, in the same regard that Kleenex® refers to tissue. Take for example their Opinel No. 8, regarded on various lists such as: "10 Essential Gardening Tools"; "Best Wood Carving Tools"; "9 Knives Any Collector Should Own"; as well as the "100 Most Beautiful Products in the World.". I mean, it doesn't get any more artistically chic than the fact that your knife was used by THE Pablo Picasso to carve out his statues. Opinel and their incredibly practical and cool knives, and tools, have been around for more than 130 years. Rooted in history with a commitment to craftsmanship, the company is still following in Joseph's footsteps nearly 130 years later, making tools designed to stand the test of time. These knives are accessible for most budgets. Opinel's affordability and simple designs continue to make them highly sought-after tools and when combined with their remarkable sharpness, equate to a truly one-of-a-kind knife that will last you a lifetime, regardless of daily use.

Photograph provided by Opinel

Care & Storage

I have very fond memories from when I learned to love the kitchen, who instilled that love in me, and why it always felt so "natural" to me. Everyone holds several childhood recollections around food, some are held so tightly to their heart that the faint smell of cookies and cakes or roasts and braises, still lingers and triggers those reflections.

While all those memories are glorious recollections of the pieces of my life which formed the person who I am today, nothing truly stands out more than 1) the affordable quality of my aunt's seemingly indestructible knives and 2) the sheer awe at the fact that she continues to have her digits perfectly intact after decades of owning extremely dull knives. Little did I know that learning how to cook with her would instill a sense of dare-devilishness in me that no cooking school or restaurant can teach.

Proper care and storage are extremely important, as it not only allows for a longer "shelf life" of this sharp utensil, but also assists in preventing permanently scarring damage, to yourself. *Don't just throw these sharp tools anywhere.* The following is a brief glimpse on proper tips to maintain your kitchen knives, in general. But, for a more in-depth review on overall knife maintenance, refer to the **"Knife Sharpening"** (page 255) and **"Knife Storage"** (page 276) sections of this book.

[Always store your knives in a safe place—out of the reach of children, please]

Cleanliness

It goes without saying, but you should always keep your knives clean. Not only for obvious hygienic reasons but also because it will extend the life of your blades, no matter how much they cost. Assuming you did spend a pretty penny on that kitchen addition, wouldn't you want to keep it for as long as possible? Well then, cleaning your knives after, *and in between*, uses with warm soapy water will do the trick. Just make sure to take the additional thirty seconds to dry them off completely, please, especially prior to storing them away. Once you begin to practice this incredibly important habit, it shall soon become second nature to you, and your knives (and wallet), will thank you later.

It is very important to make sure you don't get too comfortable with your new sharp friend by disregarding their needs and throwing them into the dishwasher or by dropping them into your kitchen sink. Even if you use the "cleanest" of dishwashing detergents, set the water temperature to cold, and flick on the gentle/china cycle… PLEASE DON'T THROW THEM INTO THE DISHWASHER. It doesn't matter what additional steps you take with your knife when it is outside of the machine; once that door gets shut, temperatures are rising and falling, and the steam and heat factor will linger through, permanently. Something so careless can cause your handles to fade, crack, split, or warp and the blade will obviously go through its own set of stressors too. Same goes for your deep kitchen sink. So many of us get lazy sometimes and just leave dishes, food, water, cups, pots & pans, and anything else you can think of just sitting in the sink, lingering with other dirty items which may have standing water, bacteria, and caked on filth. Let's try not to practice this level of "slack," in general.

I understand that life happens, some days suck, and sometimes you just don't "have enough time." I get it. But the next time you convince yourself you really don't have an additional few seconds in the day to spare, consider this: do you really want to wonder why that stain is on your blade? Was it rust caused from improper drying or is it a permanent reminder of some filth that decided to mark your blade, forever making you question what caused it? Regardless of budget, knives were made to last as any investment piece would, so care for them as such.

Sharpening & Honing

The process of owning a knife is like that of a car. From doing your research, considering budget, test driving, to safety and maintenance, all these components require a sense of responsibility from the owner. Therefore, consider adopting practices to protect your investment, provided you have not yet done so.

Generally, **do not** attempt to cut anything harder than the blade of your knife. Better yet, do not look to use your knife for something other than its intended purpose. For example, cleavers cut through bone, chef knives do not. See where I am headed?

As mentioned before, don't just throw your knives anywhere. Don't disregard them, by leaving them filthy and wet. Don't toss them into the dishwasher. Sure, some knives are made by machines in factories, but think of how they were initially made. Think of those wonderful family-owned businesses that still exist today and how they take pride in the product they create. Honor the artistic process.

Sharpening Stones & Hand/Electric Sharpeners

So, your knife needs to be sharpened and you have no idea where to start. You could take it to a professional or you could try to maintain it at home. Today there are several options available to knife owners, giving you control over the process which makes you most comfortable.

Sharpening stones come in a variety of stones and textures. These are obviously the original and primary option to consider when looking to sharpen your knife. Even if you were to seek a professional's assistance, they would most certainly use a sharpening stone. Frankly, if you're paying someone to use an electric sharpener, I would consider asking for my knives back, as it would be better for you to consider investing in one to have at home, instead. Today's hand/electric sharpeners are useful when a stone option is not readily available to you. Both have narrow guides that will aid in keeping the blade in position and there is a convenience factor that appeals to many as well. Maintenance of your blade is the "name of the game" and you should take all the necessary measures to do so. *(refer to page 255, where this is already mentioned & shows steps on how to sharpen)*

Honing Steels

Available in a variety of sizes, these rods are not meant to sharpen your blade, but rather align. I am sure we all have some visual in our minds when recalling a honing steel. Its either a chef using it in the kitchen prior to slicing through some magnificent, salt-crusted porterhouse, or it is a father flexing his culinary muscle by showing off his technique to "sharpen his knife" (sorry dad, the rod isn't making that baby any sharper).

Think of the honing steel/rod as regular maintenance for you knife, between meticulous sharpening sessions. Most honing steels consist of a coarse rod (about 12" long) and can be found in various grain textures (coarse, medium, fine-grained). There are also ceramic and diamond options but be aware that those do remove some of the steel from the edge so if not used carefully can lead to damaging wear-and-tear. *(refer to page 264, where this is already mentioned)*

Cutting Boards

Whatever you do, choose either a wooden or polypropylene board to do your cutting. Please, please, please refrain from cutting directly onto counters, metal, glass, marble, or anything else that may be similar. You may be incredibly pressed for time and a "one and done" cut must be performed on one of the surfaces mentioned; but please don't ever consider going through your prep on one these mediums. They are not only obviously dangerous, but they will also assist in the rapid dulling of your blades. Yes, you can damage your knives this way. Sometimes the mishap may be alleviated but if continuously done then your knife will remain permanently damaged, unfortunately. To prevent this disaster, make a conscious effort to ensure that your board is of a quality that will compliment your essential blade. Frankly, go the extra mile by placing a damp paper towel or kitchen towel under your board. This small effort can assure you better stability, meaning that you have taken one additional step in making sure you are safe in the kitchen.

Personally, I prefer a wood chopping board. Some may argue that it is not as sanitary, but I beg to differ, as any material of board may be considered unhygienic if one is not taking the proper steps to keep it clean. "Clean as you go," has always been the anthem preached in restaurants and culinary schools alike. I would encourage you to practice doing the same at home. This will not only maintain a clean area, but it will also ensure less of a clean up after. In fact, wooden boards are "self-healing," as small surface scratches will close back up, further preventing bacterial growth. That said, you should remain vigilant by making sure you keep up your board or even replace it once you notice that those surface marks have become deeper gouges on the board. A good option would be to consider having separate boards for separate tasks. Replace ones that are so damaged that it is extremely unappealing to even envision having any food on it. And then there is the obvious suggestion to clean your board properly. Today, there are so many fantastic, "clean" options to sanitize your cutting boards that you need not worry about any harsh chemicals.

Storage Options:

Magnetic Rack

Popular in commercial kitchens, magnetic strip holders are starting to pop up in residential kitchens too. This will be the "trickiest" of all the storage options because some strips are quite strong making for a more forceful pull, off the rack. Then you have some that might have less of a magnetic attraction, causing the knife to slip off, almost too easily. Some just outright fall off the wall if improperly attached. They certainly look cool and can give your kitchen a more industrial, "here are my knives," vibe. Should this be your option of choice, just make sure you securely fix the rack to the wall and see how your knives feel about it too.

Block

Certainly, the more traditional and readily available option that most of us are accustomed to. The knife block is meant to have a permanent presence on your kitchen counter. It is a visual reminder of how much you enjoy your time in the kitchen or how you maybe need to downsize from a block due to lack of use. Either way, this "easy" option does have it downsides. The first is that most of the time, they come as part of a set. Meaning that depending on the one you choose you will either have a modernly crafted set curated with a limited number of knives, or you will probably have several additional knives which won't even get touched during their time in your home. That said, if you are lucky enough to acquire one sans blade, then all the available slots are going to taunt you every day until you are forced to cede, and fill a collection so that the block does not feel empty. Keep in mind, also, that those divisions are deep and hard to reach for cleaning. So, if you are not doing your part to ensure that your knives are clean and dry prior to placing them back into the block, you do run the risk of damage and filth accumulating within the block. But again, because there is always someone thinking ahead, today there gorgeous block designs, which have only one large compartment, so that your knife sets may be molded into your own curation.

In-Drawer

If your counterspace is prized real estate in the kitchen, and you are going for that uber clean, minimalistic look, then you might want to consider an in-drawer option as it will keep your knives organized and out of sight. Just as with the knife block you can choose from variations with or without divisions, and you must do your part to ensure that both the knives and organizer are clean and dry. Additional steps must also be taken if considering this option. You must first measure your drawer to make sure the organizer you are considering will fit. No, they are not "one size fits all..." Secondly, choose a "safe" drawer for your storage, meaning don't go for anything too high or deep where you loose sight of your knives. It goes without saying that if you have younger children at home, you most certainly want to take additional steps to secure that drawer, as well, regardless of whether you may be teaching them proper knife safety.

Sheath

Sheaths are a great affordable option. Usually preferred most by professionals as they must transport their prized arsenal, back and forth, from their place of work to their home. Should this be the route that is best for you, consider two things: 1) As with other organizers, you want to make sure that you are cleaning and drying your knives prior to sliding them into the sheath, and that the sheath itself is clean and dry too. If not, then you will run into the same potential trouble, as with the knife block and in-drawer organizer, where accumulation of filth and/or water may result in permanent unhygienic damage to your knife. 2) If you are going to choose this option for your home, designate a safe space for your knives. Safe for you and others. I am always referring to "taking additional steps," but the reality is that knives can be dangerous tools if used incorrectly and if stored incorrectly. So, to prevent any unforeseen mishaps, choose a proper location when storing your knives away.

Photograph provided by Messermeister

Photograph provided by Messermeister.

Photograph provided by Chelsea Miller, Photographer Michael Rubenstein

Chelsea Miller Knives

Knife forging has remained traditional in the process. But knife makers are sure setting themselves apart today. From the places and backgrounds, they come from, to the materials they are choosing to use. Such is the case with Chelsea Miller. I was immediately drawn to her knives. Chelsea Miller's blades are intriguing pieces of art. It is obvious that this beautiful tool was created by someone who is looking at how to further test the limits of the knife, by attempting to evolve it, yet once more. In a world where everyone is looking for form and function to be showcased in their home, many have deemed kitchen knife designs as lackluster. Knowing that there is only so much that can be done to zhuzh up the aesthetic style of a knife while not effecting its essential purpose, Chelsea Miller has intrigued even the most creative thinkers with her artistic design.

As someone who believed they were meant to have a profession in the performing arts, Chelsea Miller's life certainly took a turn, though a dramatic element is remarkably present in all her productions. Once it became clear to her that knife making *was* her destiny, Chelsea recalled how she grew up in Vermont, where she was taught at an early age how to care for her mother's carbon steel knives. Even then, she was immediately fascinated by the everchanging patina, in a way only a child could imagine the magical possibilities of a kitchen, on a completely different level. And so, years down the line, when her father suggested she use some the various horse rasps he had lying around, Chelsea began "sculpting" away. What was revealed was an evolutionary union between two tools.

There's also an undeniable sustainability to Chelsea Miller's knives, which is truly intriguing for me. As chefs, we are always looking for ways to downsize our knife rolls or, at the very least, have items which serve dual purpose. The addition of a side rasp onto some of her pieces showcase an intentional repurposing of materials. Simply glancing at one of her knives encourages you to test the limit of your taste buds and technique. What will it slice? How much will it zest? What might it grate? This thought process is yet another facet in the beauty and wonder of cooking. The trusted bond we establish with the tools which enable and inspire us, day by day, to create, nourish and dare I say, play, is a personal choice. We may try our damned best to "follow the line" using the same tools which nostalgically remind us of why we love to be in the kitchen in the first place, but ultimately, it is what feels *best to us* which will encourage us to return to that same spot to recreate some magic.

Chelsea Miller's knives have been fashioned in way where they are fashionable, artistic pieces meant to be used for the simplest depiction of love and care—cooking. They are heirloom knives meant to be cherished until well past their vintage age. They are purposefully appealing even to those who don't seem to "understand it." In a time when we are all trying to decide what the next step in our future is Chelsea is forging a "prototype" showing what an additional element of drama can produce. It will certainly be intriguing to see what else will be introduced and the footsteps that shall be inspired following her dedication to the craft, in the future.

Photograph provided by Chelsea Miller, Photographer Michael Rubenstein

Q&A with Chelsea Miller, *Owner of Chelsea Miller Knives*

How important is the detail that goes into designing the handle of a knife, in comparison to the attention that is placed on the blade?

Wood and metal are entirely different animals. The wood prefers to be led gently whereas with metal, I'm holding on for dear life as it rattles and shakes, sparks and flakes, testing me all the time. Wood is less forgiving, pushing too hard I might lose a beautiful grain I'm trying to feature. As rough and brutal as the metal can be, though, there's always an opportunity to reshape, bend back a little.

What is your personal favorite knife, (may or may not necessarily be from your brand), and why?

My favorite knife is a chef knife that I made in the fall of 2018. I was in the middle of a showcase in Manhattan, and I had many chefs and collectors visiting to get a feel for my knives in person. Everyone had something different to say and most comments were contradictory. Some found them too light, some too heavy... I realized I had been trying to appeal to too many people rather than focus on what I like most. You'll see a clear change in shape and weight from then on. That knife I made for myself is the new standard... Until perhaps I change my mind again.

What is your preferred method of storage: block, drawer, magnet? And why?

I have several magnets on the wall in my kitchen to hold my knives. I've painted them to "disappear," the knives hover in the most beautiful way. I like to feature my knives in the same way I do artwork in my home. It gives my kitchen a warmth, an inviting atmosphere where the right tools for the job are standing ready. My countertop is also stacked with cutting boards and cookbooks, I can't stand clutter but drool over visually interesting vignettes.

What is your earliest memory of using/being introduced to a knife?

I remember my father would invite me and my sister to watch him slaughter our sheep and turkeys each year. One year he pulled us in close and with a knife opened the stomach of the newly slaughtered sheep to show us the digestive process. Seeing the grain from partially to fully digested was awe inspiring. Under his supervision he would let me use his hunting knife to clean fish we had caught. My father always had a knife on his hip. Swiss army knives were popular birthday gifts, I looked forward to each year's new features: a magnifying glass or tiny pair of scissors.

Where do you see the future of culinary knives, especially now that the world has either returned to cooking at home or begun their culinary "journey?"

I'd like to see more exclusive lines designed with a chef or restaurant in mind. Knives ought to be incorporated into the layout of a kitchen, where they live and how they fit into the overall design are important to me. I do believe we're beginning to place more value on the character of a knife.

Where do you see the future of your company?

I'm working on a reimagined knife set, modern and artistic but also accessible to all. I'm also interested in creating unique pieces that reflect the style of a space or chef. My dream is to create an entire kitchen line from knives to cooking utensils, linens, pots, spice blends, all of which are in harmony and complement one another.

Apart from the obvious, why do you think that people are so intimidated by knives or scared to use them?

Few people are taught proper knife skills or safety habits. I am often asked why there are so few female knife makers, it's for the same reason, lack of exposure. Knives are only dangerous in the kitchen if you are unpracticed.

If you could build your dream knife kit, which knives would it include and why? It can be exclusive to your brand or a combination from other brands around the world, and even historical knives you have been fascinated with.

My ultimate collection would include some of the earliest knives from around the globe. The simplicity and utility of early knives tells a story of what life was like. I'm intrigued to attempt to remake some of these and see how they could be applied to modern day cooking.

How did you fall in love with your craft and how did that influence your love of knives?

I fell in love with my craft when my father was ill. I'd come home for that period and working in his shop was the grounding experience I needed. Being able to process his illness and make the most of our limited time together, while sharing the same tools, was an experience I'll always treasure. Working with my hands I was able to tune out what was happening around me, as a result I felt better equipped to move through the world with focus and a sense of autonomy. Since then, I live each day with ease. Certainly, there are challenges, but I always have a safe place to return to in my workshop.

Favorite utensils

Spoons! I love to get lost in a spoon.

Favorite place to cook outside

At my family home there is a firepit on the edge of the beaver pond. On clear nights the moon

rises at the far end of the pond, the reflection of moon light and fire create that special seasoning.

Favorite recipe to cook outside

I love to cook with friends and family. Whatever they show up with to cook we

make room for on the fire!

Especially delicious: corn in the husk and charred eggplant.

Photograph provided by Chelsea Miller. Photographer Michael Rubenstein

Photograph provided by Chelsea Miller, Photographer Michael Rubenstein

Photograph provided by Chelsea Miller, Photographer Michael Rubenstein

Conclusion

Cooking has been significant in aiding in the evolution of man. Consider the fact that our primitive ancestors used to spend hours on end eating, which was more of an attempt to effectively consume food rather, than a social event. Discovering how to create fire enabled our ancestors to heat and cook their food, catapulting humans to evolve to the beings we are today; the knife was the catalyst that sparked that discovery. Therefore, the relationship between knife and food, knife and human, and knife and survival, has always been a true representation of evolution. This relationship "pushed" man to walk more erect, seek technology, and advance in society. While there is still much to be done, sometimes returning to our most basic tool can move us towards solving more of the complex problems of our time. Food security has always been an issue of survival for humankind. Today, not much has changed. So let us take a cue from our ancestors. Let us gather around the table, where one is open and honest over food, and contemplate the future steps of man's evolution using the same tools that once brought us "out of darkness."

I encourage you to try not just a new recipe but to also go and get yourself a quality knife to your liking and accessibility. The future of the knife is exciting, as the classic brands we have grown to trust and love are producing remarkable items. But I challenge you to go out of your comfort zone and search for novice makers who have trained under renowned industry names or familiarize yourself with those who hold such a passion for the craft that their pieces will certainly intrigue you to test out their knives. A couple of names on my radar are: Middleton Made Knives, Erica Moody, Bleinheim Forge, and countless others.

If anything, leave this section, of this book, understanding that the history of the knife and all its story is germane to the story of man. This item, tool, utensil, weapon, whatever you wish you call it, has been catapulted through history and revolutions, has undergone refinement and status, and has become part of culture and even your family memories.

Photograph provided by Chelsea Miller, Photographer Michael Rubenstein

Photograph taken by A.J., modern depiction of Nessmuk's famous drawing featured in his book Woodcraft.

Bushcraft Techniques

Note: This book is not intended to be a bushcraft/woodcraft skills guidebook. However, some general knowledge, as far as, knife techniques, wilderness etiquette, and a minimalist pack item list will be shared. I will, also, share links where good bushcraft knowledge sources can be found. Most importantly, do not be a "stickler" when performing bushcraft techniques. There is more than one way/method to accomplish the same task. The following techniques are just my personal workflow on how I like to use my knife for bushcraft.

Bushcraft/woodcraft can be considered an art as well as a science. It is an art because the techniques used to accomplish the tasks required to set up camp are all part of a skillful dance. An outdoorsman must process wood in a particular fashion, so that it may be useful to make fire, shelter, or even seating arrangements. The way wood needs to be manipulated, to harness its usefulness and maximize efficiency, is an art. Bushcraft/woodcraft is also a science, as the outdoorsman needs to understand what measurements need to be applied when processing wood. An outdoorsman should know which knots to apply and what length and height to set their rope in order to establish shelter, as well as where to set up other accommodations at camp. An outdoorsman must observe their surroundings and determine where they will acquire resources to sustain themself for the duration of their camp.

Before an outdoorsman embarks on their wilderness journey, they need to have some form of prior knowledge on the type of vegetation, wildlife, and terrain they will be dealing with so that they may "exploit it" properly and respectfully. Wilderness awareness is not just situational, as it also requires proactive and reactive behavior. The outdoorsman should educate themself through wilderness training courses, the right reading material (books, magazines, journals, articles, etc.), viewing reputable videos, and eventually building muscle memory through rehearsal drills. The wilderness can be challenging, and quite honestly, extremely harsh. An easy day trek through the woods can take a turn for the worst very quickly. There is an endless list of things that can go wrong, ranging from weather-related issues to simply taking a wrong step which may lead to injury.

The environment will dictate how you will perform on your adventure. Therefore, an outdoorsman always needs to be prepared for anything, at any given time. Mistakes will happen… we are all prone to them, whether on an outdoor adventure or simply walking through life. We are always hopeful that the mistake is a forgiving one, rather than one which can compromise your safety, or the safety of those around you. Mistakes are not failures, rather lessons learned, experience gained, and success in a bottle. The most important lesson is the one learned from a mistake. Never lose your enthusiasm and have the courage to step outside of your comfort zone more often than not.

An outdoorsman should always carry a selection of items, regardless of the amount of time they will spend on their wilderness adventure. Being prepared in case things do not go as planned is part of being proactive. This decision will, by default, improve one's outcome should any problems arise.

Here is an example of a short list of items one should always consider packing when preparing for any wilderness adventure (hiking, fishing, hunting, climbing, camping, kayaking, etc.):

Minimum Pack List:

1. Pocketknife (abide by local knife laws)
2. Pocket Multi-Tool (Leatherman or Swiss Army)
3. First Aid Kit (antiseptics, bandages, gauze, tape, tweezers, tourniquet, baby wipes, lip balm)
4. Light Pocket Poncho
5. Light Pocket Thermal Blanket (space blanket)
6. Small Flashlight (pocket-sized, preferably waterproof)
7. Small Lighter & Ferro Rod with Striker (pocket-sized)
8. Insect Repellant (pocket-sized)
9. Compass (pocket-sized) & Map of Local Area
10. Small Signaling Mirror (pocket-sized)
11. Small Whistle
12. Cap or Hat
13. Orange Bandana (used to signal or wrap a wound)
14. Pocket-Sized Field Maintenance Kit (for knife)
15. Extra Pair of Socks (at least one extra pair)
16. Sunscreen (pocket-sized)
17. 25ft of 550 Paracord
18. Small Sewing Kit (pocket-sized)
19. Stoker Flatpack Stove
20. Small Cup (titanium or stainless steel, used for boiling water)

All these items mentioned can be easily packed into a medium-sized pouch, satchel, haversack, croaker sack, or backpack, etc., and carried during your wilderness adventure. Everything combined should not weigh more than 10 lbs. This minimum pack list should accompany any additional gear required to perform any intended outdoor activities, such as hunting, climbing, fishing, etc.

In an ideal situation, there are three multipurpose tools a person should always consider carrying into the wilderness: an axe, a belt knife, and a pocketknife. Those three items will give a person a significant advantage if traversing through nature for an extended period of time. Of course, a hand saw is always a wonderful item to carry, if an axe is not available. These tools will enable a person to stay in the wilderness for more than one day, by processing wood for shelter and fire.

When building your outdoor kit or packing list, there are four key concepts to consider: Longevity, Scalability, Maintainability, and Reliability.

Longevity: Make sure the gear is operational for the duration of the outdoor trip. The gear in your kit must be within its life expectancy range, meaning the span of time that the item is safe to use. Replace any expired or broken items.

Scalability: Make sure the gear is capable of handling repeatable use for extended periods of time. Functionality should not be compromised by the number times used. Your gear should be able to exceed expectations, if needed. Your gear should be adaptable to a variety of environments and scenarios.

Maintainability: Items could be easily fixed or replaced, within a specified period, without causing an inconvenience or gap within your kit.

Reliability: Make sure you pack your kit with items that are "tried and true." These items must have a high level of merit, based on the items past performance. Know your gear and its limitations. The best way to know your gear, is to test it.

The reason one must consider the above key concepts is due to life's unpredictability; therefore, we must be proactive. When preparing, think random deployment and planned deployment. Check your kit periodically to ensure gear functionality is always at its optimal levels.

As your skills improve and you begin to understand the craft well, then you can easily accommodate one item to perform the task of several others. The idea of hiking and backpacking is to travel light. When engaging in outdoor adventures/activities the idea is to enjoy it… not rough it out.

Field Knife Maintenance Kit

In the field, there are limited resources confined solely to what we can bring or create. It is always a wise decision to include a small knife maintenance kit as part of your packing list.

I suggest including the following items as part of the kit:

1. Knife Oil (can be stored in small bottle)

2. Pocket Sharpener (Spyderco Ceramic, DMT Diamond sharpener, or Fallkniven DC3/DC4)

3. Leather Strop (a leather belt, or a pocket-sized strop)

4. Beeswax (small pocket-sized bar)

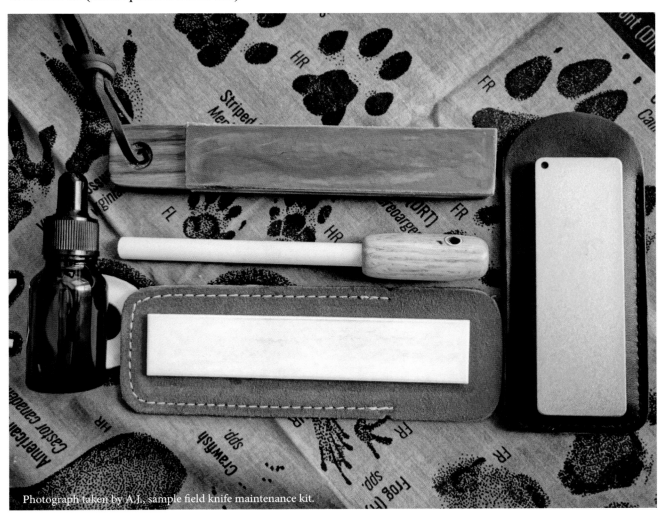

Photograph taken by A.J., sample field knife maintenance kit.

Water

Always bring enough water when heading outdoors on any adventure. Though it may seem obvious, it is always the simple things that one forgets. The amount of water you will need depends on your body weight, physical capabilities, type of adventure, weather conditions (temperature, humidity, etc.), and duration of the outdoor activity. Remember, when you are outdoors, nothing is ever "obvious." Staying hydrated should always be the first priority on everyone's mind when outdoors. Always pack a container that can be used to boil water. Boiling water from your nearest natural source will sanitize it enough to make it drinkable. Another option is packing a GRAYL® GeoPress® purifier, which can purify 24 ounces (710 ml) of water in as little as eight seconds. The filter on the device is good for 350 cycles on average.

Your body needs lots of water in order to function properly. Typically, a person can survive around three days without water. The three-day limitation depends on several factors, such as body weight, age, climate, physical activity, and overall health. Not everyone will be capable of reaching three days without water or some form of hydration source. There are also people who can manage to "squeeze through" without water for maybe a couple more days in extreme situations, but it is rare. Water is essential to sustain life, maintain functional motor skills, and keep your core temperature at normal levels. So, what happens when you are dehydrated and you do not manage to hydrate within a certain amount of time? You die.

YouTube Videos:

Coalcracker Bushcraft, "Beat Dehydration"

Living Survival, "GRAYL® GeoPress®, Best Water Filter Bottle Period!!"

Gideonstactical, "Essential To My Treks: GRAYL® GeoPress® *"*

Campfires

Please be mindful when making campfires. It is important to obey local laws, as well as be considerate of your surroundings. When building a campfire, it should be big enough to keep you warm, but small enough to easily control. Make sure the area around your campfire is clear of any debris that can easily catch fire, therefore causing the fire to spread uncontrollably. Once no longer needed, extinguish the campfire properly, including any active embers. I recommend you call the park information center before you start setting up any form of campfire. Every park is different, and their rules change frequently.

"Before starting your fire, follow these steps:

- **Know the local rules**
  Each park has their own rules on where and when you can have a campfire. Ask at the visitor center or contact the park before you visit so you know any relevant rules.
- **Know the fire conditions**
  Has it been windy and dry lately? That might mean campfires are banned, or that other special rules or restrictions are in effect. Again, contact the park when you arrive or shortly before you visit to find out if there is a burn ban or other weather-related rules you need to know." (https://www.nps.gov/articles/campfires.htm)

The above message was taken from the US National Park Service. Now, if you are in private property, then check any local advisories before you engage in setting up a campfire. Don't be the one that causes mayhem in your community, because you forgot to check the local advisories on outdoor fires. Honestly… just be safe and use common sense.

Processing Game

It is always good practice to process wild game away from your campsite to avoid uninvited guests (predators) from paying you a surprise visit. Once you are finished processing the game, clean your worksite as much as possible before walking away.

Photograph provided by ESEE Knives, Processing Game.

Cooking

Any meal prep should be performed carefully, so as to not spoil your food. Make sure to cook your food thoroughly to avoid foodborne illnesses or unwanted health conditions, such as bad indigestion, upset stomach, diarrhea, nausea, etc. In the wilderness, things can take a turn for the worst real fast.

YouTube Videos:

Wilderness Cooking, "Very Juicy And Delicious Ribeye Steak Cooked on a Rock"

Kent Survival, "Biggest Bushcraft Breakfast cooked on a Rock in the Rain"

Fisherman's Life, "Foraging a Meal Fit for a King!! Eel, Kelp, Clams, Fish, Crab, Mussels, Wild Greens"

Shelter

If you plan on spending the night at your location, pack a lightweight tarp, tent, or be prepared to build your shelter using natural resources. Your immediate environment and the location of the campsite will dictate the type of shelter you can build. It is important for an outdoorsmen to be well educated in shelter building techniques. There are several types of shelters one can build while out in the woods, from temporary to permanent, which is why I reiterate that the environment and campsite location will dictate which type of shelter is most appropriate. Here are a few to keep in mind and do some research on: Insulated Tree Well, Snow Trench, Snow Cave, Igloo, Bough Bed, Lean-To, Leaf Hut, Spider Shelter, Wickiup, Round Lodge, Ramada, and Quinzhee. Honestly, learning to make a shelter is an art. If you choose to make a shelter from a tarp, then I suggest learning four or five of the several shelter variations one can build from a tarp, such as the Adirondack, A-Frame, Arrowhead, Rectangular Pyramid, Arrowhead Wedge Cover, Basic Arch, Basic Fly Line Roof, Groundsheet, Basic Lean-To, Mushroom Fly, Bivibag Cornet, Bivibag Hunchback, Bivibag Doorway, Blue Well, Body Bag, Open Booth, C Fly Wedge, C Fly Roof, Cross Quartered Fly, Diamond Fly, Dinning Fly, Double Skin Lean-To, Envelope, Wind Shed Wedge, Wind Shed Roof, Forrester, Gunyah, Half Box, Half Cone Fly, Pyramid Fly, Hexagonal Fly, Half Pyramid Wedge, Kennel, Mountain Pod, Scallop Fly, Sentry Box, Shade House, Shade Sail, Square Arch, Star Tent, Holden Tent, Torque Tent, etc. There are many shelters one can learn to setup; it is important to understand what type of shelter to use and when.

YouTube Videos:

TA Outdoors, "15 Shelters with a Tarp"

MCQ Bushcraft & Wilderness Life, "Bushcraft Essential Knots for Shelter & Tarp Setups"

SensiblePrepper, "8 Easy Tarp Shelters for Survival"

Coalcracker Bushcraft, "10 Survival Shelter Setups in Under 10 Minutes: Oilcloth Tarp, Lean To, Plow Point, A Frame"

Campsite

Be mindful of your surroundings and only use the necessary amount of natural resources to sustain yourself and those accompanying you for the duration of your outdoor adventure. As previously mentioned, it is especially important to clean up your campsite properly and dispose of any hazardous/foreign objects accordingly. Cleaning up your campsite means that you give nature the opportunity to restore the disturbed area in order to help maintain the ecosystem we all enjoy. One must always practice good wilderness etiquette and explore responsibly.

Photograph provided by ESEE Knives, Campsite/Tent

Photograph taken by A.J., making hot coca with boys.

Photograph taken by A.J., making kindling bundles with Gerber StrongArm.

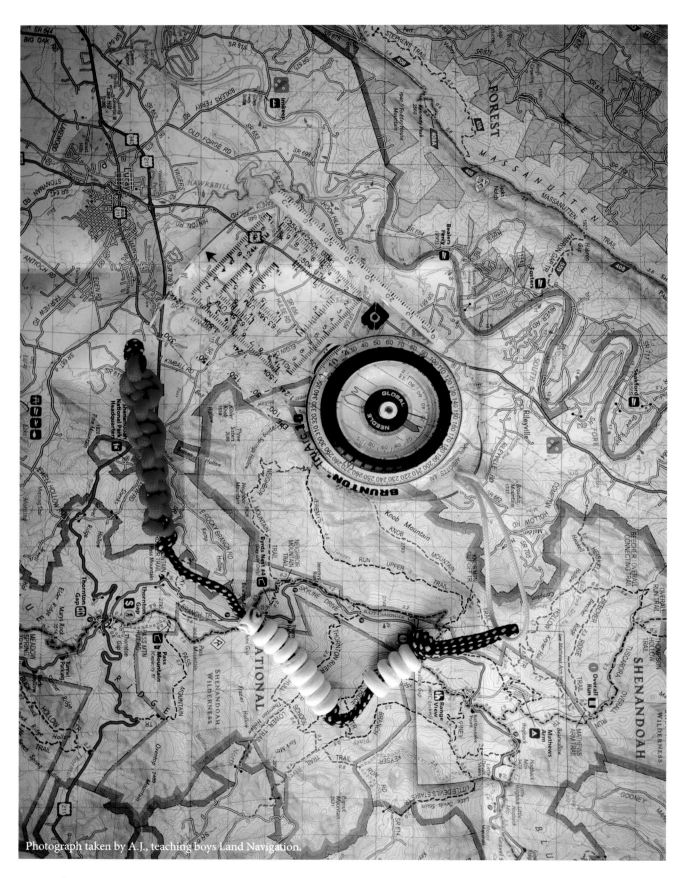

Photograph taken by A.J., teaching boys Land Navigation.

Orientation

One of the most important skills while in the outdoors is understanding the "lay of the land." Grasping your immediate environment is just the crust of the pie. The aim, when outdoors, is to divide the landscape into four core slices. These slices represent your cardinal direction: north, south, east, and west. It is not just about understanding linear directions, but also everything in between. Keep in mind that we live in a *three-dimensional + one universe*; therefore, remember to look up, down, and keep track of time. Mastery in the science of navigation is a skill that will keep you alive in the wilderness. Learn to use a compass and read a map. A good manual to read is, "*Map Reading and Land Navigation*," US Department of the Army, FM 3-25.26. The manual contains the fundamental education one would need to navigate throughout our planet.

It would NOT be wise for a person to venture into an unknown area in the woods, jungle, plains, or mountains without a map and compass. The first step is to check the declination on your compass to make sure it is correct for your current location. Orient your map with your compass by placing your compass flat on the map, with the direction of travel arrow pointing toward the top of the map. Next, rotate the compass bezel/dial so that N (north) is aligned with the direction of the travel arrow. Then, slowly rotate both the map and compass, until the compass's magnetic needle (red end) matches the map's north arrow. Basically, both the map's north arrow and the compass's magnetic needle will be pointing north. Now, find your current location on the map. Place the baseplate of the compass next to your location on the map. The intent here, is to use the baseplate as a ruler, to draw a straight line from your location to your destination. Make sure the direction of the travel arrow, on your compass, is pointing toward your direction of travel to the destination. Do NOT confuse the direction of the travel arrow, with the compass's magnetic needle arrow. Slowly rotate the compass's bezel until the orientating lines of the compass are aligned with the north–south gridlines of your map. What you are trying to do is capture the degree/bearing of travel. The angle between north and an object is called a bearing, and they are measured in degrees. Make sure that the north marker of the compass, is pointing north on the map. Look at the index on the bezel and notice the bearing you have just set. That bearing is the direction you need to follow, to reach your destination.

The line that was drawn from your current location to the destination can be used to also understand the distance you will travel. Grab a piece of paracord or piece of paper, and match the length of the line onto the paper or piece of paracord. Then lay it flat under your map's scale bar, to determine the distance.

As you begin to travel to your destination, take note of prominent landmarks around the area, so that you begin to understand the "lay of the land." It is important to know what stands between you, and your destination. Once you arrive to your destination or campsite, scope the area to make sure it is safe for you to settle. Look for signs of animal activity, such as tracks, droppings, etc.

Do not start wondering off the campsite trying to hunt, fish, or find wood for a campfire if you do not understand the "lay of the land." Take a small notebook, pen or pencil, and jot down your notes about the surrounding area. Keep a compass and knife on your body at all times. Most importantly, be ready to apply dead reckoning skills, otherwise you could find yourself in a horrible situation. A knife is your best friend in the wilderness—a trustworthy companion—that can be depended upon to save your life. Learn to wield it properly; train habitually with your knife before you embark on any journey into the unforgiving wilderness. DO NOT LOSE YOUR KNIFE. If you lose your compass, there are other methods you can use to find your way back to camp, such as the watch method, lunar method, shadow stick method, moss on trees observation, etc. But if you lose your knife, you pretty much lost your survival tool. It is not the end of the world, but… it will be harder to accomplish certain tasks without it.

YouTube Videos:

REI, "How to Use a Compass"

Coalcracker Bushcraft, "Navigation: Compass Basics"

Coalcracker Bushcraft, "Navigation: Map and Compass Duo"

David Canterbury, "Best Compass for You"

Corporals Corner, "Map and Compass (Simplified)"

STOKERMATIC, "THIS is how to use a Compass (Lensatic Compass for beginners)"

BlackScoutSurvival, "How to Use a Map and Compass"

Survival On Purpose, "How To Use A Lensatic Compass For Beginners"

The Gray Bearded Green Beret, "Primitive Navigation Techniques for Survival"

Reason I suggest viewing the above videos, is because orientation in the wilderness is extremely important, I cannot emphasize this enough.

Chopping

Chopping can be performed with large knives or axes. The style of chopping that will be covered here is the one used to fell a tree. Before engaging into any form of chopping, observe the tree and make sure there are no obstacles in the direction it will fall. Also, observe if it is already leaning toward a particular direction. If the tree is leaning toward a particular direction, then obviously this can help determine the landing area, and how it should be chopped. Develop a plan of action that makes the most sense for the particular scenario, and one that will keep you and others safe. After you have observed the area and the status of the tree, you can start chopping away. Chopping is performed by hitting the object with the cutting edge of a large knife or axe with enough pressure to sever it. This may take several heavy strikes, depending on the size of the tree. When trying to fell a tree, strike the tree trunk at a 45-degree angle to begin creating what would be a large wedge shape or v-notch. If you are felling (cutting down) a tree, you will want to make 45-degree chops on the side you want the tree to fall. The location you begin chopping the trunk should be about 12" to 18" inches from the ground. This will allow enough space between the area you are chopping and the ground. This is typically called the "first cut "or "undercut." The idea is to create this notch/cut that is about the same width of the tree. Continue to chop in this 45-degree angle, with each chop opposite each other, until you reach a depth just under half of tree's diameter. You want to end up with a triangular cutout with a flat bottom and a 45-degree slope up and out from the center of the trunk. The bottom angle should be perpendicular to the ground. Remember, the end state is a triangular cutout.

Next, you want to move to the opposite side of the area you were chopping to perform the same procedure. Now, you want the second notch/cut to be about 4" to 10" above the first notch/cut, depending on the diameter of the tree. The angle of the "second cut" or "back-cut" should be about 35-degrees, versus the 45-degree first cut. So basically, you will make a narrower triangular cutout on the opposite end. What this does is create sort of a hinge for the tree to fall on, therefore allowing it to fall on the desired location rather than rolling to another spot. Once you are about a quarter of the way, stop. This time you are going to want to exercise additional caution, as each strike will bring the tree one step closer to falling. Before you continue chopping, if the tree hasn't fallen already, give it a single push. Pay attention to the tree. If it still looks and feels sturdy, then continue chopping. Maintain the same pattern as before, (35-degree chops on the top, flat chops on the bottom). Your eyes and ears will be your greatest tools at this point. Keep a lookout for any swaying or cracking sounds and be prepared to move out of the way as fast as possible once you notice the tree beginning to fall. Stay about 12 to 25 feet away from the location where it will fall.

The size of the tree should determine the distance you want to be from the fall line, so *use common sense*. If the limb is larger than 6 inches in diameter, it might be best to consider using an axe versus a large knife (chopper). Once the tree has been felled and is flat on the ground, perform snedding/limbing(delimbing), which is the removal of the side shoots/branches and buds along the length of the tree. Practice extreme caution when doing this and pay attention to the direction of the cutting edge. It is best to stand on the opposite end of the tree, from the side you are snedding, to use the tree as a safety barrier. Finally, if you will be using it as firewood, you will crosscut the tree into ideal segments of about 14" to 16". Again, exercise extreme caution when doing this. If you have a hand saw or bucksaw, then it might be best to use it for this step, versus crosscutting with your axe.

Remember to wear the necessary safety equipment and use proper posture/form to avoid an unwanted injury. Accuracy and precision are key here. If you plan on performing this process for the first time, make sure you consult with someone that has more experience. Felling a tree is no easy task and can be extremely dangerous.

There is more than one way to chop/fell a tree. The above method is simply my preferred workflow. Below are a few links to videos that will explain this process from other people's perspective.

YouTube videos:

Schrade, "How to Chop Down a Tree Using a Survival knife."

Coalcracker Bushcraft, "Cutting Saplings: Knife only."

Buckin' Billy Ray Smith, "Logger – cutting down big tree with axe – tips."

Skillcult, "AXE ONLY Tree Processing, Saw Free Firewood."

Photograph taken by A.J., chopping tree.

Batoning

Batoning is a technique used to split small logs by placing the cutting edge of a knife on one of the two flat base surfaces of the log and repeatedly striking the spine of the knife with a thick stick or mallet. The purpose of batoning is to split the log into segments. This technique is used repeatedly until you have reduced the size of the log into multiple thin pieces of wood that can be used for kindling. This process is typically used when the logs have a flat surface to stand on and a flat surface where the knife's cutting edge may be placed. This process is a last resort because, naturally, an axe would be a better option for this task. However, a survival knife can accomplish this too, if the log's surface diameter is smaller than the size of the knife's cutting edge.

YouTube videos:

School Of Self Reliance, "Batoning Wood With A Knife."

David Canterbury, "Batoning Wood with your Knife."

Coalcracker Bushcraft, "Baton Wood Better with this Tip!"

Photograph provided by Dan Wowak, from Coalcracker Bushcraft, Batoning.

Tent Pegs

Knives can be used to carve the ends of a 5" to 7" inch stick into a spear point, which can be used as a tent peg. The other end of the peg should be carved into a blunt, round shape, as it will be the end that is hammered using a heavy piece of wood, a mallet, an axe head, or (if you have an exposed tang knife) use the pommel of your knife.

YouTube videos:

Coalcracker Bushcraft, "Tent Pegs in the Field."

The Gray Bearded Green Beret, "Bushcraft for Beginners: How to Make Tent Stakes."

Splitting Wedge

Using natural hardwood, such as Sugar Maple, Walnut, Pine, Hickory, Cherry, etc., sever a branch about 3" to 4" inches in diameter and cut the branch in four equal pieces, measuring about 6" to 7" inches in length. Proceed by carving the pieces into wedges. The wedge's flat sides should be about 45 degrees, making a V-shape point. The tail end of the wedge should be blunt/rounded or flat. The reason for the flat, rounded end is because that is the spot which will be hammered with a wooden mallet (can be made on site), axe head, or hammer. Use a small knife, hatchet, or axe to carve the wedges. The best way to use the wood wedges is to place the V-shaped tip along the natural cracks formed on the log over time and hammer the wedge(s) into the cracks causing the wood to split. If the log is large enough, it will require more than one wedge. Place the second wedge a few inches away from the first wedge and hammer it into the log.

YouTube Videos:

Far North Bushcraft And Survival, "Log Splitting The Bushcraft Way."

Skillcult, "Splitting Choice Axe Handle Blanks From An Oak Log & Shaping Wooden Wedges."

Photograph taken by A.J., spear point splitting wedge is shown in image, V-shape is preferred.

Notching/Carving

There are several notches you can do on a tree branch or log. There is the v-notch (beak notch), square notch (box notch), bow notch, whistle (flute), cross notch/lashing cross, round reduction, square reduction, round top (blunt end), dovetail notch, saddle notch, 90-degree planes, and root stripper. Each of these notch styles has an intended purpose, which we will explore more in this section.

V-notch: Used for making various traps to capture small game. It is carved nearly halfway through the stick, angles should be at 45 degrees, and come together to form a V-shape. It should be about the diameter of the stick.

Square Notch: Used for making traps, hang objects over a campfire, or to interlock small logs for building structures. It is typically carved halfway through the log, and all angles should be 90 degrees.

Bow Notch: Used for bow making. It helps hold the string in place. Make sure to smooth out the edges, so that the string does not abrade or tear.

Wedge Notch: Used to interlock logs/sticks.

Cross Notch: Used to interlock logs/sticks, in conjunction with cordage to lock the logs/sticks in place.

Round Reduction: Used for toggles, packframe, or decorative wood working.

Beam/Square Reduction: Used in log construction or in conjunction with an upright stick to create a deadfall trigger. The length of the squared carved sides should match the diameter of the stick, equally.

Dovetail Notch: Used for packframe, cooking crane, deadfall trigger device, or cabinet making for corner joints. It can be used for various applications, even joining sticks together to form square frames or creating a storage crate. The dovetail pin would need to be carved as the joining end of the other stick(s) that slides through the dovetail notch(s).

Saddle Notch: Packframe construction for joining of logs (cabin making).

90-degree Planes: Used for making traps to capture small game.

Latch Notch: Used to make traps to capture small game, such as the figure four trap.

Root Stripper: Used for hafting arrow and spear points or to remove bark from roots.

Hook Notch: Used to hang pots over a campfire to boil water or cook a meal.

Spear Point: Used to for tent pegs, spear hunting game, or spear fishing.

Round Top/Blunt End: Reduces edges, provides a clean look, and can be used as the hammering end of a tent peg. It can also be used for the rounded end of the spindle for a bow drill (Primitive Fire-Starting Method).

YouTube videos:

Coalcracker Bushcraft, "Bush Pot Suspension System." Coalcracker Bushcraft, "Cut a square notch." Coalcracker Bushcraft, "Securing Food During Survival with the L7 Trigger."

The Gray Bearded Green Beret, "18 Essential Knife and Bushcraft Skills: The Try Stick."

Try Stick

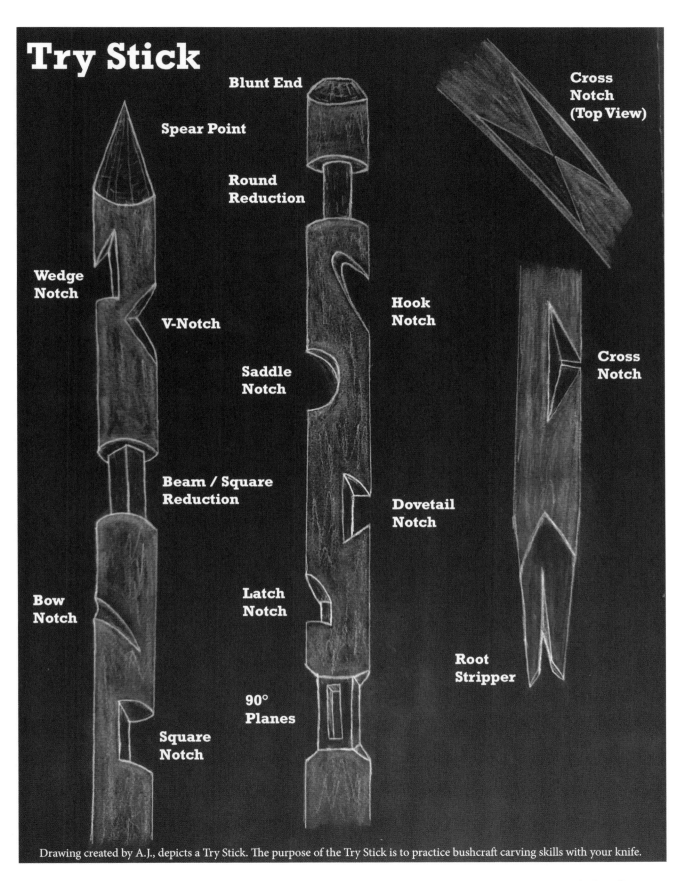

Blunt End

Spear Point

Round Reduction

Cross Notch (Top View)

Wedge Notch

V-Notch

Hook Notch

Saddle Notch

Beam / Square Reduction

Cross Notch

Dovetail Notch

Bow Notch

Latch Notch

90° Planes

Root Stripper

Square Notch

Drawing created by A.J., depicts a Try Stick. The purpose of the Try Stick is to practice bushcraft carving skills with your knife.

Traditional Fire-Starting Methods

Hand Drill

A knife can be used to carve holes on a small flat piece of wood (hearth board) that can later be used to start a fire using the "hand drill method." Ideally, the hearth board would measure about 0.50 inch in thickness with a length of about 18 to 24 inches, and be made of birch or cottonwood. It is preferred that the hearth board be made of soft wood as it produces more wood dust during friction. Use the point of your knife to carve out a hole (half-inch diameter) near the edge of a hearth board. The depth of the hole should be about half of the thickness of the wood board, roughly. Once the hole is ready, test it out with a straight, half-inch thick (diameter) knot-free stick (spindle/dowel) that is about 14 to 18 inches in length. It is best to use softwood, like cottonwood, basswood, or blue beech. It is important to make sure the spindle is long enough to avoid being hunched over for long periods of time, increasing your chances of fatigue. Round out the ends and place one of the rounded ends of the stick into the hole. Press the hearth board with your foot, to keep it in place, and rub/spin the stick between your hands. You want to use the full length of your hands, to spin the spindle. You want *consistent pressure and rapid speed*, with enough friction to generate some heat. Once you notice a little smoke, stop. Cut a small v-notch on the side of the hearth board with the point of the V-shape intersecting the hole. Make sure it is as centered as possible and large enough for dust to fall out. Place a small, thin leather pad, or thin strip of bark, under the V-notch. Put the spindle back into the hole, press the hearth board with your foot, and begin rubbing/spinning it between your hands to generate enough heat to create an ember. As more dust piles up, speed up your movement. This ember will typically drop out from the hole onto the leather pad or bark strip, so keep an eye out for it! Grab the ember, transfer it to the center of your fine tinder bundle, fold the tinder bundle over the ember, and gently blow into the bundle. If done properly, your bundle should ignite a flame.

YouTube videos:

Coalcracker Bushcraft, "Hand Drill Friction Fire."

BlackScoutSurvival, "Hand Drill Primitive Fire Making Technique – Black Scout Tutorials."

National Geographic, "How to Make a Friction Fire, Live Free or Die: DIY."

WIRED, "How to Start a Fire in a Survival Situation, Basic Instincts, WIRED."

Photograph taken by A.J., Hand Drill

Bow Drill

The hand drill method can be very tiresome and may even cause blisters on your hands, if you have not mastered the technique. A simpler method is the bow drill method. Perform the same initial procedure has the "hand drill," as far as making the hearth board and carving a hole on the hearth board with a knife. The difference is, though, that instead of your hands, you are going to use a bow (about the length of your arm, made from a semi-curved, slightly flexible wood stick, and a string, preferably nylon, attached to the ends of the stick/spindle to spin it). The best way to anchor the string is by carving a root stripper notch, as seen in the **Notching/Carving** subsection of the book, on both ends. Then wedge the string in between the root stripper notch, sliding it towards the tightest portion of the notch. Next, wrap the excess string around the top end of the stick and make a secure knot, to avoid it from coming undone. Bring the longer end of the rope to the other end of the stick, which has another root stripper notch, and perform the same procedure as above. Make sure the rope is tight. You will be left with an item that looks like a small bow which will be used to spin the spindle. Grab a small, flat, square piece of "green wood," referred to as a bearing block, which you will use to put pressure on between your hand, the stick, and the hearth board. This bearing block should be about one inch thick and about 3 to 4 inches in length. A stone may also be used as a bearing block. Carve a small hole in the center of the wooden bearing block. Place a small leather pad or leaf under the hearth board, just under the V-notch. Single wrap, or twist, the bow string around the spindle, just one twist of the rope works fine. If you do more than one twist around the stick, it may not spin successfully. Place the bearing block on you palm, and place one end of the stick in the bearing block hole. Press down on the board with your foot. Place the other end of the spindle in the hole of the hearth board, and begin moving the bow back and forth, causing the stick/spindle to spin rapidly. Make sure you have enough pressure on the stick, using the bearing block that is wedged in you palm. Once you notice enough smoke, check the hearth board to make sure the coal/ember that has formed has fallen out from the V-notch onto the leather pad, or bark strip, used to catch the ember. You want to check regularly so that you do not lose the coal/ember or that it loses its heat. Place the ember onto your fine tinder bundle, carefully fold the bundle over the ember, and gently blow until it ignites a flame.

YouTube videos:

Coalcracker Bushcraft, "Bow Drill Friction Fire with Natural Cordage."

The Gray Bearded Green Beret, "Complete Bow Drill for Beginners."

Chad Zuber, "My Bow Drill Friction Fire Technique."

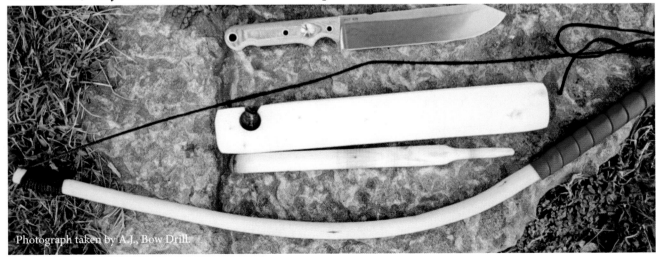

Photograph taken by A.J., Bow Drill.

Fire Plough/Plow

The fire plough method is essentially a modified version of rubbing two sticks together to generate heat through friction. Create a hearth board out of soft wood about 18 inches in length, 1 inch thick. Use your knife to form a gentle groove, or line, that runs along the length of the board. Find a stick that is strong enough to withstand some pressure without breaking, preferably made from Hazel, Cottonwood, or Birch. Gather enough tinder (dry grass, wood shavings, bark fibers, cattails, or punk-wood) and make a bird's nest. Make sure the bird's nest is fluffy enough to allow air flow. Place the tinder bundle, or leather catch pad, at the end of the board, so that the ember/coal falls onto it or can be transferred to it. Run the stick back and forth along the groove with enough pressure and speed. Consistency in the pressure and speed is key. Continue to rub or plough the tip of the stick at about a 45-degree angle back and forth along the groove. The friction will start to create a heated dust or smoldering fibers, to build up and form an ember/coal. Once you have an ember/coal, transfer it onto your tinder bundle, gently fold the bundle over the ember, and blow softly until there is a flame.

Pump Drill

The pump drill might be the hardest hand-powered device to create, but once it is made, it is the easiest of the four friction fire methods. It consists of a dowel/spindle, a narrow board (handle board) with a hole in the center, a heavy disc to act as a flywheel (counterweight), paracord, and hearth board/fire board. The heavy disc is attached to the spindle, close to the bottom end, and the handle slides over the top. The paracord is run through a small hole near the top of the spindle and attached to both ends of the handle board. The point is to wrap the paracord around the top part of the spindle, where the board will rest at its highest position. As downward pressure is applied, the paracord unwinds, causing the spindle to spin rapidly. Once the board reaches the bottom, the paracord is unwound and the pressure is exhausted. Make sure that the paracord is not too long, otherwise the handle board will drop too low. At its end state, the board must rest just above the counterweight. The counterweight keeps the spindle spinning so the paracord winds up again, around the spindle in the opposite direction, pulling the board right back up to the starting point. Repeat the motion, adding pressure downward, the handle board rises, then apply pressure downward again, etc., until smoke starts to build-up on the hearth board and an ember is created. The ember will typically fall to the ground or on whatever object you have under the hearth board to catch the ember. Transport the ember to your tinder bundle, or bird's nest, place it in the center, and gently wrap the tinder over it. Blow gently, until the bundle catches fire.

YouTube videos:

Paleomanjim, "Fore Making with Pump Drill."

Tom McElroy-Wild Survival, "Pump-Drill Primitive Fire."

Flint and Steel

This method of fire-starting is an old traditional way to ignite campfires, that dates back to the Iron Age. A high carbon steel knife blade can be used for this method, though it is not recommended because it can truly damage your blade's spine. This method will remove tiny pieces of steel to create a spark. If a steel striker cannot be used or found to strike the flint stone, then in an emergency situation, the spine of your knife's blade can be used. The blade must be of high carbon steel, such as 1095, 1080, O1, or W1, or it may not function properly. The best way to do this is to use the tip of your knife to stab a piece of charcloth onto a flat surface. Naturally, you want the spine to face you, not the cutting edge. Strike the blade's spine with a flint stone. Strike it using a fluid downward, arching motion, at an angle, to create sparks. The point of this method is to have sparks land on the pinched charcloth and create an ember. Another way is to hold the knife in place, tip down, and strike the flint stone against the blade spine using a downward motion. The intent is to drive the sparks onto a charcloth/charred material. The charcloth is then placed on your tinder bundle/bird's nest and gently folded in. Blow gently into the bundle or softly wave the bundle around so that it captures enough air to ignite a flame. Be careful, because when it finally catches fire, it can burn quick, so pay attention and have your firewood ready.

Understand that using your knife's spine is not the best option, only a last resort. The best option is using a steel striker and flint stone or quartz rock. Pinch a piece of charcloth between your thumb and flint stone. Strike the stone using your steel striker, performing a fluid downward, arching motion. All it takes is for one tiny spark to land onto your charcloth and it will ignite. Once lit, blow gently to spread the heat throughout the cloth. Place the cloth into your tinder bundle, fold it in softly, and gently blow. In as little as a few seconds, the bundle will ignite producing a nice flame.

YouTube videos:

Paul Kirtley, "How To Strike A Traditional Flint And Steel."

David Canterbury, "The Evolution of the Fire Steel."

Coalcracker Bushcraft, "Make a Flint and Steel Fire Starter Set at Home! Quick, Easy, Fun."

Coalcracker Bushcraft, "Flint and Steel Basics."

Photograph taken by A.J., Flint & Steel

Scrape/Strike a Ferrocerium (Ferro) Rod

A knife is typically not intended to be used to scrape/strike a ferrocerium rod but depending on the blade steel and type of knife, it should be ok. If your knife's blade has a 90-degree spine, it can be used to scrape the ferrocerium rod. Lay the rod on your tinder bundle, place the blade spine on the rod and apply a little pressure. Either run the spine of the knife along the side of the rod or pull the rod toward your body while keeping the knife firmly in place. Pay attention to the sparks and where they are landing; if you need to adjust your rod angle or knife pressure, do so. The point of this fire-starting method is to have the sparks land on your tinder bundle and ignite a flame.

YouTube videos:

The Gray Bearded Green Beret, "Survival Fire: How to Use a Ferrocerium Rod."

Savage Citizen, "Top 4 Mistakes When Using a Ferro Rod."

UCO, "Ferro Rod Tips and Tricks from Survival Instructor and Certified Badass, Dan Wowak."

Paul Kirtley, "How To Create Really Big Sparks With A Swedish Firesteel."

Photographs taken by A.J., scraping a ferro rod to iginite a flame on a tinder bundle that will be used to start a fire, and boil water.

Magnifying Glass

Using a magnifying glass is an extremely easy method to start a fire. There are only two things that are required to use a magnifying glass as your fire-starting method, and that is sunlight and dry tinder. Start by finding tinder, such as cattail, bark shavings, grass, chaga, or hoof fungus. Then form a bird's nest out of your fine bark shavings or dry grass. Place a cattail fluff or small thin slices of dry hoof fungus in the center of the bird's nest. Grab the magnifying glass and hover it just a few inches above your tinder. Slowly begin to change the angle of the magnifying glass until it captures the sun's light and puts a strong concentrated beam onto your pile. It might be wise to look away because it can hurt your eyes. Try to maintain a tight, consistent beam of light onto your fine tinder that is in the center of your bird's nest. If done correctly, in just a couple minutes the beam of light will heat up the tinder and it will begin to smoke. Once you notice an ember, gently fold the bird's nest over the ember and begin to blow gently into it. Remember, your bird's nest must be loose enough to allow air flow. The bird's nest should ignite shortly, and you can then place it onto your prepared location for the campfire.

YouTube videos:

Junkyard Fox, "Making Fire with a Magnifying Glass"

Photograph taken by A.J., magnifying glass

Tinder

Feather Sticks

Feather sticking is a process that can be performed by a knife or axe. Grab a dry branch from a tree or long kindling about 1 to 2.5 inches in diameter, and 10 to 12 inches long. Using the sharp edge of the blade remove the bark or outer layer, exposing the drier heartwood. Then, using the sharp edge of the blade, begin shaving off long and thin layers to create fine curls; these are referred to as "feathers." Create as many thin curls as possible. Sever the end of the branch, leaving a bundle of curls attached to a small fraction of wood. The feathers will serve as your tinder and will be used as your initial source of fuel to start a campfire. You want to place the bundle together in a pile and strike a ferrocerium rod with your knife's 90-degree spine. Place the rod just over the bundle with the end pointed at the bundle of tinder and strike it repeatedly, until enough sparks land on the bundle to ignite a fire.

YouTube videos:

Coalcracker Bushcraft, "Sticks and Feathers: Survival Fire."

The Gray Bearded Green Beret, "Feathersticks and Ferro Rods."

MCQ Bushcraft & Wilderness Life, "Bushcraft Basics Ep20: Making Fire Feather Sticks."

Photograph taken by A.J., made feathers to use as tinder.

Bark Shavings

Bark shavings are created using the 90-degree spine of a knife and rubbing the spine repeatedly on the surface of a dry tree branch or log, causing buildup of thin hair-like shavings. Bark shavings are a great source of tinder to light a fire. Remember to apply enough pressure and maintain consistency in your strokes.

YouTube videos:

Equip 2 Endure, "How to get Tinder from Cedar Tree, Quick Survival Tip."

Black Hat Bushcraft, "How to Process Tulip Poplar Sheds for 1ˢᵗ Class Tinder."

Photograph taken by A.J. Birch Bark, can be used for Bark Shavings.

Fatwood

Fatwood is typically collected from old, dying coniferous (evergreen) trees that are slowly decaying. The natural resin builds up over time, as these coniferous trees harden and begin the first stages of decomposition. As the stump wood or severed tree hardens, the resin or sap concentrates to create an all-natural, chemical-free fire starter, known as fatwood. The concentrated resin, or pitch buildup, takes an appearance of amber or yellow orange in color and seems petrified. At the core of high-quality fatwood, the color gets dark orange, almost light brown at times. Fatwood has a powerful scent of terpene (main component in turpentine). Fatwood is the best natural tinder available, because it can be lit by a spark, even when wet. The flame produced by the fatwood is windproof and burns extremely hot for a lengthy period. Some of the best tree candidates for fatwood are dying/decomposing pine trees.

To light fatwood, simply grab a piece and shave off layers as if making feather sticks. Use a ferrocerium rod and strike it with your knife's 90-degree spine. The sparks that land on the fatwood should ignite it. Obviously, there are other methods that are even easier to light fatwood, using a match or lighter, but I was just letting you know that it can be lit with a ferro rod and your knife as well.

YouTube videos:

Coalcracker Bushcraft, "Fatwood for Beginners."

The Gray Bearded Green Beret, "Finding Fatwood for Beginners."

Photograph taken by A.J., Fatwood bundle.

Hoof Fungus (Ice man fungus)

Typically, hoof fungus grows at the base of tree trunks, just over the outer layer of the bark. It is shaped like a horse's hoof, given the name, and varies in color from silver grey to nearly black. It is considered both a parasite and a decomposer. A parasite on living trees because it infects broken bark, causing rot. A decomposer, because it continues to feed on the trees long after they are dead, helping with their decomposition process. It is a non-edible fungus that is used by outdoorsmen or bushcraft experts as tinder. The Bronze Age Iceman "Otzi," discovered in Austria, (covered in earlier sections in the book), was found with four pieces of hoof fungus. Hoof fungus has been used as tinder for thousands of years. The tinder fungus must be dried out in order to be used.

The best way to light dry hoof fungus is to break apart small pieces of the fungus and use a ferro rod, match, or lighter to ignite it.

YouTube videos:

Clan Gunn Bushcraft, "Processing Amadou Tinder – Horse Hoof Fungus."

Cimbrer Bushcraft, "H) Horse Hoof Fungus."

Forrester Bushcraft, "Horses Hoof Fungus."

David Canterbury, "21st Century Longhunter Processing Tinder Fungus for Use."

Photograph taken by A.J., tree fungus, good source of tinder.

Chaga

Chaga, also known as *Inonotus Obliquus*, is a parasitic fungus that that typically grows on birch trees in cold climates. This fungus can be found in the northern hemisphere and resembles a burnt charcoal or dark clump of dirt. It measures anywhere from 10 to 15 inches in diameter and has a soft core with an orange, amber-like color. For centuries it has been used for its medicinal properties throughout northern Europe and Russia. Typically, the mushroom is ground to a fine powder and brewed as a tea beverage. Traditionally, it was used as an immunity booster, but it has also been used to treat diabetes and certain cancers. This amazing fungus is also used as a great source of tinder to light a fire. Chaga can easily catch a spark and hold an ember for some time. The best way to use this tinder source is by using the medieval "flint and steel" fire-starting method. Start by placing small pieces of the fungus onto a small leather pad or thin piece of birch bark. Place the steel striker just above the chaga. Using your flint stone, strike the steel striker using a downward motion. I know, it sounds crazy, using your flint stone as a striker. But by using your steel striker and flint in this fashion, it will help drive sparks toward the chaga. Eventually a spark will land on the fungus and ignite an ember. Once lit, place the fungus onto your tinder pile or bird's nest and gently fold the tinder or bird's nest over the ember. Blow gently into the tinder pile, until a flame ignites.

YouTube videos:

Coalcracker Bushcrafter, "Chaga for Survival - Fire Starting: Bushcraft, Survival Skills, Flint and Steel Fire"

The Gray Bearded Green Beret, "Finding Chaga Tinder Fungus in the Wild"

David Canterbury, "21st Century Long Hunter Harvesting Tinder Fungus (Chaga)"

Photograph taken by A.J., Chaga Chunks

Kapok

Kapok trees grow in the tropical rainforests of Latin America, Africa, and Asia. The trees can grow up to 70 meters tall and live for over 300 years. The tree produces a fruit, known as kapok seed pods, that are filled with silky kapok fibers, resembling cotton balls. The difference between kapok and cotton, is that kapok is highly water resistant and hypoallergenic. Kapok trees produce thousands of seedpods per season. The seedpods are harvested and the silky kapok fibers are used for duvets, mattress toppers, and pillows. Kapok fibers are highly flammable and can therefore be used as natural tinder. Kapok can be easily lit using a ferrocerium rod, match, or lighter. Be careful, because when lit, it burns very quickly.

Photograph taken by A.J., Kapok Tinder.

Punkwood

Punkwood can be found within decaying deciduous trees. Punkwood feels spongy, not mushy/soggy. The punkwood is charred using a charring tin, the same way cloth is charred to produce char cloth. The punkwood will be very brittle once charred, but it is good as a secondary option to char cloth to use with a flint and steel fire-starter kit.

YouTube videos:

Coalcracker Bushcraft, "Punkwood 101: The Basics with Ignition."

Far North Bushcraft And Survival, "Punkwood – Backwoods Tips For Fire Use."

The Gray Bearded Green Beret, "Charring Punkwood and Using Char with Flint and Steel and Solar."

Cattail

Cattail is a perennial marsh plant, typically found in wetlands, marshes, bogs, ditches, ponds, and shorelines. They flourish in areas where soil remains wet most of the year, and also, during its growing season (early spring). It is amazingly easy to spot cattail because it looks nearly identical to a corndog. The way to use cattail as tinder is to simply break it apart and use the fluff. The downside is that it burns up quite fast. That said, the fluff lights easily, even with a magnifying glass. Cattail will need to be dried appropriately, though, before using.

Photograph taken by A.J., cattail.

Marcescent Leaves

During the winter months, deciduous trees sometimes manage to retain some of their dead leaves from the fall. The dead leaves left hanging on some of the branches that dry out over the winter are called marcescent leaves. These leaves make great tinder because they remain dry on the branches versus falling off and decomposing on the ground. Marcescent leaves can be picked off the branches and made into a small tinder bundle.

Photograph taken by A.J., marcescent leaves on tree.

Jute Twine

Jute fiber is a form of bast fiber, composed of plant materials from the bark of the white jute plant. It is grown in tropical countries and harvested once a year. It is a golden-hued vegetable fiber with some flexibility unlike most other fibers. It is used to make rope or twine, among several other items. About 90% of the world's jute comes from Bangladesh and is exported to countries all around the world. It can be found on Amazon and purchased for a few dollars. It is typically sold in rolls of several yards. For bushcraft purposes, it can be used to tie down objects and tinder. If used as tinder, simply unravel, fluff it up, and make a bird's nest out of it. You can use a ferro rod, match, or lighter to ignite it.

YouTube videos:

Coalcracker Bushcraft, "The Jute Match."

IA Woodsman, "Uses For Jute Twine."

Photograph taken by A.J., Jute Twine.

Char Cloth

Char cloth is a form of man-made tinder, popoularized during medievel times. The cloth typically made of 100% plant fibers/cotton and has been charred, but not entirely burned. Cloth is folded over, rolled, or cut into small segments, and placed into a tin box or can. The tin box is then sealed and put over a campfire. The tin box will need to have a small hole punctured at the top or its side, where the smoke/steam will escape from. The tin box is left on the fire for a few minutes. Once the smoke/steam stops coming out, pull the tin box out or the char cloth will ignite and turn into ash. It is important to plug the tiny hole to prevent oxygen from getting in and igniting your char cloth. Wait for the tin to cool, then open it, and examine the char cloth. In modern day, people have decided to use an old *Altoids* tin as their charring vessel. Char cloth is nothing new; it has been used to make fires for centuries using flint and steel. As previously mentioned in this section, a segment of the char cloth is placed between your thumb and a flint stone. Strike the flint stone with a steel striker, by performing a fluid arching downward motion to generate sparks. The char cloth will eventually catch a spark and ignite. Gently place the lit char cloth into a tinder bundle and fold it in. Slowly blow air into the bundle until it begins to smoke heavy, and igniting the bundle into flames.

YouTube videos:

Coalcracker Bushcraft, "Can this traditional brass tin make char."

Coalcracker Bushcraft, "Natures Natural Fire Starter: Everything You Need to Know about Char, Flint and Steel, Natural Char."

The Gray Bearded Green Beret, "How to Make Charcloth."

Photograph taken by A.J., Char Cloth in Tin.

Cotton

Cotton balls or pads are a good source of tinder to start campfires. Some people like to soak the cotton balls or pads in hot wax to add an extra layer of protection to repel water. Other people coat the cotton with Vaseline. The cotton is then stored in a zip-lock bag or tin box/can.

YouTube videos:

SensiblePrepper, "DIY Cheap & Easy Survival Fire Starter."

GMC Crafts, "The Ultimate Bushcraft/Prepper Firestarter? Homemade. Cheap. 100% Waterproof and Reliable."

Photograph taken by A.J., cotton balls.

Bird's Nest

A bird's nest is a great way to prepare tinder bundles before introducing a lit char cloth or sparks from a ferrocerium rod. Gather dry tinder material, such as inner bark, fibrous grasses, twine, etc. Rub the material back and forth in your hands to rough it up. Begin to form a ball about the size of a fist. Form a depression in the center of the ball to develop the shape of a bird's nest. Grab the finest dry material from the tinder that was gathered and gently place it in the depression. Make sure that your tinder bundle/bird's nest is not too compact by fluffing it up a bit. It is important to understand that oxygen is one of the primary elements that feeds the fire so make sure the bundle is fluffy enough for air to circulate throughout it once lit. Light your char cloth using flint and steel, place it in your tinder bundle, and gently fold over the bundle. Blow air gently through the bundle until lit. If flint and steel is too complicated, use a ferrocerium rod to drive sparks into the bundle until lit. As a backup, always have a lighter or matches handy in the event your ferro rod fails. Once your tinder bundle is lit, begin adding kindling to keep the flames strong and healthy. The next step is to introduce firewood/logs, which is the fuel that will sustain the fire for long periods.

YouTube videos:

Coalcracker Bushcraft, "Making a Proper Fire Birdsnest."

Photograph taken by A.J., Bird's Nest

Dryer Lint

Dryer lint is a good source of manmade tinder. It can be used in the same fashion as cotton balls (with Vaseline) or simply on its own with no additives. You can use a ferro rod to ignite the dryer lint.

YouTube Videos: Survival on Purpose, "Is Dryer Lint Really The Best Fire Starter?"

Selecting Firewood

Being able to make a fire is just one step in the lifecycle of a campfire. Selecting and processing the correct wood is important because it is part of the fire sustainment process and another step that pertains to the lifecycle of a campfire. The lifecycle of a campfire can be broken down into the following steps:

1. Select a location for the campfire and prepare the site.
2. Gather and process fuel (firewood, kindling, tinder, etc.)
3. Create a flame.
4. Sustain the campfire.
5. Extinguish the campfire properly.

We have already discussed fire starting techniques using a knife in other subsections. We have also gone over wilderness etiquette and clearing a spot for the location of the campfire. This subsection will focus solely on gathering the correct wood that will aid in creating a flame and sustaining the fire for the duration of the night.

Top Ten Choices for Firewood:

Ash—White ash is one of the most user-friendly types of wood for a campfire. It is fairly lightweight, easy to split, and produces medium-to-high levels of heat. It produces around 24.2 million BTUs per cord.

Beech—Beech is an excellent choice for colder temperatures. It burns for long periods of time and produces high levels of heat. It needs to be seasoned for at least a year for best results. It produces around 27.7 million BTUs per cord.

Birch—In general, birch is a decent choice for firewood. Black birch produces the best results, with minimal downside. It is harder to split than beech and needs to be seasoned for about a year for best results. It produces about 26.9 million BTUs per cord.

Black Cherry—Cherry is a top pick because of the sweet aroma it gives off when burning. This wood is easy to split, burns well, and produces medium levels of heat. It produces around 21.1 million BTUs per cord.

Dogwood—An excellent choice because of its dense properties. It produces fairly healthy coal embers and produces high levels of heat. It is harder to split than other wood types because it is very dense. It produces about 29.1 million BTUs per cord.

Fir—Douglas Fir is a good choice for firewood because it is easy to split, produces few sparks, and has a nice aroma. The only downside is that it does produce moderate-to-high levels of smoke. It needs to season for about a year. It produces medium heat, with about 20.8 million BTUs per cord.

Maple—A decent choice for firewood. Depending on the species it can be difficult to split. It produces medium-to-high levels of heat, burns for a lengthy period of time, and produces low levels of smoke. It produces about 25.6–28 million BTUs per cord, depending on the species.

Mulberry—A good choice for firewood, because it is easy to split, produces medium levels of smoke, and medium-to-high levels of heat. As it burns it gives off a very pleasant aroma. The downside is that it produces many sparks. It produces around 25.9 million BTUs per cord.

Oak—A top choice for firewood because it produces medium-to-high levels of heat, low levels of smoke, burns for long periods of time, and produces few sparks. It is fairly easy to split and produces around 20–30 million BTUs per cord, depending on the species.

Walnut—Black walnut is an excellent choice for firewood, because it is fairly easy to split, produces few sparks, low levels of smoke, and burns for a decent length of time. It produces medium levels of heat, around 21 million BTUs per cord.

The reason it is important to discuss firewood in this book is because the last thing a person wants is to spend a great deal of time and energy chopping or batoning wood that is considered poor fuel for a campfire. It is also important to stay away from wood that can potentially damage your blade permanently.

Learning to set up your tinder and firewood is important to maintain the fire in a controlled setting and enable the fire to burn for extended periods of time. Below are a few YouTube videos that will demonstrate this process better than I can write or draw it.

YouTube Videos:

Coalcracker Bushcraft, "The 3 Processes of Camp Fire Creation – Preplanning"

Coalcracker Bushcraft, "The Best Way to Build Fire: Execution Phase and Stacked Method"

Coalcracker Bushcraft, "How to Build a Campfire: The Stacked Method"

REI, "How to Build a Fire"

Canadian Prepper, "6 Easy Campfires Everyone Should Know for Survival and Recreation"

Photograph taken by A.J., chopping firewood.

Photograph taken by A.J., kindling and firewood pile

Photograph taken by A.J., staying warm during the winter.

Wood Spoons carved by A.J.

Wood Carving

Wood carving is an art and a skill whereby one uses a cutting tool to carve functional or ornate objects from wood. It is also a necessary skill when performing bushcraft in the wilderness. In this section, I will go over a few essential knife grips to help you get started with this fun hobby. Felix Immler (bushcraft and carving expert), and Victorinox were kind enough to provide some wonderful images and great wood carving tips, which will be covered after the different carving grips.

Forehand Grip – Wrap fingers over the top of the handle, as if forming a tight fist, with the thumb wrapped underneath the handle blade facing outward. Angle the cutting edge of the blade, so that it is nearly flat against the wood object. Use your right knee as support, while working. Start cutting the wood with the bottom of the cutting edge, closest to the handle, and as you push forward, work the cutting action towards the tip of the blade. The wood will start to separate at the bottom part of the cutting edge and finish separating at the tip of the blade. It is sort of a sideways arcing motion, from bottom of the blade to top. Maintain the angle as best as possible. If you notice that your hands begin to tremble and the knife is sort of stuck in place as you begin to remove wood, the angle is incorrect, and you are likely removing too much wood at once. While using this grip, you'll notice that your elbow is doing the majority of the work. That's why some people refer to this grip as the "elbow grip."

Power Grip – This grip is easier on your elbow and forearms. The action will be concentrated mostly on your shoulder muscles. Straighten the arm with the knife. Hold the knife with the blade facing outward. Maintain the arm with the knife straight and steady. As with the forehand grip, use your right knee as support while working. Pull the wood object along the cutting edge of blade, removing material, as necessary. This grip allows for removal of larger chips with less effort. This grip is wonderful for making spear heads or tent pegs. The movement will come from the arm holding the wood NOT the arm holding the knife. Place the wood on the cutting edge and pull the wood toward you, while maintaining the arm with the knife steady and straight.

Thumb Push Grip – This grip is a modified forehand grip with thumb assist. The work will come from the thumb of the hand holding the wood. Place the wood on the cutting edge of the blade and using the thumb of the hand holding the wood, push forward, removing wood material. The knife is not to move, unless the thumb is pushing it, guiding it forward. This is a really safe way of carving because it is more controlled and there is less wood being removed. Remember, the blade is to face outward.

Palm Up Grip – This grip is also referred to as the back hand grip or chest lever. Both hands will have palms facing up. Blade facing outward, place the cutting edge on the wood object. As you bring the wood object and the knife toward your body, it will start to create a degree of separation, basically using your body as a wedge. You want to keep your forearms pressed against your chest or stomach. You want to form a small triangle, with two ends intersecting at the tip. The intersection is formed by the blade of the knife and the wood that is being cut. As you work, the intent is to begin minimizing the intersection by force; as you pull the wood along the cutting of the blade toward your body and apply consistent force on the knife slicing away from the body, while simultaneously using your body as a wedge bringing the object towards your body.

Pull Grip – This grip is typically for people who are already comfortable carving and understand how much pressure/force to apply when removing wood chips. It is a relatively easy grip, but if done incorrectly can be extremely dangerous. This is a modified forehand grip, where the blade is facing inward. Place the wood on your stomach or sternum and hold it firmly with your hand while using your other hand to place the cutting edge of the blade on the wood and begin removing wood, performing inward movements with the blade facing you. Because you are now removing wood chips with the cutting-edge inward and cutting toward your body, it is important to be extra careful and apply less force when removing wood.

Thumb Skew Grip – Think of peeling potatoes when performing this grip. Place the thumb from the hand holding the knife onto the surface of the wood object. As with the pull grip, the cutting edge will be facing you. The intent is to make small controlled inward cuts around the wood object. While placing your thumb on the wood object, make sure there is no overhang. Otherwise, as the cutting-edge moves toward you, it can injure your thumb. Be sure to hold the wood with your other hand nice and firm so that it does not slip, causing the knife to slice your thumb off. Apply light pressure and make gentle movements as you remove wood chips. This grip is not intended for the removal of large wood pieces, it is more for precision work or detailing.

All wood carving grip images taken by Sharon, as A.J. demonstrates the different grips.

*Note: Sometimes I prefer using the reverse ice pick grip when making spear points or tent pegs, instead of the power grip.

Palm Up / Chest Lever

Pull

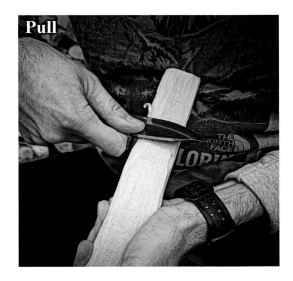

Thumb Screw

Draw

Choking Up

* **Note:** Wearing protective gear is always best. I chose to not wear gloves, so that I could better demonstrate the grips and finger placement.

Exercise extreme caution when carving/whittling to avoid injury. Working slowly and patiently is recommended. Carving/whittling is supposed to be a fun and relaxing hobby, not a stressful race to the finish line. Before engaging in this activity view instructional videos on YouTube, such as those from Felix Immler and/or Morakniv's "*The Swedish Knife Grip Sessions.*" A great book to read is Victorinox's "*Whittling in The Wild,*" by Felix Immler.

This document was provided to us by Felix Immler, from *Victorinox*.

VICTORINOX

CARVING TIPS
THE NINE KEY RULES FOR CARVING SAFELY

Learning how to handle a pocket knife correctly is essential for kids and will set them up for a lifetime of safe enjoyment. Not only will learning the safety rules help to avoid injury but it will also teach children about responsibility and discipline, both of which are crucial around knives. Here are our nine most important safety rules for children.

1. When you carve, you sit
It's very important that you are sitting down or kneeling when doing any carving or whittling. Both feet should be on the ground. The only exception would be when sawing something – here you could place a knee or a foot on e.g. a tree stump and use it to stabilize the wood you are sawing whilst the other foot remains on the ground.

2. Carve away from the body
Always make sure that the knife moves away from your body when you are carving. This is easily done in a sitting position and helps you to avoid injuries in case the knife slips. If you wish to carve a sharp tip, move the knife away from you and sideways at the same time, this helps you to create a sharp tip without needing to apply too much pressure.

VICTORINOX AG
Schmiedgasse 57, 6438 Ibach-Schwyz, Switzerland, +41 41 818 12 11, pressoffice.hq@victorinox.com, www.victorinox.com   1/3

3. An arm's length away
If you are going to carve something, ensure that no one else is within an arm's length of you. This helps you to keep a safe space around you and avoids accidents for you and for those around you.

4. Only carve with a sharp blade
Make sure your blade is sharp before doing any carving. A blunt blade means you will need to exert more pressure and the blade is more likely to slip, causing injury. You can do the paper test to see if your blade is sharp (a sharp blade should be able to cut a piece of paper easily without resistance) and if you need to sharpen your blade, a simple tool like the **Victorinox Sharpy** could help.

5. Only open one tool at a time
By far the safest way to use your Swiss Army Knife is to use only one tool at a time. Although the many tools are undoubtedly one of the attractions of our pocket knives, opening more than one at a time risks injury so be sure to close one tool before opening the next.

6. Stow your knife when you are not using it
Finished your carving adventures for the time being? Then close your blade carefully and put your knife away. This is much safer than leaving a knife lying around with the blade or with another tool open. When the pocket knife is closed and out of reach of younger children, then no one can get hurt.

7. Pass on a closed pocket knife only
Similar to rule number 6, never pass on or hand your pocket knife to someone else if a blade or other tool is still open. Be sure to carefully close the knife before giving it to someone else.

VICTORINOX AG
Schmiedgasse 57, 6438 Ibach-Schwyz, Switzerland, +41 41 818 12 11, pressoffice.hq@victorinox.com, www.victorinox.com

8. Don't carve a living tree
If you love spending time in the forest, it makes sense to respect the trees and branches within. Therefore please don't carve the trunk or branches of a living tree and leave it intact for others to enjoy.

9. A Swiss Army Knife is not a weapon
You should never ever use the Swiss Army Knife as a weapon, even if you are just playing. Our blades are sharp and could cause serious injury. Our pocket knives are intended for many purposes but violence is not one of them.

ABOUT VICTORINOX
Victorinox AG is a family business with global operations and is currently managed by the fourth generation. The company's headquarters are located in Ibach, in the Canton of Schwyz, right in the heart of Switzerland. This is where Karl Elsener I, the founder of the company, set up his cutlery business back in 1884 and, a few years later, designed the legendary "Original Swiss Army Knife." Today, the company produces not only its world-famous pocket knives, but also high-quality household and professional knives, watches, travel gear, and fragrances. In 2005, the company acquired Wenger SA, a long-established knife and watch manufacturer located in Delémont. Wenger pocket knives were integrated into the Victorinox range in 2013, so that the Wenger product portfolio today consists of watches and travel gear. Products are available online, in the company's own stores, and via an extensive network of subsidiaries and distributors in more than 120 countries. In 2019, the company achieved a turnover of CHF 480 million with a total workforce of over 2100 employees.

VICTORINOX AG
Schmiedgasse 57, 6438 Ibach-Schwyz, Switzerland, +41 41 818 12 11, pressoffice.hq@victorinox.com, www.victorinox.com   3/3

Using a Saw

A saw is an important tool not just for bushcraft, but for multiple activities that require the cutting of wood. When outdoors, I will typically rotate between my axes and my saws. Silky makes very versatile saws in all shapes and sizes. Silky saws are pull saws, so the user will be using mostly back muscles to control the sawing motion. Bahco is another brand that makes excellent hand saws. Bahco is a push and pull saw; therefore, the user will be using several muscles to control the sawing motion. Esker produces a really nice folding buck saw that can easily be put together and has a nice, comfortable grip handle.

When using a saw, keep in mind there is a little bit of effort involved, as well as taking measurements of the wood. It is important to understand that a hand saw is not a gas-powered saw; therefore, when selecting your wood for a campfire, consider a diameter that makes sense. Do not try to saw down a tree that is wider in diameter than the sawblade length. Consider a diameter that is a few inches smaller than your sawblade. Also, make sure it is not green wood, otherwise it will be impossible to burn. Use dry, seasoned wood, that will be easily to saw and burn. When sawing your wood, measure out the segments about 14" to 16" inches apart so that you end up with a nice sized log to split and use for a campfire. The firewood logs should then be split about 3" to 6" inches in width using an axe.

If you are seeking to build a structure out of the wood you gather, make sure your take proper measurements before you start sawing away. Mark your log as you take measurements, then saw on the marked spots. I typically mark my wood using the sawblade where I scrape the surface of the wood enough to create an easily identifiable spot.

Lastly, always use caution when using your tools and wear the proper safety gear. The last thing you need is to get hurt in the woods far from any hospital. The techniques used to saw wood can be found on YouTube in the following channels:

TA Outdoors, "Bahco Laplander Folding Saw Review and Test," Instructor: Mike Pullen

Corporals Corner, "Stowell's Outdoor Collapsible Bucksaw."

The Gray Bearded Green Beret, "Best Folding Saw – The Silky."

Photograph taken by A.J., using Bahco Laplander Saw.

Using an Axe to Process Firewood

Wielding an axe or hatchet is not an easy task and can require more skill than wielding a small knife. When using an axe, or hatchet, the same knife handling rules apply: maintain a firm grip, maintain eye contact with the target log and where the cutting-edge lands, keep your body parts away from the cutting edge, keep a clear blood circle, use proper technique, and most importantly, wear gloves. Eye protection is important, but not always necessary, unless the situation dictates it for safety reasons. More is always better, less may produce unnecessary stress. Pay attention to your surroundings and watch out for people that may be walking around you or objects that may get in the way from performing your full range of motion. Good practice is to form a "blood circle" and make sure no one crosses into that circle. Maintaining good posture is important when using an axe or hatchet, in addition to understanding where the axe head will end up if the target is missed. When using an axe, spread your legs shoulder width apart, bend your knees, stay low to the ground, and extend your arms out as you strike your target log. A good measure is to make sure the target log is placed on a much larger log, chopping block, or stump, that measures at least 2 feet in height from the ground. A chopping block that has good enough height is considered a safety buffer, which will prevent the axe from completing the strike's full range of motion and prevent it from potentially striking a body part, such as your leg. The impact strength, when the axe's cutting edge meets the target, is powerful. The pressure exerted from the motion will help drive the axe head through the wood. If the target log is too low to the ground and you do not have the right posture, then it will be hit with less control because the axe will be nearing the end of the strike's range of motion. In the case where the wood is too low to the ground because the chopping block is not tall enough, then I recommend getting on your knees versus standing on your feet. When striking, lean forward creating more buffer space, extend your arms properly, and maintain proper posture. The point of impact should be placed a little closer to the edge versus the center of the log. I have provide links to videos on how to use an axe or hatchet, below.

When using a hatchet, avoid swinging it like an axe because it is not built to be swung that way. A hatchet requires more skill to use than an axe because chopping or splitting wood will require different techniques. The wood will need to be laid flat, or parallel, versus on its base or perpendicular. It is recommended that the log be of smaller size than the logs typically split with an axe. The techniques used to split wood with a hatchet can be found on YouTube in the following channels:

Equip 2 Endure, "How to Use a Hatchet or Hand Axe, Skill Training," Instructor: Joe Flowers.

InnerBark Outdoors, "Axe and Hatchet Safety, How to Process Firewood," Instructor: Andy Tran.

Ray Mears & Woodlore Ltd., "Ray Mears—Choosing and using an axe, Bushcraft Survival." Instructor: Ray Mears

Photograph taken by A.J., splitting firewood with Axe.

Using a Hatchet to make Kindling

A hatchet is a fantastic tool for chopping wood and to make kindling and feathersticks (tinder). It is important to understand that using a hatchet requires a slightly different technique than when using an axe. When processing wood to make kindling, grab the wood and the hatchet together, as seen in the images below. Place the hatchet's head at the top portion of the wood. Use a firm grip and place your fingers correctly, around the hatchet and the wood, to avoid injury. Lift the wood, together with the hatchet, as seen below, and strike a log with the wood and hatchet, with enough force to split the wood.

Photograph taken by A.J., making kindlinng with hatchet.

Photograph taken by A.J., making kindlinng with hatchet.

Knots

We do not cover knots in this book, because as mentioned before, this is not a survival skills hand-book, nor a bushcraft reference guide. We cover some basic things that everyone should know, but do not dive deep into the art of self-reliance. A fantastic book to read about knots is *The Ashley Book of Knots* by Clifford W. Ashley. Another good read, if you have the additional time, is *U.S. Army TM 3-34 (FM 5-125/3)/MCRP 3-17.7J, Rigging Techniques, Procedures, and Applications*. It is import-ant for those who love exploring the great outdoors and enjoy camping in the wilderness to master a few knots. Knots are used for shelter building, fishing, tethering animals, etc. A few knots I recom-mend people to master are:

Overhand

Figure-eight

Jury-mast

Square

Sheep Shank

Angler's loop

Prusik

Double fisherman's

Clove hitch

Pile hitch

Timber hitch

Square lashing

Shears lashing

Italian hitch

Rolling hitch

Anchor bend

Tripod lashing

OVERHAND KNOT

Photograph taken by A.J.

FIGURE EIGHT LOOP KNOT

Photograph taken by A.J.

Grip Exercises

Handling a knife properly is a skill that takes time and patience to learn and master. Depending on the tasks performed, proper knife handling may take a great deal of strength. Certain exercises exist that can help improve grip strength and wrist mobility, considering that our wrists are comprised of ligaments, connective tissue, muscle, and nerves. Recall the range of motion present in our hands and wrists such as flexion, extension, adduction, and abduction. A healthy wrist can also be directly associated to healthy grip strength.

When performing the following exercises, take off any watches and jewelry from your wrist. You want your wrists bare so that you can freely move them around, without any constraints.

Stretching Exercises

A. **Wrist Rotation Movement:** Curl your fingers and make a fist, then slowly begin to rotate your wrists around in a clockwise/counterclockwise direction. Try to gently hold and stretch any angle that feels particularly tender/stiff for a few seconds. Repeat this exercise throughout the day, as needed.

B. **Prayer Hold:** Place your hands together in a prayer position in front of you and at chest level. Try to keep them at least 5 inches away from your chest. While maintaining contact with your hands, begin to lower them slowly. Go as far as you can without hurting yourself. The longer you can maintain your hands together, the better the stretch for your wrist. While maintaining this position at the bottom, slowly rotate your hands forward until you reach your limit, then slowly bring them back to the starting position. Now slowly repeat this process backwards, trying to touch the center of your chest with your fingertips. When performing these exercises, maintain the positions for a few seconds, before slowly moving your wrists back to the starting position. Be incredibly careful to not overstretch or go past your physical limitations. The purpose of this exercise is not to push through the motions rapidly, but rather, to exercise slow, mindful rotating stretches.

C. **Wall Wrist Walks:** Place your palms on a wall with your arms fully extended and fingers pointing upward toward the ceiling or sky. Try to maintain contact with the wall, as you slowly walk your hands down the wall. Bring your hands down the wall as far as you can without lifting your palms off of the wall. Once you have reached your physical limit, slowly rotate your hands outward until your fingers are pointing to the floor. Again, try to maintain contact with the wall, while slowly rotating your hands. Work with your limitations and do not try to overexert yourself, which may lead you to get hurt. With your fingers pointing downward, begin walking your hands back up the wall. Repeat this exercise as needed throughout the day.

D. **Wrist Leans:** On a comfortable surface, bend down at the knees and place your hands on the floor. Keep your arms fully extended while keeping your back straight and parallel to the ground. Slowly begin to rotate your hands so that your fingers point towards your knees. Slowly lean your body forwards and backwards, as if swaying on a rocking chair. Your palms should never lose contact with the ground and your arms need to remain straight (if arms are bending, bring hands closer to knees). When you gently lean in each direction, you should feel the stretch through to your wrist. Perform this exercise for a couple minutes only. Now, rotate your hands outward so that your left-hand fingers are pointing outward. Your wrists should be facing each other and about 10 to 12 inches apart. Slowly begin to sway left, until you feel a good stretch and slowly return to your starting point. Repeat the same steps but in the opposite direction. Continue swaying left and right, slowly, for a couple minutes, if possible. Once finished, stand up and perform the wrist rotation movement exercise for five seconds.

Strengthening Exercises

E. **Pinch Grip:** With a couple of weighted plates or a set of heavy books, pinch down with your fingertips. Do this by making an "alligator mouth" with your hands and then "bite down" on your weighted item. You will feel stress on your thumbs while performing this exercise. This is normal, as your thumb is an essential part of your grip strength. Your forearms will also begin to feel some tension. You want to perform this exercise standing straight with the items gripped by your sides. Pinch and hold for at least thirty seconds. As your grip strength improves, you can add more time or more weight to this exercise.

F. **Pull-up Bar Hold:** Stretch out and wrap your fingers around a pull-up bar or similar item. Hold the bar nice and tight before lifting your feet off the ground to perform a hang. Hang from the bar for as long as possible while maintaining a nice firm grip. The goal here is to try to hold the bar for at least fifteen seconds at a time. As you build more strength, simply add more time and repetitions.

G. **Towel Chin-ups:** Throw a pair of gym towels over a fully secure pull-up bar and then grip the towels securely with your hands. Lift your feet off the ground, hanging off the towels. Naturally, you want to grip both ends of the towel or you might fall on your face when performing this exercise. Be cautious and logical please. Maintain this hanging position for as long as possible. If new to this exercise, try to hold the hanging position for at least fifteen seconds at a time. If you desire to strengthen additional muscle groups, try performing full chin-ups by pulling yourself up to the point where your chin passes the bar and then slowly lowering back to your starting position. Repeat these exercises as necessary without overexerting yourself to the point of injury.

H. **Farmer's Walk:** With a pair of heavy dumbbells (know your limitations), walk back and forth to a certain point while holding the dumbbells by your side. If you do not have enough room to walk, stand in place for at least thirty seconds. Use extreme caution when performing this exercise, understanding your limitations and not overexerting yourself, as you may get hurt.

I. **Barbell or Dumbbell Wrist Curls:** Grab a barbell or dumbbell, and gripping it tightly, begin to slowly curl your wrists up and down. If seated, rest your arms on your thighs, allowing your wrist to hang off of your knees so that you may correctly perform the motions of the exercise. While firmly gripping the barbell/dumbbell, slowly move wrists up and down. The key here is maintaining a good, slow and steady pace. You should feel stress on your forearm muscles, but not pain. Be careful to not overexert yourself, as doing so may lead to unwanted injury.

Performing these exercises will not only improve your overall grip and mobility, but they will also strengthen your shoulders, triceps, and back. Be sure to always maintain good posture and be extra careful when performing these exercises. Take the time to perform the *Stretching Exercises* before moving onto the *Strengthening Exercises*. Having an exercise buddy present is a great option as they may help you through the movements while spotting you to prevent injury.

Photograph taken by A.J., strengthening exercises - wrist curls.

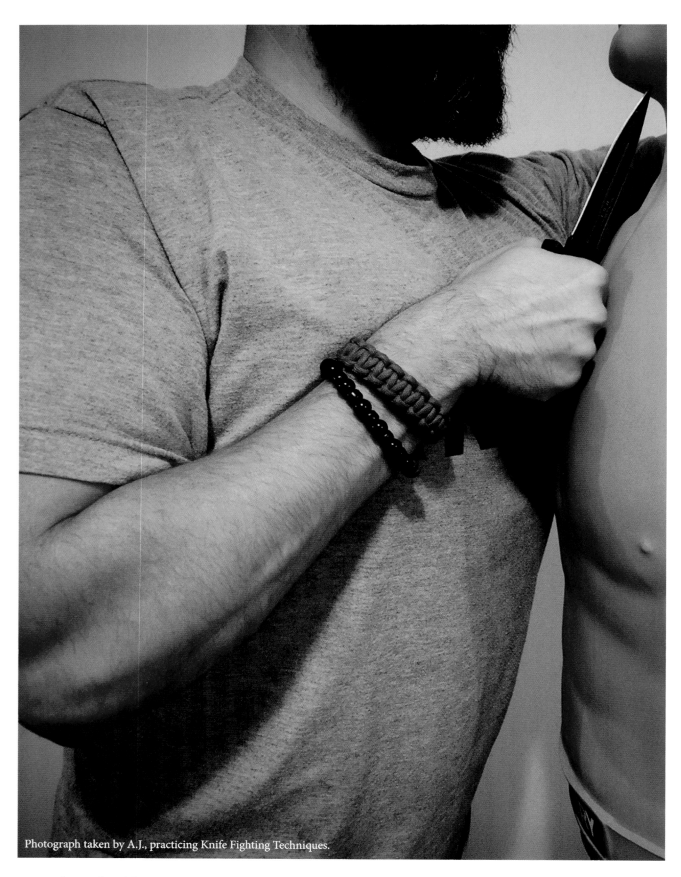
Photograph taken by A.J., practicing Knife Fighting Techniques.

Knife Fighting

Content Disclaimer: Knife fighting instruction and training is an inherently hazardous activity, under any circumstance. Knife fighting instruction, or training, requires a high level of fitness, both physically and mentally. Consult with a physician before beginning any such training related to knife fighting. Engaging in training or practice related to knife fighting comes with unique risks and hazards; therefore, it is prudent to have such risks evaluated before embarking on training or practice. Knife fighting or the use of knives can cause harm, injury, or death to you or to others; therefore, it is not suggested by this book or its authors. This book or its authors are not responsible for activities performed by the readers. All activities performed by the readers are at their own risk and the readers will assume full responsibility for the consequences that follow. Understand that a knife is a lethal weapon and breaking the law by using or carrying a lethal weapon can be punishable to the full extent of the law.

(The US Army FM21-150 was used as a point of reference for some parts in this section, along with my understanding of the human anatomy, coupled with personal knowledge obtained from boxing and martial arts training)

Knives have been used for self-defense since the Paleolithic period. The purpose of the self-defense knife never changed, but over time, the material it was made from underwent major changes. The material used to make knives evolved from a flint knapped stone to a stronger, more durable material known as bronze, and later followed by iron. A self-defense knife can be more dangerous to oneself than an opponent if the one wielding it lacks training. This book is **NOT** a self-defense book and only covers the basics of knife fighting. If the reader would like to explore knife fighting more in depth, then I suggest looking up Eskrima/Kali (FMA), Systema, MCMAP, Paranza Corta, Pencak Silat, or Tantojutsu.

Here are a few basic principles to get started:

1. **Balance.** Physical balance is the ability to sustain equilibrium and maintain an upright stance. In hand-to-hand combat, a fighter must keep their balance to both protect themselves, but also drive an effective strike. Feet should be kept about shoulder-width apart and knees flexed. Lower the center of gravity to improve balance and maintain stability. Maintain balance while moving, by using your front foot as a guide and maintaining the rear foot planted; sliding it only when engaged in movement. The front foot pushes the body backwards or laterally, with the rear foot remaining in position and sliding in the desired direction. Moving from side to side is also a possibility and is referred to as side-stepping. The point of side-stepping it to exploit weaknesses in the opponent's balance. Proper training enhances a fighter's ability to sense how to move his body in a fight to maintain balance, while exploiting the opponent's weak points.
2. **Mind Control.** A fighter must keep a clear mind to achieve mental balance. A fighter cannot allow fear or rage to overcome their ability to focus or react.
3. **Position.** The location of the fighter during a fight is just as important as the position of the opponent. When being attacked, it is vital to seek a safe position. A safe position is a location or spot where the opponent would need to move their body entirely in order strike effectively. A fighter must try to free themselves from the opponent's line of attack or blood circle. It is considered safe practice to move away from the line of attack at a 45-degree angle, either by side stepping toward the opponent or away from them. By performing counterattack measures, it enables the fighter to exploit weakness in the opponent's counterattack position. Timing and distance are also important basic principles in a knife fight.
4. **Timing.** A fighter needs to discern when the appropriate time is to perform a counterattack

measure or an effective strike. If the fighter moves too early, the opponent will decipher the intentions and adjust accordingly. If the fighter moves too late, then they will be hit by the opponent. In addition, the fighter must strike, or counterstrike, at the instant the opponent is most vulnerable.

5. **Distance.** The space between opponents. A fighter needs to position themselves where the distance is the most advantageous to them. Fighters need to adjust distance as the situation dictates, whether conducting a strike or counterstrike movement. A fighter must understand their range of motion and effective striking range as far as arms reach.

6. **Momentum.** Momentum as defined by the Oxford Dictionary is "the quantity of motion of a moving body, measured as a product of its mass and velocity." Taking momentum into consideration, a proper strike or movement has a starting point and an end point. When a movement has reached its end point, there is an outcome, or consequence, followed by a reaction. There is a short window of opportunity where an opponent's power is being directed toward a designated location, therefore allowing the fighter to adjust their movements based on the opponent's momentum, and locate weaknesses to render the opponent powerless. To put this concept into perspective, a body in motion will continue in the direction of the motion, unless impacted by another force. A body in motion creates momentum, the greater the mass in motion, the greater the momentum. A fighter needs to comprehend this principle and use it to their benefit. An opponent's momentum can be his weakness. By using their momentum against them, the fighter can place the opponent in vulnerable positions or take away balance. This principle can be applied by both parties at any given moment, therefore it is important to plan accordingly by planning several steps ahead and understand what those reactions might mean in a fight.

7. **Leverage.** In a fight, leverage is important because it is the act of using something to achieve maximum advantage. A fighter can use his body to develop a natural mechanical advantage over portions of the opponent's body. Leverage also implies, in hand-to-hand combat, applying body weight and strength into ones fighting technique/style. Applying strength and pressure at the right place and angle can destabilize an opponent. Understanding groundwork and how to apply body mechanics is a principle in hand-to-hand combat that can lead to successfully defeating the opponent.

Human Circulatory System

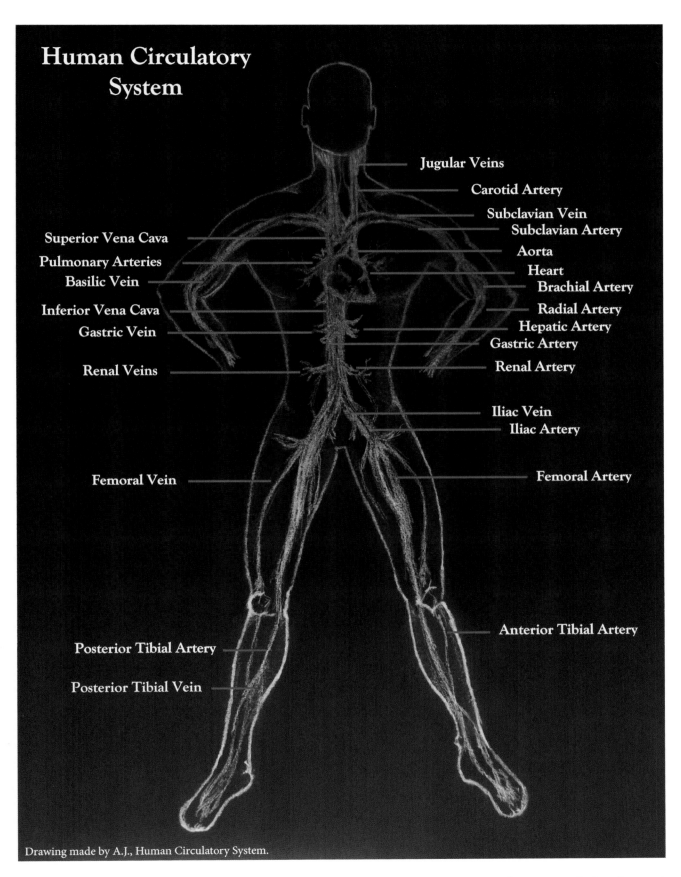

Jugular Veins

Carotid Artery

Subclavian Vein

Subclavian Artery

Superior Vena Cava

Pulmonary Arteries

Basilic Vein

Aorta

Heart

Brachial Artery

Inferior Vena Cava

Gastric Vein

Radial Artery

Hepatic Artery

Gastric Artery

Renal Veins

Renal Artery

Iliac Vein

Iliac Artery

Femoral Vein

Femoral Artery

Anterior Tibial Artery

Posterior Tibial Artery

Posterior Tibial Vein

Drawing made by A.J., Human Circulatory System.

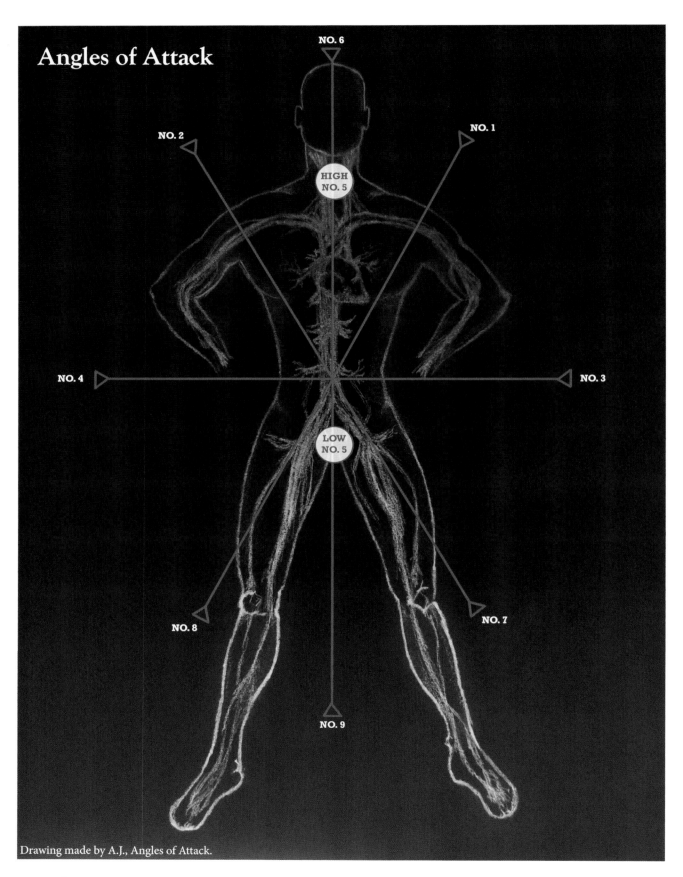

Drawing made by A.J., Angles of Attack.

Angles of Attack

In knife fighting, it is important to recognize the angles of attack because it will determine whether the slash, stab, or strike is successful at reducing the threat.

- **No.1. Angle of Attack.** A descending/falling diagonal slash or strike toward the left side of an opponent's head, neck, or torso. There are major arteries that run along the neck, such as the left carotid artery that runs lateral to the trachea. If this artery were to be damaged during a fight, it could be fatal. In addition, there are subclavian arteries that run along the left shoulder under the clavicle. The subclavian arteries supply blood to the arms. The chest area is also the major center for the circulatory system; it covers the heart, lungs, and other major organs.
- **No.2. Angle of Attack.** A descending/falling diagonal slash or strike toward the right side of an opponent's head, neck, or torso. There are major arteries that run along the neck, such as the right carotid artery that runs lateral to the trachea. If this artery were to be damaged during a fight, it could be fatal. In addition, there are subclavian arteries that run along the right shoulder, under the clavicle. The subclavian arteries supply blood to the arms. The chest area is also the major center for the circulatory system; it covers the heart, lungs, and other major organs. Puncturing/piercing the chest area with a knife would produce a critical wound to the opponent.
- **No.3. Angle of Attack.** A horizontal slash or strike to the left side of an opponent's torso in the ribs, flank area, or hip region. Vital organs are located on the left side of the torso and any damage to these organs can be fatal.
- **No.4. Angle of Attack.** A horizontal slash or strike to the right side of an opponent's torso in the ribs, flank area, or hip region. Vital organs are located on the right side of an opponent's torso and any damage to these organs can be fatal.
- **No.5. Angle of Attack.** This area is divided into upper and lower; upper being the neck area, lower being the groin area. It is directed toward the opponent's front. A strike, slash, or stab in this area can be fatal.
- **No.6. Angle of Attack.** A strike downward onto an opponent's head. This is typically done with a knife's pommel, also referred to as a pommel strike.
- **No.7. Angle of Attack.** An upwards/skywards diagonal slash or strike toward an opponent's lower-left side. This area covers the left anterior iliac crest and left lower quadrant of the torso. Major arteries run along this area, such as the inferior mesenteric common iliac and lower areas of the superior mesenteric. Within this area towards the inner thigh, there are major veins, such as the femoral arteries. In the foot, towards the rear just above the heel bone is the Achilles tendon. Damaging the opponent's Achilles tendon would greatly reduce their level of mobility.
- **No.8. Angle of Attack.** An upwards/skywards diagonal slash or strike toward an opponent's lower-right side. The inner thigh contains major veins, such as the femoral arteries. Towards the rear of the foot, just above the heel bone, is the Achilles tendon. Damaging the opponent's Achilles tendon would reduce their level of mobility greatly.
- **No.9. Angle of Attack.** A strike, slash, or stab, upwards/skywards toward an opponent's groin area.

The human body is very vulnerable with major arteries, veins, organs, muscles, and connective tissue located in every direction. Knife fighting requires a great deal of training, not only to learn how to strike but also protect yourself from a strike. Knife fighting is probably one of the bloodiest forms of attack and not for those easily deterred by the sight of blood. For additional knowledge on knife fighting, it would be wise to take a martial arts course that focuses on knife fighting styles, reading books, and watching instructional videos. Lots of practice is especially important, because it is the muscle memory and fast reaction that will keep you alive. It is important to understand that knife fighting is a form of self-defense, just like any other fighting style. If engaged in such activity, be careful, mindful, and ready for the consequences that follow.

Photograph taken by A.J., Hammer Grip.

Knife Grips

There are several knife grips to consider when knife fighting. Only a few will be covered in this book. Keep in mind that different knives equate to different grip styles. Some knife fighting techniques and grips are weapon specific, therefore, learning to master a few grips is important.

FROWARD GRIPS

Hammer Grip. One of the strongest grips for thrusting a blade into an opponent's torso. If seeking deep penetration versus a shallow cut, then this grip is the best choice. The hammer grip is a common grip used to stab an opponent, where the fingers and the thumb completely wrap around the handle. The edge is typically oriented away from the wielder. This grip does have drawbacks, especially if the opponent has some understanding of self-defense; they wait for right moment when weaknesses in the grip are more exposed and strip the knife away. That is why being able to interchange grips in a knife fight is important. This grip is also used for pommel strikes that can cause deadly blows to an opponent's temple or shatter bone, such as the nose, cheeks, or skull.

Saber Grip/Fencers Grip. The saber grip is often referred to as the sword grip, which is common among experienced skilled fighters. This grip allows similar mobility to the hammer grip. Most fighting knives are developed taking this grip into consideration, where the knife guards are designed to protect the fingers from sliding onto the cutting edge. The thumb is placed on the spine of the knife handle at the guard or where the knife extends from the handle. This grip enables the wielder to apply good force for strong cutting and reach. The downfall of this grip is the fact that there is a visible gap between the fingers and the thumb, allowing for a weaker grip.

Finger Support Grip. The finger support grip is often used for skinning game. It is a blade forward grip in which your index finger supports the upper spine of the blade. This is a good grip when using small knives to make precision cuts. This is the least effective grip of all in a knife fight. Due to the style of grip, it is easy to lose control of the knife.

Modified Saber Grip/Pinch Grip. This grip places the thumb on the side of the knife handle or on the side of the blade in a pinching fashion. By placing the thumb this way, it orients the blade horizontally in the hand. The edge typically faces left. This grip enables good mobility and is more easily capable of entering between the ribs. In the event you hit a rib with this grip, the rib is likely to split, enabling entry to the lungs or other vital organs. Good inward slashing and thrusting is possible with this grip.

Filipino Grip. This grip is like the saber grip, with the difference that it places the thumb on the spine of the blade. This grip enables deep cutting and power slashing. The thumb aids in guiding the blade's cutting edge toward key target areas with more precision. Similar to the saber grip, there is a gap between the fingers and the thumb, creating a weaker grip.

REVERSE GRIPS

Ice Pick Grip. This grip is the most comfortable grip of them all. It is used particularly for stabbing downward. Like the hammer grip, it is used when seeking to penetrate deeply into the opponent. The cutting edge is oriented toward the wielder, with the tip down. This grip also enables for hook and pull strikes, ripping away at anything in its path. This is not the type of grip opponents want to try and kick the knife out of the wielder's hands, or they will find the tip of the blade stuck to their leg.

Ice Pick Grip with Thumb Support. In this grip the knife is held using the ice pick grip, but with the thumb on the pommel for added support when striking downward. This grip is mostly used with knives that have weak guards or no guard at all. Placing the thumb on the pommel will help your fingers from sliding onto the cutting edge.

Ninja Grip/Forearm Grip. This grip is a favorite among martial artists because of the element of surprise. The knife is held like the ice pick grip but the blade rests against the underside of the forearm. This grip hides the knife from plain sight and allows for vertical, horizontal, and back slashes. Speed and surprise are the two key factors with the grip. If the opponent realizes the style of grip, they may already know what they need to do—strip away the knife.

UNCONVENTIONAL GRIPS

Palm/Finger Assist. This grip places the pommel of the knife on the palm of the hand with the index finger placed along the spine of the blade. This grip is typically used for small knives. It is a common grip for field-dressing/skinning game. The finger assist provides the wielder with good accuracy when thrusting or slicing. The index finger guides the blade to the target areas.

Punch Grip. This grip is not uncommon unless the knife is specifically designed to be used as a push dagger or punch dagger. The punch grip places the knife between the middle and ring finger, with the pommel resting on the palm. This grip enables the wielder to easily punch through flesh and bone into critical organs.

Edge In or Edge Out

The hammer grip or the ice pick grip can be used with the cutting edge facing in or out, depending on the fighting style.

Grip photographs taken by A.J.

HELLE
NORWAY

Knivar for eit liv i det fri
Knives for the outdoors

HELLE.COM

Photograph taken by A.J., Superstitions - Add a coin with a gift knife.

Knife Superstitions

Add a Coin with a Gift Knife

Various cultures believe that one must never gift a knife, without a coin, in exchange. Gifting a knife without a coin in return, can symbolically "sever" the relationship. Therefore, to avoid this, include a copper coin (penny) with the gifted knife and ask the receiver to return the coin to you as a form of "payment" for the knife. A small token to maintain your relationship.

Never Open a Knife, You Cannot Close

It is considered bad luck to open a knife and have someone else close it, or to close a knife that someone else has opened. This pertains particularly to foldable knives and sheathed knives. It is widely believed that the one who exposes the blade must return the blade to its original position.

Be Careful of Falling Knives

Some cultures believe that if a knife falls and sticks to the ground, it signifies bad luck for the owner.

Others, though, believe that when a fallen knife sticks to the ground, it symbolizes good luck for the person who is in the direction of how the knife leans.

No Stirring

Many believe that nothing should ever be stirred, neither liquids or food, with your knife, as it may lead to stirring up trouble in your life.

Tasted Blood

Ancient traditions would say that you never really take ownership of a knife until it has "tasted" your blood. They also believed you should never re-sheath a combat knife after a battle if it has not drawn blood.

The Afterlife

Anglo-Saxon cultures believed a loved one should never be buried without a knife, which gave them protection when arriving to the other side.

Crossing Blades

One should never cross knives, as it means several things (mostly bad), in different cultures. For example, crossing a knife or eating utensils in Ireland, anticipates a fight or argument happening soon. In Italy, the crossing of knives insults the symbol of the holy cross.

However, in most countries it is socially understood that when one crosses their utensils after a meal, it symbolizes that one has completed their meal.

Pregnancy

Some cultures believe that sliding a knife under a pregnant woman's mattress will lead her to have a boy.

Similarly, others insist that placing a knife under the bed during childbirth eases labor pains.

Bedtime

In China, it is believed that sleeping with a knife under your bed will scare away bad spirits.

Likewise, in Greece, it is said that if you put a knife with a black handle under your pillow it will keep away nightmares.

Steel Knives

Owning a knife made of steel is said to protect you against misfortune, curses, and fairies.

No Playing with Knives

In Romania, if you play with a knife they say the angels will run away from you.

Your Front Door

Some believe that thrusting a knife through the front door of a house may bring additional protection.

No Sharpening After Dark

Some cultures believe it is bad luck to sharpen your knife once the sun goes down.

Wedding Gifts

Never gift a knife, or set of knives, as a wedding gift, as it can lead to chaos in the marriage.

Table Manners

In Russia, never eat or lick food from your knife, because it may make you angry like a dog.

Likewise, other cultures say to never lick food off a knife, as it may make you a cruel individual.

Housewarming

Never gift a knife, or set of knives, as a housewarming gift because then the gifted shall become an enemy.

Lover

Receiving a knife as a gift from a lover means your love will soon come to an end.

Fishing or The Fisherman

In Iceland, it is said that when cleaning fish, should the knife fall to the ground and land with the blade pointing toward the sea, then the fisherman will have a bountiful haul on their next fishing trip. But if the knife falls with the blade pointing toward land, then on the next fishing trip he shall return empty handed.

The Chef or Bad Luck Cook

Some cultures believed that if you cross your spoon with your knife after eating, then you did not enjoy the meal and wish bad luck to the cook.

Hunting

Some hunters believe that you should never let a woman handle the knife you use to kill game, not including the knife you use to dress your game.

Manners

It is bad manners to hand a knife to a person with the blade pointed toward the receiver. Instead, hand the knife with the handle pointed toward the receiver.

Photograph taken by A.J., Superstitions - boys handinng each other a blunt carving knife.

Purchasing a Knife

When purchasing a knife, it is important to remember that there is no such thing as the perfect knife. It is unrealistic to think that you will find one that can do it all or have it all. However, there is such a thing as the perfect knife for the appropriate occasion. There are knives that can help us achieve a desired outcome at particular tasks in certain environments, under certain conditions. That is the reason we should have a diverse collection of knives, to optimize our versatility.

By now, you should have a pretty good understanding of knives and can make an informed decision about the style of knife you need and the best steel for the job. If you still have doubts or concerns, feel free to reach out to us via our website www.knifebible.com or our Instagram account @knifebible. We would be happy to answer any questions.

Here is a short list of places we like to purchase our knives from:

1. DLT Trading: www.dlttrading.com
2. Smoky Mountain Knife Works: www.smkw.com
3. KnivesShipFree: www.knivesshipfree.com
4. KnifeWorks: www.knifeworks.com
5. Knife Center: www.knifecenter.com
6. Blade HQ: www.bladehq.com
7. Knife Joy: www.knifejoy.com
8. Knives of the North: www.knivesofthenorth.com
9. Aventuron: www.aventuron.com
10. The Knife Connection: www.theknifeconnection.com

Photograph taken by A.J.

Conclusion

Turn over enough stones, and you will start to realize that human civilization would not be what it is today without knives. There is a partnership that lives intertwined in the veins of mankind and the steel of the blades, which helped create our civilization. We crawled out of our dark, frigid caves and with our handmade tools, stood a chance to fend for ourselves in the unforgiving wilderness, blanketed with beasts of burden. If at any point civilization was threatened and there was a need to start anew, knives would be the tools used to fight our way to a new beginning.

Do yourself a favor and invest in a good quality, fixed blade knife, whether it be for kitchen or bushcraft. Appreciate the work of art you hold, as it is an heirloom meant to be handed down for years to come.

Photograph provided by Opinel

"Every time I hold a knife, a nostalgic feeling slowly drapes over me. There is an honest connection… I cannot explain it. It connects to my body, filling me with ambivalence… a spiritual relationship experienced, solely, when reunited with an old friend. It is the missing piece to the puzzle that completes me, as a man."

—A.J. Cardenal

To The Wanderer

There is more to life, than what we assume.

Take a long walk in the woods, in places so densely majestic and uncanny, they make you shiver. Bathe under the infinite rays of sunlight, that break through the treetops. Stop, for a second and bend down to dig your fingers into the soil. Feel the grains of the earth rolling through your fingertips. Smell the fuel that feeds life into our mother planet. Take a deep breath, hold it in for a bit, then slowly release the air back out... you are here. Alive, free, and adventurous. Live wild, passionately, and soulfully. Feed your soul, by taking that hair-raising first step into the unknown. Find yourself under the shades of beautiful evergreens and the cool, purified air. You are man, and the wilderness is your original playground. Inspire, to be inspired. Praise, to be praised. Give, to be given. Fight, to earn a freedom that no one can take away. Sing your way up to higher grounds and earn that badge of courage. Live, as if today were your last day on earth. Never live in silence and always be vigilant. Help those less fortunate. Gift others a little reassurance... a fighting chance, to break free from the shackles that keep their souls imprisoned. Sprinkle your path in life with small acts of kindness. Quite simply, be humane. Along the way, you will notice how short life is and the ripples you've caused moved others through the pond we consider, the lifeblood of humanity. Whistle while you work. Learn a new skill and share your knowledge with the ones you love. Know that you are not alone in this world. Just look out your window and notice the life that surrounds you, in its many forms, joining you on this journey. When encountered with loss, understand that we are also blessed with an opportunity, a second chance to adjust things a little more on our path. Take the first step. I promise, you will find your true self along the way.

Photograph taken by Sharon Steel, Olympic Mountains, Washington

SOCIAL MEDIA HIGHLIGHTS

Above and Below images taken and provided by Kyle Baysinger, @kylessharpcreations.

SOCIAL MEDIA HIGHLIGHTS

Above and Below images taken and provided by Rive Knives.
@riveknives www.riveknives.com

JANKA HARDNESS RATING BAR CHART

Wood Species   **Hardness Value**   *When considering wood handle scales use this chart.

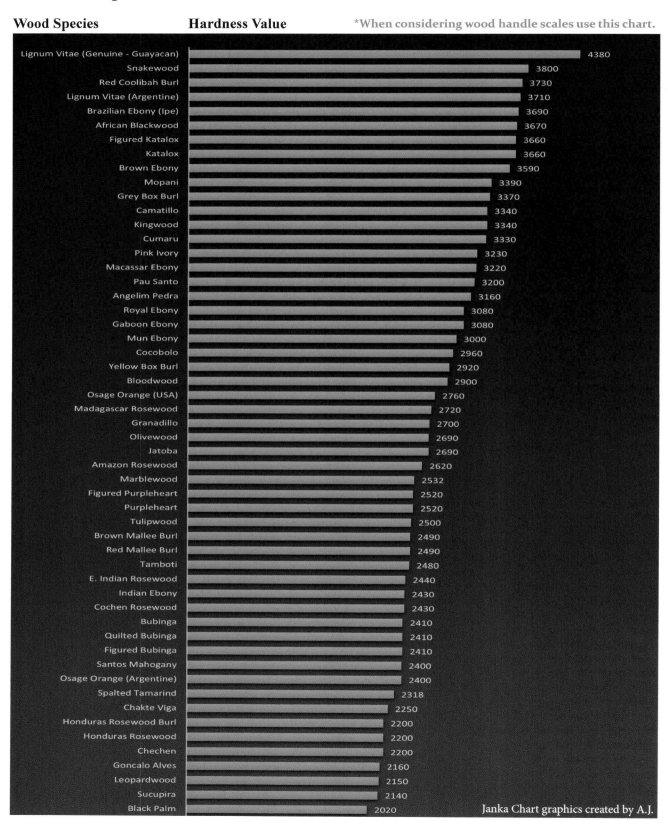

Wood Species	Hardness Value
Lignum Vitae (Genuine - Guayacan)	4380
Snakewood	3800
Red Coolibah Burl	3730
Lignum Vitae (Argentine)	3710
Brazilian Ebony (Ipe)	3690
African Blackwood	3670
Figured Katalox	3660
Katalox	3660
Brown Ebony	3590
Mopani	3390
Grey Box Burl	3370
Camatillo	3340
Kingwood	3340
Cumaru	3330
Pink Ivory	3230
Macassar Ebony	3220
Pau Santo	3200
Angelim Pedra	3160
Royal Ebony	3080
Gaboon Ebony	3080
Mun Ebony	3000
Cocobolo	2960
Yellow Box Burl	2920
Bloodwood	2900
Osage Orange (USA)	2760
Madagascar Rosewood	2720
Granadillo	2700
Olivewood	2690
Jatoba	2690
Amazon Rosewood	2620
Marblewood	2532
Figured Purpleheart	2520
Purpleheart	2520
Tulipwood	2500
Brown Mallee Burl	2490
Red Mallee Burl	2490
Tamboti	2480
E. Indian Rosewood	2440
Indian Ebony	2430
Cochen Rosewood	2430
Bubinga	2410
Quilted Bubinga	2410
Figured Bubinga	2410
Santos Mahogany	2400
Osage Orange (Argentine)	2400
Spalted Tamarind	2318
Chakte Viga	2250
Honduras Rosewood Burl	2200
Honduras Rosewood	2200
Chechen	2200
Goncalo Alves	2160
Leopardwood	2150
Sucupira	2140
Black Palm	2020

Janka Chart graphics created by A.J.

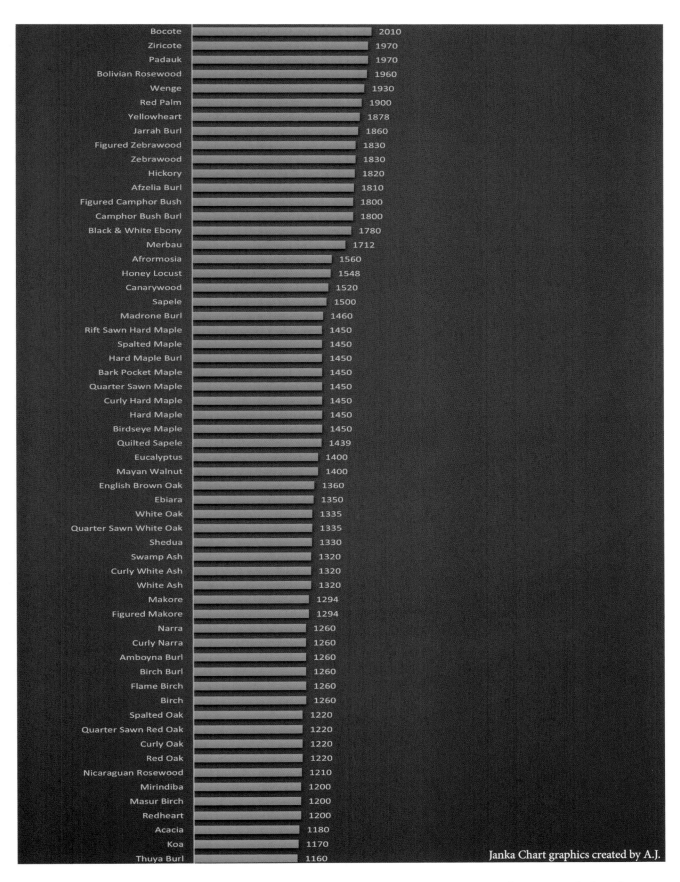

Wood	Janka
Bocote	2010
Ziricote	1970
Padauk	1970
Bolivian Rosewood	1960
Wenge	1930
Red Palm	1900
Yellowheart	1878
Jarrah Burl	1860
Figured Zebrawood	1830
Zebrawood	1830
Hickory	1820
Afzelia Burl	1810
Figured Camphor Bush	1800
Camphor Bush Burl	1800
Black & White Ebony	1780
Merbau	1712
Afrormosia	1560
Honey Locust	1548
Canarywood	1520
Sapele	1500
Madrone Burl	1460
Rift Sawn Hard Maple	1450
Spalted Maple	1450
Hard Maple Burl	1450
Bark Pocket Maple	1450
Quarter Sawn Maple	1450
Curly Hard Maple	1450
Hard Maple	1450
Birdseye Maple	1450
Quilted Sapele	1439
Eucalyptus	1400
Mayan Walnut	1400
English Brown Oak	1360
Ebiara	1350
White Oak	1335
Quarter Sawn White Oak	1335
Shedua	1330
Swamp Ash	1320
Curly White Ash	1320
White Ash	1320
Makore	1294
Figured Makore	1294
Narra	1260
Curly Narra	1260
Amboyna Burl	1260
Birch Burl	1260
Flame Birch	1260
Birch	1260
Spalted Oak	1220
Quarter Sawn Red Oak	1220
Curly Oak	1220
Red Oak	1220
Nicaraguan Rosewood	1210
Mirindiba	1200
Masur Birch	1200
Redheart	1200
Acacia	1180
Koa	1170
Thuya Burl	1160

Janka Chart graphics created by A.J.

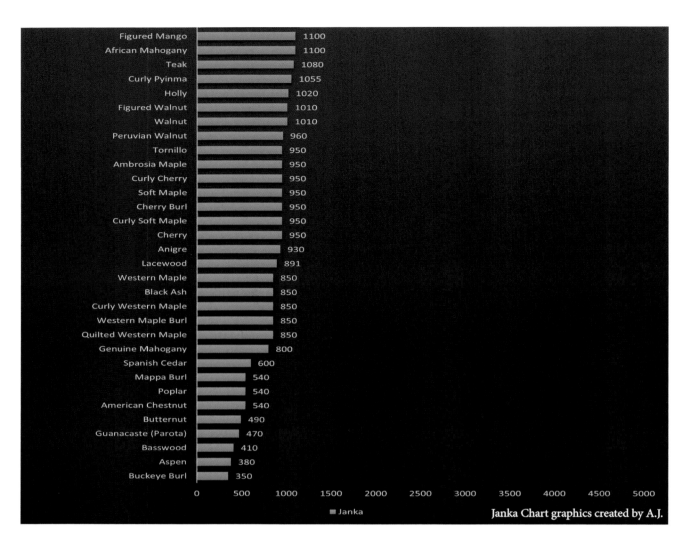

Janka Chart graphics created by A.J.

Janka Hardness Test

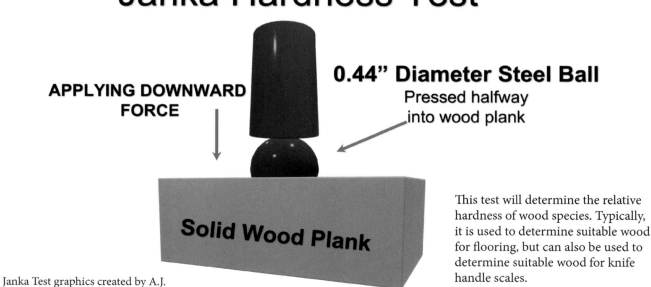

APPLYING DOWNWARD FORCE

0.44" Diameter Steel Ball
Pressed halfway into wood plank

Solid Wood Plank

This test will determine the relative hardness of wood species. Typically, it is used to determine suitable wood for flooring, but can also be used to determine suitable wood for knife handle scales.

Janka Test graphics created by A.J.

Angle Sharpening Guide

Common Angles

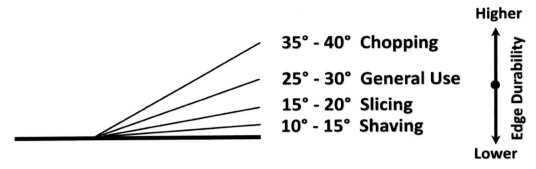

35° - 40° **Chopping**

25° - 30° **General Use**

15° - 20° **Slicing**

10° - 15° **Shaving**

Higher

Edge Durability

Lower

Purpose	Types
Chopping	Cleaver, Machete, Heavy Use Knives, and Some Axes.
General Use	Hunting Knives, Survival Knives, Sport Knives, Tactical Knives, Some Axes and Hatchets.
Slicing	Culinary Knives (Boning, Carving, Chef, Fillet, Pairing), Everyday Carry (EDC), and Pocket Knives.
Shaving	Razor Blades, Scalpels, and X-Acto Knives.

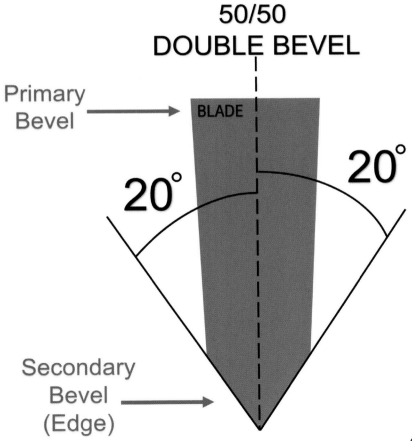

50/50 DOUBLE BEVEL

Primary Bevel → BLADE

20°   20°

Secondary Bevel (Edge) →

Graphics created by A.J.

Rockwell Hardness Test

History: The Rockwell Hardness Scale is named after the Rockwell Brothers (Hugh and Stanley Rockwell). They were metallurgists working at a ball bearing factory in Connecticut, in the early 1900s. They saw the need for a device to accurately measure the strength of different metals/steels. Stanley Rockwell patented the method in 1914. In 1919 he amended the patent to include a Rockwell scale chart. There are several Rockwell Scales, but the one we are most familiar with in the Knife Industry is the Rockwell C Scale.

How it works: Using a diamond indenter, a specific amount of static force is applied to a metal surface/steel sample for a set time, while using precise measuring procedures and recording the data. Two tests are recorded; the first being the "minor load" test, which is used as a baseline for calculations. The second test uses a major load, which is basically a heavier degree of force applied to the metal surface or steel sample. The value from the minor load is then subtracted from the vale of the major load. The final value is then transferred to the Rockwell C Scale, where its corresponding value becomes the metal's Rockwell hardness indicator/number.

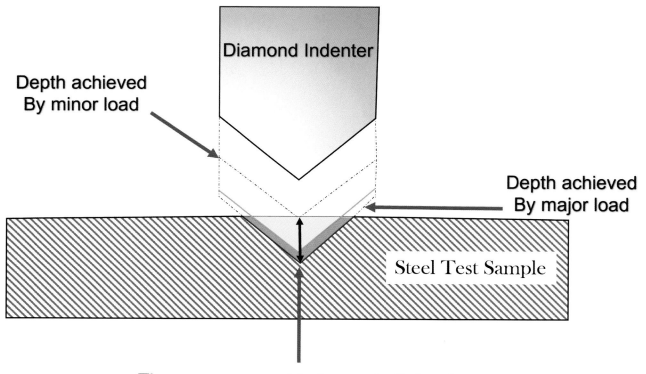

Depth achieved By minor load

Diamond Indenter

Depth achieved By major load

Steel Test Sample

The measurement between both loads (minor and major), is the basis of the hardness test reading. Essentially, the smaller the difference, the harder the material.

Rockwell Graphics created by A.J.

Note: The harder the surface, the less of a difference between the minor and major load tests, which also means the higher RC/HRC rating the steel will have. A rating below 55 typically relates softer steels. Steels that rate above 64 are considered very hard steels, which equates to high tensile strength, stay sharp longer, are easier to sharpen, but have higher brittleness.

Knife Companies List:

A

Ahti

Adler German Axes

Al Mar Knives

Allen Putman

Ambush Knives

American Knife Company

American Tomahawk Company

Andersson & Copra

Andre De Villiers

Antonini Knives

Anza Knives

Arno Bernard

Artisan Cutlery

Attleboro

B

Bark River Knives

Baskett Custom Knives

Bastenelli

Battle Horse Knives

Bear & Sons Knives

Becker Knife & Tool

Benchmade Knife Company

Bestech Knives

Bill Blade

Bill Ruple Knives

Black Dragon Forge

Blackjack Knives

Blue Grass Cutlery

Boker Knives

Bradford Knives

Brian Efros Knives

Brian Tighe & Friends

Brisa

Brous Blades

Bubba Blade

Buck Knives

Burke Knives

C

Camillus

Case Knives

Casstrom

Castillo Knives

Cattaraugus Cutlery

Chaves Knife & Tool

Chelsea Miller Knives

Chris Reeve Knives

CIVIVI Knives

Cold Steel Knives

Colonel Blades

Colonial Cutlery International

Coltellerie Berti

Columbia River Knife & Tool Company (CRKT)

Condor Tool & KnifeCrouch Knives

Cumming Bladeworks

Curtiss Knives

D

Dan Peters Custom Knives

Dan Tope Knives

Dark Side Blades

Dawson Knives

DEFCON Knives

Demko Knives

Dexter Russell, Inc.

Doug Ritter

DPx Gear

E

Emerson Knives

Enrique Pena Knives

EnZo Knives

ESEE Knives

Esker

Estwing

Erapuu

F

Fallkniven

Ferrum Forge

Finch Knife Company

Fiddleback Forge

Fiskars

Fox Knives

Fred Perrin Knives

G

Gerber

GiantMouse

Gransfors Bruk

Great Eastern Cutlery

Grimsmo Knives

GT Knives

GTI Knives

H

Halfbreed Blades

Hallmark Cutlery

Hammer Down Forge

Havalon Knives

Hawkins Knives

Heibel Knives

Helle

Hen & Rooster Knives

Heretic Knives

Hinderer Knives

Hoffman Blacksmithing

Hogue Knives

Honey Badger

Hults Bruk

Hunt Knives

Hyken Knives

I

Iain Sinclair

Iisakki Jarvenpaa

J

J. Hoffman Knives

J. A. Henckels

Jake Hoback Knives

J.E. Made Knives

Jerry Moen Knives

Jim Coffee Knives

Jimmy Lile Knives

Joe Loui Customs

Joe Watson Knives

Joey Roman Knives

K

KA-BAR

Kansept Knives

Karesuando Kniven

Kellam Knives

Kershaw Knives

KeyBar

Kikuichi CutleryKizer Knives

Kizlyar Supreme Knives

Knight Elements

Knives of Alaska

Knob Creek Forge

Koenig Knives

Koster Knives

Krein Knives

L

Laurin

Leatherman

Les George Knives

LionSTEEL

Lon Humphrey

L. T. Wright Knives

M

Marbles

Maher and Grosh Knives

Mantis Knives

Marifione Custom Knives

Marttiini

Marvin Solomon Custom Knives

Maserin

Master Cutlery

McNees Custom Knives

Mcusta Knives

Medford Knife & Tool

Messermeister

Microtech Knives

Mikov Knives

MKM

Morakniv

Mummert Knives

My Parang

N

Nago Higonokami

Nordsmith Knives

Novinc Knives

O

Ohta

Olamic Cutlery

Old Forge Knives

Old Hickory

Ontario Knife Company

Opinel

Osprey Knife & Tool

Otter Knives

Outdoor Edge Cutlery

P

Paragon Knives

Pena Knives

Pete Winkler

Piranha Knives

PMP Knives

ProTech Knives

Puma Knives

Purgatory Ironworks

Q

QSP

Queen Cutlery

Quickhatch Knives

R

Randall Made Knives

Rapala

Rat Worx USA

Red Horse Knives

Real Avid

Real Steel Knives

Reate Knives

Red River Knives

Revo Knives

Rick Hinderer Knives

Robby Bowman

Robert Klaas

Robesen

RMJ Tactical

Rockstead Corporation

Roselli

Rough Ryder Knives

Ruike Knives

Ryan W Knives

S

Sawmill Cutlery

Scagel

Schatt & Morgan Cutlery Co.

Schmuckatelli

Schorsch Custom Knives

Schrade Cutlery

Shun Cutlery

Skelton Bladeworks

Silky Saws

Silver Stag

Skelton Bladeworks

Smith & Sons

Snody Knives

Snow & Neally

SOG Knives

Spartan Blades

Spyderco Knives

Smith Handforged Knives

Steel Will

Stromeng

Swan Lake Knives

T

Timor Cutlery

T.M. Hunt

Todd Hunt

Toor Knives

TOPS Knives

TRC Knives

Tuyaknife

U

Uncle Henry

United Cutlery

V

V Nives

Valkyrie Knives

Vehement Knives

Victorinox Swiss Army

Viper Knives

W

Wachtman Knife and Tool

We Knife Co.

Weatherford Knife Company

White River Knives

William Henry

Winkler Knives

Wood Jewel

Work Tuff Gear

Woox

Wusthof Knives

Z

Zero Tolerance Knives

Zieba Knives

Zoe Crist Knives

Zwilling J. A. Henckels Knives

Use Your Knife

Knives are meant to be used, maintained, and cherished. These multipurpose tools are our dependable companions, that help us accomplish a plethora of tasks and even help us defend ourselves in life threatening moments. Use your knife, because you will grow to love it more, knowing that it made you a more self-reliant person. Every scratch it acquires is a memory, a story, a way in which life personalizes your knife. The patina it builds over time is a symbol of wisdom, one that mirrors the wisdom of its wielder. Enjoy your knife for what it is... the very tool that gave humans the ability to protect themselves, forage the planet, process game, build settlements, and lead empires.

Stay Sharp, Stay Tuned...